"I have profitably used *Moral Choices* as a central textbook in my Christian Ethics courses since it first came out in 1995. This new edition builds on the strengths of the previous editions by deepening the analysis, bringing the discussions up to date, and adding a needful new chapter on ethics and economics. The book remains clear, readable, well-informed, biblical, and pertinent for the moral questions and challenges facing Christians today."

Doug Groothuis
Professor of Philosophy, Denver Seminary

Moral Choices is characterized by particular strength in its discussion of ethical methodology, its approach to bioethical and business ethics issues, its accessibility and readability, its use of cases and discussion questions, and its engagement with a wide range of both secular and Christian thinkers through the ages. It is conservative and evangelical while remaining irenic and dialogical."

—David P. Gushee
Distinguished University Professor of Christian Ethics
Mercer University

"Scott Rae is one of the leading evangelical ethicists in North America, and this thoroughly updated version of *Moral Choices* features the excellence we have come to expect from his pen. Based on its breadth of coverage, depth of insight, and accessibility of style, it is now the go-to text for colleges and seminaries. It is also a must-read for pastors and laypersons who want to be informed about the ethical issues of our day. I highly recommend it."

J. P. Moreland
Distinguished Professor of Philosophy, Talbot School of Theology

"This is a well-crafted introduction to Christian ethics. Professor Rae exhibits in his work the very virtues that he extols his readers to emulate. His love of learning, Christ,and the good, the true, and the beautiful comes through loud and clear. Although one may find oneself disagreeing with Professor Rae, as I do on a few issues, you will be more informed, challenged, and enlightened as a consequence of reading this book."

Francis J. Beckwith
Professor of Philosophy and Church-Studies, Baylor University, and
Author of Defending Life: A Moral and Legal Case Against Abortion Choice

textbook*plus*⁺

Equipping Instructors and Students with
***FREE RESOURCES** for Core Zondervan Textbooks*

Available Resources for Moral Choices

Instructor Resources

- Instructor's manual
- Exams
- Presentation slides
- Sample syllabi

Student Resources

- Chapter videos
- Exam study guides
- What does it mean to be human?

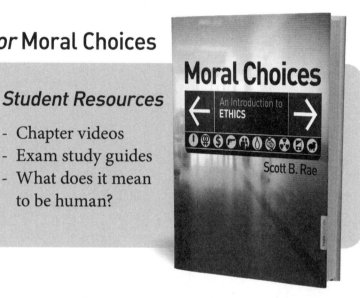

*How To Access Resources

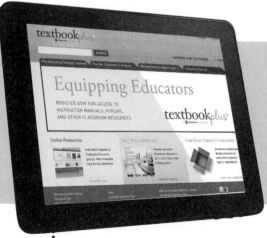

- Go to www.TextbookPlus.Zondervan.com
- Click "Register Now" button and complete registration process
- Find books using search field or "Browse Our Textbooks" feature
- Click "Instructor Resources" or "Student Resources" tab once you get to book page to access resources

www.TextbookPlus.Zondervan.com

Moral Choices

An Introduction to
ETHICS

Scott B. Rae
Third Edition

ZONDERVAN®

ZONDERVAN.com/
AUTHORTRACKER
follow your favorite authors

ZONDERVAN

Moral Choices
Copyright © 1995, 2000, 2009 by Scott B. Rae

This title is also available as a Zondervan ebook.
Visit www.zondervan.com/ebooks.

Requests for information should be addressed to:

Zondervan, *Grand Rapids, Michigan 49530*

Library of Congress Cataloging-in-Publication Data

Rae, Scott B.
    Moral choices : an introduction to ethics / Scott B. Rae - 3rd ed.
        p. cm.
    Includes index.
    ISBN 978-0-310-29109-1 (hardcover)
    1. Ethics. I. Title.
BJ1012.R32 2009
170 — dc22   2009005151

Cover design: Scott Lee Designs (scottleedesigns.com)
Interior design: Matthew Van Zomeran

Printed in the United States of America

13 14 15 16 17 18 19 20 /DCI/ 27 26 25 24 23 22 21 20 19 18 17 16 15 14 13 12 11 10

Contents

Acknowledgments

Special thanks and appreciation are due to a number of important people who enabled this third edition to become a reality. Thanks to my colleagues at Talbot School of Theology, particularly in the philosophy department, for their intellectual stimulation and encouraging friendships — you guys provide a great environment in which to work. My deans at Talbot, Dennis Dirks and Mike Wilkins, provide substantial encouragement for writing and flexible schedules in order to finish projects and meet deadlines. Special thanks to Jim Ruark at Zondervan, who has overseen the editing of all three editions of *Moral Choices* — thanks for your thorough and careful work. You have made each of the three editions better. I have much appreciation for Katya Covrett, my senior editor at Zondervan, for her initiative and creativity in proposing the changes for this edition.

Many thanks to Zondervan for their desire to publish a third edition of this book. I trust that it will continue to be a useful tool, now more beneficial with the updates made for this new edition.

To my wife, Sally, and my sons, Taylor, Cameron, and Austin — thanks for your patience with me when I was getting this finished. You all are such an encouragement, and I am grateful for all that you mean to me.

I dedicate this third edition to my late father, Walter B. Rae, who taught me about morality from the way he lived.

Publisher's Preface

The teaching of ethics and morality has never been more challenging than it is today. Each morning of this twenty-first century seems to bring with it a news story or societal revelation that forces us to cogently think through ethical ramifications that even Solomon would have difficulty discerning.

Moral Choices is an introductory textbook written at an accessible level that allows students to clearly enter a field of study that otherwise could quickly become a quagmire. Use it with confidence in the classroom as it presents some of the most pressing moral issues facing us today, including abortion, euthanasia, homosexuality, war, capital punishment, reproductive technologies, and moral authority.

About the Author

Believing "morality ultimately issues from the character of God," Dr. Scott Rae, in teaching this subject, combines biblical studies with ethical relevancy while maintaining a timely and current perspective on such topics as "connecting the law and morality," "natural law in Christian ethics," "the social dimension of Old Testament ethics," and "the biblical background of abortion."

Writing Style

Readers will appreciate the book's succinct approach to these weighty matters. It does not deteriorate into theoretical jargon or obtuse philosophies. Rather, it unpacks key terms and distinctions in ethics to help readers become more familiar with this new territory.

Organization

As new subjects are introduced and discussed, they are headlined in bold text for easy reference. Ethical dilemmas are exposed, and the author makes the case both for and against them, allowing readers to see both sides. Sidebars highlight how historic figures, documents, and events have influenced thought and dialogue about ethics.

Each chapter ends with (1) a concluding paragraph to assist students in comprehending what has just been taught; (2) a "For Further Reading" section to recommend resources for advanced study of these subjects; and (3) endnotes to facilitate the overall flow of reading for readers while also providing academic clarity to the text.

Model

This book offers a practical ethical model for readers to make daily moral decisions. It also presents case studies to show how to apply that model in various sticky circumstances.

Indexes

Nearly four hundred key people, topics, and terms are alphabetically indexed to their page numbers, assisting readers in quickly locating important information. A Scripture index is also included for finding the biblical bases for discussions in the book.

Goals

Moral Choices not only introduces ethical matters to students, but also helps them develop a practical discerning framework as they face moral and immoral issues outside the classroom every day.

Chapter 1

Introduction: Why Study Ethics?

In Plato's classic work *The Republic*, the myth of Gyges sets out the question, Why be moral? Gyges was given the opportunity to live life as an invisible entity, able to do anything he wanted to do with no one ever discovering what he had done. That is, he could do whatever he wanted and would be assured of getting away with it. Given the chance to live life like this, the question Plato raises is, Would a person want to be moral?[1] After a good deal of dialogue, Plato concluded that being moral was inherently valuable, apart from any additional benefits it produced or harm that it enabled a person to avoid.

How would you respond to the question, Why be moral? Since the moral life and moral decision making are the focal points of this book, this question is foundational. If you decide that being moral is not very important, then you probably will not spend much time reading this or any other book on ethics. But if being moral is important to you, the content of this book will be helpful in shaping how you view morality.

Most people, when they are genuinely honest with themselves, associate doing well in life with being a good person. Having moral character is still essential to most people's conceptions of what makes a person flourish in his or her life. For example, it is difficult to imagine a person being considered a success in life if he has gained his wealth dishonestly. It is equally difficult to call a person a success who is at the top of his profession but cheats on his wife, abuses his children, and drinks too much. On the other hand, we rightly hold up a person like Mother Teresa as a model of living a good life, even though she lacked most material goods that society values. One of the principal reasons for being moral is that it is central to most concepts of human fulfillment. For the Christian, being moral is critical to a life that seeks to honor God. We could say that being moral is inherently good because it is foundational to a person's flourishing in life, since doing well in life and being a good person still go together for most people.

The same holds true for society as a whole. Most people would not want to live in a society in which morality was unimportant, in which conceptions of right and wrong carried little weight. In fact, it is unlikely that any sort of civilized society could continue unless it had concern for key moral values, such as fairness, justice, truthfulness, and compassion. Ethics are important because they give direction to people and societies who have some sense that they cannot flourish without being moral.

Many thoughtful observers of today's culture are growing increasingly concerned about a breakdown in morality, particularly among students and young adults. They cite phenomena such as drug use, alcoholism, teenage pregnancies, violence, juvenile delinquency, crime, and sexually transmitted diseases as evidence of the moral fabric of society coming unraveled. The alarming number of school shootings, in which students are killing their peers—such as the tragedies at Virginia Tech University in 2007, Northern Illinois University in 2008, and the continuing incidences of these shootings at high schools—only adds to the concern.

Ethics are crucial because moral questions are at the heart of life's vital issues. Morality is primarily concerned with questions of right and wrong, the ability to distinguish between the two, and the justification of the distinction. Closely related are such questions as, What is a good person? What things are morally praiseworthy? What constitutes a good life? and What would a good society look like? These are fundamental to your view of the world. You cannot formulate an adequate worldview without providing answers to these moral questions.[2] Practitioners in a wide variety of professions, whether or not they realize it, deal with moral questions. For example, morality is fundamental to politics, since politics and the law concern the way in which people ought to order their lives together in society. In addition, medicine and the sciences, such as genetics and molecular biology, have numerous moral overtones because they deal with the morally charged areas of life and death. Further, business provides a variety of ethical minefields that can challenge the integrity of the men and women who are striving to succeed in an ever more competitive global economy.

Ethics are also important because you face moral choices every day. Every so often you will face emotionally wrenching moral dilemmas that have no easy answers. Many decisions you will make on a day-to-day basis also involve questions of right and wrong, some of which may have easy answers but are difficult to carry out. Ethics provide the basis on which you make those decisions. Most people have an idea of what sorts of things are right and wrong. Explaining why you think something is right or wrong is altogether another question. The basis on which you make moral choices is often as important as the choices themselves. Yet few people have thought through the way in which they justify their conceptions of right and wrong.

Finally, ethics are important in facing a number of issues, including abortion, euthanasia, same-sex marriage, war, and capital punishment. Debates on issues such as these seem endless and irreconcilable, and they promise to continue far into the future. What many of these issues share is a fundamental disagreement over the ultimate source of moral authority. Some individuals hold that moral authority is ultimately a human construction, while others insist that moral authority comes from some transcendent source that is beyond human beings, such as a revelation from God or nature.[3] As you read the newspaper and various news magazines and listen to television news, you will be increasingly aware of the importance of these issues. You will also notice that, apart from legal intervention, most of these issues are no closer to being resolved today than they were ten years ago.

Not only does intractable debate characterize these issues, but society has a general sense of bewilderment over a number of other issues. Many of these involve matters of science and technology that have run far ahead of ethical reflection. For example, genetic testing, gender selection, various reproductive technologies, and the use of human embryonic stem cells in the treatment of certain diseases all involve moral dilemmas that are far from resolved. Most observers in these areas acknowledge that technology has outpaced society's ability to determine the moral parameters for its use. There is a general sense that ethics are necessary for dealing with our increasingly technological society.

More people have an interest in ethics today than at any other time in the recent past. Some of that interest is due to the complex issues spawned by technology, while others have an alarming sense of a general moral decline in society. In addition, the numerous scandals that have rocked the business community and other professions have left some to ask if "business ethics" and "professional ethics" are indeed oxymorons. Some people are aware of the need to stress values in various educational arenas, including public schools. Many are also realizing that the value-neutral approach to education at all levels is not working, and some even suggest that such value neutrality is impossible. Although there is a greater emphasis on character in view of well-publicized business ethics failures, ethics helps determine which character traits are admirable and worth cultivating.

These reasons for the importance of studying ethics all presume that there is such a thing as genuine moral knowledge. But that notion is being increasingly called into question in philosophy today as a result of the cultural dominance of the worldview of *naturalism*. Among other things, the naturalist holds that all reality is reducible to that which can be perceived with one's senses—that is, there is nothing that is real or that counts for knowledge that is not verifiable by the senses. As a result, moral knowledge has been reduced to the realm of *belief* and is considered parallel to religious beliefs, which the culture widely holds are not verifiable. The theist maintains that moral knowledge is genuine knowledge in the same way that scientific knowledge is real—that the notion that "murder is wrong" can be known as true and cannot be reduced to subjective opinion or belief without the risk of all morality being subjective. The theist argues that no one lives consistently, as though morality is entirely subjective, and that moral truths do exist and can be known as such.[4]

Overview of the Book

As you read this book, you will be exposed both to foundations in ethics and to the application of those foundations to the most pressing moral issues of the day. Believing that morality ultimately issues from the character of God, I find the most critical and foundational element of ethics to be the direction that God provides, both in his Word (i.e., special revelation) and outside his Word (i.e., general revelation). Chapter 2 will outline the distinctive elements of Christian ethics. This entire book could be about Christian ethics. Some works are entirely devoted to this subject. Here you will simply get a synthesis of the main parameters of biblical ethics.

Throughout the ages, many philosophers, even some whose inquiries predate the written Scriptures, have wrestled with the questions of right and wrong and arrived at somewhat different answers. Recognizing, then, that the Bible is not the only source of ethical inquiry, chapter 3 provides an honest look at alternative ethical systems, such as relativism, utilitarianism, and ethical egoism. We will also examine the major figures who systematized them, including Plato, Aristotle, Augustine, Aquinas, and Kant. These must be brief, but I have included resources, especially original sources, should you wish to study any of these individuals or systems further. For each alternative approach to ethics, I will offer a description of the system and its major advocate, a presentation of the strong points of the system, a comparison of it with Scripture, and a critique of the system, both from within the system itself and from the perspective of Christian ethics. In order to be able to converse with an increasingly secular world about ethics and morality, you need exposure to the ways in which other people have done ethics. Some of these approaches contain truth that ultimately comes from God, even if the people formulating the alternative are unaware of it. Also, for the sake of clarity, I have tried to use terms in a manner consistent with their use in secular works on ethics.

Chapter 4 contains a model for making moral decisions and illustrates its use on some particularly knotty moral dilemmas. This model can be used in virtually any setting and does not require any particular worldview commitment for its profitable use. I offer this model not as a type of computer program for generating correct moral decisions, but as a guideline to ensure that all the key bases are covered when you make moral decisions. This chapter begins to build the bridge from theory to application that will be more clearly defined in subsequent chapters.

Chapters 5 through 12 deal with some of the current issues that are hotly debated both among individuals and in society. Discussion in these chapters will recognize the way these issues affect people individually (personal ethics) as well as how they affect public policy (social ethics). Since medical ethics involves some of the most frequently debated and complex issues, chapters 5 through 8 discuss such issues as abortion, reproductive/genetic technologies, and assisted suicide.

Staying within the arena of ethics pertaining to life and death, chapter 9 addresses the issue of capital punishment. Chapter 10 addresses the subject of sexual ethics, which includes sexual orientation, same-sex marriage, and birth control. Chapter 11 takes up the issue that has been debated longer than any other, the morality of war, which has some new questions raised, particularly in the aftermath of 9/11 and the ongoing war on terrorism. Chapter 12 will address the intersection of ethics and economics, with an introduction to business ethics and a brief look at the moral assessment of the economic system of global capitalism.

Introducing Key Terms and Distinctions in Ethics

One of the difficult aspects of studying a subject like ethics is that you are introduced to many terms with which you are unfamiliar. For example, new members of the hospital ethics committee with whom I consult are often unfamiliar with terminology customarily used by ethicists. So, to keep you from the initial shock of jumping headfirst into a new subject, this section will introduce you to some of the key terms that you will often see as you read this book.

Most people use the terms *morality* and *ethics* interchangeably. Technically, morality refers to the actual content of right and wrong, and ethics refers to the process of determining right and wrong. In other words, morality deals with moral *knowledge* and ethics with moral *reasoning*. Thus, ethics is both an art and a science. It does involve some precision like the sciences, but like art, it is an inexact and sometimes intuitive discipline. Morality is the end result of ethical deliberation, the substance of right and wrong.

Major Categories

Four broad categories have traditionally fallen under the heading of ethics. They include (1) *descriptive ethics*, (2) *normative ethics*, (3) *metaethics*, and (4) *aretaic ethics*. Normative ethics will be the primary concern in this book.

First, *descriptive ethics* is a sociological discipline that attempts to describe the morals of a particular society, often by studying other cultures. Anthropologists often use it in their fieldwork to describe the moral distinctives of other cultures.

Second, *normative ethics* refers to the discipline that produces moral norms or rules as its end product. Most systems of ethics are designed to tell you what is normative for individual and social behavior, or what is right and wrong, both generally and in specific circumstances. Normative ethics *prescribes* moral behavior, whereas descriptive ethics *describes* moral behavior. When we examine important moral issues in later chapters, we will be trying to establish a set of norms to apply to that particular issue. When most people debate about ethics, they are debating normative ethics, or what the moral norms should be and how those norms apply to the issues at hand.

Of course, ethics is not the only normative discipline.[5] For example, the law produces legal norms but not necessarily moral ones, although law and morality probably overlap significantly. In addition, there are norms of good taste and social acceptability, which we call etiquette. Further, religion produces behavioral norms, often defined by a religious authority such as a pastor or other church official, that govern one's relationship to God. In chapter 2 we will see that Christian ethics includes a substantial overlap between duties with respect to a person's relationship to God and duties with respect to the people around him or her.

Third, *metaethics* is an area of ethics that investigates the meaning of moral language, or the epistemology of ethics, and also considers the justification of ethical theories and judgments. For example, it focuses on the meaning of the major terms used in ethics, such as *right, good,* and *just.* The primary focus of technical philosophers, metaethics has been receiving more attention from a popular audience today since more people are insisting that the language of right and wrong is nothing more than an expression of personal preferences. Accordingly, some will argue that the judgment that homosexuality is wrong is not a statement about right and wrong but simply a personal distaste for homosexuality. Morality is thus reduced to matters of taste and preference and has little to do with right and wrong. We will look at this later in chapter 3 when we discuss emotivism.

Fourth, *aretaic ethics* is a category of ethics that focuses on the virtues produced in individuals, not the morality of specific acts. Also known as *virtue theory*, it is growing in popularity today. The term *aretaic* is taken from a Greek term that is translated "virtue." Recognizing that there is more to the moral life than simply making right decisions, many people believe that matters of virtue and character are equally, if not more, important than the way in which we resolve moral dilemmas.

When discussing whether someone or something is moral, it helps to be very specific. Normally, making a moral judgment involves at least four specific considerations.[6] First, you should consider the *action* itself. This is usually the focus of a moral judgment but hardly the only aspect of moral evaluation. Second, you should evaluate the *motive* of the person (called the "moral actor") performing the action. In some cases the motive is the only difference between two otherwise identical actions. For example, your motive in giving something to someone is often the only difference between a gift and a bribe. Of course, sometimes you might not be able to determine the motive, in which case it cannot be assessed. Third, you should evaluate the *consequences* of your actions and decisions. Bear in mind, however, that actions may be inherently right or wrong, regardless of the consequences. For example, slavery in the pre–Civil War South was wrong regardless of how slavery benefited the Southern economy, because human beings are not objects that should be bought and sold. We will discuss this further in chapter 3 when we get to utilitarianism. Fourth, although a bit more difficult to do than the previous three considerations, you should attempt to evaluate the *character* of the moral actor. Character is the tendency of a person to act in predictable ways over time. Virtue theorists have led the way in insisting that any ethic that does not concern itself with character and virtue is incomplete and reduces ethics to merely a preoccupation with actions, specifically moral dilemmas that people do not often face.

We evaluate character more often than we think. For example, when we decide who we can trust, we are making an assessment of that person's character, determining whether he or she is a trustworthy person. We certainly evaluate character when we make decisions about who we will marry, since character is critical to a good marriage. And we are usually asked to evaluate character when we write letters of reference for people. So the assessment of character is not something that should be foreign to us, though we realize that, like our judgment of motives, we may not have all the information we need to make an accurate assessment. In those cases our appraisal must remain somewhat tentative.

Ethical Systems

Ethical systems may be classified as either *action-oriented* systems or *virtue-based* systems. Under these two major divisions are three subcategories by which ethical systems may be further classified: *deontological* systems, *teleological* systems, and *relativism*. Most of the technical terms have to do with the action-oriented systems.

First, *deontological* systems are systems that are based on principles in which actions (or character, or even intentions) are inherently right or wrong. There are three primary deontological systems: (1) *divine command theory*, (2) *natural law*, and (3) *ethical rationalism*. The Christian will tend to be more deontologically oriented because of the emphasis in Christian ethics on the commands of God as moral absolutes and guiding principles. But Christian ethics will have a substantial place in it for an ethic of virtue, since a major part of the Christian moral life involves emulating the character traits of Christ and exemplifying the fruit of the Spirit (Gal. 5:13–24).

Second, *teleological* systems are systems that are based on the end result produced by an action. Since the consequences rather than principles determine right actions for teleological systems, no action is inherently right or wrong in a teleological system. Whether an action is right or wrong depends on the consequences produced by that action. If it produces more beneficial consequences than harmful consequences, it is moral. If not, it is immoral. The primary form of teleological ethics is called *utilitarianism*, which holds that the action that produces the greatest good for the greatest number is the moral choice. More specifically, utilitarianism defines the good generally as the greatest pleasure, or preference satisfaction, and seeks that for the greatest number. Another form of teleological ethics is called *ethical egoism*, which maintains that the right thing to do is whatever is in a person's self-interest. Thus, for the ethical egoist the only consequence that matters is whether it advances his or her own self-interest.

Third, *relativism* refers to an ethical system in which right and wrong are not absolute and unchanging but relative to one's culture (cultural relativism) or one's own personal preferences (moral subjectivism). Both forms of relativism are widely embraced today. With the current emphasis on multiculturalism and appreciation for the cultural diversity that exists in much of the world, and the importance of a culture's values in its self-definition, it should not surprise us that there is a movement toward accepting all cultures' values as equally valid, which is the definition of cultural relativism. Moral subjectivism is advocated every time someone says, "Whatever is right for you is okay, but what's right for me is also okay!" Such moral subjectivism is frequently seen in one's view of sexual morality, in which a person is particularly sensitive to having a view forced on him or her, thus reducing sexual ethics to personal preference. This view of morality is often associated with a postmodern view of the world, in which objective truth and objective morality are called into question.[7]

Morality and the Law

As you might expect, there is substantial overlap between what is legal and what is moral. Most, if not all laws, have some moral overtones to them. For example, even laws such as one regarding driving on the correct side of the road imply a respect for life and property. We rightly assume that the person who drives on the wrong side of the road and ignores other similar traffic laws has respect for neither life nor property. Most people hold that for laws to be valid, they must have some connection to widely shared moral principles; that is, a law that violates society's widely held values cannot be a valid one. Thus, in most cases there is a significant connection between law and morality.[8]

As a general rule, we will assume that the law is the moral minimum. Obeying the law is the beginning of our moral obligations, not the end. Be careful about the person who insists, "If it's legal, then it must be moral." That view is that the law is the moral maximum, not the minimum. There are many things that are immoral that are not illegal. Take adultery for example. Most people would agree that cheating on one's spouse is immoral, but no one (at least in the West) goes to jail for it. In addition, lying is immoral in most cases; but only in certain contexts, such as a court of law, would someone be prosecuted for lying. In most cases violating the law is immoral, except in rare cases where the law requires a person to do something that is unethical. For example, if the law required physicians to perform abortions for everyone who requested one, many physicians would consider that an immoral law, and they would be free to engage in civil disobedience — that is, they would follow their norms of morality, violate the law, and take whatever consequences the law meted out. But cases of civil disobedience are somewhat rare today, but when they occur, the person may follow the biblical dictum that "we must obey God rather than men" (Acts 5:29).[9]

So the law is the moral minimum. It is the moral floor, not the ceiling! The majority of our most interesting moral dilemmas occur when confronted with the question of how far beyond what the law requires our morality demands us to go. In other words, how far beyond mere compliance with the law do my moral convictions tell me I have to go? Most of the pressing demands of morality are in those spaces where the law is not definitive, where the law is silent, or where the law allows one to do something unethical.

However, many things that are unethical ought also to be illegal. For example, fraud is immoral, and most forms of fraud are also illegal, and justifiably so. I'm sure you can think of many other immoral activities that should be illegal, such as murder, child abuse, and sexual assault. Be careful of the person who insists, "You can't legislate morality!" Whether that statement is true depends on what is meant by "morality." If moral beliefs, motives, or intentions are meant, then those certainly cannot be legislated. In fact, the First Amendment, which guarantees freedom of religion and speech, was written to keep the state out of the business of imposing beliefs on its citizens. That is, it was to protect the church from the state, *not* to protect the state from the church. A person's genuine moral intent is changed by persuasion, not coercion, since intent has to do with one's free choices. But if by *morality* one means "moral behavior," then that can be, and is, legislated virtually every day around the world. Some cultures, such as Islamic cultures, use the force of law more routinely to enforce private moral behavior among consenting adults. But virtually every law is the imposition of someone's morality, given the overlap between most laws and the moral principles that undergird them.

Some of the issues we will take up in the later chapters raise this question of whether a moral position should also be legislated in terms of public policy. For example, issues such as abortion, assisted suicide, human cloning, genetic privacy, and same-sex marriage raise important questions of what public policy should be on these matters. A variety of interest groups, including religious ones, attempt to influence what the law should be on these and other issues.

When religious groups or individuals get involved in public policy, it invariably raises questions about "the separation of church and state." As originally intended, the First Amendment that established religious freedom only prohibited the federal government from establishing federally supported and federally sanctioned churches, as had been done in Europe with disastrous results that included religious wars and harsh religious persecutions. The First Amendment guaranteed religious freedom by prohibiting the establishment of a national church. The government was supposed to be neutral toward all religious groups. This clearly emphasized freedom of religion.

From the separation of church and state, it did not follow that the state was to be neutral or hostile toward religion in general. Many of the Founding Fathers who wrote parts of the Bill of Rights were very clear that a democracy needed the moral restraints and the grounding for rights that religion provided.[10] The Founding Fathers never imagined a society in which the state would be neutral or hostile toward religion in general. As A. James Reichley of the Brookings Institution said:

> The founders' belief in the wisdom of placing civil society within a framework of religious values formed part of their reason for enacting the free exercise clause. The First Amendment is no more neutral of the general value of religion than it is on the general value of the free exchange of ideas or an independent press. The virtually unanimous view among the founders [is] that functional separation between church and state should be maintained without threatening the support and guidance received by republican government from religion.[11]

Until recently, religious groups have freely attempted to influence public policy without anyone objecting that they are violating the separation of church and state.

Conclusion

You will undoubtedly be introduced to other new terms and ideas as you read this book. But don't let the terminology intimidate you. Every thoughtful person should be concerned about and interested in ethics, since it addresses the ultimate questions about the good life, the good person, and the good society. As Socrates said in Plato's *Republic*, "We are discussing no small matter, but how we ought to live."

Review Questions

1. How would you answer the question, Why be moral?

2. What is the myth of Gyges, and how does it relate to the question, Why be moral?

3. How are ethics important in fields such as business, medicine, and politics?

4. How would you distinguish between ethics and morality?

5. What are descriptive ethics, normative ethics, metaethics, and aretaic ethics?

6. When a moral assessment is made, what must be assessed besides the action?

7. What is the difference between deontological and teleological systems of ethics?

8. How would you describe the relationship between morality and the law?

Chapter 1 Notes

1. Technically, the *Republic* is concerned with the question of justice—in Gyges's case, whether a person would still desire to be just. But for Plato, justice for an individual was closely associated with virtue, so the illustration still fits the question, Why be moral?

2. When a person converts to Christianity, he or she not only enters a relationship with Christ and inherits eternal life, but also adopts a worldview—a set of lenses through which to view the world. Other critical worldview questions include What is real? (metaphysics); How do we know that which we know? (epistemology); What happens to a person after death? Where is history going? and What kind of a thing is a person? (anthropology). For more discussion on the subject of one's worldview, see James W. Sire, *The Universe Next Door*, 4th ed. (Downers Grove, Ill.: InterVarsity, 2004); J. P. Moreland, *Love Your God with All Your Mind* (Colorado Springs: NavPress, 1998); and Nancy Pearcey and Phillip E. Johnson, *Total Truth: Liberating Christianity from Its Cultural Captivity* (Wheaton: Crossway, 2001).

3. For further detail on the issues currently being endlessly debated and the two sources of moral authority, see James Davison Hunter, *Culture Wars* (New York: Basic Books, 1992); and *Before the Shooting Begins: Searching for Democracy in America's Culture War* (New York: Free Press, 1994). See also James Davison Hunter and Alan Wolfe, *Is There a Culture War? A Dialogue on Values and American Public Life* (Washington, D.C.: Brookings Institution, 2006); and Peter Kreeft, *How to Win the Culture War* (Downers Grove, Ill.: InterVarsity, 2002).

4. For further discussion of this topic, see R. Scott Smith, *Virtue Ethics and Moral Knowledge* (London: Ashgate, 2003); and Robert Audi, *Moral Knowledge and Ethical Character* (New York: Oxford University Press, 1997).

5. See Louis Pojman, *Ethics: Discovering Right and Wrong* (Belmont, Calif.: Wadsworth, 1990), 4–5.

6. Ibid., 7–10.

7. For further reading on the impact of postmodernism and ethics, see Douglas Groothuis, *Truth Decay* (Downers Grove, Ill.: InterVarsity, 2000). See especially chapter 8, "Ethics without Reality—Postmodernist Style."

8. For further reading on the relationship between law and morality, see these works: H. L. A. Hart, *Law, Liberty and Morality* (London: Oxford University Press, 1963); Lord Devlin, *The Enforcement of Morals* (London: Oxford University Press, 1965); the debate between Hart and Harvard law professor Lon Fuller in Hart's, "Positivism and the Separation of Law and Morals," *Harvard Law Review* 71 (February 1958): 593–629; and Fuller's "Positivism and Fidelity to Law," *Harvard Law Review* 71 (February 1958): 630–72. The debate is summarized in Scott B. Rae, *The Ethics of Commercial Surrogate Motherhood: Brave New Families* (Westport, Conn.: Praeger, 1994), 126–29.

9. See the writings of Martin Luther King on this subject, especially his "Letter from a Birmingham Jail," in his book *Why We Can't Wait* (New York: Signet, 1964).

10. Here is a sample of the Founding Fathers' view of religion in public life: *Thomas Jefferson*: "Can the liberties of a nation be thought secure when we have removed their

only firm basis, a conviction in the minds of the people that these liberties are the gift of God?" It seems clear that, as Jefferson wrote in the preamble to the Declaration of Independence, rights and liberties are ultimately theologically grounded and need religious nurture in order to be maintained. He further stated that "religion should be regarded as a supplement to law in the government of men and as the alpha and omega of the moral law."

James Madison, writing in the government charter for the Northwest Territory, said, "Religion, morality, and knowledge, being necessary to good government and the happiness of mankind, schools and the means of learning shall forever be encouraged." Here Madison, representing Congress, is calling upon the government to promote religious and moral education, which today would be considered a violation of the separation of church and state.

George Washington, speaking in his farewell address at the end of his second presidency, said, "Where is the security for property, for reputation, for life if the sense of religious obligation desert the oaths, which are the instruments of investigation in courts of justice? And let us with caution indulge the supposition that morality can be maintained without religion. Whatever may be conceded to the influence of refined education on minds of peculiar structure, reason, and experience forbid us to expect that national morality can prevail in exclusion of religious principle."

Benjamin Franklin, writing in his plan for public education, said, "[History shows] the necessity of a public religion, the advantage of a religious character among private persons and the excellency of the Christian religion above all others, ancient or modern. [The great mass of men and women] have need of the motives of religion to restrain them from vice, to support their virtue, and to retain them in the practice of it until it becomes habitual." All of the above citations are from A. James Reichley, *Religion in American Public Life* (Washington, D.C.: Brookings Institution, 1985), 89–106.

11. Ibid., 113.

Chapter 2

Christian Ethics

Despite modern departures from it, the Judeo-Christian system of morality has had a profound impact on societies around the world from its inception. Many people who do not hold to the particulars of a Christian worldview nonetheless view Christian ethics as a valuable set of moral guidelines and ideals for society. Even people who deny key Christian doctrines, such as the deity of Christ, will admit that Jesus was both a compelling moral example and insightful moral teacher. In this chapter you will be introduced to the major emphases in Christian ethics as outlined in both the Old and New Testaments. You will also be exposed to other concepts central to a Christian ethic, such as natural law, deontological ethics, and virtue theory. You will read briefly of some objections to Christian ethics, such as the classical "*Euthyphro* dilemma," in which the questioner asks, "Does God command things because they are good, or are things good because God commands them?"

At its heart, Christian ethics is a blend of both virtues and principles. Morality is ultimately grounded in the character of God—that is, the ultimate source for morality is not God's commands but God's character. The virtues, or character traits, that are made clear by God's character and further clarified by Jesus' character, are the ultimate foundation for morality from a Christian worldview. God's commands are derived from his character. God issues the commands that he does because he is the kind of God that he is. For example, God commands that we love our neighbors, ultimately not because "love makes the world go 'round," though that result is surely a good thing, but because he is that kind of God. In addition, God mandates that we be forgiving people not primarily because forgiveness restores relationships, though that is certainly true, but because God is fundamentally a forgiving God. The virtues, then, are primary, and the moral principles, or God's commands, are derived from them.

The Bible makes a clear connection between God's character and his commands. Perhaps the most evident one is the preamble to the Ten Commandments, in which God prefaces the commands with the statement, "I am the LORD your God, who brought you out of Egypt, out of the land of slavery" (Ex. 20:1). Then the commands commence. God emphasizes that the commands follow from who he is, from his character, and specifically from how he acted on Israel's behalf. The second commandment, which prohibits idolatry, is based on God being a jealous God—he is zealous for his people's loyalty (v. 5). God calls his people to be holy, because that is the kind of God he is (Lev. 20:26). The New Testament insists that followers of Jesus "be perfect ... as your heavenly Father is perfect" (Matt. 5:48), and that the church avoid partiality because God is an impartial God (James 2:5–8). Other examples of this link between God's commands and his character

Augustine

Augustine is widely considered to be the dominant contributor to ethical theory during the transition between the ancient world and the Middle Ages. He attempted to formulate an explicitly Christian ethic for a world that was just beginning to experience Christianity.

After searching for a worldview that would hold together for him, he converted to Christianity from a life of hedonism in 386. He wrote a wide variety of works, both philosophical and theological. As he grew older, his interest turned more toward the Scriptures and pastoral work and away from more technical philosophy, although his ministry in the church was always strongly influenced by his background in philosophy. From about 390 until the end of his life, he worked as a priest and later served as a bishop in North Africa. Perhaps his two best-known works are the *Confessions* and his work in social ethics, *The City of God.* He was the first Christian to systematically develop Christian ethics and he suggested that virtue was acquired by means of God's grace through the gospel, the sacraments, and the ministry of the Holy Spirit within the soul of the believer.

Augustine held that all being is good because it is created by a good God. Evil as an independent entity does not exist but is only the privation of good. Happiness, or blessedness, to use Augustine's term, consists in community and fellowship in the kingdom of God. The supreme good for a human being is eternal life—that is, the perfect enjoyment of God for eternity.

In his social ethic, Augustine conceives of two radically different communities with two different ideas of what is good, the city of God and the city of man. Believers are the residents of the city of God, and the world apart from God's grace inhabits the city of man. Because of his strong view of the effects of sin on institutions, he recommended a minimal role for the state, to maintain order and secure justice as best as was possible in a fallen world.

include the principle of generosity to those in need, based on God's generosity in Christ toward individuals (2 Cor. 8:7–9), the principle of forgiveness, based on God's forgiveness in Christ (Eph. 4:32), and the critical principle of love of neighbor, based on the notion that "God is love" (1 John 4:8).

Other types of moral reasoning supplement the primary place of virtues and principles. Just as the Bible is not a tightly structured systematic theology but a mixture of different theological emphases presented in a variety of literary styles, so too, Scripture is not a systematically arranged ethical theory, but a mixture of different types of moral reasoning presented in a variety of literary contexts. The Bible makes use of a diversity of types of moral reasoning in an attempt to supplement the primary emphasis on virtues and principles. For example, the Mosaic law is heavily deontological, with its emphasis on principles that are, of course, ultimately dependent on God's character. The prophets reflect this, too, in that their preaching is essentially reminding the people of the parts of the law that they have forgotten or high-handedly disobeyed. But there are other types of moral reasoning used in the Bible.

The Wisdom Literature contains a measure of utilitarian reasoning. For example, many of the Proverbs contain explicit descriptions of the consequences of certain actions and character traits. The writers of the Proverbs appear to praise wisdom because of the good consequences it produces, while they warn against folly because of the harmful consequences it produces. To be sure, the Wisdom Literature is ultimately grounded in the Law and thus ultimately grounded in principles. The Wisdom Literature, then, does not attempt to use utilitarianism as a self-sufficient system for discovering morality, but the appeal to principles is supplemented by appeal to consequences, a use of both utilitarian and deontological methods. The reason this is done is because of the universal audience of the Wisdom Literature. The intended readership of the Wisdom Literature extended outside the community of Old Testament Israel. As a result, the authors could not rely on the same style of reasoning that other authors used with Israel. In fact, conspicuous by its absence in the Wisdom books are many themes that characterize the Law, such as the Promised Land, the sacrifices, the religious festivals, and the fine points of the Law, all of which were compelling only to the nation of Israel. In appealing to other cultures, the authors needed to use a style of moral reasoning that would enable them to present a compelling case to the diverse audience they were addressing. Consideration of consequences enabled them to do just that. That is not to say that the Wisdom books are utilitarian in their view of morality. They do not ground right and wrong in consequences, but use the outcomes to help make their case for the way of wisdom.

The Bible also appeals to ethical egoism and self-interest, specifically in the covenant blessings and cursings in Deuteronomy 27–30. Here God reveals to

Moses that Israel's agricultural prosperity and national security are dependent on their national obedience to the covenant. Thus their loyalty to the covenant will result in certain blessings, while their disobedience will lead to certain cursings. Accordingly, Israel would have a high degree of national self-interest to obey the Law. The prophets repeatedly refer to the blessings and cursings of the covenant in their attempts to call Israel back to faithfulness to God, suggesting that the covenant cursings and blessings form a significant aspect of Old Testament ethics. In addition, the New Testament suggests that receiving the gospel message is in one's self-interest in that it enables a person to avoid a Christless eternity. Further, it is implied that obedience to God is in one's long-term self-interest, even though it may be accompanied by short-term adversity and persecution. Again, this is not to say that Scripture uses egoism as a self-sufficient ethical system, but rather, that the appeal to virtues and principles is supplemented by an appeal to self-interest.

Finally, the Bible also appeals to natural law, or the revelation of God's moral values outside the pages of Scripture. For example, the book of Proverbs defines right and wrong (wisdom and folly) by observations drawn from nature (Prov. 6:6–11; see also Ps. 19:1–6) and human relationships (Prov. 24:30–34). Natural law is not strictly limited to observations from nature, however. It refers to universal moral principles that are not specifically derived from special revelation. The oracles to the nations (e.g., see Isa. 13–23; Jer. 46–51; Ezek. 25–32) are good examples of biblical appeal to natural law. Unlike Israel who had the Mosaic law, these nations lacked the Law and are still condemned for many of the same transgressions as Israel, including injustice, violence, and oppression of the poor. We can conclude, therefore, that these nations were somehow aware of their crimes; otherwise, God could not be just in holding them accountable for their crimes. The means by which God made them aware of these moral obligations is general revelation, or natural law. Thus in the Scripture, natural law supplements the ethics provided by special revelation.[1]

What seems to be absent from the diversity of styles of moral reasoning is any appeal to relativism, either cultural relativism (in which morality is determined by the cultural consensus) or moral subjectivism (in which right and wrong are determined by one's individual tastes and preferences). Because of the transcendent source for Christian ethics, it is presumed that morality cannot be confined to the dictates of culture, not to mention a person's subjective preferences. There is a presumption of universality to Christian ethics that comes from the virtues and principles being grounded in God's character and commands respectively. Because of this transcendent grounding, the biblical authors find it difficult to see morality as anything but universally applicable. There are gray areas in which the biblical principles are not clear and areas that the Scripture does not directly address. In those cases not giving offense to certain cultural norms is considered important

(Rom. 14–15; 1 Cor. 8). But that only comes into consideration when the overriding virtues and principles are not determinative of the morally right course of action. Nowhere in Scripture does a cultural norm take priority over a clear mandate from God's character or biblical principles. Culture is certainly taken into account when it comes to *applying* the virtues and principles, but that is a far different matter than culture *determining* what the moral norms ought to be.

Old Testament Ethics

The Old Testament contains a rich resource of material for ethical reflection, beginning with the Ten Commandments and moving through the Wisdom Literature to the prophets' searing moral condemnation of Israel for their idolatry and resulting moral shortcomings, including violence, oppression of the poor, injustice, and sexual immorality. The Ten Commandments are the foundation, of which the rest of the law of Moses is an expansion. The Wisdom Literature, especially the Proverbs, takes the general principles of the Law and applies them to both Israel and an international audience. These books encourage following the way of wisdom, which includes growing in positive character traits such as prudence, humility, teachability, and purity. The prophets address mostly the nation of Israel, essentially preaching the law to them and calling the people to change their lives in accordance with the Law.

It is true that much of the Mosaic law was superseded by the coming of Jesus and is not addressed to the community of God's people today in the same way it was addressed to the nation of Israel. Of course, the ceremonial law, especially the sacrifices, have been made obsolete by Jesus' sacrificial death on the cross (Heb. 8–10). But much of the civil law is no longer in effect either, because God's people have been "released from the law" (Rom. 7:6). But the Bible affirms that all Scripture is profitable (2 Tim. 3:16–17), even though not all of it is directly addressed to issues facing the community today. Part of the hermeneutical task that is foundational to ethics is to properly read Scripture to determine the moral norms that are applicable for today.

This task is complicated by the fact that the Bible was written to a very different culture, which spoke different languages and wrestled with very different issues than we do today. In one sense, all Scripture is culture-bound; that is, it was written with a particular set of cultural understandings and spoke to issues that may seem foreign today. Part of the interpretive task is to discern what general principles or virtues can be gleaned from the specific teachings of the Old Testament Law and Prophets. Of course, some aspects of Old Testament ethics are directly applicable, such as the command to love God with all one's heart, soul, and strength (Deut. 6:4–6). But other aspects, such as commands that have to do with the Year of Jubilee, require discovering a broader, more general principle or virtue that can then be applied to a contemporary problem or issue. For example, we don't offer the sacrifice of thanksgiving today because we are not under the ceremonial law. But the underlying principle, that God's people should regularly recognize and celebrate God's goodness to them, cultivating the virtue of gratitude, can be drawn from the texts that command these offerings. We would then apply the more general principle of offering gratitude to God but do it in different ways than by offering a sacrifice. Perhaps we would have a public service of thanks to God on a monthly basis in our church or in our families.

Although there is a rich reservoir of material in the Old Testament and many miscellaneous laws governing life in Israel, some emphases do reoccur regularly throughout the teaching of the Law, Wisdom Literature, and Prophets. I have tried to synthesize these emphases, while realizing that the following summary statements do not exhaust the richness of Old Testament ethics.

The Law as the Core of Old Testament Ethics

The foundation of Old Testament ethics is the law of Moses. Some scholars use the term *Law* more narrowly to refer to the Ten Commandments (Ex. 20:1–17; Deut. 5:1–21). We will use it more broadly to refer to the first five books of the Old Testament, the Pentateuch, but especially to the material found in Exodus 20–40, Leviticus, and Deuteronomy 5–30. The Law sets out the fundamental principles and commands for Israel and consists of three primary parts: (1) the moral law, or the Ten Commandments; (2) the civil law, which governed social relations and institutions; and (3) the ceremonial law, which governed Israel's worship of God. When referring to Old Testament ethics, most scholars use the moral and civil law as the foundation. The ceremonial law is often considered a part of Israel's religious ritual and not strictly related to ethics.

Much of the remainder of the Old Testament ethics can be seen in relation to the Law. In the Poetic Literature, especially Psalms, worship is often presented as a response to the revelation of God in the Law. The Wisdom Literature attempts to take the general demands of the Law and make them persuasive to an international audience, without any of the features directly related to Israel, such as the sacrificial system, the Promised Land, the covenants, and the tabernacle or temple. The Prophets appeal to the Law as their primary point of reference in making their indictments against Israel.

One major difference between the Law and the Prophets is that the Prophets make a general appeal to the broad overarching principles in the Law, namely, avoiding idolatry and maintaining justice, in contrast to the detailed specifics in the Law. These are key concepts for Old Testament ethics, reflecting the emphasis of the Ten Commandments on both worship and social relations, or on one's relationship with God and with other people in the community. Rarely do the Prophets address the people with the specifics contained in the Law. Essentially they are preaching the general principles contained in the Law, and they frequently direct attention to the cause-and-effect relationship between obedience and agricultural prosperity in the covenant blessings and cursings of Leviticus 26 and Deuteronomy 27–30.

In the Old Testament, Israel was a theocracy,[2] a nation in which the law of God was automatically the law of the land. Accordingly, all morality was legislated. No distinction was made between law and morality, as one could find in a pluralistic society. The church today, however, is not under the civil and ceremonial aspects of the Law as was Old Testament Israel. Even though this distinguishes biblical Israel from modern, nontheocratic Western nations, a case can be made for Israel as a model for a biblical social ethic. This assertion is based on the premise that the principles underlying the Law are still valid and applicable for the church today.

The Ten Commandments as Moral "First Principles"

The Ten Commandments (also known as the Decalogue) are widely and correctly considered the foundation of morality, not only for Christian ethics, but in the judgment of many in the culture, the foundation for social morality. Many cultures have ethical mandates that are parallel to much of the Decalogue, which suggests that God's fundamental moral laws were knowable to the surrounding cultures and that those cultures were also accountable to them (see the discussion of natural law later in this chapter). Thus the term "first principles" is used to describe them—they are those principles that are clear and evident, even to people without access to Scripture. The Ten Commandments are found in two places in the law of Moses—in Exodus 20:1–17 and its parallel in Deuteronomy 5:1–22. Both occasions for the giving of the Ten Commandments were crucial points in Israel's history. The first giving of the Ten Commandments (Ex. 20) came following the miraculous exodus from Egypt and was considered the core on which the remainder of the Mosaic law was based. The second giving of these commandments (Deut. 5) occurred at the end of Israel's wilderness wanderings and just prior to their entry into the Promised Land. Both instances were preceded by God's miraculous and overwhelming provision for the people, thus illustrating God's providential care for his people, which is summarized in Exodus 20:2, which says, "I am the LORD your God, who brought you out of Egypt, out of the land of slavery" (also Deut. 5:6).

The purpose for each delivery of the Ten Commandments, as well as the rest of the Law, was to shape the nation of Israel into a society that would reflect God's righteousness and compassion both individually and culturally. In the preamble to the Ten Commandments, in Exodus 19:6, God lays out the goal for the Law in general, to create a "kingdom of priests and a holy nation." The Ten Commandments were the foundation necessary to accomplish this goal.

The first tablet of the Ten Commandments contains the first four commands, which outline a person's obligations to God. By contrast the second tablet lists moral responsibilities to others. In the first four commands, God requires that he be their only God (Ex. 20:3; Deut. 5:7), that they do not attempt to reproduce his image in the form of an idol (Ex. 20:4–6; Deut. 5:8–11), that they do not misuse God's name (Ex. 20:7; Deut. 5:11), and that they devote a Sabbath to God as a day of rest and devotion (Ex. 20:8–11; Deut. 5:12–15). The final six commands deal with obligations to others and the community, beginning with those closest to a person—his or her family. To honor one's parents is integral to long life in the land (Ex. 20:12; Deut. 5:16). The final five commandments include prohibitions of murder, adultery, theft, bearing false witness (or most forms of lying), and covetousness (or envy) (Ex. 20:13–17; Deut. 5:17–21). Virtually every culture has prohibitions that parallel these last five commands, demonstrating how central these commands are not only for Christian ethics but also for cultural stability. These are considered basic moral obligations that respect life, marriage and family, property, and truth telling. It is not hard to imagine that a culture that does not adhere to these final five commandments would have difficulty maintaining its ongoing stability. Even the general prohibition that mandates truth telling is critical, because if one cannot expect the truth in his or her verbal communication, it will not be long before meaningful communication becomes very difficult, if not impossible.

Obedience as Personal Loyalty to God

Even though obedience to the precepts of the Law was strongly emphasized as one of the means by which Israel was to be set apart, obedience was not seen as an end in itself. Rather, obedience to the Law was seen primarily as loyalty to God. This emphasis made Old Testament ethics different from the other legal codes of the ancient world. Although the Law shares some similarities with other codes of the ancient world, such as the Babylonian Code of Hammurabi, it is also quite distinct from them in that it is person-centered. A critical emphasis in Old Testament ethics is that God is a person who stands behind the precepts, a concept that is expanded by Jesus in the Gospels in his repudiation of Pharisaic legalism. The emphasis is on obedience to a Person, not just to a command. For example, even the first line of the Ten Commandments refers to God as the one who delivered the Hebrews from slavery in Egypt. Accordingly, this summary statement of what God had already done on their behalf provides a motive for the people of God to remain loyal to him (Ex. 20:2–3). The indicative statements about who God is and what he has done for Israel provide the basis for the imperatives of the Law, which outline the proper and expected response to God's kindness and faithfulness.

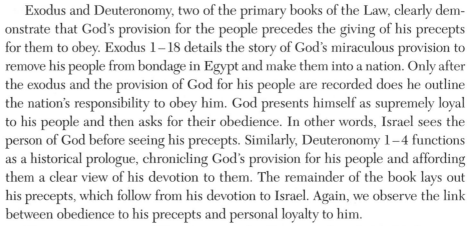

Exodus and Deuteronomy, two of the primary books of the Law, clearly demonstrate that God's provision for the people precedes the giving of his precepts for them to obey. Exodus 1–18 details the story of God's miraculous provision to remove his people from bondage in Egypt and make them into a nation. Only after the exodus and the provision of God for his people are recorded does he outline the nation's responsibility to obey him. God presents himself as supremely loyal to his people and then asks for their obedience. In other words, Israel sees the person of God before seeing his precepts. Similarly, Deuteronomy 1–4 functions as a historical prologue, chronicling God's provision for his people and affording them a clear view of his devotion to them. The remainder of the book lays out his precepts, which follow from his devotion to Israel. Again, we observe the link between obedience to his precepts and personal loyalty to him.

The overall structure of Deuteronomy also illustrates the relationship between obedience and loyalty. The structure is based on the format of the suzerainty treaty, which was used consistently throughout the ancient world at this time.[3] This treaty form first lays out the commitment of the king to his subjects and then stipulates what he expects of the people. Inherent in the treaty is the connection between loyalty to the king and obedience to his precepts. Perhaps one reason this type of treaty form was used to structure Deuteronomy was to strengthen the link between obedience to God's commands and loyalty to the person of God. The prophets speak to this connection when they compare Israel's idolatry to a form of spiritual adultery. Ultimately what was grievous to God was the loss of his relationship with the people, which was evidenced by their long-standing disobedience to his commands.

Holiness as the Unifying Theme of Old Testament Ethics

The central concept that unifies Old Testament ethics is holiness.[4] The Hebrew term for "holy" derives from the Hebrew word *qadosh*, which means "set apart." This is the root concept of the New Testament idea of sanctification.[5] Israel is set apart as a nation to reflect the character of God in their worship, their social relations, and their institutions. One of the primary reasons that God issued his commands was to set Israel apart from its pagan neighbors. This is what Exodus 19:6 means when it refers to Israel as a "holy nation" and a "kingdom of priests." This call for national and individual holiness is grounded in the character of a holy God. God called Israel to be set apart from their neighbors because God is set apart ("You are to be holy to me because I, the LORD, am holy," Lev. 20:26). Vivid examples of how God desired Israel to be set apart occur in the specific commands in Deuteronomy that are aimed at producing a contrast between Israel's practices and those of the other nations in the ancient Near East. The following examples will illustrate this.

First, Deuteronomy 17:16–17 places limitations on the person who would eventually occupy the office of king in Israel. He must not acquire great wealth, military might, or national security alliances (through intermarriage with foreign women), since these would undercut his dependence on God for personal and national security. Throughout the ancient world at this time, the king was virtually deified, and limits on his sovereignty were rare. The king of Israel, however, was to bow before the sovereignty of God. Due to these limitations placed on Israel's king, the surrounding nations knew that he was not a god, but only a servant of the living God.

Second, the treatment of women captured in the course of warfare illustrates how the Law set Israel apart from its neighbors. In much of the ancient world, women who were taken captive by a victorious army were subject to a wide variety of sexual offenses. Israel, however, was obligated to treat them humanely and with respect. If an Israelite wanted to marry a captive woman, he could do so. But the Law strictly prohibited Israelites from selling these women as slaves, either for domestic or sexual purposes (Deut. 21:10–14).

Third, the treatment of other slaves was also to be humane, in contrast to much of the ancient world. After six years of service, slaves were to be released (unless they wanted to remain with the family), and upon their departure their master was to provide for them liberally rather than leave them destitute (Deut. 15:12–18). The treatment of the poor in the land was similar (Lev. 25:25–29, 35–43; Deut. 15:1–11).

The primary way in which Israel was to be set apart for God was in its worship. The Law repeatedly prohibited Israel from worship rituals that contained any compromise with the Canaanite religious practices of their neighbors. For example, sorcery, spiritism, witchcraft, and divination, all of which were associated with Canaanite idolatry, were forbidden in an effort to distance Israel from the worship patterns of their neighbors (Deut. 18:9–13).

The first two of the Ten Commandments explicitly prohibit worshiping false gods (Ex. 20:1–6). Other prohibitions contained in the Law may forbid certain practices simply because the practices resembled the worship practices of Israel's pagan neighbors. For example, when Aaron's sons offered "unauthorized fire" in the tabernacle, God took their lives (Lev. 10:1–5). Although this passage has various interpretations, the one that is most consistent with God's harsh treatment of the priests is that perhaps they introduced a pagan religious ritual into the worship of God in the tabernacle. Likewise, the prohibition in Exodus 23:19 ("Do not cook a young goat in its mother's milk") may have nothing to do with kosher laws or good health practices. Instead, the practice may be prohibited because it resembled a Canaanite religious ritual. In addition, because the worship of the Canaanite god Baal frequently involved sexual immorality, illicit sexual relations are prohibited (Lev. 18; Num. 25:1–3).[6] God's desire for Israel to be set apart for him was central to Old Testament ethics. This is the reason why Israel's request to have a king like all the other nations (1 Sam. 8) undercut God's purpose for Israel to be a "kingdom of priests" and a "holy nation."

The Overlap of Personal and Social Ethics

Because Israel was a theocracy, in the Old Testament there was substantial overlap between personal and social ethics. Today ethicists usually separate ethics into personal ethics (concerning individual ethical decisions) and social ethics (concerning morality for groups, namely, the broader society). A social ethic mandates morality for the society at large or the degree to which individual moral positions should also be moral obligations for the society at large. Whether those ethical norms are enforceable by the law is a different question, though in Old Testament Israel, there were actions that were immoral but not punishable by the civil law, such as covetousness.

The abortion debate effectively illustrates the contemporary distinction between personal and social ethics. Many pro-choice advocates insist that though you can be personally opposed to abortion, to say that abortion is wrong for society as a whole is a different question, particularly when it comes to the law enforcing the social ethic. This type of reasoning has also been applied to adultery and homosexual behavior. In the case of murder, however, everyone — regardless of background, culture, or religious tradition — believes that it is wrong and should be wrong for everyone in society. In this case there is an overlap of personal and social ethics. In the Old Testament, personal and social ethics were more overlapping. What was moral for the individual (personal ethics) was also generally moral for the society (social ethics).

The emphasis on individual morality occurs most frequently in the Wisdom Literature. Perhaps this is because the Wisdom books are addressed universally in a way that the Law was not. The Wisdom Literature was written more for an international audience, and the Law was addressed to the covenant community of Israel. Thus personal and social ethics overlap less in the Wisdom Literature because the bonds of community are not emphasized as much as they are in the parts of the Old Testament addressed directly to Israel.

The Social Dimension of Old Testament Ethics

God's design for Israel as a kingdom of priests and a holy nation was to be an ideal society. The Law mandated individual behavior, and in doing so, it structured the society. The very structure of Israel's society was to reflect their relationship with God. It was assumed that the Law addressed the structures of both society and individuals. Consequently, much of the Law comes under the heading of civil law, which governed social relationships and established institutions that would ensure a proper ordering of society and maintain justice within the society (see, e.g., Ex. 21–23; esp. 20:12–17; Lev. 18–20, 25; Deut. 19–25). Since the economic aspects of life in the Promised Land presented great challenges to the Israelites in their attempt to be obedient to God, much of the civil law addressed issues concerning property and economics. The ceremonial part of the Law was also well developed (see Ex. 24–40; Lev. 1–10, 22–23; Deut. 5–16).

The prophets also develop the social dimension of Old Testament ethics. They frequently accuse Israel of violating the social aspects of the Law. Charges of oppression, perversion of justice, and exploitation of the poor were all reminders that the people had both personally sinned and set up structures in their society that violated the Law (Amos 4:1; 5:11–13; Mic. 2:2; Hab. 1:4). Not only do the prophets look back to the Law, but they also look forward to the consummation of the kingdom for the social dimension of Old Testament ethics. In most of their visions of the kingdom of God, the prophets emphasize a rightly ordered society as well as a people who worship God properly. Perhaps the clearest examples of this are the Servant Songs of Isaiah (chaps. 42, 49, 50, and 53), especially in 42:1–4, where the Servant-Messiah (Jesus) will bring about justice, or a proper ordering of society. Whereas Israel failed in the ordering of society, the Servant-Messiah will succeed.

Leviticus 25, where much of Old Testament real estate law is codified, provides several examples of the way in which the civil law structured social relations in Israel. Since the land was central to the Old Testament agricultural economy, this section of the Law is very important. This passage establishes several important institutions, including the sabbatical year (vv. 1–7), the Year of Jubilee (vv. 8–24, 35–46), and the law of redemption (vv. 25–34, 47–55). The sabbatical year legislation mandated that the Israelites were to let the land rest every seventh year by not planting crops on it. This was a visible means by which the Israelites demonstrated to their neighbors their trust in God to provide food for them in the years in which they did not harvest crops.

The Year of Jubilee (Lev. 25:8–24, 35–46) was an even more radical institution established by the Law. Every fiftieth year, all land was returned to its original owners and all slaves were released. Leases on land were priced according to the proximity to the Jubilee, that is, more expensive if the Jubilee was far off, less expensive if the Jubilee was near. The purpose of the Jubilee was to regularly redistribute the land. This prevented the inordinate accumulation of land and provided an opportunity for a person to make a living from the land, the primary means by which people supported themselves in an agricultural society.[7] This institution also demonstrated that the land belonged to God and thus could not be permanently bought and sold (v. 23).

The law of redemption (Lev. 25:25–34, 47–55) functioned like the Jubilee, only more regularly and not quite as radically. This law required that if a person became so impoverished that he had to sell his land or sell himself into slavery in order to survive, the nearest relative had the legal obligation to buy the land or the person and return the land to the individual or allow the person to avoid slavery and work independently. In addition, if at some point after he had sold his land or himself, he obtained the means to buy his land back or buy himself out of slavery, he had the right to do so and could not be refused. As a last resort, at the Jubilee, his land automatically reverted back to him, as would his status as a free man. The law of redemption is applied in the book of Ruth, as Boaz not only redeems Ruth (a different law of redemption known as levirate marriage, in which the nearest relative was required to marry a childless widow to carry on the lineage of her deceased husband and provide for her support) but also the property that belonged to her husband prior to his death.

Another real estate law that structured a type of welfare system was the law of gleaning (Lev. 19:9–10), which mandated that when harvesting one's field, the owner was to leave the perimeter of the field unharvested and only go through the field one time to gather the crops. The unharvested edges and the crops that were dropped or missed on the first pass were to be left for the poor and the immigrant to harvest for themselves. This set up a kind of "workfare," providing for the needs of the poor but also requiring that they take initiative and work for it. This too is applied in the book of Ruth when Ruth as a widow seeking support is allowed to glean in Boaz's field.

Other examples of laws that structured Israelite society include prohibitions of usury (Ex. 22:25; Lev. 25:35–37),[8] of moving boundary stones that delineated a person's property (Deut. 19:14; 27:17), and of perverting the legal system by showing bias, accepting bribes, or committing perjury (Ex. 23:1–2; Deut. 18–20; see also the ninth commandment in Ex. 20:16, which prohibited bearing false witness). The Law regulated both individual behavior and societal structures, producing institutions that were based on Israel's covenant relationship with God for the purpose of developing an ideal society that would bear corporate witness to the reality of God in Israel's midst.

The Pursuit of Justice

Throughout the Old Testament, God's people were called to stand against injustice because God is a God of justice, whose heart breaks when the poor and vulnerable are victimized by the powerful. The paradigm throughout the Old Testament for God being for the poor and rescuing the oppressed is the exodus, and is a consistent reminder to Israel of God's rescue. It became the model for how Israel was to treat the vulnerable among them (Lev. 19:33 — applied to immigrants, and

Deut. 24:17–18—applied to the widow, orphan, and immigrant). Further, one of the reasons for keeping the Sabbath was that God had rescued them from the continual work of being slaves in Egypt (Deut. 5:12–16).

God set up Israel under the Mosaic law with laws and structures in place to protect the vulnerable. The Law was structured to proactively prevent exploitation of the poor and vulnerable. Traditions such as the law of gleaning (Deut. 24:19–22), the Year of Jubilee and obligation of land redemption (Lev. 25), and laws about loans to the poor, including usury laws (Deut. 24:10–18), set up society so that the poor were protected from those who would exploit them. Israelites were not to take economic advantage of the poor, and the law was structured to prevent this. This is one of the primary components of Israel being a "kingdom of priests" and a "holy nation" set apart for God (Ex. 19:5–6). The way they lived in a just society was to be a testimony to their neighbors of the reality of God in their midst.

In the Psalms, God is repeatedly portrayed as the rescuer of the oppressed, weak, and poor—that is a fundamental aspect of who he is (Pss. 10:16–18; 35:10; 72:12–14; 82:2–4; 103:6; 140:12; 146:5–9; see also Jer. 20:13). In these psalms, justice and mercy go together. Showing mercy alone, after the fact, is only part of what God does for the poor. God also proactively takes up the cause of the

An Evangelical Manifesto

Published in mid-2008, in anticipation of the upcoming presidential election, the Evangelical Manifesto is a declaration of evangelical identity and commitments. Its purpose is to challenge the community to rethink its identity and place in public life and reform its behavior. Drafted by prominent Christian leaders such as Os Guinness, Richard Mouw, and Dallas Willard, it is a strategic plan for evangelical engagement in the twenty-first century.

A significant part of the manifesto is an encouragement to rethink the role of faith and public policy. They put it this way: "Called by Jesus to be in the world, but not of the world, we are fully engaged in public affairs but never completely equated with any party, partisan ideology, economic system, class, tribe or national identity." As a result, the draft attempts to "repudiate two equal and opposite errors into which many Christians have fallen recently. One error has been to privatize faith, interpreting and applying it to the personal and spiritual realm only.... The other error, made by both the religious left and the religious right in recent decades, is to politicize faith, using faith to express essentially political points that have lost touch with biblical truth." The draft attempts to urge a more civil participation in public life that has the potential of more clearly reflecting Christ in public engagement.*

*See www.anevangelicalmanifesto.com.

poor and pleads the case of the vulnerable. This is why the proverb can make the claim that "he who oppresses the poor shows contempt for their Maker, but whoever is kind to the needy honors God" (Prov. 14:31). Similarly, the people are to speak up and defend the poor (Prov. 31:8–9). The prophets routinely admonish the people and leadership to *defend the cause* of the poor. This mandate is often linked to fundamental aspects of our life with God and doing what is right (Isa. 1:11–17—seeking justice is linked to *doing right*; Isa. 58:5–8—seeking justice is linked with *true religious observance*; Jer. 22:13–17—seeking justice is linked with *knowing God* (see also Prov. 28:5); Isa. 42:6–7—seeking justice is linked with *being a light to the Gentiles*). Justice is also connected with the coming of the Messiah in his kingdom (Isa. 42:1–4; 61:1–2).

Injustice against the vulnerable and failure to advocate for them and take up their cause also characterizes a society that has gone spiritually astray (in the Old Testament, it is a society that has given itself over to idolatry, a key evidence of which is institutional injustice—Isa. 1:21–23; Jer. 5:26–29; Ezek. 22:6–13, 29).

This emphasis is echoed in the Minor Prophets. Amos, for example, condemns the idle rich and pronounces judgment on Israel for their promotion and toleration of social injustice (2:6–8; 4:1; 5:11; 8:4–6). He sees social injustice when those who have money and power use their resources and position to take advantage of the poor and vulnerable. There is no distinction in the Prophets between institutional and individual oppression of the poor. Social injustice and sexual sin are considered equally egregious sins in the eyes of God (2:7). Micah likewise condemns those who use their power to exploit the poor. Such injustice is considered a primary identifying characteristic of a society or community that has gone spiritually astray and, in the Prophets, is a cause of God's judgment (2:1–3; 3:1–4, 9–12). By contrast, Micah points out what should be obvious to the people—that God requires those who follow him to act justly (literally, "do justice"), love mercy, and walk humbly with God (6:6–8). This is in contrast to the empty religious ritual so prevalent in Old Testament Israel. God desires justice more than religious ritual. Zechariah also calls the people to repentance, a part of which is a call to promote compassion and justice for the poor and vulnerable (7:8). Malachi echoes this call by putting a concern for justice toward the poor on the same level with those who engaged in false religion and sexual sin (3:5).

New Testament Ethics

In the New Testament the emphasis is not as much on institutional morality and social ethics as it is on a morality for the church. With the coming of Christ, the people of God are no longer under the Law. The ceremonial law has been superseded by the death of Christ, and the civil law no longer applies directly because the primary agent of God's work in the world is the multinational, multiracial church, as opposed to the theocratic nation of Israel.[9] Thus, for the church, not only has the way that a person relates to God changed, but the way in which God views the mission of his people has also changed. Although the broad objective—to glorify God by bearing witness to his rule over the earth—is the same in both Testaments, the way in which it is achieved is different. Under the Law, Israel was literally "one nation under God." The church, however, is a multiethnic body of believers for whom national boundaries are irrelevant. The church is to bear witness to the reality of God by the type of community that is experienced in it, as was the case in Old Testament Israel. But the commands of the New Testament do not provide the same institutional framework to the church as the Law did for Israel. That does not mean that the gospel has no social element, but rather that the New Testament church did not attempt to structure institutions and effect social change in the same way that the Old Testament did.

This does not mean that the church should not attempt to effect institutional change in society today. That, in fact, is an aspect of the kingdom of God inaugurated by Jesus. The kingdom in the Old Testament clearly had both an individual and a social dimension (Isa. 2:2–4; 11:1–9; Mic. 4:1–5). When Jesus preached that "the kingdom of heaven is at hand," he did not indicate that he was changing the Old Testament concept of the kingdom in any significant way. The disciples and others who heard his message seemed to understand the kingdom in its Old Testament context. When the kingdom is fulfilled in its entirety at Jesus' second coming, it will have both an individual and social dimension.

Most of the Old Testament texts that prophesy the coming kingdom envision a kingdom with a social aspect, one in which the resulting society is rightly ordered, being free from injustice, oppression, and exploitation of the poor. The institutions that reinforced an unjust society would be dismantled. If the kingdom had a social dimension at its inception and has a social dimension at its culmination, then it seems logical to assume that in the interim, a social dimension will be important too.

Even though the New Testament does not emphasize a social dimension as much as the Old Testament, it does not follow that the gospel completely lacks a social aspect. Many things that the New Testament church did not overtly endorse or encourage are openly and justifiably supported in the church today. For example, the fact that the early church did not build hospitals, orphanages, or other similar institutions (not to mention church buildings or seminaries) does not mean that later church support of these was inappropriate. Just because the New Testament church did not focus on institutional social change does not imply that it is an inappropriate action for the church today. Part of the reason the church did not engage in social change was due to its role as a persecuted minority in the first century, relatively powerless to effect social change under the tyranny of the Roman Empire. Rather, the church affected change in the only way genuinely available, by the formation of countercultural Christian communities throughout the ancient world that lived together in community and modeled the virtues in a way somewhat analogous to the kind of "ideal society" to which God called Israel in the Old Testament.

Some argue that social change is not the realm of the community of God's people in the New Testament era, because the social order will deteriorate prior to the consummation of the kingdom with the return of Jesus. This aspect of ethics is often made analogous to "rearranging the deck chairs on the *Titanic*," suggesting the futility and poor stewardship involved. The counterargument to this is that such a diagnosis can also be made of the church's role in evangelism. People will reject the gospel message increasingly as Jesus' return draws closer. But no one suggests that such a reality means that the mandate to proclaim the gospel be abandoned. In fact, quite the opposite is true. For the church's focus on social change, just because society may be moving in the morally wrong direction has little to do with whether there is a mandate for social change. In addition, the Bible calls God's people to be faithful to its mandates and leave the impact up to the work of God in the world.

Mandates for social change, in addition to the proclamation of the gospel and making disciples, can all be envisioned under the general heading of the Great Commission (Matt. 28:19–20), since Jesus made it clear that his followers were to "make disciples . . . teaching them to obey everything I have commanded you." As you will see in the rest of this section, Jesus' teaching continues the mandate for justice and social impact that began with the Old Testament Law and Prophets.

As was the case with Old Testament ethics, entire books have been written on New Testament ethics. In this section, therefore, we will attempt to synthesize the main emphases in the New Testament's description of the moral life. Constructing any kind of system of New Testament ethics is difficult because so little of Jesus' teaching on ethics is developed systematically.[10] Also, Paul's and the other apostles' contributions on ethics are often given in response to specific problems in the churches and are not necessarily universally applicable or binding. Just as it is difficult to systematize the theology of the New Testament, so it is with New Testament ethics. The following is offered as the main emphases of New Testament ethics.

An Ethic of Virtue — Becoming Like Jesus

Although the New Testament greatly emphasizes principles, it also places high value on virtue, thereby reflecting the blend of virtues and principles that characterizes Christian ethics. The Gospels and Epistles never envision the moral life as simply doing the right thing—as the religious leaders emphasized—apart from developing character and virtue. The virtues centered around those of Christ, and the development of character was synonymous with becoming more like Christ.

In terms of virtue theory, the ideal person will model Christ. The New Testament is clear that the moral obligations for the follower of Jesus are subsumed under the notion of "becoming like Christ." For example, Christ's followers are to imitate his humility and obedience to the will of his Father (Phil. 2:5–11). They are to emulate Christ in his suffering and death, providing a model of submission to authority (1 Peter 2:22–24). Further, the believer is called to imitate Paul, who in turn imitates Christ (1 Cor. 11:1). The great promise to those who follow Jesus is that they have been predestined to be "conformed to the likeness of [God's] Son" (Rom. 8:29). Believers are called to be "imitators of God," and it was assumed that the audience knew that Jesus was the earthly manifestation of God (Eph. 5:1).

The fruit of the Spirit (Gal. 5:22–23) and the deeds of the flesh (vv. 19–21) provide an initial list of the virtues and their opposing vices. The vices are expanded in Mark 7:20–23 and 1 Corinthians 6:9–10. The virtues are often explained as character traits that must be "put on" just as the vices are to be "put off" as part of imitating Christ's character (Eph. 4:20–32; Col. 3:1–11). Perhaps the reason why there is no systematic discussion of the virtues is because they are illustrated

The Politics of Jesus

Although some in the Christian community disparage the attempts of the church to influence culture and government, most who adhere to a Christian ethic accept that religious people have some role in impacting public policy. But how that manifests itself and what sort of policy positions result from such a commitment vary widely. There is new debate over what it means for Christian ethics to intersect with specific public policies. Some of the long-standing consensus positions include opposition to abortion on demand and same-sex marriage. In addition, there have been long-term efforts to return religion to the public schools and support for public displays of religious symbols. However, new issues are emerging that threaten to divide the religious community. These include immigration reform, global climate change, global public health and AIDS, international human rights, and worldwide poverty relief. There is serious debate on what position is consistent with Christian ethics but also on the most prudent means to accomplish public policy goals.*

*Lisa Miller, "An Evangelical Identity Crisis," and Michael Gerson, "A New Social Gospel," *Newsweek*, November 13, 2006, 28–43; Stephanie Simon, "Evangelical Agenda Fight Is Heating Up," *Los Angeles Times*, March 10, 2007, A1.

so well in the Gospel accounts of the life of Christ. The apostles did not need to describe much further what was already so well depicted in the narrative accounts of Jesus' life. Whatever the reason, it is clear that any ethic that claims consistency with the New Testament must include its emphasis on cultivating virtue, namely, the virtues exemplified in Jesus' life.

An Ethic of Love

Any account of New Testament ethics that does not include love as the central virtue is surely incomplete. Jesus and the apostles take the central command of the Law, "Love the LORD your God with all your heart and with all your soul and with all your strength" (Deut. 6:5), and develop an ethic of love for God and one's neighbor. The parable of the good Samaritan (Luke 10:25–37) defines one's neighbor as anyone who has a need that person can meet, and applies the principle to those outside the church as well as to fellow believers. When an astute young lawyer asked Jesus about ethical and spiritual priorities, Jesus replied that a person's chief duties were to love God and one's neighbor as oneself (Luke 10:25–29; see also Matt. 22:34–40, where Jesus similarly answers the question of the hostile religious leaders). Paul summarizes the entire Law under the heading of love, suggesting that love fulfills the Law (Rom. 13:8–10; Gal. 5:14).[11] Similarly, Jesus insists that the world will know that he is who he claims to be by the way love is practiced in the community (John 13:35).[12] In John's epistles, John extends this notion, arguing that it is inconsistent to say that a person loves God without practicing a life of love (1 John 3:17; 4:7). Love is considered the ultimate expression of the virtues involved in following Jesus and the indicator of how substantial the commitment to one's faith is.

Principles Reapplied, with Virtues

Although the virtues are the ultimate grounding for moral principles, the New Testament places great emphasis on principles expressed in God's commands. Jesus essentially deepens and reapplies the principles of the Law that were misused by the Jewish religious leaders. For example, in the Sermon on the Mount (Matt. 5–7) he does not nullify the Law (5:17–20; John 10:33–35). Rather, he critiques the Pharisees for their misunderstanding and misapplication of it. He extends the requirements of the Law and promotes to both the religious leaders and the general population a deontology that is both action and intent oriented. Jesus teaches in the Sermon on the Mount that the intention is just as important as the action, and that a correct action with the wrong intention is not a correct action at all. The Pharisees exemplify some of the abuses of an unbalanced commitment to principles with their system of rigid rules and insensitivity to both the people involved and the consequences of such strict attention to rules.

For example, when Jesus is criticized in Matthew 12:1–14 for healing a man with a withered hand on the Sabbath, he is grieved at their blind adherence to rules and resulting lack of compassion for the man. Jesus makes it clear that he is rejecting not the Sabbath command, but the Pharisees' misreading of it. Had the religious leaders had a notion of virtue (of compassion) in addition to their principles, they might not have been so callous to the man who needed healing. In addition, when Jesus is criticized in Mark 7:1–20 for not following the religious traditions of the Jews, he responds with an example of how that tradition can actually produce harm. Mark 7:11 refers to the tradition of "Corban," a term that translates a Hebrew word that literally means "offering." In Jesus' day, Corban referred to something devoted to God, and in this case it involved money. Since the money was devoted to God, it could not be used for anything else, including financial assistance for one's own needy parents. Jesus' critique here involved correcting their rigidity with the element of virtue, here the virtue of loyalty to family. In rebuking the Pharisees for their rigid misapplication of the Law, Jesus sought a radical change in the primary perspective of ethics among first-century Jews. He rejected a rigid and callous commitment to principles that were not consistent with the Law. He aimed for a deontology that accurately applied the Law, combining a commitment to principles with the virtue of compassion for people.

For Paul and the apostles who wrote the Epistles, the emphasis on virtues and principles is much the same. It emerges not in confrontations with the Pharisees, but in conflicts with other heretical deviations from the gospel. For example, when Paul confronts the adherents of Jewish-Christian legalism (the Judaizers) in Romans and Galatians, he affirms a primary principle of the Christian moral life—spiritual growth cannot be accomplished by one's individual effort alone. Rather, it happens by grace through faith, in the same way a person originally came to saving faith (Gal. 3:1–3). Also, in Colossians Paul confronts the heresy of incipient Gnosticism, or the glorification of knowledge as the means by which the spiritual elite achieve spiritual perfection. He affirms the principle that spiritual maturity takes place not by knowledge alone but by the working of "Christ in you" (Col. 1:27). Even in areas in which there are no clear-cut moral rules, the "doubtful things" or morally gray areas (Rom. 14–15; 1 Cor. 8–10), Paul appeals to the principle of not offending one's weaker brother. There is no backing away from use of principles on the part of the apostles, since it was such a clear emphasis in Jesus' ministry. The apostles' primary ethical goal was to accurately represent Jesus' teaching and apply it to relevant problems in the church.

This is perhaps seen most clearly in 1 Corinthians, where Paul addresses specific problems by an appeal to principles. To their divisiveness (chaps. 1–4), he applies the principle of the unity of the body of Christ. To their immorality, he applies the principle of maintaining sexual purity in the church (chaps. 5–6). To the question of marriage and singleness (chap. 7), he applies the principle of being content in whatever state one is in. To the question of meat offered to idols (chaps. 8–10), he applies the principle of not offending the weaker brother. To the question of worship in the church and spiritual gifts (chaps. 12–14), Paul applies the principle that things in the church are to be done in an orderly fashion so that the entire church is built up. Paul appeals to the church to practice principles that they already know, thus living life consistently with the principles established by Christ and the virtues modeled by him.

Members of the Kingdom — People of the Cross/Resurrection

In the New Testament, ethics follows from what membership in the kingdom demands. Ethics and discipleship overlap significantly. Little distinction is made between the moral and the spiritual life, except that the former deals mainly with the believer's responsibility to the church and the world, while the latter relates to one's worship of God. A consistent pattern emerges in the New Testament in that Jesus and the apostles would initially preach the message of the kingdom and then its ethical implications. But the ethical implications are addressed quickly, since it was inconceivable to the early church that someone would profess Christ and not adhere to the moral demands of life in the kingdom.

A good example of this occurs in the gospel of Matthew. After the events of Jesus' birth and preparation for ministry (Matt. 1:1–4:11), Jesus comes boldly proclaiming that "the kingdom of heaven is near" (4:17). The first disciples are gathered (4:18–22), then large crowds begin to follow him (4:23–25). Shortly after crowds gather and his message gains popularity, he preaches the Sermon on the Mount (chaps. 5–7), where he presents the ethical demands of life in the kingdom. Likewise, the material on sanctification, or the spiritual life, in the book of Romans (chaps. 6–8; see also chaps. 12–15, which address more practical moral problems in the church) is not presented until after the doctrine of justification by faith is outlined and defended (chaps. 1–5). Paul taught that the attempts of unregenerate people to be moral fall far short of what God requires. Neither Jesus nor Paul viewed such attempts as substitutes for membership in the kingdom.

What membership in the kingdom looks like was powerfully shaped by the cross and resurrection of Jesus. The New Testament authors consistently appeal to the death of Jesus as the example of virtue and the model for individual behavior. For example, just after Peter makes the critical confession of Christ as Messiah, Jesus tells his followers that their lives must resemble his at the cross. He uses the metaphor of taking up one's cross as the defining component of following him (Mark 8:18–34). The apostles echo this when Paul tells the Philippians that they must imitate Christ's humility as exhibited on the cross (Phil. 2:6–11). He further invokes both themes of the cross and resurrection when he outlines our spiritual foundations by the notion that we have died and been raised up with Christ. Thus believers are to count themselves dead to sin and alive to God (Rom. 6:1–11). This is parallel to Paul's admonition to the Colossians to live for Christ, when he insists that God's people have died with Christ and been raised with him. As a result, they were to live differently, putting to death the vices of their former lives and adopting the virtues of their new life in Christ (Col. 3:1–14). Similarly, Peter exhorts the church to be shaped by the example of Christ on the cross, particularly in their dealings with the surrounding culture (1 Peter 2:18–25). The cross and resurrection of Jesus defined the early Christian community and illustrated the virtues of Jesus that they were to imitate.

New Testament Ethics: A Special Place for the Poor

The preferential place of the poor is a particular emphasis in Jesus' teaching that is consistent with the admonitions of the Old Testament prophets. The poor and others outside the social mainstream are some of the people with whom Jesus spent most of his time (other than time with his disciples). Thus he modeled as well as verbally taught this ethical imperative. This emphasis surely reflects the Old Testament stress on the institutions of the Law that were designed to take care of the poor in the land of Israel. He realizes that the poor will always exist in society (Matt. 26:11), but the implication is to take care of them, not ignore them. The poor are singled out as the special recipients of the gospel (Matt. 11:5; Luke 4:18) and are blessed (Luke 6:20), perhaps because the materially poor most easily grasped the notion of spiritual poverty (Matt. 5:3). The Epistles encourage caring for the poor, especially the poor in the church, being sensitive to their vulnerability, and treating them with esteem, not contempt (Rom. 15:26; 2 Cor. 8:1–7; 9:1–15; James 2:1–13).

Jesus captures the importance of caring for the poor in Luke 14:12–14. When one gives a banquet, the poor and the marginal members of society should be invited instead of one's friends, because a person's friends will inevitably repay the invitation, whereas the poor lack the material means to repay. Thus one is to invite the poor since they cannot repay, trusting God for a reward in heaven (v. 14). Doing this forces the host to show unconditional grace toward the poor and models the unconditional love with which God loves each believer. The church's concern for the poor is one of the clearest illustrations of God's unconditional care for the individual person and perhaps is one of the reasons why such care for the poor is mandated.

Faithfully following Jesus involves taking up the cause of the poor. In the Gospels Jesus announces the coming of the kingdom of God by continuing the Old Testament theme of concern for the poor. For example, in his first act of public ministry in Luke's gospel, Jesus cites Isaiah 61:1–2 as being fulfilled in his coming, the evidence for which is that the good news comes to the poor (Luke 4:14–21). Similarly, when the followers of John the Baptist ask Jesus if he is the promised Messiah, Jesus points to the evidence of the marginalized being healed and taken care of (Matt. 11:2–6).

Jesus continued the Old Testament theme of caring for the poor and expected his followers to do the same (Matt. 25:31–46). Here the command to care for the poor is connected to a person's commitment to Jesus himself, echoing Proverbs 14:31 ("Whoever is kind to the needy honors God"). Jesus was well known for his relationships with the marginalized, including foreigners, women, children, and the poor. Jesus intervened aggressively to correct an injustice when he cleansed the temple. He threw out the money changers, who were using a religious cloak to oppress the poor and those from other lands (John 2:12–17). He rebuked the religious leaders for neglecting justice, which Jesus called one of the "weightier matters of the law" in favor of empty religious rituals (Luke 11:42). Though it might not look as if Jesus confronted institutional injustice, remember that the political and religious systems in first-century Israel were virtually identical. The religious leaders were also the political leaders, holding political power under the Romans. Thus, when Jesus attacked the religious status quo, he was also confronting the social-economic-political status quo.

The early church followed this example in fulfillment of the Great Commission. That is, combating injustice is part of the final command Jesus left his disciples ("teaching them to obey everything I have commanded you," Matt. 28:19–20). In Acts one of the clearest identifying marks of the church's "growth" is its commitment to the poor, even though the majority of early believers were poor themselves. Two of the three "snapshots" of life in the early church concern taking care of the poor (Acts 2:42–47; 4:32–37).

The Epistles continue to urge the church to take care of the poor (2 Cor. 8–9). In Old Testament fashion, James connects true religion to taking care of widows and orphans in their distress (James 1:27), urges the church to avoid favoring the rich over the poor (2:1–7), and charges them to take care of those who need help as an indication of one's faith being the real thing (2:15–17). This is echoed in 1 John, where John connects a heart for the poor with the love of God being in us (3:17–18). James finally urges the wealthy in the church not to use their wealth or position to take advantage of the vulnerable (James 5:1–6).

The Dynamic: The Indwelling Holy Spirit

This emphasis stands in sharp contrast with the prevailing opinion in the world of the New Testament. The Jewish religious leaders relied on spiritual discipline to develop holiness, and the Greeks depended on education to produce morality. The

New Testament assumes that both are insufficient. Instead, it provides an internal source that assists in decision making and enables one to mature spiritually. This theme is introduced in the Gospels (John 13–17) and developed in the Epistles, particularly those of Paul. For example, Romans 8 discusses the role of the Holy Spirit in producing sanctification in the individual believer. The person without the Spirit is not able to welcome spiritual things into his or her life (1 Cor. 2:14). The process of being transformed from one stage of glory to the next comes ultimately from the Spirit (2 Cor. 3:18). Believers who "live by the Spirit" will produce the fruit of the Spirit (Gal. 5:16, 22–23), and will not satisfy their innate inclination to sin. Clearly, the New Testament envisions moral and spiritual maturity only in connection with the internal ministry of the Spirit who transforms a person from the inside out.

Divine Command Theory

Given the place in biblical ethics for God's commands and the assumption throughout Scripture that his commands are to be obeyed, an emphasis on God's commands, or biblical principles, is an important part of Christian ethics. Frequently, when Christians stress God's commands in their system of ethics, they sometimes advocate what is called a "divine command" theory of ethics. A divine command system is one in which the ultimate foundation for morality is the revealed will of God, namely, the commands of God as found in Scripture. Traditional divine command theory is a somewhat different view than we advanced earlier, that God's character, not his commands, is the ultimate source of moral norms. Nevertheless, God's commands do have a significant place in Christian ethics, though logically subordinate to God's character. That is, one can recognize God as the source of divine commands without adhering to a strict divine command theory. Given the place for God's commands in a system that blends virtues and principles, some of the objections to a divine command theory of ethics must be considered.

Of course, Christian ethics is not the only religious moral system with an emphasis on divine commands. Judaism, Islam, neoorthodox Christianity (as represented by Karl Barth and Emil Brunner), and many of the ancient polytheistic religions place great importance on divine commands for their ethics. In fact, the original philosophical tensions raised by divine command ethics came from the classical Greeks during the time of Plato. In his well-known dialogue, the *Euthyphro*, Plato asks the question that must be addressed by every adherent of divine command theory: Does God (in Plato's case, the gods) command things because they are good, or are things good because God commands them? In other words, do God's commands make something right or indicate that it is right? If one answers that God commands things because they are good, it would seem to make God's commands redundant, simply reinforcing what is already obvious and available to everyone. But if one answers that things are good because God commands them, then God appears arbitrary, and he would be free to command anything, even those things that violate society's widely held moral principles.

For example, if things are good because God commands them, then he could command that we torture babies, and that would be good simply because he commanded it. But that seems strongly counterintuitive for most people, and the average person would have great difficulty worshiping that kind of God. This view is known as ethical voluntarism, and when critics attack divine command morality, they usually target ethical voluntarism.

Islamic ethics is considered to be one example of ethical voluntarism. Muslims hold very strongly to the sovereignty of Allah, and consequently, they believe that he cannot be accountable to anyone or anything. Because of this understanding of Allah, it is consistent for Muslims to hold that such a sovereign being can command whatever he desires, and that, in and of itself, makes it good. Critics of Islamic ethics insist that this makes Allah arbitrary and gives him freedom to be even capricious in his commands. To see the God of the Bible in this way makes most Christians uncomfortable, because the Scripture portrays God as bound by his character, which makes him unable to command certain things. Therefore ethical voluntarism appears to be inconsistent with the biblical portrait of God.

The other side of the question posed in the *Euthyphro* is to insist that God commands things because they are good. This is the view of historic, rabbinic Judaism and of Roman Catholic ethics as developed by Thomas Aquinas. God is not free to command anything he so desires, but is restricted by his character. This condition does not undermine God's sovereignty, but prevents him from acting in a way inconsistent with his own character. Thus morality is not grounded ultimately in God's commands, but in his character, which then expresses itself in his commands. Another way to state this is that whatever a loving God commands is good. In other words, anything that God commanded that was consistent with his character, which is love, would be good. Should God hypothetically command that we were to torture babies, it would not be good, and believers would not be accountable for obedience to it.[13] This solution avoids the charge of ethical voluntarism by linking God's commands with his character. That is, the notion of the good is based on God's eternal and unchangeable character.

Goodness and General Revelation

Another way to approach this problem as presented in the *Euthyphro* is to see God's commands in Scripture (special revelation) in conjunction with his moral values expressed outside of Scripture (general revelation). This aspect of Christian morality is commonly called natural law and will be outlined in more detail below. Natural law posits that moral precepts exist prior to God's commands given in special revelation, and that objective moral values exist outside of special revelation. These concepts are logically independent of Scripture and are thus indirectly revealed by God in creation. Objective goodness has always existed since it is rooted in God's character, but it is revealed through natural law prior to God giving human beings the Bible. The Christian notion of goodness includes more than just what is revealed in the Bible. It also includes what God has revealed by general revelation. Just as God has revealed truths about the sciences outside of Scripture, he has also revealed truths about morality outside of Scripture.

Natural law is simply general revelation in the area of moral values. This idea is important for developing a divine command theory that does not make God an arbitrary commander. Not only must his commands be consistent with his character, but they must also be consistent with the values he has revealed in general revelation. If it is reasonable to believe in a God who can reveal himself in special revelation in the Bible, then neither is it unreasonable to believe in a divine command theory in which God's commands must be compatible with general revelation. To take this view, one would obey a divine commander without being a traditional divine command theorist or ethical voluntarist.[14]

Problems with Divine Command Ethics

Even if one accepts this as the way to resolve the *Euthyphro* dilemma, there are still two problems with divine command ethics that must be addressed. First is the problem raised by many critics of Christian ethics that calling God "good" presupposes a prior notion of goodness that must be independent of God and religion.[15] However, this criticism confuses two different philosophical categories, namely, *epistemology*, or one's knowledge of something, and *ontology*, or the essential nature of a thing. Just because a person must know something about what is good before calling God good, it does not follow that goodness is essentially independent of God. If I am traveling to San Francisco from my home near Los Angeles, I must look on a road map to find it before I arrive there. But surely it does not follow that the road map is logically prior to the city of San Francisco. My knowledge of San Francisco is not logically prior to the existence of that city. In the same way, just because I must know something about goodness before I can tell that God is good does not mean that morality is independent of God.

A second problem with divine command theories arises when there is an apparent conflict between two commands in Scripture. For example, during World War II, when Corrie ten Boom gave sanctuary to Jews in her native country of the

Netherlands, the authorities often asked her if she was hiding Jews in her home. If she told the truth, the Jews would have been taken to extermination camps. But if she lied, they would have been saved. Here she was faced with a genuine moral dilemma, or a conflict of commands. She had a moral duty to tell the truth, but she was also responsible for preventing harm when it was in her power to do so, especially when it involved saving life. What was she morally obligated to do?

Consider the example of Rahab in Joshua 2. Here Rahab the prostitute was commended for her faith in sheltering the Israelite spies sent on a reconnaissance mission to the Promised Land. The authorities directly asked her if she knew the location of any Israelite spies. Not only did she tell them that she did not know where the spies were, but she also sent them after the Israelite spies in the wrong direction. She was actually hiding them in her attic. She is included in God's "hall of faith" in Hebrews 11, and though she is never directly commended for her lie, she is praised for her act of faith in providing a safe refuge for the spies. Clearly, part of providing that refuge was deceiving the authorities who were after the spies.

When divine commands genuinely conflict, there are usually three ways to resolve the conflict.[16] In using these alternatives, one must recognize that a true moral conflict exists and not rationalize away a clear command of Scripture that one simply does not want to obey.

The first alternative is to maintain that no conflict actually faces the believer. This is known as *nonconflicting absolutism.* The person who holds this position reasons as follows: since an infallible God inspired his inerrant Word, no such conflict of commands is possible. To admit to a conflict would compromise the character of God by admitting that he is capable of giving commands that conflict. That is, if God's commands are indeed absolutes, then there cannot be any exceptions. Neither can those commands be ranked in any kind of a hierarchy. This particular model for ethics claims that when the absolutes of the Bible are properly interpreted, they will not conflict with other absolutes. Thus one way out of moral "dilemmas" would be to appeal to God's providence to open the way out. According to this view, Corrie ten Boom should have told the truth and trusted God to work out his will for the Jews she was hiding. Critics of this view cite the example of Rahab mentioned above as an example of a moral conflict that invalidates this view. A second way to deal with these dilemmas would be to capture the intent of the command more clearly. For instance, the command not to bear false witness is not a blanket prohibition against lying, but a prohibition against malicious lying. Thus Rahab and Corrie ten Boom did not face a moral dilemma at all—their deception was justified because it was not a malicious lie.

A second alternative is to admit that real moral conflicts do exist, but sin is still sin, even when a person is faced with competing obligations. Advocates of this view hold that because we live in a fallen world, real moral conflicts can and do occur. Moral dilemmas are due not to any flaw in God's character or commands, but to the existence of sin and depravity in the world in which the commands are to be applied. God's law is absolute, moral conflicts are inevitable in a fallen world, and people have the duty to do the lesser evil. But it is still evil, for which forgiveness is available for the Christian. Thus Corrie ten Boom should have lied to protect the Jews, the lie being the lesser of two evils facing her. Then she should have immediately bowed at the foot of the cross and asked God for forgiveness for lying. The problem that is often raised against this view is that having a duty to sin in certain situations is morally problematic. It is hard to imagine that a person can be morally culpable for something that could not be avoided and about which the person had no choice.

A third alternative, known as *graded absolutism*, or *hierarchialism*, is similar to the second. Like the second view, this alternative also holds that moral conflicts are real due to life in a fallen world. However, the option chosen is not evil, and it is not correct to say that the person chose the "lesser evil." The choice is a morally justifiable option, not sin. A person has the obligation to do the greater good and is not morally culpable for doing what could not be avoided. This view recognizes that God's laws are absolute, yet there are higher and lower laws, or a hierarchy, within God's laws. For example, God's command to the apostles to preach the gospel was over his command to be in submission to the state (Acts 4:13–20). Jesus makes reference to the "more important matters of the law" (Matt. 23:23–24), a reference to the greater importance of justice, mercy, and compassion over the law of tithing. This view attempts to combine the nature of God's commands, the reality of life in a fallen world, and a proper understanding of moral accountability. Thus, in this view, Corrie ten Boom would have been morally justified in lying to protect the lives of the Jews she was harboring.

Natural Law in Christian Ethics

The notion of natural law is a controversial one in moral philosophy in general and in Christian ethics in particular. It is controversial in philosophy because it refers to an ethic that is transcendent and not a human creation, because the concept of natural law has been used historically to oppress some groups such as women, and because it implies a "God's-eye view" of morality that many find inconsistent with a pluralistic and postmodern view of morality.

In addition, natural law is controversial in Christian ethics too. Its development has historically been primarily the domain of Roman Catholic philosophers and theologians. The Reformers and those who followed them were skeptical of natural law for two reasons, even though they did believe in general revelation or the idea that God could reveal some things about himself outside of the Bible. First, they believed that sin made it difficult to discover morality apart from the clear revelation of God in the Scriptures. Second, they believed that the Bible was the central source of moral and spiritual authority. The Reformers held that the Catholic view of natural law undercut both of those crucial doctrines. A second group of critics were the twentieth-century Protestant neoorthodox theologians (e.g., Karl Barth and Emil Brunner) who argued that natural law undercut the centrality of Christ for the moral life.

Critical Issues
Concerning Natural Law

For Christian ethics, natural law is an important concept at the heart of the debate over several crucial questions:

1. To what degree can moral values be known apart from special revelation? What is the relationship between reason and revelation in ethics? If one holds to a concept of natural law, then objective moral values do exist apart from

Thomas Aquinas

Thomas Aquinas (1224–1274) was born and raised in Italy, studied under Benedictine monks as a child, and attended the University of Naples before joining the Dominicans, the order of preachers in the Roman Catholic Church. His advanced study in philosophy and theology took place primarily at the University of Paris. After receiving his doctorate there, he began a twenty-year period as an active teacher in Paris and Italy (1252–1273). The best known of his works is the multivolume *Summa Theologica*. His work on ethics is only a part of this massive work.

One of Thomas's fundamental ethical concepts was the notion of the public good under law. Ethics was much more than simply one's inner attitude, as was the case with the Stoics.

The good is based on his concept of natural law, that is, the natural tendencies of a thing. This includes a consideration both of its end and its function. These were considered to be natural and thus ordained by the creator God. Happiness is knowing God and loving the good, while evil is that which interferes with it.

Thomas held that the principles of natural law are self-evident precepts from which practical reason deduces moral maxims. Natural law imprints its structure on beings and therefore determines its inclinations to proper acts and ends. Natural law can be known by reason and is accessible to everyone, regardless of an individual's relationship to God.

Aquinas saw human beings as essentially social beings. He reasoned that even if the fall had not occurred, government and the state would still have a place. Thus his social ethic left more room for the state to intervene to improve the lot of society. For Aquinas, institutions exist to encourage the development of good people.

Scripture, and reason works together with revelation to discover moral values. If one denies the existence of natural law, then all legitimate moral values are derived from Scripture, and reason functions only to interpret and apply God's revelation in the Bible.

2. To what degree can a person be good without the special grace of God? For adherents of natural law, people can be good without saving grace, but for those who deny its legitimacy, the only way people can be called good is if they are believers who have received God's redeeming grace.

3. To what degree is Christian ethics distinctive from nonreligious ethical systems? To what degree is there common ground between Christian and non-Christian morality? For those who hold to some form of natural law, Christian ethics has substantial overlap with non-Christian ethical systems. There is little distinctive content to Christian ethics, since the nonbeliever is called to most of the same acts and character attributes to which the Christian is called. The distinctiveness of Christian ethics has more to do with the motive for ethics and the way that one's ethic is justified than the actual content of moral behavior. For the person who minimizes the role of natural law, Christian ethics constitutes a different and higher standard of morality than any secular morality.

Ultimately, the degree to which one holds to natural law will determine the way in which one can try to persuade the world to adopt Christian ethics. If natural law is not a viable concept, then believers can only talk to the world with the gospel, and they would likely hold that the social mission of the church is unimportant or is to be accomplished by a community that produces social change indirectly, by the witness of its life together in community.[17] But if natural law is viable, then the church can engage in a legitimate social mission and Christian activism on moral issues that can complement the proclamation of the gospel.

Defining Natural Law

One of the most difficult aspects of natural law is defining it. The term is used in two primary ways today. First, it refers to general, objective, and widely shared moral values that are not specifically tied to the special revelation of Scripture. Values such as justice, fairness, respect for an individual's dignity, the obligation not to harm another, truth telling, and the respect for life in prohibitions against killing are some examples of virtually universal values whose origins predate Scripture.[18] Oxford University theologian John Macquarrie has put it this way: "In fact the very term 'natural law' is misleading if it is taken to mean some kind of code. The natural law is not another code or system of laws in addition to all the actual systems, but is simply our rather inaccurate way of referring to those most general moral principles against which particular rules or codes have to be measured."[19] These values are a consensus that comes out of the observations and conclusions of humankind over the centuries. In the same way that God has revealed truth about the sciences in creation and revealed truth in the observations of humankind in the social sciences, natural law refers to God's revelation of morality from all sources outside of Scripture. In this sense, natural law is general revelation applied to moral values.

A more specific form of natural law in which specific moral rules are codified is used predominantly in Roman Catholic circles. For example, the Catholic view of reproductive ethics, especially contraception and the use of reproductive technologies to alleviate infertility, uses natural law reasoning to reach conclusions about their validity. Here natural law is tied to what is natural in creation. For example, since the natural process of reproduction that God ordained in creation begins with sexual relations and progresses from conception to pregnancy to birth, anything that interferes, interrupts, or replaces this natural process is morally wrong. This explains why Catholic teaching prohibits contraception, abortion, and most reproductive technologies.

This specific form of reasoning should be evaluated on a case-by-case basis. Most Protestants tend to reject this form of reasoning when applied to contraception or reproductive technologies, but embrace it when dealing with issues such as genetic engineering, in which medical researchers are cautioned against "playing God" and interfering with his created order. In particular, evangelicals use natural law reasoning in voicing opposition to homosexuality. According to many evangelical groups, homosexual relationships are not legitimate because they are unnatural—that is, they are against the created order that God ordained. Thus, before dismissing this more specific form of natural law, evangelicals need to recognize how frequently they invoke it in their arguments on different social issues.

The Biblical Basis for Natural Law

Perhaps the central passage in the Bible that affirms natural law in the broad sense is Romans 2:1–16. After Paul appeals to creation to point out the sin of the nonreligious, and, interestingly, to oppose homosexuality, he proves that the moralistic person is also condemned before God because of his sin (Rom. 1:18–32). As it applies to natural law, the heart of this passage is in Romans 2:14–15, where Paul states: "Indeed, when Gentiles, who do not have the law, do by nature things required by the law, they are a law for themselves, even though they do not have the law, since they show that the requirements of the law are written on their hearts, their consciences also bearing witness, and their thoughts now accusing, now even defending them."

God appears to hold those without the Law accountable for their sin in the same way that he holds the Jews accountable (Rom. 2:17–29). For God to legitimately hold the world accountable for sin, they must have access to God's standard of morality, even if they lack special revelation. This would be natural law, or general revelation applied to morality. God has revealed these values outside of Scripture and made them accessible to those who lack the Scriptures. Paul's teaching in Romans 2 parallels the oracles to the nations (Isa. 13–27; Jer. 46–51; Ezek. 25–32; Amos 1–2) in which the prophets condemn Israel's pagan neighbors, who did not have the Law, for many of the same things he condemned Israel, who did have the Law. Unless the nations have access to God's law apart from the written Law, it is hard to see how God can be just in holding them accountable for that which they have no knowledge.[20]

In the Old Testament, the concept of wisdom opens the door for at least the more general form of natural law. The Wisdom Literature suggests two sources of wisdom: natural and revealed. Although revealed wisdom (God's wisdom in the Scripture) claims authority by being God's Word and natural wisdom (God's wisdom revealed outside of Scripture) appeals to empirical evidence for its authority, both are legitimate and authoritative.

Clarence Thomas's Appeal to Natural Law

Among all the unusual occurrences that took place in the 1992 confirmation hearings of United States Supreme Court Justice Clarence Thomas was his belief in a concept called *natural law*. Once he mentioned it in the course of answering a question, many members of the Senate Judiciary Committee expressed immediate concern, and protests went up from numerous special interest groups, namely, feminist groups. Why did his reference to natural law raise so much concern?

First, natural law refers to an ethic that is transcendent rather than an ethic that is a human creation. In a culture permeated by naturalism, this is not a welcome view of morality.

Second, the concept of "nature" has been used historically to oppress women and minorities. In the Middle Ages "nature" was used to maintain a static social order in which everyone had his or her place, especially women. It is likely that the feminist and gay rights groups that opposed Judge Thomas had this in mind.

Third, the term *natural* is a widely debated term today, subject to all sorts of misapplications. Perhaps the claim about what is natural implies a God's-eye view of morality, considered hopelessly out of date by modern philosophers. This may be what many people objected to about Thomas's use of the term.

Scripture affirms that there is a fixed order that governs the natural physical world (Jer. 31:35–36; 33:20–21, 25–26). Many of these laws of nature have been discovered by physics, astronomy, chemistry, and biology. Creation psalms like Psalm 19, which praises God for the way he has revealed himself in creation, reflect this idea. In Proverbs 8:22–31, it is clear that God's wisdom was intimately bound up with creation (see also Prov. 3:19–20). The Hebrew term translated "fixed order" in Jeremiah 33:25 derives from a term that means "cut in, inscribe, or decree." This same Hebrew word is elsewhere translated as "law" (e.g., Lev. 18:4). In other words, what is "cut in" the cosmos is one source of what is "cut in" the commands of God, a reference to the Ten Commandments being cut, or carved, in stone when originally given to Moses. God's wisdom is expanded in Proverbs 8:32–36 to include interpersonal and especially moral knowledge. It is "inscribed" in nature and can be discovered by reason. The writer draws conclusions about one's character and morality based on adherence to God's wisdom that is "inscribed" in creation, suggesting that God's wisdom in creation includes moral knowledge.

The message of the Proverbs is that living in harmony with this order brings peace (*shalom*) and well-being, but living at odds with this order is folly and brings self-destruction. Proverbs 8:32–36, which personifies wisdom and refers to it in the first person, puts it this way:

> Now then, my sons, listen to me [wisdom];
> blessed are those who keep my [wisdom's] ways.
> Listen to my instruction and be wise;
> do not ignore it.
> Blessed is the man who listens to me,
> watching daily at my doors,
> waiting at my doorway.
> For whoever finds me finds life
> and receives favor from the LORD.
> But whoever fails to find me harms himself;
> all who hate me love death.

Since this passage directly follows Proverbs 8:22–31, which links God's wisdom and the creation, it is the moral and spiritual conclusion drawn from the reality of God's natural wisdom. Notice that all of the references to God's wisdom in creation precede the existence of any special revelation of Scripture. The concept of wisdom then suggests that God has revealed objective moral values outside of Scripture, or natural law.

Thus Scripture and God's natural wisdom are two sides to God's wisdom. Although the wise sage responsible for Proverbs was under inspiration, this does not negate the fact that the sage gained these insights from his own observations. Two specific proverbs make the link between the sage's observations and moral conclusions drawn from them. In Proverbs 6:6–11 the sage observes the diligence and forethought of the ant and draws a conclusion about diligence and laziness. Likewise, Proverbs 24:30–34 draws the identical conclusion, repeated verbatim, from observation of a lazy person and the consequences of laziness. Hence, observations drawn from the physical and interpersonal worlds are some of the sources for gleaning God's natural wisdom and drawing appropriate moral conclusions. The goal of the sages was to discover and transmit those values embedded in creation through God's cosmic wisdom. They discovered them by observations of nature (what Roman Catholics call the "order of nature") and by reason (what they call the "order of reason").[21]

	Ultimate Source	Immediate Source	Primary Interpreter	Basis of Authority
Special Revelation	God	Scripture	Priest	"Thus says the Lord!"
Natural Wisdom	God	World	Wise Sage	"It works!"

The Limits of Natural Law

Many of the criticisms of natural law relate not to its existence, but to how it can be reliably known. With their strong view of sin and depravity, the Reformers held that natural law was virtually useless, since the capacity of fallen human beings to discern it apart from Scripture was so flawed that no separate moral principles could be confidently known. The ability of fallen human beings to discover natural law has been corrupted by the fall, particularly their ability to use morality to mask self-interest.[22]

Special revelation is needed because it is not always clear if something is natural because of sin or creation. For example, death is a natural process that everyone experiences, but the Bible is clear that death is not part of God's original design; it results from the entrance of sin into the world (Rom. 5:12–14). In addition, many aspects of the spiritual life do require special revelation, such as those that relate to salvation and eternity. Although natural law does help reveal some moral obligations, the proper motive, the context, and the justification of Christian morality depend on further insights gained from Scripture. Certainly, what some might refer to as natural law can and does conflict with Scripture. In these cases Scripture is the final arbiter. All of natural law is consistent with Scripture, but not all of it is contained in Scripture, although Scripture clarifies some of it.

Natural Law and Jurisprudence

Much of the contemporary debate and redefinition of natural law is being done by law professors and legal scholars. Specifically, they are asking, "What makes a law just?" and "On what basis are human rights to be protected?" There are two schools of thought on the relation between natural law and the law.[23]

First, the legal positivists hold that there is no essential relationship between law and morality. Laws are valid simply because they are creations of recognized institutions. Perhaps legal positivists are motivated by the fear that if there were too close a link between law and morality, then certain groups might impose their morality with the force of law.

Second, the school of moral realism is committed to the idea that laws that do not correspond to objective values are nonlaws, or invalid laws. For law on any level to be accepted as valid, it must relate to objective moral truths.[24] Ultimately, for the Christian there are objective values that are grounded in the creative activity of God, revealed in general revelation, deduced by reason and experience. They are also substantially revealed in Scripture, which is the final authority in cases of conflict. Of course, the clearer revelation is found in Scripture, but it is supplemented by natural law, which provides a common ground between Christian and non-Christian ethics. This enables effective dialogue with the world about the substance of Christian ethics. Natural law provides the means by which Christian ethics are made persuasive to a secular world.

For Further Reading

Budziszewski, J. *What We Can't Not Know: A Guide*. Dallas: Spence, 2003.

Clark, David K., and Robert V. Rakestraw. *Readings in Christian Ethics. Vol. 1: Theory and Method*. Grand Rapids: Baker, 1994.

Grenz, Stanley. *The Moral Quest*. Downers Grove, Ill.: InterVarsity, 1998.

Hollinger, Dennis P. *Choosing the Good: Christian Ethics in a Complex World*. Grand Rapids: Baker, 2002.

Wright, Christopher J. H. *Old Testament Ethics for the People of God*. Downers Grove, Ill.: InterVarsity, 2004.

Review Questions

1. What is the connection between virtues and principles in Christian ethics? List some biblical texts that spell out this connection.

2. What modes of moral reasoning are used in Scripture? Which are primary? Which are supplemental?

3. What mode of moral reasoning is not found in Scripture?

4. What is the unifying theme of Old Testament ethics?

5. Give some examples of Old Testament laws that structured institutions in ancient Israel.

6. Give some of the biblical support for the mandate to pursue justice for the oppressed and vulnerable.

7. Explain the role of the Holy Spirit in Christian ethics.

8. What is the central virtue in Christian ethics?

9. What is the *Euthyphro* dilemma? How would you begin to resolve it?

10. How would you resolve a conflict of values such as faced Rahab and Corrie ten Boom? Do you consider those values in conflict at all?

11. How would you define natural law?

12. Why have some been critical of the concept of natural law?

13. What is the biblical basis for natural law?

14. How would you distinguish between the legal positivists and the moral realists?

Chapter 2 Notes

1. This will be developed later in this chapter.

2. Most contemporary examples of theocracies are in the Islamic world. Nations such as Iran and Saudi Arabia derive their constitutions and their judicial systems from the Koran.

3. For further reading on this treaty form, see Meredith Kline, *The Structure of Biblical Authority* (Grand Rapids: Eerdmans, 1972).

4. For further discussion of this, see Walter C. Kaiser Jr., *Toward Old Testament Ethics* (Grand Rapids: Zondervan, 1983).

5. The Greek term used in the New Testament for sanctification, *hagiazo*, is derived from the Hebrew term *qadosh*.

6. Sexual relations outside marriage are also prohibited in the Law because they violate God's design for marriage, sexuality, and procreation set up in Genesis 1–2. Romans 1:18–31 clarifies this link to the order of creation.

7. Contrary to the suggestions of many liberation theologians and evangelicals of a more liberal political and economic persuasion, the Jubilee does not necessarily provide a redistribution of *income*, only *opportunity*. Neither does the Jubilee provide a justification for anything like socialism, because its principal purpose was to ensure that no one was without the resources necessary to earn a living. If a person squandered the renewed opportunity provided by the Jubilee, there was no automatic entitlement to the community's goods.

8. Usury was quite different in Old Testament times than today. See the discussion of this in chapter 12.

9. This is not to say that the Law has no relevance for the church today or that it must be applied in terms of broader principles. It is still applicable to the church, although it is no longer directly addressed to the church.

10. The exceptions to this are in the Sermon on the Mount (Matt. 5–7) and Paul's teaching on the spiritual life in Romans 5–8.

11. Interestingly, in these two passages, Paul uses the command to love one's neighbor as oneself as the fulfillment of the Law, not the command to love God. Perhaps this is to suggest that one's moral and spiritual priorities are not to be viewed hierarchically, but as simultaneous responsibilities. For further discussion, see J. Grant Howard, *Balancing Life's Demands* (Portland, Ore.: Multnomah, 1983).

12. For more on this point, see Francis Schaeffer, *The Mark of the Christian* (Downers Grove, Ill.: InterVarsity, 2007). This classic work has been reissued in the IVP Classics series.

13. For further development of this view, see Robert Merrihew Adams, "A Modified Divine Command Theory of Ethical Wrongness," in Gene Outka and John P. Reeder, eds., *Religion and Morality* (New York: Anchor, 1973), 318–47.

14. Most critics of religious morality assume that if divine commands are an important component of one's ethical system, one must be an ethical voluntarist. But that is not necessarily the case, as the above discussion has shown. Thus, when Christians encounter criticism of their ethics, they must be sure that the critic has not set up the straw man of the ethical voluntarist.

15. For example, see Kai Nielsen, *Ethics without God* (New York: Prometheus, 1985), particularly chapter 2, for a larger description of this criticism of Christian ethics.

16. Adapted from Norman L. Geisler, *Christian Ethics* (Grand Rapids: Baker, 1989), 86–110.

17. See, for example, the work of John Howard Yoder in *The Politics of Jesus* (Grand Rapids: Eerdmans, 1972) and *The Priestly Kingdom* (Notre Dame, Ind.: University of Notre Dame Press, 1984).

18. For a catalog of these values traced historically, see the appendix in C. S. Lewis, *The Abolition of Man* (New York: Macmillan, 1947).

19. John Macquarrie, "Rethinking Natural Law," in Charles E. Curran and Richard A. McCormick, eds., *Readings in Moral Theology*, Vol. 7: *Natural Law and Theology* (New York: Paulist Press, 1991), 239.

20. For further exegetical study on the biblical basis for natural law, see Alan F. Johnson, "Is There Biblical Warrant for Natural Law Theories?" *Journal of the Evangelical Theological Society* 27 (June 1982): 185–99.

21. For further detail on this distinction, see Richard Gula, *Reason Informed by Faith* (New York: Paulist Press, 1989).

22. For more on this, see Reinhold Niebuhr, *Moral Man and Immoral Society* (New York: Scribner, 1932).

23. The classic debate between the positivists and realists took place in the pages of the *Harvard Law Review* between Oxford professor H. L. A. Hart and Harvard law professor Lon Fuller. See H. L. A. Hart, "Positivism and the Separation of Law and Morals," *Harvard Law Review* 71 (1958): 593–629; and Lon Fuller, "Positivism and Fidelity to Law: A Response to Hart," *Harvard Law Review* 71 (1958): 630–72.

24. On the connection between law and objective morality, see Arthur A. Leff, "Unspeakable Ethics, Unnatural Law," *Duke Law Journal* 1229 (1979).

Chapter 3

Ethical Systems and Ways of Moral Reasoning

As people in our contemporary culture wrestle with ethical decisions, they employ a wide variety of methods of moral reasoning. One obvious place to observe this is in the debate over various social issues. One of the primary reasons why many of these debates remain unresolved is that often the participants are applying different methods of moral reasoning.

Imagine that you are listening to a community panel discussion on the morality of physician-assisted suicide. The participants are (1) an eighty-year-old man with terminal cancer and approximately six months to live; (2) the head of the local chapter of the Hemlock Society, an organization that advocates assisted suicide; (3) a physician who specializes as an oncologist, that is, a cancer specialist; (4) a Catholic priest who is an outspoken opponent of euthanasia; (5) an atheistic philosophy professor from the local college; (6) an attorney; and (7) a Protestant minister. Each one will use a different type of moral reasoning in presenting his respective position, and each will offer a brief opening statement to define and defend his position.

Participant 1: The Eighty-Year-Old Man with Terminal Cancer (Ethical Egoist)

All this moral discussion of euthanasia really bothers me. You see, for me it all boils down to the fact that I am the patient, and what I want should be the thing that counts. It's my interests that really matter here, not whether euthanasia violates the Hippocratic Oath or the sixth commandment ("Thou shalt not murder"), or what consequences allowing euthanasia produces for the general society. I am the patient and the one most directly affected, and that's why it should be my decision. Whatever is in my best interest in terms of euthanasia should be okay.

Participant 2: The Head of the Local Chapter of the Hemlock Society
(Deontologist)

I am in substantial agreement with our first participant, though for a different reason. I, too, support euthanasia, or physician-assisted suicide, but from a slightly different perspective. One of the fundamental principles, or rights, that Western societies have affirmed for centuries is the right of individual autonomy and self-determination, that is, the right of people to make private choices concerning their lives without interference from the state. Surely matters of life and death for people are so private that they ought to have the freedom to do as they choose without undue interference from the authorities, as long as no one else is harmed. This is a fundamental right that is based on the principle of respect for persons and individual bodily integrity. I appeal to this fundamental moral principle in order to affirm my support for euthanasia.

Participant 3: The Physician Who Specializes as an Oncologist
(Utilitarian)

In most cases I, too, support euthanasia, but for still different reasons than we have heard so far. You see, I hold that it is not necessarily principles that determine right and wrong, but the consequences produced by the actions in question. If a particular course of action or decision produces the best set of consequences, then it seems to me that it should be allowed. To put it another way, the action that produces the greatest balance of benefits over harms is the one that is the most moral. So, in the case of euthanasia, I think that the first two participants have framed the question incorrectly. What is important to determine is whether active euthanasia would produce the greatest good for the greatest number of people. I can see that allowing physician-assisted suicide could produce a lot of good for the people involved. It would relieve the patient of needless suffering, stop the family's anxiety about their loved one's condition, end a needless drain of the family's financial resources, and allow everyone involved to get on with their lives. Now, there may be situations in which euthanasia may produce, on balance, more negative than positive consequences. In those cases it should not be allowed. We should be cautious in setting hard-and-fast rules that don't fully consider the consequences.

Participant 4: The Catholic Priest
(Deontologist)

I am opposed to all euthanasia because of a principle that is foundational to our civilization. Even for those without any religious inclination, the principle "Thou shalt not kill" is still one of the core values on which most civilized people agree. Now I also happen to believe that this principle comes from God, but a person does not have to believe in God to accept the importance of this moral rule. I hold that active euthanasia is killing an innocent person, and that is something our society should not allow, regardless of the person's desires. Underlying the moral rule "Thou shalt not kill" is the more important principle of respect for the dignity of a person. Now again, I believe we should respect people because they are made in God's image, but you don't have to believe in God to accept such a basic moral principle. People have an innate tendency toward self-preservation, and that is one of the basic reasons it is immoral to take innocent life. You see, like my opponent at the Hemlock Society, I, too, hold a high place for principles, but I differ on how they are applied. For me, the principle of respect for persons does not mean that we should necessarily let them do whatever they want to do. What it does mean is that we should never take innocent life, because life is sacred, and when it shall end is not our prerogative.

Participant 5: The Atheistic Philosophy Professor (Emotivist)

I hate to throw a monkey wrench into this whole discussion, but in my view, all of the participants so far are trying to do the impossible. So far each person has attempted to make some kind of determination of what is right or wrong in the case of active euthanasia. I don't think this is possible. They are really using the language of right and wrong to mask their own personal preferences. What I mean is that anytime a person says that something is right or wrong, all they are saying, and can say, is that they either like or dislike the action or position under consideration. It is obvious that the elderly gentleman and the representative of the Hemlock Society are really saying that they personally approve of euthanasia. It is equally obvious that the priest is really saying that he personally disapproves of euthanasia. We should be honest and admit that we're only talking about our preferences, and that we're simply using moral language to give greater persuasive power to our argument.

Participant 6: The Local Attorney (Relativist)

I wouldn't go quite as far as my professor friend, but I do think he's moving in the right direction. I'm not prepared to say that there is no such thing as genuine right and wrong, but I do think that there is no universal, absolute standard of right and wrong. What is moral depends on the situation and on what the cultural consensus of right and wrong is at that time. In the case of euthanasia, if the culture has reached a consensus that it should be allowed, then I see no reason why it should not be allowed. Conversely, if the culture is opposed to the practice, I see no good reason why euthanasia should be forced on them. I know that in the Netherlands, for example, the majority believes that euthanasia is right, and that should be respected. We could say that it is right for them. But in the state of Utah, where there are so many religious Mormons, or in the Bible Belt, where there are so many conservative Christians, the culture will undoubtedly be against euthanasia, and that should also be respected.

Participant 7: The Protestant Minister (Virtue Theorist)

I'd like to put a slightly different slant on the issue of euthanasia. You see, I believe that there's more to morality than simply making decisions when a person is faced with a moral quandary. There is more to the moral life than simply doing the right thing and making the correct decision. We cannot neglect the place of an individual's character, or virtue, when considering ethical questions. In my view, the important questions still have not been asked. For example, what does a person's desire for active euthanasia tell us about that individual's character? What does support for euthanasia, or opposition to it, say about our society? Does it say that we as a society lack compassion for the suffering terminally ill, as proponents of euthanasia suggest? Or does it say that we have lost some of our reverence for life and our commitment to care for the dying, as opponents of euthanasia would suggest? These are very important questions that cannot be ignored in any discussion about the morality of euthanasia.

Each person on this panel has argued his position using a distinctive method of moral reasoning from a specific ethical system (each participant's method is noted in parentheses above). The positions represented are the main positions adopted by people when applying moral reasoning to the moral issues currently debated in society. As you witness the news media's coverage of various debates over ethical issues, watch for the various methods utilized by those engaged in the debates. If you are very observant, you will likely detect the regular use of most of the systems discussed in this chapter.

The major types of moral reasoning can be grouped roughly into two primary categories. The first includes those who see morality as essentially a human creation, that is, morality that is *created* by human beings. A second group includes those who see morality as something that *transcends* human nature, that is, morality that is not a human creation but that is *discovered* by a variety of means (e.g., reason, intuition, and divine revelation). Most of the ethical systems outlined in this chapter are distinctly human creations (utilitarianism, egoism, relativism). But some involve views of morality as something to be discerned, such as many forms of deontological ethics and some forms of virtue theory. However, neither deontology nor virtue ethics *necessarily* involves principles and virtues that arise from a transcendent source. The relevant principles/virtues can also be human creations. In fact, even religion-based forms of ethics can be human creations if the view of the Bible or other specific "book" of that religion is viewed as a solely human-generated work. So people who view the Bible as nothing more than the reflections of human beings could hold to a moral theory based on the Bible but still see the principles and virtues as human creations only.

Any ethical system involves both a personal and intellectual commitment to follow its dictates. Any particular view of morality commits a person, whether he or she knows it, to a certain view of the world. It commits a person to a certain view of *metaphysics*, or the nature of reality, of which moral values are a part, especially those that claim to have a transcendent source. It also commits a person to a certain view of *epistemology*, or theory of knowledge, because moral responsibility is linked to a person's knowledge of the rules of morality produced or discovered by a particular system. Questions of epistemology are especially important for moral systems that appeal to a transcendent source of moral authority, because how a person discovers moral values is critical to the viability of such a moral system. Support of a particular moral system also commits one to a certain view of *anthropology*, or view of human nature, because of the connection between one's ethics and a person's ability to live up to that ethical standard.

Throughout much of intellectual history, Christian ethics (discussed in chapter 2) has intersected with other attempts to explain and ground morality. Christian moral philosophers have made significant contributions to the history of ethics and have dominated the moral landscape during some time periods. For example, Augustine was the dominant figure during the beginning of the Dark Ages, as was Thomas Aquinas during the Middle Ages. However, competing visions of morality have always existed. Rival ways to determine right and wrong have always been around, though in different historical periods, some were more dominant than others. In some cases moral philosophers devised ethical systems to replace Christian ethics as the moral system of the masses. Some of these thinkers sought to undermine Christian ethics by providing an account of morality independent of God's special revelation in the Bible. Other philosophers simply attempted to bypass any specifically religious input for morality.

As I suggested in chapter 2, Christian ethics is a blend of virtues and principles but also employs some other types of moral reasoning in order to support the primary role of virtues and principles. It is one thing to utilize some of the moral theories discussed in this chapter as a supplement, for example, in order to be more persuasive in one's presentation. But it is very different to appeal to any one of these systems (egoism, relativism, utilitarianism, etc.) as the sole determinant of morality. We should recognize that some ethical systems not specifically grounded in Scripture have insights to offer to the Christian ethicist. For example, Thomas Aquinas, the principal architect of medieval Roman Catholic morality, was influenced by both the philosophy of Aristotle and the theology of Augustine. In fact, Muslims and Jews who were contemporaries of Aquinas were similarly influenced by Aristotle.

For the remainder of this chapter, I will analyze each of the ethical systems used by the panel participants, highlighting the positive elements of each system as well as offering a critique of each.[1]

Ethical Egoism

Ethical egoism is the theory that the morality of an act is determined by one's self-interest. Actions that advance self-interest are moral, and those that do not are not moral. A common misunderstanding is that an ethical egoist is someone who

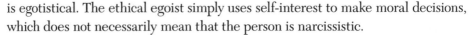

is egotistical. The ethical egoist simply uses self-interest to make moral decisions, which does not necessarily mean that the person is narcissistic.

In addition to Participant 1, who made his moral decision about euthanasia based strictly on his self-interest, many other contemporary examples illustrate the practice of ethical egoism. For example, medical doctors frequently make

Thomas Hobbes

Hobbes lived in England for most of his life (1588–1679), absent only during a brief exile in France away from political turmoil in England. He was very interested in and heavily influenced by geometry and mechanistic psychology, and these disciplines played a significant part in the formation of his ethics. He is best known for his shortest work, *Leviathan*, which summarizes a good deal of his ethical and political theory.

His personal ethics are clearly based on the nature and constitution of a human being. He has an atomistic view of human nature in which, parallel with science, man is viewed as a small, isolated, individual machine. The good is defined in terms of the individual and the individual's self-interest. Hobbes assumed that aversions and appetites are constant. For example, he assumed that all people desire peace. This is one of his principal laws of nature. According to Hobbes, since people share desires such as freedom from the fear of death and the enjoyment of prosperity, universal goods must exist, the basis for a universal ethic.

Happiness for Hobbes derives from his notion of desire and the good. Happiness is not the repose of a satisfied mind, as in the classical definition of contemplation. Human beings are always in the process of attaining happiness but cannot finally attain it. Happiness is in the pursuit — that is, in the progress from one desire being satisfied to another. Hobbes called this "a perpetual and restless lust for power that ceaseth only in death" (from *Leviathan*).

Because of this ever-increasing lust for power, we exist in a state of war, what Hobbes called the *state of nature*, or the war of all against all. His laws of nature are premised on the assumption that there is no security in the state of nature. Thus one is to desire peace so that all other desires can be met.

The laws of nature that exist are all related to furthering one's self-preservation. These laws establish covenant-keeping, liberty, justice, gratitude, modesty, equity, and mercy as the principal virtues. Hobbes called these laws of nature "immutable and eternal" and considered them binding.

Hobbes viewed society as a voluntary association, where free and equal individuals clash to maximize self-interest. The goal of government is to provide order to safeguard one's pursuit of self-interest. He inaugurated the idea of government by consent, but an absolute ruler, which he called Leviathan, was needed to protect man from others.

decisions based on their potential exposure to medical malpractice suits. In many cases nothing is inherently wrong with the desire to avoid lawsuits. My point here, however, is simply to illustrate the use of ethical egoism in making moral decisions. For the physician who is an ethical egoist, the right thing to do is what will protect him from being sued, or what is in his self-interest.

Another example of ethical egoism is what we commonly call "whistle-blowing." This occurs when an employee's superiors ask the employee to do something that the employee believes is immoral, such as falsifying data, offering bribes, or deceiving customers or regulators. The employee may refuse to fulfill the request and instead may "blow the whistle" on the company, revealing the immoral and, at times, illegal practice that they have been asked to do. In most cases, however, whistle-blowers lose their jobs and are blacklisted from the industry, leaving them unable to support themselves and their families. In short, whistle-blowing often has devastating results for the employee. When deliberating about blowing the whistle, many employees become ethical egoists, using their own self-interest as the determining factor for what they should do in the situation.

Appeal to rational self-interest is used in the Bible as a way of motivating people to be obedient to God. For example, the covenant blessings and curses set forth in Deuteronomy 27–30 promise Israel agricultural prosperity and military peace as consequences of obedience, and threaten the opposite should the nation turn to idolatry and disobey God.[2] What is in Israel's national self-interest is clearly a motivation for doing the right things. Other examples of this use of self-interest include becoming a Christian and receiving eternal life as a result, which is clearly in a person's self-interest. Doing altruistic acts because of the good feelings we receive is egoistic. Some have even suggested that the Bible is entirely egoistic and simply changes the categories of what constitutes a person's self-interest. However, that is too strong a statement. While the Bible never condemns self-interest, it does require that it be balanced with concern for others (Phil. 2:4). It is one thing to occasionally appeal to rational self-interest as the Bible does, but quite another to claim that egoism is a sufficient ethical system, as do thoroughgoing ethical egoists. We will examine this latter claim in the following paragraphs.

In ethical egoism one's only moral duty is to one's own self-interest. This is not to say that a person should avoid actions that help others, since a person's interests and the interests of others can coincide. It may be that helping others may be a means to the end of a person's own self-interest. It is also not to say that one's short-term interests are primary. One may forgo an immediate advantage to insure long-term interests. Thomas Hobbes, the original egoist, suggested that to prevent the pursuit of self-interest from destroying society, people should voluntarily give up some of their freedom to pursue their interests so that each one's long-term interests might be protected.

In Support of Egoism

The principal arguments offered in support of ethical egoism are as follows:[3]

1. *Looking out for others is a self-defeating pursuit.* Looking out for others is self-defeating for three reasons. First, the egoist claims that we know only our own needs, and we have much less ability to understand or meet the needs of others. Second, being concerned with the needs of others invades their privacy. Third, people find it demeaning to accept the help of others. Interestingly, the logic of this argument is actually very *unegoistic*. The argument runs like this: (a) We ought to do whatever will promote the best interests of others; (b) this will happen best if we all pursue our own interests exclusively; (c) therefore, each of us should adopt the policy of pursuing our interests exclusively. The end result is that we act like egoists but reason like altruists. Following this argument to its logical end, we would have to conclude that we are not egoists at all, but altruists with a strange view of what makes for the general welfare.

2. *Ethical egoism is the only moral system that respects the integrity of the individual human life.* This is the argument of the most well-known spokesperson for egoism, the libertarian novelist-philosopher Ayn Rand.[4] Her argument is as follows: (a) Since a person has only one life to live, this life is of supreme importance; (b) the ethic of altruism regards the life of the individual as something that one must be ready to sacrifice for the good of others; (c) thus altruistic ethics does not take seriously the value of the individual human; (d) egoism, which allows each person to view his own life as having ultimate value, does take the individual human seriously; (e) therefore, ethical egoism ought to be accepted. The problem with this argument is that it portrays the two alternatives of self-interest and altruism as polar extremes and mutually exclusive.[5] In her view, altruism demands that one's interests have no value, when in reality one's self-interest can be balanced with a concern for others. When the argument is presented in this way, it is easy to see how egoism can have appeal, since the alternative is so unattractive. Very few people would choose a life in which they could never look out for their own interests.

3. *Egoism is the hidden unity underlying our widely accepted moral duties.* The egoist accepts that people can genuinely look out for others yet tries to explain it as an outworking of self-interest. For example, doing harm to others is to be avoided so that others will be more inclined not to harm us. Truth telling is in our interest because people will trust us and be truthful with us. Likewise, keeping promises or entering into mutually beneficial arrangements, or contracts, is in our interest. One could reply that this is only a general rule, since one might gain from harming another or lying or breaking promises or contracts. When this is so, the obligation not to harm others cannot be drawn

from egoism. Also, one could argue that altruism is to one's advantage. But it does not follow that this self-interest is the only, or even the most fundamental, reason for doing something altruistic. It only proves that it is also to my advantage to do something altruistic. To derive a duty from self-interest, one would have to prove that self-interest is the only motive for being altruistic.

Problems with Egoism

Not only can one rebut the main arguments for ethical egoism, but also one can point out other problems that it has. First, egoism has no means to settle conflicts of interest between individuals and groups without appealing to some other system. What happens when my self-interest conflicts with yours? All the egoist can do to resolve the conflict is to reassert his basic premise of self-interest. To think that interests never conflict is naive. Yet this assumption seems to be necessary if ethical egoism is to be a viable system.

Second, ethical egoism ultimately collapses into anarchy. For example, Hobbes's system required an absolute monarch (whom he called *Leviathan*, the title of his work that explains this concept) to keep egoism from disintegrating into anarchy. Yet there were no guarantees that the monarch would not also pursue his own self-interest too. It takes great faith to believe that some kind of "invisible hand" mysteriously works all things out.[6] Again, for the system to work, it requires resources outside of itself. To make egoism work, one must assume some sort of internal mechanism to control egoism. The Bible teaches that depravity drives people toward selfishness, whereas common grace and the image of God counter that drive. For the believer, the resources also include the indwelling Holy Spirit to counteract depravity.

Third, egoism is an arbitrary ethical system.[7] It divides people into two groups and says that the interests of one group count more than the interests of the other. For example, both anti-Semitism and racism illustrate this. Advocates of those ideologies insist that the interests of their group count more than the interests of Jews or any other race different than their own, simply because of the difference in race. In general, treating groups differently is justifiable if there are relevant differences between the groups. An anti-Semite or racist cannot point consistently to any criteria that justify anti-Semitism or racism. Egoism advocates that we divide the world into two groups—me and the rest of the world—and that we regard the interests of the first group as more important than the second, but putting myself into such a privileged category simply cannot be justified.

Fourth, ethical egoism is often built on the false premise of psychological egoism, that is, the notion that individuals are only capable of acting in their self-interest, and that genuine altruism does not exist. This premise is false for two primary reasons. First, sometimes we simply act spontaneously without any concern for self-interest. For example, people who perform feats of heroism generally do them by instinct, without any thoughts of possible recognition. In addition, in our closest human relationships, namely, friendship, marriage, and parenthood, we often sacrifice our well-being and interests for those we love. The egoist will insist that on the surface your actions only look like altruism. But if you look at the deeper, unconscious motives, you find that your motives are entirely egoistic. At this point, however, egoism becomes an untestable theory. This reveals the deepest flaw of egoism, since the egoist has announced his determination to interpret people's behavior in a way that corresponds to his theory no matter what they do. Thus nothing that anyone could do could count as evidence against the theory. However, the argument could just as easily be turned around by saying that at the deepest level, one's motives are altruistic, not egoistic. Further, this argument confuses a motive and a benefit. Just because someone receives a benefit from an altruistic act, it does not follow that it is the motive for doing the act. We would actually hope that people receive good feelings from doing altruistic things even though that may not be the entire motive.

Fifth, ethical egoism as a sufficient system ignores the fact that the Scriptures call believers and unbelievers to a balance of self-interest and altruism. We are called to care for the needs of others because they are comparable to our own and because a significant part of being a disciple of Christ is following his altruistic example. Believers are called to be servants, and that invariably involves periodically putting others' needs ahead of our own and in rare circumstances can involve laying down one's life for another. It does not, however, obligate believers to neglect their legitimate self-interest. The Bible does not call believers to ignore self-interest in the way that ethical egoists claim it does. The claim that the believer "must deny himself and take up his cross and follow me" (Mark 8:34) refers to denial of one's ownership of oneself, having turned that over to God. It does not mandate that one should not care at all for self-interest. One should remember that at times even Jesus separated from the crowds to seek solitude with his heavenly Father. Hence the Bible seems to suggest that self-interest has a legitimate place, but it needs to be balanced by a compassionate concern for the interests of others.

Utilitarianism

Utilitarianism is what is known as a teleological system (taken from the Greek word *telos*, which means "end," "goal"), in which the morality of an act is determined by the end result. In fact, sometimes utilitarianism and teleological ethics are used interchangeably. Utilitarianism commonly argues that the moral choice is the one that produces the greatest good for the greatest number of people, or the moral choice is the course of action that produces more good consequences than harmful ones. Thus this type of moral reasoning is also called *consequentialism* because of its overriding emphasis on the consequences of an action.

Utilitarianism has its roots in the philosophies of Jeremy Bentham (1748–1832) and John Stuart Mill (1806–73). Bentham held to a hedonistic utilitarianism, which maintains that the most moral acts are those that maximize pleasure and minimize pain. Mill developed his approach away from hedonism and toward a more general concept of maximizing the general happiness or the greatest good for the greatest number. When it was proposed, utilitarianism was a radical theory, since it divorced morality from divine revelation and from any view of nature. According to utilitarianism, moral behavior no longer required faithfulness to divine ordinances and rigid moral rules.

Utilitarian modes of moral reasoning are widely applied to many of the currently debated moral issues. Most of the public policy in the United States and Western Europe is still decided on overwhelmingly utilitarian grounds. As was evident from Participant 3 in the euthanasia debate, a good deal of the discussion about active euthanasia is conducted on utilitarian grounds, where principles take a backseat to consequences. If, on balance, euthanasia provides more beneficial consequences for more people, then a utilitarian would consider it to be the most moral choice. Another example of utilitarianism is when a company considers closing plants or laying off workers to maintain their competitive position in the marketplace. While acknowledging that this will produce harm for some, the company justifies such measures by asserting that it is safeguarding the jobs of the

Jeremy Bentham

Jeremy Bentham (1748–1832) was one of the founders of classic utilitarianism, with John Stuart Mill. He was trained as a philosopher and a lawyer, who didn't practice law but was instead involved in legal reform. He wrote voluminously on a variety of subjects, ranging from morality to political philosophy to religion. He put forth his principle of utility as a means of assessing the merits of particular laws that were in force, especially applied to prison reform. His principle of utility involved primary consideration of pain and pleasure, the two "sovereign masters" of nature. His view of happiness involved the maximization of pleasure and minimizing of pain, or achieving the greatest balance of pain over pleasure. In terms of moral theory, any action that produced a greater balance of pleasure over pain was good, sometimes called hedonistic utilitarianism. He actually proposed a system of measuring pleasure over pain. His view of the general morality was that actions and laws should be crafted to produce the greatest happiness for the greatest number.

rest of the employees. Keeping the company in business, management argues, will produce greater benefits than harms.

The Appeal of Utilitarianism

The appeal of utilitarianism rests on a number of factors. First, it is a relatively simple theory to apply. All one must do is weigh the anticipated good consequences of an action against its anticipated harmful ones and see if the bottom line produces a greater balance of benefits over harms. If it produces greater benefits, then it is the most moral course of action. Second, it avoids the rigidity of deontology, that is, it keeps morality from being reduced to abstract principles that must be strictly followed, regardless of consequences produced by them. Without question, deontological, principle-based systems can be legalistic and can sacrifice people at the expense of holding to one's principles. Third, it doesn't require special appeal to any religious authority for morality; rather, it appeals to nonmoral criteria for determining the good. This makes it a logical choice in an increasingly secular Western world, in which people are growing more skeptical of religiously based morality. Many people in society view the divorce of morality from religion as a good thing, and see utilitarianism as a substitute for divisive moral systems based on religion. Also, the presumed neutrality of utilitarianism has special appeal to a world that still prides itself on being value free and objective. Fourth, most people know intuitively that the consequences of one's actions must be taken seriously. No matter how tenaciously one holds to principles, one must take the consequences of one's actions into account to have a fully functioning moral system. Utilitarianism enables one to do just that, since the consequences of an action determine its morality.

Utilitarianism may be divided into two primary schools known as *act utilitarianism* and *rule utilitarianism*. Act utilitarianism uses the consequences of any given course of action to determine its morality. In doing so, the act utilitarian treats each moral decision separately and weighs the consequences of each isolated act. Rather than depending on a separate calculation of consequences each time one needs to make a moral decision, rule utilitarians have formulated moral rules to guide them in decision making. The rule utilitarian formulates rules based on the tendency of certain actions to produce a predictable set of consequences. For example, sexual assault would be an immoral act, not because of any virtue or principle that prohibits it, but because sexual assault, every time it occurs, produces more harmful consequences than beneficial ones. The rule utilitarian could say the same about many other actions, such as truth telling, promise keeping, murder, fraud, and deceit. Thus a rule utilitarian appears very similar to a deontologist, yet they have entirely different foundations for their rules.

Although utilitarianism has appeal, especially in a secular society, it also has shortcomings. The most common charge against utilitarianism is that it cannot protect the rights of minorities, and sometimes it can even justify obvious injustices when the greater good is served. For example, in the pre–Civil War South, slavery was clearly justifiable from a utilitarian point of view. It provided cheap labor that made the South very prosperous and clearly benefited more people than it harmed. But no one today would justify slavery on any grounds, let alone utilitarian ones. The good consequences that it produced appear not only irrelevant, but callous toward the suffering endured by so many slaves. The reason that slavery was immoral has little to do with the balance of consequences. Rather, it has to do with a universal principle that directs us to safeguard the basic rights and dignity of people, ultimately because they are made in the image of God.

Also, utilitarianism can justify obvious injustices, such as contriving evidence against an innocent person to prevent widespread social unrest that would result in loss of life and substantial property damage. On strictly utilitarian grounds, framing an innocent person is not only justifiable, but morally obligatory, in order to prevent significant harmful consequences. But most people have a deep intuitive sense that framing the innocent is wrong, regardless of the consequences.

A utilitarian may reply that the cases cited beg the question, since they assume the priority of the principles of justice and fairness. Here it is crucial to demonstrate

John Stuart Mill

Mill (1806 – 73) was, with Jeremy Bentham, one of the ideological founders of utilitarianism and one of the most influential thinkers of his time. He was trained as a philosopher and economist, and throughout his life he wrote on subjects such as logic, metaphysics, political philosophy, and ethics. His utilitarian ethics had much in common with Bentham's, though it was not identical. He too held to a view of right and wrong that was tied to the consequences that action produced, and he sought to take morality out of the realm of religion and its theological grounding. But his view of utility was somewhat broader than Bentham's. Mill distinguished between pleasure and happiness, and further between types of pleasures. For Mill, an action is morally right if it produces a greater balance of good consequences over harmful ones. Like Bentham, he proposed a political philosophy that gave high regard to the individual but also gave attention to the common good. For example, he regarded property rights as important but not absolute. They could be altered if sufficient considerations of the common good warranted. This falls out of his view that the good is what provides the greatest balance of good consequences to the greatest number. Both he and Bentham were social reformers who conceived of a new way to think about morality and social policy. They were called radicals in their day and advocated a political philosophy that was oriented toward autonomy, individual rights, and the good of society as a whole.

to the utilitarian how difficult it would be to live with the implications of his or her theory.

The utilitarian may also take the position of a rule utilitarian instead of an act utilitarian. This prevents individual actions from being judged by the principle of utility. Rather, the rule utilitarian would approach the situation differently. The rule utilitarian would not reason as an act utilitarian, but would step back from the situation and ask, "What rules of conduct tend to promote the greatest good for the greatest number?"

Given two societies, one that had a rule against bearing false witness and another that did not, from the perspective of utility the first one would clearly be the better one. By appealing to the rule against bearing false witness, the person would conclude that he or she should not frame an innocent person to quell a riot. Thus the utilitarian has shifted the focus from the justification of individual actions to the justification of general rules (on the principle of utility) to avoid the charge of injustice. Whether the utilitarian has avoided the charge of injustice is not clear, however, since it could be argued that a society that periodically uses false witness in specific circumstances to prevent widespread social unrest might be a good society. It is not clear that the retreat to rule utilitarianism can help ease the tension created by act utilitarian situations.

Problems with Utilitarianism

Even if the utilitarian can escape the charge of justifying obvious injustices, this system has other problems. First, not only are the consequences of actions difficult to predict and measure, but the notions of benefit and harm are not value neutral. What may be a benefit or a harm to one person may not be to another. It is not entirely accurate to say that the utilitarian uses nonmoral criteria to evaluate the morality of an action. In many cases one must appeal to principles to give substance to the idea of a benefit or to arbitrate competing claims about a benefit. In other words, the utilitarian must appeal to principles to determine what constitutes a good or harmful consequence. What makes an outcome harmful or beneficial thus depends on a prior commitment to principles. It seems that the utilitarian must "smuggle in" principles to give substance to the notions of harm and benefit. For example, why should we conclude that a murder victim has been harmed? What makes that a harm if his or her life is not sacred, possessing intrinsic human dignity? It's true that someone is harmed when murdered, but what makes that harmful is that the principle of the dignity of persons is violated. You could make a similar argument for other actions that produce harms, such as the above example of sexual assault.

Second, utilitarianism lacks criteria to direct the distribution of benefits in a group. It tends to be an aggregate theory in that what really counts is the overall amount of benefit—that is, the greatest good for the greatest number. The distribution of benefits is just as important, if not more so, as the overall amount of benefit accorded to the aggregate group. For example, a particular policy may increase the prosperity of the group as a whole yet concentrate its benefit among the most privileged in the group. The utilitarian cannot make a judgment on the distribution of those benefits, only how the policy impacted the group as a whole.

Third, utilitarianism offers no place for the idea of individual merit.[8] For example, an employer promotes a responsible employee rather than an irresponsible one, not because it serves the general utility, but because the responsible employee has earned it. Without being guilty of discrimination, we recognize merit as a reason for treating people in different ways, regardless of the consequences for treating people that way.

In spite of these problems with utilitarianism, it is important to take the consequences of actions and decisions seriously, since there may be times when an appeal to principles will not resolve a dilemma. In addition, a consideration of consequences may be a compelling way to construct an argument about a specific moral issue to a diverse culture.

Deontological Ethics

Deontological systems of ethics are principle-based systems, in which actions are intrinsically right or wrong, dependent on adherence to the relevant moral principles or values. What distinguishes various types of deontological systems is the source of the principles that determine morality. In chapter 2 both the notion of divine commands and natural law were discussed and were determined to be important components of a Christian ethic.

Nevertheless, there are deontological systems that are not dependent on any religious grounding. Most notable of these is what is known as *ethical rationalism*, the moral theory of Immanuel Kant.

Underlying his moral system are three critical assumptions. First, to have a valid moral system, one must have power to constrain people without being deterministic. In other words, reason must have the power to motivate action, but it must also leave one genuinely free not to do one's duty. In contrast to Hume, reason governs the passions, not vice versa.

Second, what is a valid duty in circumstance X is the same for all rational beings. This is his principle of fairness and is foundational to his central concept known as the *categorical imperative*. He does acknowledge relevant differences among people, but the point is that moral obligations do not vary based on the circumstances. Here Kant appears to be anticipating the utilitarians, such as

Bentham and Mill, for whom morality depended on the consequences of an action, which depended largely on one's circumstances.

Third, people cannot change their moral obligations or duties merely by changing their desires. Moral imperatives based on desire are what he called hypothetical imperatives. A true moral imperative is what he called categorical, since it is not based on some desire.

Kant's system revolved around the notion of the good will. This is his first proposition on the nature of morality. The good will is seen as being the key to being worthy of happiness. In this notion, he reversed the emphasis of the classical Greek philosophers, that virtue would essentially bring one well-being. For Kant, happiness followed if one was morally worthy of possessing it. The good will is capable of acting from motives other than the desire to be well off. It recognizes that one's duty is inherently good apart from any consequences that it produced. What makes the good will good is that it operates independent of consequences. He cited two cases in which one can have a bad will that produces good results and a good will that produces bad results. Kant reasoned that since one cannot control all the consequences, moral worth cannot depend on things that are beyond the control of the individual making the moral decision. The good will is the will that acts for the sake of duty. Thus the idea of duty is set up in accordance with the above three assumptions. One's duty can be contrary to one's inclination but does not have to be. For Kant, being moral is more than acting according to one's inclination.

Immanuel Kant

Widely regarded as one of the greatest philosophical minds and contributors to ethics, Kant lived during the height of the Enlightenment (1724 – 1804). He was raised in Prussia and educated at the University of Königsberg, where he later spent most of his teaching career. He wrote voluminously about metaphysics, logic, epistemology, philosophy of religion, and ethics, and enjoyed an outstanding reputation throughout Europe during his lifetime.

Kant devised a principle-based ethic, centered not on a religious system, but on reason alone. He represents the epitome of Enlightenment ethics in that he attempted to construct an adequately grounded ethical system based on the use of reason alone. His system was not dependent on divine revelation, either special or natural. Also, it was not based on any particular view of human nature, since nature could be interpreted in many different ways. Insisting that a valid moral system must be independent of empirical observation, his ethics were in part a response to the ethics of Hume, his contemporary.

Actions are determined by desire, by inclination, or by what Kant calls a *maxim*. A maxim is the plan of action where an individual in circumstance X does act A to bring about result R. But the result is not what gives the act worth, because one does not control all the results of one's actions. Therefore the question is raised, What is it about the maxim that makes the will good?

The good will is the only unconditional good. The good will is one that acts from duty. The value of an act done from duty is not in its consequences. Hence it must be from its maxim. But what distinguishes the good maxim from the bad? The good maxim must be able to motivate every rational being in the specified circumstance. Thus it must have something that is the "same for all." This is the form of the law, or its ability to be universalized. In other words, all beings can act on the maxim without making it impossible for any to act on it. So, what Kant called the categorical imperative is not based on circumstances.

Within his concept of the good will is the idea of the contradiction of the will. This assumes that if everyone did it, no one would ultimately be able to do it. In his test for universalizability, he asked, "Would it be fair, or could we live with it if everyone did this?" The categorical imperative is often applied in a bit different way, by asking, "Could we live with a state of affairs if everyone did not do things that Kant suggested are to be universal maxims?" For example, if everyone violated the duty to tell the truth, could we live with the kind of society that would inevitably result from this? Kant calls this the principle of universalizability.

To put it another way, he might ask, "Are you ready for your action to be regarded as the equivalent of a law of nature?" Thus we are constrained to do something because we respect the law that can be universalized, and we feel a sense of duty as a result. Duty and inclination are not necessarily opposed, but a moral act is one done out of duty, not simply because one wants to do it. Moral maxims must be categorical, that is, they must be binding and independent of one's desires. This categorical imperative actually has four different formulations, which are listed below:

1. Act only according to that maxim by which you can at the same time will that it should become a universal law.
2. Act as though the maxim of your action were by your will to become a universal law of nature.
3. Act so that you treat humanity, whether in your own person or in that of another, always as an end and never as a means only. From this formulation the fundamental principle of respect for persons is derived. (This is one of the most significant legacies of the ethics of Kant.)
4. Do no action according to any maxim that would be inconsistent with its being universal, and thus act only so that the will through its maxims could regard itself at the same time as universally law-giving. This is what he calls his principle of

autonomy. Since we derive the principles from our own rational nature, we are autonomous and self-determined, and thus by our actions we "legislate" morality. Moral constraint is thus possible without individuals losing their genuine freedom of moral choice.

To summarize, no will is morally good because it does what it wants to do. A motive other than the passions must exist: respect for law. Free from determination, the rational will acts on the basis of respect for law. But since not all are purely rational beings, human beings *ought* to act under the constraint of the categorical imperative. The moral purpose of reason is to illuminate us to our "ought," independent of sensation. The highest good for Kant is both happiness and being worthy of it. That is achieved by adherence to duty.

Kant's categorical imperative in particular and his ethical system in general have come under considerable criticism on three primary points. First, Kant appears to have been overly optimistic about the ability of reason to formulate universal absolutes. Kant held that rational persons using their faculties could reason themselves to precisely the same moral rules. This seems to run counter to the degree of moral diversity that exists in the world today. Such diversity cannot be accounted for simply in terms of rationality, which suggests that there are other factors beside reason that contribute to moral norms. Kant is widely considered the apex of modernity with its virtual worship of reason, a project that has been widely judged to have failed. Despite its other shortcomings, postmodernism has rightly called the supremacy of unaided reason into question, here because the wide variety of moral values and how they are weighted calls into question the adequacy of reason alone to formulate universal principles.[9]

A second line of criticism of Kant comes from the results of the categorical imperative. According to Kant, when properly applied, the categorical imperative gives one absolute moral rules, which is the goal. That is, it produces an exceptionless moral system—there are never any exceptions to Kantian formulated moral rules. Kant himself suggests that even when confronted with the need to lie in order to protect an innocent person who is about to be killed, one still has an unqualified duty to tell the truth. Yet this seems very problematic and illustrates one of the tensions of absolutist deontological moral systems in general—they cannot deal with scenarios when principles conflict. I discussed this in chapter 2 in connection with divine command theories of ethics and resolved it there by suggesting that there are occasions when principles need to be weighted and ranked. This runs counter to a Kantian deontology, which presumes that there is never a conflict in one's moral duty if properly ascertained. For a deontological system to avoid being excessively rigid and unbending, it makes more sense to hold to prima facie principles (literally, "at first glance") that have periodic exceptions to them when they come into conflict with other principles. This is not an absolutist deontological system, nor is it Kant's formulation, but it seems to fit our intuitions about our duty when moral rules conflict.

A final criticism of Kant is that his categorical imperative is only a procedural morality and does not offer any guidance in terms of the content of morality. That is, it is a necessary part of formulating moral rules but not sufficient to tell us what the rules ought to be. One can properly devise consistent absolutes, but the categorical imperative cannot tell us why those absolutes may be considered right or wrong. For example, Kant's procedure can tell us that we ought to have a rule against actions such as deception or adultery, but it can't tell us why specifically those things are wrong.[10] A procedural notion such as the categorical imperative cannot provide much to clarify the material content of morality.

Emotivism

The debate over moral issues such as euthanasia, abortion, and homosexuality illustrates the overlap between moral judgments and personal preferences. For example, many people who say that homosexuality is wrong actually mean that they find it distasteful or disgusting. This is another way of describing ethical subjectivism (see the following section on relativism). The subjectivist holds that morality depends on how an individual feels about an action. When someone makes the statement that "X is wrong," the subjectivist will conclude that the person simply disapproves of X, since morality to the subjectivist is in the eye of the beholder. Many of the same criticisms of ethical relativism also apply to ethical subjectivism.

Emotivism goes beyond subjectivism and is a theory about metaethics, that is, the language of morality. The emotivist holds that moral language simply expresses a person's emotions about a subject. Hence nothing that anyone says in moral language can be true or false. The emotivist considers ethical statements to be attitudes masquerading as facts. Emotivism as a moral theory has its roots in the moral philosophy of David Hume, who held that morality is a matter of sentiment rather than fact.

There is an essential difference between the subjectivist and the emotivist. For the subjectivist, moral judgments are reports or statements of fact about the attitude of the person who says them. For the emotivist, moral judgments are not facts at all, but emotional expressions about an action or person. The subjectivist will say, "Homosexuality is wrong!" This means, "I disapprove of homosexuality." For the emotivist, the same statement means, "Homosexuality, yuck! Boo!" Emotivism is thus a more sophisticated theory than subjectivism. Both share the idea that moral judgments are not normative statements and that objective moral facts are nonexistent.

Philosophical Developments in Emotivism

Two philosophical developments contributed to the rise of emotivism. The first was a reaction to a moral theory called *intuitionism*, in which morality was directly intuited by the person making the moral decision. Since intuitionism seemed arbitrary to many philosophers and therefore untenable as a moral theory, emotivists went a step further than intuitionists. They claimed that the language of morality expressed one's emotions about the situation or person under consideration but that nothing was said about what was right or wrong.

A second philosophical development that contributed to emotivism was the rise of *logical positivism*. Logical positivists claimed that only two types of statements are possible: (1) analytical statements, such as definitions, and (2) factual statements that are empirically verifiable. In other words, the only things that can be considered as facts are definitions and statements that can be either proven or

David Hume

Hume was born and raised in Scotland (1711 – 76) and was not an academic philosopher by profession. He was a historian as well as a philosopher and wrote a history of Great Britain in addition to his numerous philosophical works. Among his treatises in philosophy, he attempted a complete philosophical system titled *A Treatise of Human Nature*. He wrote about metaphysics, epistemology, anthropology, philosophy of religion, political philosophy, and ethics. He was a very popular person in literary circles during his lifetime, although he received much criticism for his philosophical works.

Hume's ethics come out of his overall worldview, which is known as empiricism — that is, the only matters of fact are those discernible by the senses. Thus moral facts and moral sense as perceptible objects do not exist. The rules of morality are not derived by reason. Moral distinctions are independent of reason, and, for Hume, reason is only the slave of the passions.

In fact, reason is inert when it comes to determining the morality of an action. Hume compared vice and virtue with sounds, colors, heat, and cold. They are not qualities in objects but perceptions in the mind. Morals have to do with sense, not reason. Reason can only determine means to accomplishing ends. Reason only serves the passions, and they are not subject to reason. Reason is also powerless to incite action necessary to actually do the good.

Reducing morality to matters of opinion or feeling is at the heart of Hume's project. The reason his theory is important is that it is widely followed today. Morality is becoming increasingly subjective and is losing its propositional nature as people in our culture insist that judgments of right and wrong are merely individual subjective feelings or opinion.

disproven empirically. According to the logical positivists, moral judgments are more than definitions and are not empirically verifiable; therefore, they cannot be factual statements. All they can be are statements that simply express and arouse emotion.

Therefore, for the emotivist, moral language has three purposes.[11] First, it expresses emotions or feelings. This is the primary use of moral language. Second, it is imperative — that is, it is used to lend authority to a command to someone to do something. Third, it is persuasive; it is used to influence another's actions, primarily by bending another's will to fit one's own. Emotivism does give us something positive, a reminder that moral language is emotionally charged and can be used improperly to manipulate people under the guise of getting them to do the right thing. Unfortunately, because moral language is so emotionally charged, people often dismiss it today as too divisive or incapable of verification.

Problems with Emotivism

Emotivism as a moral theory can be criticized in three primary ways.[12] First, the verification theory of meaning, which is the foundation of logical positivism, has problems. Specifically, it fails its own test of meaning. Emotivism maintains that the only statements capable of having meaning are those that are empirically verifiable, but this underlying principle is itself not empirically verifiable. There is no good reason to limit meaningful statements to those that are verified empirically.

Second, emotivism is actually a theory of the use of moral language, not of its meaning.[13] The emotivist has jumped from a theory of use to a theory of meaning without any justification for that leap.

Third, emotivism cannot account for the place of reason in ethics. Emotivism sets up a false dichotomy, as the following demonstrates:

   (a) Either there are moral facts like there are scientific facts, or
   (b) values are nothing more than expressions of our subjective feelings.

But there is another possibility; namely, moral truths are truths of reason, or a moral judgment is true if it is supported by better reasons than the alternatives. From a Christian worldview, we would also say that moral truths are also truths of revelation and that there is a strong connection between the facts of creation and the facts of morality. Good reasons usually resolve moral disagreements, but for the emotivist, giving good reasons and using manipulation would essentially be the same thing. There is no good reason to assume that moral language is not also factual language or that moral judgments are just expressions of emotion or preference rather than cognitive statements. It should not be surprising that ethical statements are not empirically verifiable, since right and wrong are not empirically observable qualities. But neither are they simply emotive expressions.

Relativism

Ethical relativism became popular as a result of the findings of cultural anthropologists, who observed that different cultures have widely varying moral codes and concepts of right and wrong. Its key advocates include anthropologists, such as William Graham Sumner, Ruth Benedict, and Melville Herskovits, and philosopher John Ladd.[14]

As these scholars studied different cultures, they discovered the lack of a uniform concept of right and wrong. For example, some cultures practice polygamy, while others practice monogamy. Some cultures consider it a moral obligation to give one of their children to an infertile couple. Some cultures, such as certain Eskimo groups, practice euthanasia and infanticide in ways that seem ghastly and immoral to many other cultures. Among the Auca Indians of South America, treachery was considered the highest virtue. In fact, after sharing the gospel with the Aucas, the missionaries were shocked to learn that the Aucas saw Judas as the hero of the gospel, not Jesus. In colonial India, the Indians burned widows following the death of their husbands, which was a widely practiced custom considered to be morally legitimate. What the natives of Polynesia considered as taboo astonished Captain Cook's sailors. Despite the fact that the women had much freedom in the area of sexual relations, the natives considered it taboo to eat a meal with someone of the opposite sex. Today female circumcision is practiced widely in Africa and the Middle East, a practice that many Western feminists refer to as mutilation. These illustrations offer merely a sample of the various ways in which people conceived and practiced morality.

In response to these observations, scholars drew new conclusions about the nature of morality. In view of such moral diversity, they suggested that it was impossible to believe in universal moral values. Such moral diversity called into question ethical systems that posited absolute, unchanging moral principles that could be universally applied. The more "enlightened" way of viewing morality was to allow for morality to be relative to the culture. Rather than being universal, morality was seen as relative to the cultural consensus.

Different Forms of Relativism

Some anthropologists, however, merely pointed out the differences between the moral codes of various cultures. This is what we called, in chapter 1, "descriptive ethics," which is not a normative discipline at all. That is, this is only a descriptive enterprise, and there is no attempt to draw normative ethical principles out of their observations. They looked at the diversity of ethical standards and concluded that different cultures in the world have widely differing standards of right and wrong. But many other anthropologists espoused a normative form of relativism called *cultural relativism.* This is the primary form of relativism and holds that all values are culturally created and therefore are not objective, universal moral principles applicable to all cultures and time periods. In other words, the culture determines the values and sets the moral norms. So whatever is the cultural consensus on morality determines what is moral for that culture. Whereas the history of ethics has shown how sociological conditions have strongly influenced the emphases of different thinkers, the ethical relativist says that morality is actually dependent on the cultural context in which one finds oneself. Consequently, there are no objective, universal moral principles that are binding for all cultures and time periods.

As a result, any practice that is the cultural norm is moral for that culture, and someone from another culture cannot make a judgment on that practice, since for the relativist, there are no norms that transcend culture. So, for the custom of female circumcision, for example, since that is the norm for that culture, that makes it moral. Someone from outside that culture cannot make a criticism or negative assessment of such a practice, since that person is outside the culture. It is often said, "It's a Middle Eastern thing (or substitute another culture)—you wouldn't understand." And since you couldn't understand, you can't make a judgment on the practice.

Cultural relativism is sometimes referred to as *conventionalism*, which maintains that cultural acceptance determines the validity of moral norms. While morality may need cultural acceptance to function properly, it is quite another thing to insist that cultural acceptance *determines* the validity of its values. In practice little difference exists between cultural relativism and conventionalism. In both instances the culture determines the morality, and the standards of that culture are considered normative for that culture without being universal.

A second form of relativism practiced today is *moral subjectivism*, which says that morality is determined by the individual's own tastes and preferences. Expressed in its popular form, ethical subjectivism says, "What's right for me is right, and what's right for you is right," even if the person is referring to two diametrically opposed actions. One could say, "Being faithful to one's spouse is right for some people, but open marriage is right for others." This view of morality is often applied to sexual morality where one's moral code for sexual behavior is considered a private matter and where one can subjectively and individually determine what is right. It's not hard to see how cultural relativism could reduce to subjectivism, as the size of the relevant culture shrinks, ultimately ending up a culture of one person, hence subjectivism.

A third form of relativism smuggled into the popular culture is called *situation ethics*. Popularized by Joseph Fletcher in the 1960s and 1970s, situation ethics holds that all morality is relative to the situation in which one finds oneself, and one's moral obligation is to do the loving thing in that situation. Technically speaking, situation ethics is not relativism, since the law of love actually functions as an absolute. (As biblical support for his position, Fletcher repeatedly cites Romans 13:8, "Owe nothing to one another, except to love one another" [Fletcher's paraphrase]).

Situationists often cite the classic case of the woman in the Nazi concentration camp who asked a guard to impregnate her so that she could be released to her family. Unless she were ill or pregnant, she knew that she would remain in prison. So she decided to become pregnant to be reunited with her family. Situationists will argue that her illicit affair was justifiable, since love for her family motivated her act. In determining the morality of her action, the situationist views the act of adultery as irrelevant.

Cultural relativism, the view that morality is determined by the cultural context in which one finds oneself, is the predominant form of relativism today. It is widely applied in the popular culture in two principal areas, namely, international business and multiculturalism.

One of the most significant challenges to doing business in other parts of the world comes from cultural relativism. Imagine yourself as a business executive responsible for expanding your firm into international markets. As a result of different ethical standards of doing business, you will be faced with the temptation to offer bribes to high government officials to secure access to the market for your product. Although bribes are considered immoral and illegal in much of the West, your clients in this new market will expect them as a normal part of doing business. What will you do? Will you adhere to what you consider to be a universal standard that does not permit bribery? Or will you adopt the philosophy "When in Rome, do as the Romans do" and justify offering bribes because that is acceptable in that culture?

Imagine now that you are a project manager for a large construction company that is expanding its business into the third world, where safety and environmental standards are significantly lower than in the United States. By adopting lower safety standards, your company can save a great deal of money, but it presents safety hazards for some of the people living in the community. Do you build according to higher safety standards, or do you simply follow the inferior codes of the foreign country and increase your company's profits? All kinds of things once considered immoral can now be justified if one becomes a relativist and uses culturally acceptable standards.

So as not to be pointing an accusing finger at other countries and cultures, imagine a situation that frequently occurs here in our own country, the United States. In an attempt to avoid paying higher income taxes, businesspeople will claim deductions for expenses that they did not have. Dishonest activities, such as padding expense accounts and falsifying other data, are often done simply because they are considered permissible in the context of the corporate world. The fact that "everyone else does it" is taken as permission to perpetuate such blatant corruption.

A second principal area where ethical relativism is applied is in multiculturalism, which is a movement that seeks to foster greater appreciation of and tolerance for cultures different than one's own. This takes the form of things like cultural exhibits and education to avoid language and other behavior that offends particular cultural groups. Relativism has been perhaps inadvertently associated with multiculturalism, since in order to take any culture seriously, one must come to grips with its values. Failure to take a culture's values into account may actually result in trivializing it. Once you begin to promote tolerance and understanding of a culture's distinct values, you must take the next logical step, which is to accept their values as equally valid as yours, which is a textbook definition of cultural relativism. In the name of appreciating cultural diversity, one accepts the values of a culture as normative within that culture. Then it becomes more difficult to make value judgments about a culture for fear of creating offense and not appearing tolerant. In many circles, if you are not a relativist, you are accused of being ethnocentric and even a cultural imperialist.

An extreme example of this occurred when an Arab-American family moved to California from the Middle East. When the adult daughter expressed her desire to ⟨ ⟩usband, the girl's father insisted that her marriage be arranged by ⟨ ⟩ng to traditional Middle Eastern custom. When the girl refused ⟨ ⟩r engagement to a man of her own choosing, her father took ⟨ ⟩ considered appropriate to his Middle Eastern background—he ⟨ ⟩nor killing," considered necessary in the father's culture in order ⟨ ⟩ reputation of the family. When he was on trial for murder, his ⟨ ⟩argued that since his behavior was normative in his Middle East-⟨ ⟩morality of his action should be determined by his cultural con-⟨ ⟩rds, the attorney appealed to cultural relativism to attempt to ⟨ ⟩s action.[15]

⟨ ⟩ of Relativism

⟨ ⟩ophical shortcomings, ethical relativism does have appeal, par-⟨ ⟩opular culture. The first appeal of relativism is based on the ⟨ ⟩at morality does not develop in a sociological vacuum. Some ⟨ ⟩are formed either in reaction to or affirmation of the social conditions of the time. Unfortunately, these values can be mistaken for absolute standards when in reality they are little more than cultural biases dressed up in moral language. Slavery during the Civil War era aptly illustrates this. Although it was clearly immoral for human beings to own and mistreat other human beings, many Southerners attempted to justify slavery, sometimes on biblical grounds. Created to supply cheap labor in the agricultural South, slavery was deemed moral, and the right to own slaves was regarded as an absolute right. In reality, slavery was merely a cultural creation that was regarded as an absolute moral right.

A second appeal of relativism comes from the way it is presented. Frequently relativism is presented as though it and its opposite, absolutism, are the only two valid alternatives. The absolutist rigidly holds to absolute moral principles and does not allow for any exceptions, regardless of the circumstances. This is clearly not an attractive or realistic position to hold; and if relativism is presented as the only alternative to this kind of absolutism, it is not difficult to see why people would prefer relativism. It is better to see morality on a continuum, with absolutism at one extreme and relativism at the other. One can hold to objective moral principles and not be a complete absolutist, that is, one can be what is called a "prima facie" absolutist, literally, "at first appearance." While recognizing the importance of unchanging, objective, moral principles, the prima facie absolutist allows for periodic exceptions to general principles. On selected issues, most people who hold to the importance of principles would admit exceptions. For example, many people would agree that in the rare cases when a pregnancy presents imminent danger to a woman's life, it is justifiable to end the pregnancy. Similarly, if someone breaks into my house with a loaded gun and asks where my wife is, I am not obligated to tell him the truth. Thus the relativist's appeal rests on a false dichotomy.

A third appeal of relativism comes from the emphasis on multiculturalism, mentioned above. This trend emphasizes tolerance for the distinctives of other cultures, including values, which moves one strongly in the direction of being a relativist. Yet most people realize that limits must be drawn somewhere and that some standards must transcend culture if society is to arbitrate between competing cultural values. This has deeper philosophical roots in a postmodern view of truth, knowledge, and morality. Postmodernism insists that all knowledge is received through one's cultural lenses. As a result, it is impossible to have an objective view of truth. And since there can be no such thing as objective truth, making any kind of claim for similarly objective and universal moral norms is considered futile by the postmodernists. It would be difficult to overestimate the impact of postmodern thinking on the resurgence of relativism in the culture today. The postmodernist's radical skepticism concerning the reality of truth and knowledge exacts a heavy price when it comes to morality. The postmodernist conclusion that moral values are simply human conventions that reflect one's cultural lenses and matrices of power renders morality as little more than a subjective enterprise in a futile search for a consensus. At best the postmodernist can embrace cultural relativism in recognition of the social agreement on a particular set of values that is useful only for that social group. Postmodernism also has a significant impact on Christianity in general since their denial of *metanarratives* (which means that there is no one dominant worldview or any way to judge between competing worldviews) renders the gospel message just another religious opinion.

The postmodernist's view of truth, knowledge, and morality has also been vigorously challenged by a variety of critics, some of whom are religious thinkers, but many simply recognize the flaws in the postmodern view of the world without approaching it from any particular religious view of the world. Two primary criticisms have been raised of postmodernism.[16] The first is to insist that just because one sees the world through a particular set of lenses (or biases), it does not mean that he or she is incapable of rationality or objectivity. It may make being rational and objective more difficult, but it does not make it impossible. If bias actually made it impossible to objectively assess reasons and evidence for a view, then we would be left in the odd position of not being able to objectively teach or investigate anything that we believed in. Nor would we be able to teach what we opposed!

A second problem with postmodernism as a worldview is that it is self-refuting. Either the postmodernist thinker presents his or her views as being true and rational, and thereby sensible and worth adopting, which is a denial of the central premises of postmodernism, or the postmodernist advocate does not offer his or her position as true, which does not provide any compelling reasons for accepting it over other worldviews.

A fourth appeal of relativism comes from the modern emphasis on scientific objectivity. When applied to morality, this takes the form of value neutrality, presumed by the culture to be a good thing, though increasingly the objectivity of scientific inquiry is being called into question even in the hard sciences by postmodernists. Yet scholars are increasingly recognizing that value neutrality is actually a myth, and even if it were possible, it may not even be desirable. In the popular culture, a person who holds to absolute values that transcend culture is perceived at best as somewhat unenlightened and at worst as a narrow, rigid fundamentalist. Given this alternative to relativism, it is not surprising that relativism has appeal.

Weaknesses of Relativism

In spite of its appeal and widespread use in the popular culture, relativism has significant philosophical shortcomings. First, in terms of the observations of the cultural anthropologists who developed relativism, the degree of moral diversity is overstated and the high degree of moral consensus is understated. A good deal more moral consensus exists among cultures than was first believed. Anthropologist Clyde Kluckhohn has noted the following:

> Every culture has a concept of murder, distinguishing this from execution, killing in war and other justifiable homicides. The notions of incest and other regulations upon sexual behavior, the prohibitions on untruth under defined circumstances, of restitution and reciprocity, of mutual obligations between parents and children—these and many other moral concepts are altogether universal.[17]

A second weakness of relativism is related to the first. Many of the observations of moral diversity were differences in moral practices. For example, take the historical tradition of some tribes of Eskimos to practice a form of euthanasia. One can argue that the principle being followed is the same as that in the West—that of respect for one's elders. But the way in which that norm is applied is very different, based on their religious view that a person goes to the eternal state in the condition in which he or she dies. Under that view, they would consider allowing a person to die in a hospital, full of tubes and technologies and in a frail, chronically diseased condition, a terrible wrong. It seems clear that diversity in practice does not necessarily equal diversity in underlying values or principles. Much less moral diversity exists at the level of principles than many anthropologists think they have observed. A person who holds to the reality of objective moral values can easily account for many, though not all, varieties in practices from the perspective of the underlying principles.

A third weakness of relativism is that cultural relativism as a normative system cannot be drawn from the observations of the cultural relativist. Cultural relativism as a moral system does not follow simply from the empirical data of moral diversity among cultures. Just because different cultures have different moral standards, even if the degree of moral diversity is not overstated, it does not follow that there is no such thing as absolute values that transcend culture.

A fourth weakness of relativism is that it provides no way to arbitrate among competing cultural value claims. This is important as many countries recognize the high degree of cultural diversity in their populations and therefore the inevitable clash of cultures. For example, as the Middle Eastern population of Europe continues to grow, creating cultural enclaves in Western European countries, clashes of cultures are becoming more common, sometimes leading to violence. The archbishop of Canterbury, the head of the Church of England, has made the controversial suggestion that European countries must find accommodation with Islamic law codes and allow Islamic law to have its place in the law of the various European countries.[18] The relativist can offer very little to resolve these kinds of conflicts since the relativist can neither condemn either group nor umpire their competing claims.

The fifth and most serious charge against relativism is an extension of the fourth weakness. The relativist cannot morally evaluate any clearly oppressive culture or, more specifically, any obvious tyrant. Cultures that relegate women to the status of second-class citizens cannot be evaluated by the relativist, since morality is dependent on the cultural context. Similarly, the relativist cannot pass judgment on someone like Hitler, who oppressed a minority with the permission, if not approval, of the majority, since no moral absolute that transcends culture exists to which the relativist can appeal as a basis for that judgment.

A sixth weakness of relativism is that it allows no room for moral reformers or prophets. Since the reformer stands against the cultural consensus that is supposed to determine the valid moral values for the relativist, the relativist cannot offer the praise due most moral reformers. The relativist can only explain the moral reformer as an example of the clash of cultures. Yet moral reformers often stand alone, apart from any support from the culture, until the movement gathers momentum.

A final objection to relativism is the charge that its central premise, namely that moral absolutes do not exist, is a self-defeating statement, since the premise itself is an absolute. However, the relativist could respond that the premise is only a formal absolute, not a material one — that is, it is a statement that describes the procedure of relativism, not a moral principle that is absolute. While that distinction is correct, the relativist still has a moral absolute that makes the system self-defeating, namely, the absolute of tolerance and respect for the values of other cultures. The relativist could hardly tolerate any culture that had intolerance as one of its central virtues.

Virtue Theory

All of the normative theories examined thus far are action-oriented ethical systems. The exception to this is emotivism, which is a theory about moral language, rather than a theory that attempts to provide moral direction. Most ethical theories in modern times have focused on doing the right action or making the right decision when confronted by a moral dilemma. Many of the major debates in ethics have revolved around the basis for determining what is the right action, whether consequences or principles provide that basis, and whether the right action is universal or relative.

Virtue theory, which is also called aretaic ethics (from the Greek term *arete*, "virtue"), holds that morality is more than simply doing the right thing. The foundational moral claims made by the virtue theorist concern the moral agent (the person doing the action), not the act that the agent performs. Dating back to Plato and Aristotle, the tradition of virtue theory is a long one, including the Epicureans, the Stoics, the New Testament Gospels, and Thomas Aquinas. With the collapse of the medieval worldview during the Renaissance and Enlightenment periods, one of the unfortunate casualties was Thomas's emphasis on Aristotelian virtue theory.

Some virtue theorists hold that virtue theory can stand alone as an adequate system of ethics. Others hold that virtues and moral rules or principles are interdependent, but exactly how they fit together is a point of debate. In the face of both natural law and divine commands, it is difficult to see how the Christian could not embrace some sort of deontological ethics. But it is equally difficult to see how the Christian could ignore virtue theory in favor of act-based ethics, given the emphasis in the New Testament on developing the character of Christ, which would seem to precede action. As suggested in chapter 2, the virtues are logically prior to principles in that the virtues emerge out of God's character, and

Plato

Plato lived from roughly 426 to 347 BC. He came from a wealthy, aristocratic family that allowed him the luxury of study. His background likely contributed to his somewhat negative appraisal of democracy. He was a close associate of Socrates. Accordingly, Socrates plays a role in most of Plato's writings, and a prominent role in some of Plato's writings on ethics. At some time during the 370s he founded the Academy, a place of higher education where he taught through his well-known method of dialogue and questioning. Aristotle was a member of the Academy during the last twenty years of Plato's life.

Most of Plato's writings consist of his "dialogues," which actually bear more resemblance to monologues. He wrote roughly twenty-five of these dialogues, and the most well known and widely read of these is *The Republic*. In this work he presents much of his ethical theory, although many of the other dialogues contain material that deals with ethics.

The emphasis in Plato's thought is not on rights, moral principles, or consequences, but on questions of the soul. His moral philosophy is not concerned with whether certain actions are right or wrong, but with whether one is a good person. What is today called "virtue theory" dominated classical ethics, and Plato was the consummate virtue theorist. He and other Greek moral theorists thought that they could know the good person, that is, the right way to live one's life in general. They were more concerned with one's character and virtue than with any action-based theory of ethics.

For Plato life was parallel to a craft or skill — that is, the right way to live life was parallel to a right way to perform a craft or skill.

that moral rules and principles are those that are consistent with the outworking of God's virtue.

Some of the main differences between virtue ethics and act-oriented ethics are an emphasis on being rather than doing, an emphasis on who a person should become more than what a person should do, the importance of following people with exemplary behavior instead of following moral rules, an emphasis on a person's motive in place of action, and a stress on developing character more than simply obeying rules. Virtue theory is an ethic of character, not duty. These emphases are certainly consistent with the biblical emphasis on becoming more like Christ in character. One could also argue that act-oriented systems do not adequately produce moral people, not to mention spiritually mature people. It would seem that some component of virtue theory is needed to supplement act-oriented systems. Given the biblical emphasis, it would appear that act-oriented ethics alone give a person an overly narrow view of the moral life.

In Favor of Virtue Theory versus Act-Oriented Ethics

Advocates of virtue theory have pointed out some of the shortcomings of act-oriented ethics.[19] First, they reduce ethics to solving moral dilemmas and difficult cases that most people encounter infrequently. This is a reductionistic view of morality in which ethics has been moved to the extremes of life. The real substance of the moral life, the day-to-day decisions that people must make, is ignored.

Aristotle

Aristotle continued in the Platonic tradition of the virtuous person but spelled out the specific virtues and a psychology of moral behavior in much more detail. He spent much of his life (384–322 BC) in the political world because his father was the physician to Amyntas II, King of Macedon. Aristotle assumed leadership in the Academy of Plato after Plato's forced suicide and remained there until 342 BC, when he accepted the invitation to become the personal mentor for Alexander the Great. After this three-year assignment, he established schools in the different areas of Greece in which he resided.

Aristotle wrote voluminously, both on the popular level and the more sophisticated scientific and philosophical level. He wrote on a wide variety of subjects, including logic, physics, psychology, natural history, and philosophy. The core of his philosophical writings included works on metaphysics, ethics, and politics. He considered ethics and political philosophy to be inseparable, and thus his *Politics* is a logical extension of his three works on ethics, namely, the *Nicomachean Ethics*, the most well-developed ethical treatise; the *Eudemian Ethics*; and the *Magna Moralia*.

Second, the virtue theorist points out that moral duties involve attitudes as well as actions. It is ludicrous to say that two people who perform the same right action but with different attitudes are both equally worthy of praise. Act-oriented ethics focus on the act and tend to minimize the dispositions and character of the moral agent. Thus act-oriented ethics is a truncated view of the moral life, particularly for the Christian, who is commanded to develop virtuous character. One of the primary moral rules emphasized in Scripture is to cultivate virtue (Gal. 5:22–23).

Third, act-based systems provide little motivation for doing the right thing.[20] This is especially true of the apex of action-based morality, the system of Kant, who held that the good will was the will that performed its moral duty for the sake of duty. According to most virtue theorists, action-oriented ethics are largely negative prohibitions that involve hair-splitting distinctions that do not usually move people to action.

Fourth, action-based systems can become legalistic and encourage people to hide behind a facade of morality. They may actually mitigate against cultivating long-term adherence to moral principles.

Finally, act-based ethics overemphasize individual autonomy, or the ability of people to arrive at their moral duties by reason or revelation alone.[21] Since virtues are usually developed in some sort of a relationship or community, virtue theory gives proper emphasis to the communal context of ethics.

Virtue Theory on Its Own

Some virtue theorists hold that considerations of virtue are sufficient in and of themselves, and thus all act-oriented systems of ethics are unnecessary. Typically, a virtue theorist develops a theory in three stages. First, one must develop some conception of the ideal person or the purpose of a person. Without this first stage,

The Golden Mean

Aristotle's specific virtues derive from his concept of the *mean*. He is perhaps best known for this way of describing the virtues, popularly known as the "golden mean." A virtue is the mean between two extremes of behavior or emotion, usually between the extremes of excess and deficiency. For example, courage is described as the mean between rashness (an excess) and cowardice (a deficiency). Temperance is the mean between overindulgence (an excess) and self-denial (a deficiency). Other virtues include liberality, honor, gentleness, friendliness, and truthfulness. The ethic of the mean is an ethic of moderation that produces happiness. The mean is not merely the middle, but a mean that is relative to a person's circumstances.

virtues that the theorist determines to be essential would appear ungrounded, suspended in philosophical midair. For the Christian, this first stage is defined by the example of Jesus, considered the paradigm for virtue. Second, the theory involves developing a list of virtues necessary for achieving the person's proper purpose as outlined in the first stage. Third, people need to be shown how they can develop these virtues, either by divine grace, training, discipline, emulation, education, or a combination of these. For the virtue theorist, the moral virtues must be lived and cannot be taught in isolation from real life.

According to Aristotle, virtues are those habits that enable one to live well in the community. They are tied to the end of a human being, which is to use reason in pursuit of the good life. He defined virtues in terms of the golden mean, that is, between the two extremes of excess and deficiency. Virtues are developed by exposure to virtuous people — by watching and imitating them. This parallels the emphasis in Christian ethics on imitating Christ and developing his character, although a Christian's ultimate purpose differs from that described by Aristotle.

Problems with Virtue Theory on Its Own

Nevertheless, any virtue theory standing alone, without a partnership with moral rules or principles, will have problems. The classic criticism of virtue theory is that it fails to give adequate guidance for resolving moral dilemmas. Whether this criticism is entirely fair is debatable, since it does seem possible to use considerations of virtue to make difficult moral decisions. It does not offer the clear directions provided by a rule-based system, but that is not to say that it gives no direction.

A virtue theory that stands alone, however, does have one primary problem. Since virtue theory relies on the emulation of ideal individuals in order to develop virtue, and since we have no way of observing or evaluating a person's character apart from that individual's actions, some emphasis on one's actions is essential in order to recognize a virtuous person. Virtue ethics seems to presuppose that you will simply know that a person is virtuous when you meet one, a debatable assumption at best. Two other related problems include the inability of virtue theory to make sense out of cases in which good people do harmful actions and the inability of virtue theory to provide any way for society to notice when good persons have gone bad, since the theory emphasizes the person's character as opposed to actions. A final criticism of virtue theory is that virtue ethicists are overly optimistic about the power of virtue to stem social evils. Since notions about what constitutes virtue are so diverse, society must depend on rules that are based on principles to maintain social order.

Virtue Theory in Relation to Principles

Many other virtue theorists hold that virtues and principles must somehow coexist. They hold that virtues without principles are blind, but principles without virtues are impotent to motivate people to action.[22] The debate is whether virtues derive from principles (called the *correspondence view*) or complement principles as equals (called the *complementary view*).[23] According to the correspondence view, moral rules obligate people to perform certain actions, regardless of whether they possess the requisite virtues. Thus the virtues must be secondary and the principles primary. Virtues are dispositions to obey the rules or perform certain actions. Each virtue corresponds to a moral principle that governs the action that exhibits that virtue. The virtues do not have intrinsic value, only instrumental value. Their role is to motivate one to perform right actions and eliminate wrong actions. Principles help one evaluate the act, and virtues help one evaluate the moral actor. Both are important, because those with particular virtues are more likely to perform the right actions.

According to the complementary view, however, people have a moral obligation to be a certain kind of person, and whether it results in action is irrelevant in many cases. Some rules require action, but some require virtue. Virtues are more than simply dispositions to act in certain ways, since they include attributes that do not necessarily involve action. To be sure, the only way we can tell if a person has those virtues is when they issue in action. Christians do not consider moral virtues to be derivative or to lack intrinsic value. Right consists in doing the right thing with the right motive and attitude. It is insufficient to do the right thing for the right reason if the underlying attitude is absent. Virtues are a constitutive element of the good life and especially of being like Christ. Therefore a complementary view of virtues and principles would appear to be more consistent with Scripture. The virtues are logically prior to principles, insofar as God's character expresses itself in virtues, and moral rules and principles then are those that are consistent with the outworking of God's virtues.

Conclusion

Most of the moral systems described and critiqued in this chapter are still widely embraced in the contemporary culture. As you encounter the debate of different moral issues in public, observe which methods of moral reasoning those in the debate employ. The shortcomings of these systems illustrate the need for a method of moral reasoning that is based on general revelation, natural law, or special revelation. The Bible does employ different types of moral reasoning, but nowhere does it suggest that any of the systems mentioned in this chapter are all-sufficient.

Blending divine command, natural law, and virtue, the biblical emphasis seems to be a combination of virtue theory and deontological ethics with periodic appeal to egoism and utilitarianism.

For Further Reading

Audi, Robert. *Moral Knowledge and Ethical Character*. New York: Oxford University Press, 1997.

Beckwith, Francis J., and Gregory Koukl. *Relativism*. Grand Rapids: Baker, 1998.

Carson, Thomas L., and Paul K. Moser. *Morality and the Good Life*. New York: Oxford University Press, 1997.

MacIntyre, Alasdair. *After Virtue*. Notre Dame, Ind.: University of Notre Dame Press, 1984.

Pojman, Louis P. *Ethical Theory: Classical and Contemporary Readings*. Belmont, Calif.: Wadsworth, 1995.

Review Questions

1. Which of the moral theories presented in this chapter are action-oriented theories? Which one is *not* a normative ethical theory?

2. How does virtue theory differ from other action-oriented moral theories?

3. What other philosophical commitments must be made as a result of one's moral theory?

4. Ethical egoism determines right and wrong on what basis? Give some examples of ethical egoism in use in the culture at present.

5. What is the Bible's view of the pursuit of one's self-interest?

6. What are the primary arguments that support ethical egoism? What are some of its shortcomings?

7. What makes ethical egoism an arbitrary system? Do you agree?

8. What does psychological egoism refer to? How is it different from ethical egoism?

9. What does it mean that utilitarianism is a "teleological system"?

10. Who are the philosophers who systematized utilitarianism?

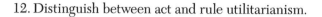

11. How does utilitarianism determine right and wrong? Give some examples of utilitarianism being used in public policy today.

12. Distinguish between act and rule utilitarianism.

13. Summarize some of the shortcomings of utilitarianism.

14. Which philosopher popularized a nonreligious form of deontological ethics?

15. Explain the categorical imperative.

16. What is the principle of universalizability?

17. What is meant by emotivism?

18. What is emotivism actually a theory about?

19. For the emotivist, what are moral judgments really about?

20. What are the shortcomings of emotivism?

21. How did the observations of moral diversity contribute to the popularity of relativism?

22. What is the definition of cultural relativism? How is that different from moral subjectivism?

23. How does international business raise the issue of relativism?

24. What is the connection between multiculturalism and relativism?

25. What is a prima facie absolutist?

26. What is the appeal of relativism? What are its shortcomings?

27. How does virtue theory differ from other action-oriented theories?

28. What is the relationship between virtues and principles? How are the correspondence and complementary views of this different?

Chapter 3 Notes

1. The reader may notice that deontological systems, or ethical systems based on principles, are not outlined in as much depth as the other types of moral reasoning. This is because, of the three main types of deontological system—Kant's categorical imperative, natural law, and the divine command theory—the latter two are discussed in chapter 2. I will present and critique Kant's system in this chapter.

2. See also Ephesians 5:29, "No one ever hated his own body, but he feeds it and cares for it."

3. James Rachels, *The Elements of Moral Philosophy* (Philadelphia: Temple University Press, 1986), 67–73.

4. See her classic exposition of ethical egoism in *The Virtue of Selfishness* (New York: Signet, 1961).

5. Louis Pojman, *Ethics: Discovering Right and Wrong* (Belmont, Calif.: Wadsworth, 1990), 48.

6. In his defense of capitalism as an economic system, Adam Smith employed ethical egoism to some degree in his justification of it. He argued that there was an "invisible hand" that coordinated each person's pursuit of self-interest and made it work for the common good. It should be recognized that Smith held to an *enlightened* self-interest, presumably self-interest regulated by Christian morality as the key to making capitalism work. See his classic work *The Wealth of Nations* for further discussion of this.

7. Rachels, *Elements of Moral Philosophy*, 76–78.

8. Ibid., 102–3.

9. For an insightful critique of autonomous reason in the history of the West, see Francis A. Schaeffer, *Escape from Reason* (Downers Grove, Ill.: InterVarsity, 1968; reissued as IVP Classic, 2007).

10. Pojman, *Ethics*, 149.

11. Ibid., 145–46.

12. Ibid., 147.

13. This is the point made by Alasdair MacIntyre in chapter 1 of his *After Virtue*. His critique of modern ethics is that emotivism is philosophically bankrupt and essentially all that remains after the Enlightenment efforts to create morality by reason alone have failed. See MacIntyre, *After Virtue*, 3rd ed. (Notre Dame, Ind.: University of Notre Dame Press, 2007).

14. Their main works in this area are as follows: William Graham Sumner, *Folkways* (New York: Ginn, 1906); Ruth Benedict, *Patterns of Culture* (New York: New American Library, 1934); Melville Herskovits, *Cultural Relativism* (New York: Random House, 1972); John Ladd, ed., *Ethical Relativism* (Belmont, Calif.: Wadsworth, 1973).

15. Neal Gabler, "Moral Relativism: You Don't Get It," *Los Angeles Times*, June 14, 1992, M1–2.

16. I am indebted for these two points of critique to J. P. Moreland and William Lane Craig, *Philosophical Foundations of a Christian Worldview* (Downers Grove, Ill.: InterVarsity, 2003), 144–52.

17. Clyde Kluckhohn, "Ethical Relativity: Sic et Non," *Journal of Philosophy* (1955): 52. See also E. O. Wilson, *On Human Nature* (New York: Bantam, 1979).

18. Interview with Archbishop of Canterbury Rowan Williams, BBC Radio 4, *World at One*, February 7, 2007.

19. Some of the main works on virtue theory are Edmund Pincoffs, *Quandaries and Virtues* (Lawrence: University of Kansas Press, 1986); Richard Taylor, *Ethics, Faith and Reason* (New York: Prentice-Hall, 1985); Philippa Foot, *Virtues and Vices and Other Essays in Moral Philosophy* (Blackwood, N.J.: Blackwell, 1978); James Wallace, *Virtues and Vices* (Ithaca, N.Y.: Cornell University Press, 1978). Two very helpful collections of essays on virtue theory are Robert Kruschwitz and Robert Roberts, eds., *The Virtues* (Belmont, Calif.: Wadsworth, 1987); and P. A. French, T. E. Uehling, and H. K. Wettstein, eds., *Ethical Theory: Character and Virtue*, Midwest Studies in Philosophy, vol. 13 (Notre Dame, Ind.: University of Notre Dame Press, 1988).

20. Pojman, *Ethics*, 116.

21. Ibid., 119.

22. Ibid., 126.

23. Ibid., 124–30.

Chapter 4

Making Ethical Decisions

Case 1: Business Ethics: Stopping Patent Violators

You work for a large multinational company that makes and distributes automotive parts. You are the product manager for a handful of specific products, such as spark plugs, starters, and fuel injectors that are marketed in the United States and Canada. Your company invests substantial sums of money each year in research and development that result annually in new products and improved quality of existing products. In the past few years, low-priced imitation auto parts, primarily but not exclusively from China, have flooded the market, resulting in significant loss of market share for your company and other market leaders, so that some have been forced to lay off employees. The makers of these "knock-off" products do not invest in research and development in order to innovate. They simply copy the designs of the more established companies. They then produce them at far lower costs and sell them at much lower prices, easily undercutting competitors. These companies are operating without respect for intellectual property laws and are violating patents held by the traditional market leaders. Your company is alarmed at the extent to which these knock-off products are making inroads with your long-term customers. You have just recently been appointed to lead the team that will deal with the imitation products that are threatening your company.

In the next few months, you will be attending a very large trade show, which will bring automotive buyers and sellers from all over the world. These imitation sellers will be at the trade show marketing their products, as will your company. The imitation sellers are aware that they violate patents, and as a result, they carefully guard their display products and literature, in the attempt to prevent companies like yours from gaining information about their knock-offs. In fact, if they know you work for your company, they will give you no information or cooperation.

Your strategy is to use a false identification at the trade show to gather information and sample products to take back to your design engineers for their analysis. This strategy is necessary to prove that these other companies are violating your company's patents. Once you have proof, you will be in a legal position to effectively counter patent violations. At the trade show, you will be assuming a fictitious name while working for a nonexistent company. You have instructed your team to lie to the sellers, and you have even trained them to distract the sellers working their booths in order to have others on the team steal their samples. This plan violates the trade show policy and your company's ethics standards. You have reservations about the plan because it involves intentional and substantial deception about your identity as well as theft of the sellers' property. On the other hand, the knock-off makers are stealing intellectual property and undermining the livelihood of your company's employees.

In this situation, what should you do as the team leader? Which is the morally right course of action? Does stopping patent violators justify lying and theft? An equally important question in this situation is, How would you decide what to do? The process of making a moral decision can be as important as the decision itself, and many ethical decisions that people face are so complex that it is easy to exhaust oneself talking around the problem without actually making any progress toward resolving it. "Where do I start?" is the question asked by many people facing moral dilemmas. People who are faced with these decisions often need direction that will enable them to move constructively toward resolution.

A Model for Making Moral Decisions

To address adequately the ethical dilemmas that people regularly encounter, I will present a procedure for making moral decisions. I offer it not as a formula that will automatically generate the "right" answer to an ethical problem, but rather as a model designed to make sure that the right questions are asked in the process of ethical deliberation.

Given the ethnic and religious diversity of our society, the model used for making ethical decisions should be able to accommodate a variety of different moral and ethical perspectives. The model presented here is not tied to any one particular perspective but can be used comfortably with a variety of cultural, ethnic, and religious backgrounds. Although this model is consistent with the Bible and allows for use of biblical principles, it is not a distinctively Christian model. As you will see, it is heavily oriented toward virtues and principles, with consideration of consequences in a supporting role.

As we mentioned earlier, what makes many moral dilemmas so difficult is that the Bible does not always address an issue clearly, if at all. More general biblical virtues and principles may be brought to bear on the issue at hand. In these instances, however, there is often disagreement about which biblical principles and virtues are applicable and how they apply to the specific issue under discussion. Further, it may be that the virtues/principles conflict in any given scenario. These tend to be some of the most difficult ethical dilemmas because they involve making choices and weighting the virtues/principles that have a bearing on the case. Appeal to principles and virtues alone will not necessarily resolve any particular case. Thus, insisting that all ethical dilemmas be resolved simply by appeal to biblical principles and virtues seems to oversimplify things. Certainly, appealing to the Bible, either a specific text(s) or more general principles, can conclusively resolve many moral questions, but in some cases that does not happen.

Perhaps the first question to be sure to address has to do with *defining an ethical dilemma*. I often ask people how they would know if they were facing an ethical dilemma, and not surprisingly, they frequently are unable to answer this question. It may be that people miss some of the ethical dilemmas they face because they are not sure what to look for. Here is the definition of an ethical dilemma: *An ethical dilemma is a conflict between two or more value- or virtue-driven interests.* You must be sure to identify the parties in the conflict, what their interests are, and what virtues and values underlie those interests.

Following is a list of the elements of a model for making moral decisions:[1]

1. Gather the Facts.

Frequently ethical dilemmas can be resolved simply by clarifying the facts of the case in question. You may find that you have a different sort of dilemma, not a moral one. For example, you might discover that you have a communication breakdown that has created the dilemma that can be solved simply by facilitating a conference that brings clear and timely communication. Or you may find that you have a strategic dilemma instead of a moral one, where the issues involved are morally neutral. When you have a genuine ethical dilemma, gathering the facts is the essential first step that must be taken prior to any ethical analysis and reflection. In analyzing a case, we need to know all of the available facts. Later, we may need to acquire additional information pertaining to the case. Thus, to make an intelligent ethical decision, one needs to ask two primary questions: What do we know? and What do we need to know?

2. Determine the Ethical Issues.

Ethical issues are stated in terms of legitimate competing interests or goods. These competing interests are what actually create an ethical dilemma. Remember, an ethical dilemma is defined as a conflict between two or more value/virtue-driven interests. That is, moral values and virtues must support the competing interests in order to have a genuine ethical dilemma. If you cannot identify any underlying virtues/values, then you may have some other kind of dilemma, not a moral one. Participants in these dilemmas normally hold to their positions with substantial passion because they are driven by deeply held ethical values and virtues. The issues should be presented in an X versus Y format in order to reflect the competing interests in a particular ethical dilemma.

3. Determine What Virtues/ Principles Have a Bearing on the Case.

In any ethical dilemma, certain virtues and moral values are central to the competing positions. It is critical to identify these principles and, in some cases, to determine whether some principles are to be weighted more heavily than others. Clearly, biblical principles should be weighted more heavily. Also, the virtues and values that speak to the case may come from a variety of sources, such as the Constitution or natural law (those almost self-evident values that are widely shared), which would supplement the applicable biblical principles. In a diverse cultural context, it may be that values may come from other religious traditions or widely held values from that particular culture.

4. List the Alternatives.

Part of the creative thinking involved in resolving an ethical dilemma involves developing alternative courses of action. Although you will probably rule out some alternatives without much thought, in general, the more alternatives that are listed, the better the chance that your list will include some very good ones. In addition, you may come up with some creative alternatives that you had not considered earlier.

5. Compare the Alternatives with the Virtues/Principles.

At this point the task is one of eliminating alternatives according to the moral principles that have a bearing on the case. In many instances the case will be resolved at this point, since the principles will eliminate all alternatives except one. In fact, the purpose of this comparison is to see if a clear decision can be made without further deliberation. To do this involves satisfying all the relevant virtues and values. If a clear decision is not forthcoming, the next part in the model must be considered. At the least, some of the alternatives may be eliminated by this step of comparison. Often, in order to make a clear decision, you must weight one or more virtues/values more heavily than the others. When weighting certain virtues/

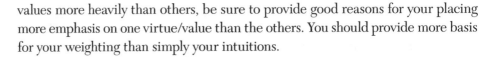

values more heavily than others, be sure to provide good reasons for your placing more emphasis on one virtue/value than the others. You should provide more basis for your weighting than simply your intuitions.

6. Consider the Consequences.

If the principles do not yield a clear decision, then a consideration of the consequences of the remaining available alternatives is the next step. Here the task is to take the viable alternatives and attempt to predict both the positive and negative consequences of each. In addition, one should try to estimate how beneficial are the positive consequences and how severe are the negative ones, since some consequences will be clearly more substantial than others.

7. Make a Decision.

Deliberation cannot continue indefinitely. At some point you must make a decision. Realize, too, that ethical dilemmas often have no easy and painless solutions. Frequently, the decision that is made is one that involves the least number of problems or negative consequences, not one that is entirely devoid of them. Be careful of trusting your "sleep-well quotient." You may make a good decision and still not sleep well, because these dilemmas are often very difficult and don't lend themselves to easy solutions.

Applying the Model

Using the preceding model, let's return to the case of the patent violators. Here we will illustrate how to apply the model and clarify the meaning of each of the elements in the model. Two additional cases will be presented and analyzed in the framework of this model to ensure that it is clear and can be used profitably.

Case 1: Stopping Patent Violators

1. Gather the Facts.

The relevant facts in this case are as follows:

- Your company makes automotive parts and invests significantly in research and development.
- Your company holds numerous patents for their innovative auto parts.
- Your company's market share is being undercut by low-priced imitation products that violate your legally held patents.
- Other market leaders have been forced to lay off employees as a result of this foreign competition.

- You are in charge of some product distribution in the United States and Canada.
- You have recently been put in charge of the team that will address the problem of foreign competition.
- Your strategy involves lying about your identity and stealing the competitors' products at an upcoming trade show.
- Getting the knock-off products back to your company's engineers is critical to proving that your patents are being violated.
- Your strategy violates the trade show policy and your company's ethics standards.

Information you need to know:

- Would the trade show officials approve of your plan if you disclosed it to them prior to the start of the trade show?
- Is the company willing to make an exception to its ethics policies in this situation?

2. Determine the Ethical Issues.

The primary parties that have a stake in this situation are your company, your team, and the imitation sellers. Lesser parties include the trade show officials. Your company's interest is in the prevention of theft of intellectual property. The imitation sellers' interest is maintaining respect for their private property at the trade show. The ethical dilemma involves a conflict between the interests of your company and the imitation sellers (the trade show officials have an interest in preventing illegal activity on the part of your team at their trade show).

3. Determine What Virtues/Principles Have a Bearing on the Case.

You can invoke a variety of virtues and values as relevant to this case. First is the norm of truth telling, grounded in the biblical mandate to avoid giving false witness. A second is the norm of respect for private property. This applies to your company, given your plan to steal the imitation sellers' samples. But it also applies to the imitation sellers' violation of your company's patents. There is also a principle of loyalty to your company and compassion for potentially laid-off employees. But there is a principle of respect for the law and the policies of the trade show officials as well. Further, you must deal with the virtue of personal integrity involved in violating your company's ethics standards. In addition, there seems to be a principle of justice that has a bearing on this issue, since you are motivated in part by company loyalty but also in part by your desire to see fairness win out and the patent violators receive just deserts.

4. List the Alternatives.

A first option is to proceed with your strategy to conceal your identity, mislead the sellers, and steal their products. A second and related alternative is to seek the permission of the trade show officials to disguise your identity and obtain the samples you need. If such permission were granted, then you would not be acting contrary to the trade show regulations. But you also run the risk of exposing your strategy and not receiving permission, which would it make the first option very difficult to proceed with. A third option is to avoid deception and theft and seek to enforce the patent violations in some other way.

5. Compare the Alternatives with the Principles.

There does not seem to be an alternative that satisfies all of the principles/virtues. Thus there is not a clear decision that can produce a "win-win" solution where all the relevant virtues/values are fulfilled. To reach a decision at this point will involve weighting the principles/virtues according to good reasons. One could weight the values of private property and truth telling more heavily, because to steal the competitor's samples violates the law and sets up a very slippery slope that could justify other more clearly immoral activities to achieve important company objectives. But one could also weight justice and fairness more heavily and conclude that the prohibition against theft might not apply as rigidly since the products you would be stealing are imitations of your company's products. The claim that the imitator company is protected by private property considerations could be debatable. You might even make the argument that you are not stealing at all since the product is actually yours to begin with. Let's assume for the moment, however, that appeal to virtues/principles will not resolve the dilemma at this point.

6. Consider the Consequences.

- If the first option is taken, and you decide to hide your identity and steal their samples if possible, then a number of positive consequences are likely—you will obtain the necessary materials for your engineers to analyze and present evidence of patent violations. You will also contribute to stopping patent violations and help protect your company from illegal competition. In addition, you will likely increase the morale of your team by succeeding at something critical to the company's remaining competitive. Your success could embolden other market leaders to more aggressively confront patent violators. But negative consequences could also result. You could get caught and risk public relations embarrassment, censure from the trade show, and possibly criminal charges for theft.

- With the second option, to seek approval of the trade show officials for your plan, if you receive permission, you could temper some of the potential negative consequences. You would not run afoul of the trade show rules, and you would be less likely to risk prosecution if caught. But you may not receive permission, and the result in that case would be to make your plan much more difficult to accomplish. The positive consequences would likely remain the same.
- With the third option, you have no risk of embarrassment or violation of the law/trade show regulations, but you would not obtain any of the potential benefits either.

7. Make a Decision.

What would you decide in this case? Which virtues/principles are the weightiest? Would you include others? Which alternatives are the most viable? Would you suggest others? Which consequences seem to be the severest? Do you think others will occur? Does the fact that the imitation makers are violating patents make it acceptable to steal their products in order to prove it? Where might that type of reasoning lead in the future in other situations?

At some point, however, you need to realize that you must stop deliberating and make a decision, as uncomfortable as that may be. For the Christian, prayer should be made throughout this process of deliberation and while working through any decision. The Bible promises God's wisdom for dealing with trials and difficult situations (James 1:1–5), as well as God's strength to do what is right.

Case 2: Medical Ethics

A sixty-seven-year-old Latino woman who does not speak any English comes into the medical center with a diagnosis of stage 2 non-Hodgkin's lymphoma, a type of cancer, for which chemotherapy has been prescribed as the preferred course of treatment. She had been in generally good health prior to the onset of her current condition. At the time of admission, she appears to be fully competent and capable of making her own decisions. She knows that something is wrong with her and appears anxious and fearful at the prospect of what getting well will involve.

Her family accompanies her and stays with her consistently after her admission. That family includes a son and daughter, both married. They are clearly a loving and caring family who want what is best for their mother. She is a widow and has been living with her son and daughter-in-law for the past three years. The son feels a good deal of responsibility to take care of his mother and considers himself quite close to her. He is the translator for the patient, and virtually all information that the physicians and the patient exchange must go through the patient's son.

He insists that only a minimal amount of information be given the patient out of a fear that she will give up on living and resign herself to dying, thus contributing negatively to the treatment. It appears that cultural values are at the root of his desire to protect and take care of his mother.

The patient has not been told of her specific diagnosis or the effects of chemotherapy. All that she appears to have been told by her son is that she is sick and that the treatment will cause her to become sick to her stomach and lose some of her hair. If you were the physician in this case, what would you do? Would you follow the family's wishes since they seem to be based on significant cultural values that you are not familiar with, or go against them and tell the patient what you think she needs to know, even if it means that she gives up the fight as her family fears?

1. Gather the Facts.

- The patient is a sixty-seven-year-old Latino widow who does not speak any English and cannot communicate with the physicians or nurses.
- Her family includes a son and daughter, both married. She has been living with the son and daughter-in-law for the past three years. The son serves as her translator and is very caring and concerned for her well-being.
- Her diagnosis is stage 2 non-Hodgkin's lymphoma, a form of cancer, for which chemotherapy has been prescribed.
- She has been in generally good health prior to the onset of her current condition.
- She has not been told of her specific diagnosis or the treatment she will undergo, out of the family's fear that she will not want to live. She has been told of some of the anticipated side effects of the treatment by the nurse who conducted her initial interview.
- She appears to be fully competent and capable of making her own decisions.
- The cultural factors that are influencing the family to withhold important information from her are primarily the value of protecting a loved one, especially when that loved one has contracted serious illness.
- She is anxious and fearful at the prospect of her examination and treatment. She appears to know something is wrong with her.

2. Determine the Ethical Issues.

This case involves a conflict between patient autonomy, specifically the right to give informed consent for treatment versus what a caring family thinks is best for the patient. The children clearly believe that if their mother is told of her condition, she will resign from life and succumb to the disease. Thus patient autonomy conflicts with the obligation to do good to the patient.

The nursing staff faces an even more difficult dilemma in cases like these, since they are bound by physician orders. Their conflict is adherence to physician orders versus duty to protect the integrity of the patient (by helping ensure informed consent).

3. Determine What Virtues/ Principles Have a Bearing on the Case.

A variety of principles and virtues are relevant to this case. First is the right of the patient to give informed consent to her treatment, especially for something as invasive as chemotherapy. This right is recognized in the law and is based on a broader principle of patient autonomy, which is grounded in a right of bodily integrity—a right to control what is done to a person's body. The ultimate reason that individuals have these rights is out of and for the fundamental dignity of the person, which comes ultimately from human beings being made in God's image.

In conflict with that principle is the obligation of the medical team to act in the patient's best interest. This is grounded in the virtue of beneficence, which creates the obligation to do good for the patient whenever one can. A further virtue that has a bearing on this case is that of compassion for a suffering patient. The virtue of compassion creates the obligation to do what is in the patient's best interest. However, the family can also appeal to compassion and what they think is in their mother's best interest. The application of these virtues and principles will be shaped by what exactly the patient's best interest looks like. Does it mean acting so that she doesn't give up fighting for her life? Or does it mean relieving her distress at what she is going through?

A third principle involved is respect for the family's wishes and culture. This comes out of the virtue of humility, which suggests that the physicians and nurses not assume that their way of handling this patient is necessarily and uncritically superior to how the family is treating her. Of course, there are limits to this, and part of the dilemma in this case is to determine how heavily to weight this respect for their cultural values. These cultural components include some very important virtues, such as family loyalty, care for one's elders, and the cultural norm that the eldest male in the family is the head of the family and thus responsible for important decision making. The family's culture puts a high priority on the virtue of caring and defines it as taking the burden of decision making off of the patient. The responsibility of caring extends to decision making in their culture because the family views the disease as a very heavy burden that the patient must carry. As a result, the family's obligation to care includes taking as many of the other burdens off of their loved one as possible, including decision making.

Other principles include the responsibility of nursing staff to adhere to physician orders and the responsibility of all of the staff to obey the law concerning informed consent.

4. List the Alternatives.

The first alternative is to attempt to convince the family and perhaps the physician as well of the seriousness of the treatment and her right to know why she needs it. If that fails, the next step could be to ask the family to participate in an ethics committee case conference in order to persuade them to disclose the information. Regardless of what alternative is chosen, these discussions, both with the family and with the broader ethics committee, should be held prior to making any further decisions. Should these discussions fail to resolve the dilemma, then one alternative is to override the family's wishes and inform the patient of her condition and course of treatment.

By contrast, after these initial discussions, the physicians and nurses could accommodate the family's wishes and continue to withhold information from the patient. This would involve allowing the son to remain as her translator and begin treatment without her knowing her diagnosis or prognosis.

A third alternative is to wait for the patient to inquire about her condition, at which point you would encourage her to ask pointed questions to her family and physician. This would have to be done through another translator.

A fourth alternative is somewhat more direct with the patient. You could bring in another translator and, with the son in the room, ask her if she wants to know the details of her condition, outlook, and treatment. This alternative will likely meet with strong objections from her son, and he will likely take it as a significant cultural offense.

5. Compare the Alternatives with the Virtues/Principles.

It may be that a clear decision can be reached here. The first steps should be to pursue all avenues to persuade the family to allow open disclosure by the physician or to disclose the information themselves. If those are exhausted and the dilemma is still unresolved, the remaining alternatives would be to either withhold or disclose the information to the patient. Disclosing the information could occur directly, by telling the patient outright through another translator, or more indirectly, by asking the patient through another translator if she wants to know her diagnosis and treatments. The more indirect alternative satisfies the values of patient autonomy by giving the decision back to the patient herself. However, if she wants her son to make these decisions for her, this alternative allows her the opportunity to make that clear. If that is her answer, then virtually all of the important virtues/principles are satisfied. Since the disease and treatment are both fairly serious, and since it is hard to be sure if the family's fear of her "giving up" is justifiable, the indirect alternative would tilt the balance in favor of patient autonomy and thus toward disclosing the information, if that is what the patient so desires. Such a decision would still run contrary to the cultural background of the family, in which the oldest male has decision-making authority, but it would allow for adherence to informed consent, allow the patient to speak for herself, and respect her dignity.

For the nursing staff, the resolution may not be as forthcoming if the physician continues to side with the family and withhold information. One viable option for nursing staff would be to request that care of this patient be transferred to another staff member who can accommodate the family's and the physician's request.

6. Consider the Consequences.

If the option of *disclosing the information* directly is taken, the following are some of the likely consequences:

- The family will feel alienated from the physician and the medical center because their cultural values have been violated.
- The family may take the patient to another facility that will comply with their wishes.
- The patient may "give up" on life and succumb to the disease.
- The patient may feel relieved and empowered that someone is finally telling her what is happening to her.

If the option of *continued withholding of information* is taken, here are some of the likely consequences:

- The patient will continue to be fearful and anxious about her treatment.
- The patient will find out the information at some point, creating a breach of trust.
- The family will be satisfied and their cultural values respected.

If the option of *asking the patient if she wants to know her situation* (through another translator) is taken, the following are some of the likely consequences:

- The family will be offended at the breach of their cultural values respecting the decision-making authority of the oldest male.
- The patient will be afforded the opportunity to speak for herself and give consent if she so desires. If she desires to do that, the law concerning informed consent will be followed. If she wishes to have her son make those decisions for her, the medical center is still following the law and the cultural value is respected.
- The patient will be relieved either way, knowing that her wishes have been considered.

7. Make a Decision.

This case forces us to think through the limits of respecting a family's wishes and the limits of respect for cultural diversity. How far do we go in accommodating a family's appeal to its cultural mores, and on what basis do we draw lines? Clearly, one line that can be drawn is when the patient's medical care is compromised, or when respecting the culture involves jeopardizing the patient's best interest or her dignity as an individual. Here it seems that the alternative that involves asking the patient if she wants to know the details of her situation satisfies most of the virtues and values at stake and produces the best balance of consequences too.

Case 3: International Business Ethics

You work for an international construction company that does business in many other parts of the world. You are head of a sales team that markets your company's construction services in Asia and the Middle East. Many of your projects are contracts with national or local governments to build public facilities, such as highways, government buildings, and other infrastructure, such as bridges. Sales negotiations for these projects usually involve a number of government officials who have to give their approval for the projects to move forward. The specific project you are working on involves construction of a multibuilding office complex for a provincial government. You have been informed that to complete the contract and begin construction, you must pay "pledges" to a handful of officials in order to finalize the deal for your company. These "pledges," or as you consider them, bribes, are a normal part of doing business in this part of the world, and most companies who do business successfully here pay them without hesitation. The payments go into the personal accounts of the officials. Payments like these are illegal under U.S. law, but the risk of being detected is low, and you are aware that many companies, including yours, make these payments regularly to ensure that business gets done. The project will bring in $100 million in revenue, and the "pledges" amount to a total of about $5 million when all the necessary officials have been paid. You have the authority either to make the payments or to refuse to make them. But if you refuse, the chances of obtaining the contract are not good, and the company has told you that if this contract doesn't come through, some from your team might have to be laid off. The government will award the contract to the company that will pay the "pledges." The first payment of $1 million is due at your next meeting. Will you pay the "pledges," or not?

1. Gather the Facts.

The relevant facts are as follows:

- You head the sales team that does marketing and sales in parts of the world where bribery is common.
- The current project is a $100 million project, which requires $5 million in bribes to be paid to specific government officials for their personal benefit.
- Payment of these bribes is common and expected in this part of the world but illegal under U.S. law.
- You have the decision-making authority in this case.
- Your company will support whatever decision you make but reminds you that this contract is very important. Your company does not have a policy in writing on requests for payments such as these.
- You feel pressure to make these payments, knowing that if you don't secure the contract, some of your team might have to be laid off.
- You did not initiate these payments in order to obtain a competitive advantage, but you know that paying them will give you a much favorable position over all other competitors.

2. Determine the Ethical Issues.

The ethical issue in this case revolves around the conflict between adhering to the law and fair competition versus loyalty to your company, especially the members of your team. Your company has the obligation to its employees and shareholders to secure business, and you feel this obligation, particularly to your team. However, you are concerned about the unfairness of making these payments and the advantage it will give your company.

3. Determine What Virtues/ Principles Have a Bearing on the Case.

The primary principle that is relevant is that of fairness, or fair competition. The reason bribery is illegal for U.S. companies is that it promotes an unlevel playing field for competition. However, you have a competing value in loyalty to your company, and you are motivated by the virtue of compassion for your team members, some of whom will be out of jobs should you fail to obtain this contract.

4. List the Alternatives.

Here the alternatives seem straightforward. You can make the payments and expect that you will obtain the contract, or you can refuse to make the "pledges" and most likely open the door for some other company to get in ahead of you. If

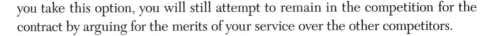

you take this option, you will still attempt to remain in the competition for the contract by arguing for the merits of your service over the other competitors.

5. Compare the Alternatives with the Virtues/Principles.

This may be an example of a situation that could be resolved at the level of the facts. The exact nature of these payments will determine whether they violate any of the above virtues/principles. Since you did not initiate these payments, you might argue that they do not constitute bribery at all. Rather, they could be more analogous to extortion, in which a person uses a position of power to demand favors from those subject to his or her exercise of authority. By contrast, you could also argue that these payments do amount to bribery, since you could walk away from the contract (a costly decision, which increases the coercive element of the payment). The payments further do result in your company's getting a major competitive advantage, the very problem that laws against bribery intend to avoid. If the payments are extortion, then it may not be a violation of any principle to pay them, analogous to payment of ransom. It clearly is wrong to demand extortion, but it is less clear that it is wrong to pay it. If that is the case, then there is no moral dilemma, and you can pay the extortion and hopefully obtain the contract. However, if the payments are indeed bribery, then they would violate one of the key principles, and you would have to continue to resolve the dilemma.

At this point you would consider weighting the virtues/principles. Which of the competing virtues/values should take priority? You can make a strong case for weighting adherence to the law and fair competition more heavily, since fairness is such an important value. However, you could also make a case for loyalty to your company and especially to your team since the consequences of not obtaining the contract will involve some layoffs. What is important at this step is to see that the case can be resolved if one or more virtues/values can be considered to carry more weight than the others.

6. Consider the Consequences.

- If you do decide to make the payments, the likely consequences will be that you will secure the contract, other payments may be necessary at other points in the construction, your company will profit, and no one from your team will need to be laid off. You will also be in violation of U.S. law, and if your violation is detected, it could result in substantial fines and a public relations embarrassment. You could also be accused of contributing to a culture of corruption in that particular region or country.

- If you refuse to make the payments, your chances of obtaining the contract are significantly lower, putting some members of your team at risk of being laid off and hurting your company's financial stability. It is possible that you could still compete for the contract on the merits of your company's service, especially if it becomes known that your company does not engage in or respond to requests for bribery. You will not be in violation of U.S. law and will not be at risk for sanctions that accompany bribery charges.

7. Make a Decision.

This is an example of a case that could be resolved once a factual determination is made. If these payments are bribes, then a good case can be made for obeying the law with the principle of fairness on which it is based. But if the payments are not bribery, then the law and notion of fairness would not apply, or would not be weighted as heavily. Usually payments that give a competitive advantage are more like bribery than extortion, since with extortion the option to walk away from the situation normally does not exist. But with this contract, the company doesn't have to pay the bribes. They can simply move on to the next opportunity and compete on their merits. We will revisit the subject of bribery in chapter 12, which deals with the intersection of ethics and economics.

Conclusion

My hope is that this model offers a helpful way of ensuring that all of the relevant questions are asked when attempting to resolve an ethical dilemma. It is not, however, a formula or a computer program that will automatically enable a person to easily resolve ethical dilemmas. But when faced with what appears to be a confusing maze of facts and feelings, this model will provide you with some guidance in the decision-making process.

Chapter 4 Notes

1. I have adapted this model from the seven-step model of Dr. William W. May's course Normative Analysis of Issues, taught at the School of Religion, University of Southern California.

Chapter 5

Abortion and Embryonic Stem Cell Research

On January 20, 1973, the United States Supreme Court decided the landmark *Roe v. Wade* case that legalized abortion. For pro-choice advocates, the decision amounted to the emancipation of women from having to carry unwanted pregnancies to term. For pro-life supporters, on the other hand, the decision was tantamount to an assault on the most vulnerable segment of society, the unborn. Since that decision, the abortion debate has intensified, and it shows no signs of being resolved. It is still the debate that defines the current cultural conflict in America and will likely remain so in the foreseeable future.

The long-standing abortion debate has expanded into other areas as well. For example, there is controversy about abortions that occur late in pregnancy, known as partial-birth abortions. Pro-life advocates cite these as particularly egregious examples of callousness toward life and the unborn, and pro-choice advocates resist any restriction on the constitutional right of women to procure abortions.

As medical technology develops, there is increasing interest in research on embryos, mainly to harvest their stem cells, which scientists envision for numerous useful treatments for a variety of debilitating diseases. There is also debate about abortion and public policy—that is, whether abortion should be illegal if one considers it immoral. Most pro-life advocates are encouraging changes in the law, but some suggest that though they view abortion as immoral, the coercive force of the law should not be imposed on women seeking abortions.

The literature on the subject of abortion is vast, from both pro-life and pro-choice perspectives, and on both popular and scholarly levels. It would take some time to become familiar with all of it. Many philosophers, lawyers, theologians, and ethicists have devoted much of their professional lives to pursuing the abortion

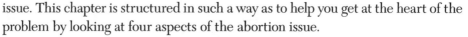

issue. This chapter is structured in such a way as to help you get at the heart of the problem by looking at four aspects of the abortion issue.

The first aspect of the abortion issue concerns the legal background that has developed since the *Roe v. Wade* decision in 1973. Four more key Supreme Court cases will be presented, with special emphasis on the two most recent cases, which restrict abortion rights while affirming the basic direction of *Roe v. Wade*. The second aspect is the biblical background. We will review the contribution of the Bible to the issue. The third aspect is an analysis of pro-choice arguments for abortion rights. The fourth aspect of the problem deals with the issue of personhood and asks the question, At what point in the process of gestation does the unborn become a person? Finally, we will look at some of the related issues, such as embryonic stem cell research. You will notice that the material on the moral status of fetuses and embryos is also relevant to the discussion of reproductive technologies, addressed in chapter 6.

The Legal Background of Abortion

Although numerous legal battles have been carried out in the courts over different aspects of the abortion issue, the cases that have reached the Supreme Court are the most influential in setting the terms of the debate and the general direction of its outcome. Five specific cases have been particularly important both in establishing the legal right of a woman to obtain an abortion and in limiting that right. Beginning with the *Roe v. Wade* decision that initially legalized abortion and continuing through to the *Planned Parenthood v. Casey* decision that affirmed but limited the right to abortion, the abortion debate has continued to focus on the courts rather than on the U.S. Congress or state legislatures.

Roe v. Wade (1973)[1]

In this landmark case, Norma McCorvey* (Jane Roe) claimed she had been raped and that Texas law was forcing her to continue her pregnancy, even though she had been impregnated against her will. Although she later admitted that she had not been raped but had become pregnant due to birth control failure, the Court ruled that Texas laws prohibiting abortion except to save the mother's life were unconstitutional. Such laws were claimed to violate the due process clause of the Fourteenth Amendment of the Constitution, which protects a person's right to privacy. The idea of privacy was extended to a woman's womb, allowing her the right to end her pregnancy.

---

*In August 1995 McCorvey changed her views about abortion, quit her job at a Dallas women's clinic, and joined a church pastored by a leader of Operation Rescue, an outspoken pro-life organization (operationrescue.org).

The Court ruled that although a woman does have a constitutional right to an abortion, the state also has an interest in protecting the woman's health and the potential life of the fetus. The Court saw this as growing and becoming compelling as the pregnancy progresses. They therefore divided pregnancy into three trimesters and held that the state has different interests during each of the trimesters. The justices affirmed a woman's unquestioned right to abortion on demand during the first trimester of pregnancy. After the first trimester, however, the state may regulate abortion in ways that are reasonably related to the health of the mother, for example, by requiring that abortions be done in licensed medical facilities by licensed medical personnel. Thus, after the first trimester, abortion is available but not entirely on demand. After viability (i.e., the point at which the fetus can live on its own outside its mother's womb), due to the state's interest in the potential life of the fetus, the state may regulate and prohibit abortion, except in cases necessary to preserve the life or health of the mother. Although the decision did not technically legalize abortion on demand, *Roe v. Wade* along with its companion case, *Doe v. Bolton*, would eventually make abortion on demand legal throughout pregnancy.

Doe v. Bolton (1973)[2]

In a companion case decided on the same day as *Roe v. Wade*, the Court struck down a Georgia law that limited abortions to accredited hospitals, required the

The "Jane Roe" in *Roe v. Wade*

Norma McCorvey was the plaintiff in the landmark 1973 case of *Roe v. Wade*, which legalized abortion. Her remarkable transformation from *Roe* supporter to pro-life activist is well documented and is a touching story of her own personal redemption. One little-known fact about her is that, contrary to her testimony in *Roe*, she was not raped, and thus her abortion was not due to the fact that she was pregnant as a result of sexual assault. She became pregnant due to consensual sex. However, she did come from a very rough family background and was pregnant with a very unwanted pregnancy. Following her success as a *Roe* plaintiff, she was active in pro-choice advocacy and clashed repeatedly with pro-life supporters in her hometown of Dallas. Then, as fate would have it, or as some would say, in the providence of God, pro-life pastor and Operation Rescue leader Flip Benham moved into the house next door to her. Over time Benham and other leaders reached out to her, bringing her to faith in Christ. One of the most significant changes in her life was her move from pro-choice to pro-life activist. She started her own ministry, Roe No More, and has a special passion for crisis pregnancy clinics.*

*From www.leaderu.com/norma/.

approval of the hospital abortion committee and confirmation by two other physicians, and limited access to abortion in Georgia to state residents. Again citing the woman's right to privacy, and for the first time, the physician's right to conduct medical practice, the Court declared the statute unconstitutional. Any attempts to limit the woman's right to obtain an abortion must be consistent with what the Court called "a compelling state interest," of which there was none in this case.

An exception in the Georgia law allowed for abortion in the case that a continued pregnancy would either endanger the pregnant woman's life or threaten her health. The decision about a threat to the woman's life or health was made according to the "best clinical judgment" of the physician. The right of the physician to exercise judgment in this way constituted a significant broadening of the *Roe v. Wade* decision and made abortion on demand available throughout a woman's pregnancy. The *Roe v. Wade* decision allowed states to prohibit abortion after viability, except when continuing the pregnancy threatened the life or health of the mother. The decision in *Doe v. Bolton* expanded what was meant by the life and health of the mother.

The Court interpreted the health of the mother to include much more than simply her physical health. It also included her psychological and emotional health. Thus, if she would be significantly harmed emotionally by continuing the pregnancy, the physician could authorize an abortion. The Court put it this way: "That statute [the Georgia law in question] has been construed to bear upon the psychological as well as physical well-being.... We agree that the medical judgment [of the woman's physician] may be exercised in light of all factors — physical, emotional, psychological, familial and the woman's age — relevant to the well-being of the patient. All these factors may relate to health [of the pregnant woman]."[3]

Thus the Court ruled that if the physician sees the pregnancy as a threat to the woman's health in virtually any way, he or she can authorize an abortion at any stage of the pregnancy. If continuing the pregnancy would affect the emotional health of her family (the familial factors cited by the Court), an abortion could also be justified. The way in which the Court expanded the idea of the woman's health and how the fetus can threaten it opened the door to abortion for virtually any reason. This decision, along with the *Roe* decision, established a constitutional right to abortion on demand.

Planned Parenthood v. Danforth (1977)[4]

The case of *Planned Parenthood v. Danforth* struck down limits on the freedom to obtain an abortion according to the standards set down in *Roe v. Wade*. At issue was a Missouri law that required that a woman's husband also consent to the abortion, and that the parents of a minor child consent to her abortion. The Court ruled that a woman's right to abortion cannot be limited by the requirement that a spouse or parent of a minor child must grant prior consent. The Court ruled that the decision to abort must be left to the pregnant woman and the best medical judgment of her attending physician, and that blanket provisions of consent were overreaching and therefore unconstitutional. For many opponents of abortion, it was inconceivable that a pregnant teenager could obtain an abortion without either her parents' consent or even their knowledge. Accordingly, this decision created substantial controversy.

Webster v. Reproductive Health Services (1989)[5]

Webster v. Reproduction Health Services marked one of the first significant limits to the right to abortion. The Court reversed decisions by the District Court and the Court of Appeals and upheld a Missouri law that prohibited the use of public funds or medical facilities for "nontherapeutic" abortions (i.e., abortions not necessary to safeguard the life of the mother). The Court held that the right to abortion established in *Roe v. Wade* does not obligate the state to pay for abortions for women who cannot afford them. The denial of public funds to secure an abortion does not violate *Roe v. Wade*, since it places no governmental obstacle in the path of a woman seeking an abortion. It simply leaves her the same choices as if the government had decided not to operate any public hospitals at all. In addition, the use of public funds for childbirth, which is constitutional, and not for abortion does not violate *Roe v. Wade*, since states are allowed to make value judgments in their allocation of public funds.

Whereas the Hyde Amendment prohibited the use of federal funds for abortions, *Webster v. Reproductive Health Services* concerned the right of states to prohibit the use of their tax dollars to pay for abortions. Proponents of abortion argued that the right to obtain an abortion is an empty right if a woman cannot afford it and if the state refuses to help her pay for it. The Court ruled that the responsibility of government, at any level, to pay for abortions does not follow from the woman's right to obtain an abortion free from state interference. The Court rightly distinguished between a negative and a positive right. Negative rights are the rights to be left alone, to be free from governmental interference (in this case, in procuring an abortion). In other words, the state cannot place deliberate obstacles in the way of a woman who desires an abortion. A positive right is a right that also obligates someone to provide it for you (in this case the state that provides the funds to pay for the abortion). As outlined in *Roe v. Wade*, the right to an abortion is a negative right, a right to be left alone and free from interference in pursuing an abortion. That negative right does not obligate the state to provide a way for a woman to obtain the abortion.

Planned Parenthood v. Casey (1992)[6]

The most recent challenge to *Roe v. Wade* concerned a Pennsylvania law and was considered by abortion opponents to be the best opportunity for the Court to actually overturn *Roe v. Wade*. At issue in the case were the provisions of the law that required a twenty-four-hour waiting period before the abortion (during which time a woman must be given information about the procedure and risks of abortion and about the probable gestational age of the fetus), parental consent for a minor seeking an abortion (although the law provided a way to bypass that requirement by getting a judge's consent, called the judicial bypass), and notification of the woman's husband of her decision to obtain an abortion. A woman could be exempt from all of these requirements in cases of "medical emergency."

Sensing that this case was a challenge to the basic tenets of *Roe v. Wade*, the Court went to great lengths to reaffirm the basic direction of that decision and to continue to safeguard a woman's right to choose an abortion, much to the disappointment of pro-life advocates. The Court reasoned that abortion rights are consistent with the notion of the right to privacy that emerges out of the idea of liberty in the Constitution. They further reasoned that abortion rights are consistent with the ideas of personal autonomy (the right to make one's major life decisions for oneself) and bodily integrity (the right to have one's body left alone), parallel to the right to refuse medical treatment. These arguments constitute a significant part of the pro-choice position that will be examined more closely in the next section.

However, the Court did uphold some of the provisions of the Pennsylvania law, much to the dismay of pro-choice advocates. First, the Court upheld the twenty-four-hour waiting period in which the woman would be provided information about the risks of abortion (both to the woman and the fetus) and the probable age of the fetus. Even if the information presented (which had to be presented fairly and in a way that was not misleading) resulted in the woman choosing childbirth over abortion, it did not constitute an undue burden to a woman seeking an abortion. Second, the Court also upheld the parental consent with judicial bypass provision of the law as reasonable. Third, the Court declared the spousal notification provision of the law invalid because of the risk that it could pose to a woman and because it would be a significant obstacle for some women in obtaining an abortion.

Thus both pro-life and pro-choice advocates were disappointed with the ruling. Pro-life supporters felt as if the best chance to overturn *Roe v. Wade* had been lost and vowed to continue the fight in state legislatures across the country. Pro-choice supporters were disappointed at the restrictions the Court upheld, believing them to be undue burdens on women seeking abortions. The legality of abortion appears to be safe for the time being, however, with *Roe v. Wade* having survived the challenges to its constitutionality. That makes the place of moral debate and persuasion even more important and underscores the significance of the biblical data and the moral arguments used in the debate.

The Biblical Background of Abortion

Although the Bible never specifically states that "the fetus is a person" and "Thou shalt not have an abortion," it is misleading to insist that the Bible has nothing to say about the moral status of the unborn. The general tenor of Scripture is resoundingly pro-life. Although some texts on the surface appear to support a pro-choice position, such support is not borne out by further examination of the texts in their context.

The Bible clearly prohibits the taking of innocent life in the Sixth Commandment: "You shall not murder" (Ex. 20:13). Applying this directly to the unborn involves begging the question about the moral and ontological status of the unborn. That is, to apply this to the unborn involves a further argument that the embryo/fetus in the womb constitutes a person who possesses the right to life. It is indisputable that God is deeply involved in fashioning the unborn in the womb and thus deeply cares about the unborn. From the Bible's perspective, abortion is thus seen as an unjustified interference in God's sacred role in the womb. When abortion occurs, it involves not only the termination of a pregnancy, but also the termination of the very work of God in the womb. However, that is not the same thing as claiming that the unborn are persons and that abortion is ending the life of an innocent person. Given his role as Creator of the entire universe, God is involved

Partial-Birth Abortion

Opponents of abortion cite one particular method of terminating a pregnancy as an example of the "right to choose" taken to an extreme. Abortion rights advocates argue that the procedure is used only in emergency late-term abortions and should remain legal. The procedure involves partially delivering the fetus breech (legs and torso first) but leaving the skull in the womb — then the physician makes an incision at the base of the skull and removes by suction the brain tissue of the fetus, instantly causing its death. Abortion opponents routinely refer to this as a form of infanticide, even though some (admittedly a small part) of the fetus is still technically in the womb. How frequently and for what reasons these types of abortion occur is a matter of debate. President George W. Bush signed a bill into law in 2003 prohibiting the procedure, though it does contain an exception in the case of a threat to the mother's life. The U.S. Supreme Court upheld the law in a 2007 decision. The ban on partial-birth abortions does not mean that all late-term abortions are illegal — just the specific procedure known as the partial-birth abortion.

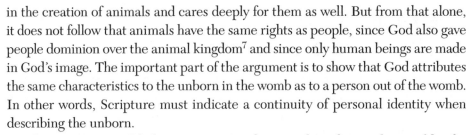

in the creation of animals and cares deeply for them as well. But from that alone, it does not follow that animals have the same rights as people, since God also gave people dominion over the animal kingdom[7] and since only human beings are made in God's image. The important part of the argument is to show that God attributes the same characteristics to the unborn in the womb as to a person out of the womb. In other words, Scripture must indicate a continuity of personal identity when describing the unborn.

The passages cited below are not an exhaustive list of texts that could refer to abortion, but they represent the clearest indications of a continuity of personal identity that begins at the earliest point of pregnancy and continues into adulthood. Some of the relevant passages use conception and birth interchangeably. Others suggest that the same characteristics of adults are applied to the unborn.

Examples of where the Bible uses conception and birth interchangeably include Job 3:3, which states, "Let the day perish on which I was to be born, and the night which said, 'A boy is conceived'" (NASB). This poetic passage employs what is called *synonymous parallelism*, in which the second line of poetry restates the first one, essentially saying the same thing in different language. This type of parallelism suggests that the child who was "born" and the child who was "conceived" are considered the same person. In fact, the terms "born" and "conceived" are used interchangeably here, suggesting that a person is in view at both conception and birth. What was present at birth was considered equivalent to what was present at conception. This is strengthened by the use of the term "boy" in the second half of the verse, which speaks of conception. The woman did not conceive a thing or a piece of tissue, but a "boy," a person. The Hebrew term for "boy," *geber*, is also used in other parts of the Old Testament to refer to a man (Ex. 10:11; Deut. 22:5; Judg. 5:30). Thus, in the same sense that an adult man is a person, the individual conceived in Job 3:3 is a person.

Other passages that seem to use conception and birth interchangeably include Jeremiah 1:5, where God says, "Before I formed you in the womb I knew you, before you were born I set you apart; I appointed you as a prophet to the nations." Here it seems clear that God had a relationship with and an intimate knowledge of Jeremiah in the same way he did when Jeremiah was an adult and engaged in his prophetic ministry. In the womb he was called to be a prophet, something that was commonly done with other prophets when they were adults. That is, there is more to this text than the simple parallel between conception and birth. It also describes God knowing the unborn in the same way he knows a child or an adult, thereby attributing something characteristic of adults to the unborn. However, one should be careful not to take the parallelism too far in this text, since it would extend the argument for personhood farther than one might want and suggest preexistence. A similar text occurs in Isaiah 49:1, which states, "Before I was born the LORD called me [literally, "from the womb the LORD called me"]; from my birth he has made mention of my name." Again the parallel suggests that conception and birth are used interchangeably, but the text adds to this the idea that the person in question was both called and named prior to birth, indicative of a personal interest that parallels the interest God takes in adults. Since the person in view in Isaiah 49:1 is the Suffering Servant, Jesus Christ, this passage may be a reference to the preexistence of Jesus. Perhaps the clearest indication that the unborn are objects of God's knowledge may be found in Psalm 139:13–16, which clearly shows that God is intimately involved in forming the unborn child and cultivating an intimate knowledge of that child.

Some people may object to the use of these texts, suggesting that all of these refer only to God's foreknowledge of a person prior to birth. However, in passages such as Job 3:3, the person who eventually grows into an adult is the same person who is in view in the womb. Although it is true that these passages use poetic devices to make their point, one cannot dismiss such texts simply because they are using figurative language. Poetry is difficult to interpret in many places, but just because it uses figures of speech is no reason to minimize their contribution. Figurative language always is making some kind of literal point, and though it is not appropriate to take figures of speech in a woodenly literal way, they do have an underlying literal point that is being made, which, in the above texts, is the parallel between conception and birth.

Psalm 139:13–16 describes the intimate involvement of God in the formation of the unborn. From a Christian worldview, this should be sufficient to discourage abortion, since it interrupts the sovereign work of God in the womb. However, the psalm further teaches a continuity of personal identity from the earliest points of pregnancy forward. The psalmist who is intimately known by God in the first few verses is the same person who was described as intricately formed in the womb by God later in the psalm. And he is the same person who at the end of the psalm, requests God to search him and know his heart. Some raise the objection that Psalm 139 speaks only of the *development* of a person in the womb, not of the fact that what is in the womb is indeed a person. However, these texts suggest that in the womb from conception is a person with potential for development, not merely some being that will develop into a person at some point in the gestational process. These texts, particularly Psalm 139, strongly suggest a continuity of personal identity that runs from conception to adulthood.

Two other passages highlight this continuity of personal identity. Psalm 51:5 says, "Surely I was sinful at birth, sinful from the time my mother conceived me." Here David is confessing not only his sins of adultery with Bathsheba and premeditated murder of her husband, Uriah the Hittite (see 2 Sam. 11–12), but also his innate inclination to sin. This is a characteristic shared by all people, and David's claim is that he possessed it from the point of conception. Thus the inherent inclination to sin is attributed both to adult persons and the unborn. Using synonymous parallelism similar to that in Job 3:3, David appears to treat birth and conception as practically interchangeable terms. Finally, the Greek term for "baby," *bréphos*, is applied to a child still in the womb in Luke 1:41–44 as well as to the newborn baby Jesus in Luke 2:16.

Perhaps a more explicit reference to the significance of the birth of the baby (*bréphos*) Jesus comes from the visitation of Mary to Elizabeth in the early days of her pregnancy. Mary visits Elizabeth (Luke 1:39–56) only a few days after she has found out that she is pregnant with Jesus. The account of the angel's announcement (vv. 26–38) indicates that Mary left in haste to visit Elizabeth and share this news with her. Allowing for travel time of roughly two weeks, we perceive that when she arrives at Elizabeth's home, Mary is in the very earliest stages of her pregnancy, with a fetus that is less than three weeks old. Upon arrival at Elizabeth's home, Mary is immediately recognized as "the mother of my Lord" (v. 43). Even though she is carrying a very early stage fetus (in fact, at this point in the pregnancy, most expectant women do not even know they are pregnant), she is clearly recognized as a mother, and by implication, Jesus is recognized as her son, a baby. Further, John the Baptist leaps in Elizabeth's womb, perhaps signifying his recognition of the significance of Jesus' conception and in utero development.

What is clear is that all of the parties involved in this narrative—Mary, John, and Elizabeth—recognize that something very significant is occurring that is bound up with Mary being pregnant with the Messiah. The significance of the incarnation, though likely not grasped in its fullness, is nonetheless recognized, not at Jesus' birth, but far earlier, in the earliest stages following conception. That is, the incarnation is recognized as having begun months prior to Jesus' actual birth. From the earliest points of life in the womb, Mary and Elizabeth realize that the incarnation has begun. This lends support to the notion that the incarnation began with Jesus' conception and that the Messiah took on human form in all of its stages, embryonic life included.

The general tenor of Scripture appears to support the idea that the unborn is considered a person by God, being described with many of the same characteristics that apply to children and adults. However, a handful of passages seem to indicate that the unborn is less than a full person, and that the Bible does not consider the unborn to be the equivalent of an adult in terms of its essential personhood. The primary text that calls this into question is Exodus 21:22–25, which records a specific law designed to arbitrate a very specific case. "If men who are fighting hit a pregnant woman and *she gives birth prematurely* [has a miscarriage] but there is no serious injury, the offender must be fined whatever the woman's husband demands and the court allows. But if there is serious injury [i.e., to the woman], you are to take life for life, eye for eye, tooth for tooth, hand for hand, burn for burn, wound for wound, bruise for bruise" (emphasis added).

Some suggest that since the penalty for causing the death of the fetus is only a fine, whereas the penalty for causing the death of the mother is death, the fetus must not be deserving of the same level of protection as an adult person. It must have a different status, something less than that full personhood that merits a life-for-life penalty if taken. This argument assumes that the phrase "gives birth prematurely" should be translated "has a miscarriage." If that is the correct translation, then the argument that the unborn are viewed differently may have more merit, because of the difference in penalty. However, there is significant debate over the translation "gives birth prematurely." The most likely translation is "she gives birth prematurely" (so NIV), implying that the birth is successful, creating serious discomfort to the pregnant woman but not killing her or her child. The normal Hebrew word for "miscarriage" is the term *shakal*, which is not used here. Rather, the term *yasa* is used. It is normally used in connection with the live birth of one's child. The fact that the normal term for miscarriage is not used here and a term that has connotations to live birth is used suggests that the passage means a woman who gives birth prematurely.[8] This would make more sense of the different penalties accruing to the guilty party. Perhaps the phrase "if there is serious injury" (v. 23) could apply to either the woman or the child, so that if the woman actually did have a miscarriage, the punishment would be life for life.

The Arguments for the Pro-Choice Position

The pro-life position has in effect only one argument, based on the notion that the unborn is a person, which must be answered. Throughout the past two decades, however, pro-choice proponents have put forth a number of arguments to support a woman's right to choose abortion. In the next section, we will examine the pro-life claim that the unborn has personhood from the point of conception. Here we will examine the various pro-choice arguments that have been articulated both in popular and scholarly forums.[9] Most of the arguments for abortion rights commit the logical fallacy known as "begging the question," or assuming the conclusion one wishes to reach without offering any evidence for its validity. For example, in order for their various arguments to work, pro-choice advocates assume that the fetus is not a full person. The pro-life advocate will rightly point out the question-begging fallacy so as to focus the debate on the central issue—the personhood of the unborn.

1. A woman has the right to do with her own body whatever she chooses.

That a woman has the right to do with her own body whatever she chooses is by far the most frequently presented argument in favor of abortion rights. It is the fundamental principle of the pro-choice movement—the woman's right to choose. This is foundational to the woman's constitutional right to privacy and was appealed to by the Court in the *Casey* decision when they referred to the preservation of a woman's bodily integrity and to her personal autonomy to choose abortion. Many people who personally oppose abortion and would never have one themselves nevertheless support a woman's right to choose abortion on the basis that it is her body and therefore her choice.

In response, I would note that a person's right over his or her own body is not absolute. In most states, prostitution is illegal, and nowhere is it legal to pour illegal drugs into one's body. In addition, the fetus is technically not part of the woman's body. It is a genetically distinct entity with its own genetic code, and early on in the pregnancy it has its own heart and circulatory system. In many cases it also has a separate gender identity that is present from the moment of conception. It would be difficult to account for the presence of a differently gendered "part" of the woman if the fetus is a part of the woman's body. This argument confuses the fetus *being attached to* the woman carrying it and *being a part of* the woman carrying it. It does not follow that just because the fetus is attached to its mother by an umbilical cord that the fetus is a part of her in a way that denies its own separate identity. To put it differently, this argument confuses the fetus living inside the woman with being a part of her. Again, these are not the same, and being a part of her does not follow necessarily from the fact that the fetus lives inside of her.

This argument further begs the question of the nature of the fetus by assuming that it is less than fully human. If pro-choice advocates did not assume this, this argument could not stand. Historically in Western society, when life and freedom (choice) have been in conflict, life always has taken precedence. Only if the fetus is not a person does a woman have a right to make a choice that would result in its death. But if the fetus is a person, then very few freedoms would take precedence over its right to life. The pro-choice advocate may respond that I am also begging the question by assuming that the fetus is indeed a person. That is true, but it is done only in order to show the question-begging nature of this argument. That is, only if one assumes that the fetus is not a person will the argument work. But that is the heart of the debate, and any argument that assumes what is central to the issue cannot be considered valid.

2. If abortion becomes illegal, we will return to the dangerous days of the "back alley" abortion providers.

The argument that if abortion becomes illegal we will return to the days of the "back alley" abortion providers takes one back to the days prior to the *Roe v. Wade* decision, when most abortions were illegal and women had to go to less than ideal settings to obtain them, thereby putting their health at significantly greater risk. Unlicensed physicians allegedly performed these abortions in "back alley" clinics with varying degrees of safety. Desperate to be relieved of an unwanted pregnancy, women would thus endanger themselves in the process of obtaining an abortion. No one, the argument goes, would want to go back to those days, and if the pro-life movement has its way, that is exactly where society will be heading.

In response, this argument also begs the question, since one must assume that the fetus is not a person. Otherwise, the person advancing this argument would be arguing that society has the responsibility to make it safe to kill people who have the right to life. Unless the fetus is a person, this argument has little force, for if it is a person and abortion amounts to killing a person, the issue of making it safe for a person to do so is not only irrelevant, but it is absurd. The only way that the safety of the mother can be a legitimate concern is if the fetus is not a person and if abortion is comparable to any other type of surgery in which a part of the woman's body is removed.

This argument also seems to overstate the potential danger to women receiving illegal "back alley" abortions. The statistics on the number of women who died procuring illegal abortions are clearly inflated, at times even by the admission of pro-choice advocates.[10] For example, according to numbers available from the Bureau of Vital Statistics, roughly forty women died from such abortions in 1972, the year prior to *Roe v. Wade*. In fact, the number of deaths from abortion-related consequences has decreased consistently since 1942.[11] It is misleading to insist that the majority of illegal abortions were performed by unqualified physicians, since prior to 1973 roughly 90 percent of illegal abortions were performed by licensed physicians in good standing with their state medical boards.[12]

Closely related to this argument is the argument that any substantial prohibition of abortion is unenforceable. To enforce any such law would likely involve intolerable invasions of privacy and would force physicians to break their covenant of confidentiality with their patients. But again, this argument begs the question by assuming that the fetus is not a person, for if it is, then making it safe and legal to abort a fetus does not follow at all. In addition, it can be shown that prior to 1973, restrictive abortion laws were quite enforceable and were effective in limiting abortions. Since 1973 roughly 1.5 million abortions have been performed annually. Prior to 1973 roughly 100,000 abortions were performed annually. This does not mean that enforcement would be free of all difficulties, but it does not follow that abortion should not be limited because of these difficulties.

3. Forcing women, especially poor ones, to continue their pregnancies will create overwhelming financial hardship.

The argument that forcing women to continue their pregnancies will create overwhelming financial hardship is based on the idea that economic hardship will likely result from women being without the option of abortion to control the size of their families. Without safe and legal abortion, these women will be condemned to a life of poverty and financial burden, which is also unfair to the children that they bring into the world.

In response, this argument also begs the question by assuming that unborn poor are not persons. This argument can work only by making such an assumption. Otherwise, this argument could be used as a basis for exterminating all those people who are financially burdensome to society. Obviously the reason that society does not do this is that the financially burdensome are persons with the right to life, and their burden to society is irrelevant to their continuing right to life. Only if the fetus is not a person can we say that financial burdensomeness is a criteria for elimination. This argument also confuses finding a solution with eliminating the problem. The solution to unwanted pregnancies is not to eliminate them; by comparison, we could easily solve the problem of poverty by exterminating all the poor. It is better to view adoption as one of the solutions to the problem and recognize that hardship, no matter how severe, cannot justify intentionally killing someone.

4. Society should not force women to bring unwanted children into the world.

Closely related to the economic hardship argument is the argument of the unwanted child. This argument is broader, encompassing pregnancies that are unwanted for more than reasons of financial hardship. Abortion helps society prevent bringing unwanted children into the world, and thus prevents child abuse and child neglect.

In response, this argument also begs the question by assuming that the fetus is not a person, because if it is, then surely abortion is the worst imaginable form of child abuse. In addition, one cannot determine the value of a child based on the degree to which he or she is desired. If anything, the fact that a child is unwanted is more of a commentary on the parents than the child, and if the fetus is a person, whether it is wanted or not is irrelevant to its right to life. Perhaps the issue of the homeless offers a parallel. They are not wanted in many communities, but the reason they are not eliminated has nothing to do with that. They are persons with the right to life, and one cannot solve a problem by eliminating it. Therefore, this argument hinges on the pro-choice advocate's ability to demonstrate that the fetus is not a person, not on the fact that the pregnancy is unwanted.

Statistics show that since 1973 child abuse has increased substantially, even with the termination of approximately 1.5 million unwanted pregnancies annually. It may be that the incidence of child abuse is unrelated to liberal abortion laws. If anything, it could be that the callousness toward the fetus engendered by liberal abortion laws has carried over into a greater societal tendency toward child abuse. No evidence shows that being unwanted is necessarily linked with being abused. In fact, some studies have shown that the great majority of abused children were wanted by their parents, and adopted children experience a higher incidence of child abuse than nonadopted children.[13]

5. Society should not force women to bring severely handicapped children into the world.

That society should not force women to bring severely handicapped children into the world is the argument from the deformity of the fetus, which can be detected in utero through the process of amniocentesis. This is becoming more routine in prenatal care, and frequently genetic counselors assume that a woman will have an abortion if tests reveal a deformed fetus. Pro-choice advocates consider it unfair and insensitive to force a woman to carry a pregnancy that she knows will result in a severely deformed child.

In response, abortions in the case of deformity are a relatively small percentage of the overall number of abortions performed annually. These are clearly some of the most difficult cases in the abortion scenario. At best, they only support the right of a woman to have an abortion in these difficult cases, but they do not support the right of a woman to choose abortion as a fundamental right. In general, difficult cases do not make the general rule — that is, they do not support the right of a woman to choose abortion on demand.

This argument also begs the question of the personhood of the fetus, since this argument can only be valid if we assume that the fetus is not a person. But if the fetus is a person, then this argument can be used to justify killing all the handicapped. There is no moral difference between aborting a handicapped fetus and executing handicapped children. Yet no one accepts the right of parents to kill their handicapped children, precisely because they are persons. Unless the assumption that the fetus is not a person is true, the argument collapses. Thus this argument must rest on whether the fetus is a person, not on the handicapped status of the fetus. In addition, it is presumptuous to say that a handicapped life is not worth living and should be aborted. This may be true in rare and very extreme cases, such as anencephaly, where the child is born with only a brain stem and no other part of the brain. But this extreme case cannot be used to justify abortion in cases of more moderate deformities, such as mild Down syndrome. No evidence supports the notion that unhappiness necessarily accompanies disability.

6. Society should not force women who are pregnant from rape or incest to continue their pregnancies.

The argument that society should not force women who are pregnant from rape or incest to continue their pregnancies is related to the previous one and is one of the most emotionally compelling arguments for a woman's right to choose abortion. Since the woman had sex forced on her against her will, it is argued that she should not be forced to continue a potential pregnancy. This is not a case of carelessness, but rather a lack of consent to sex that made her pregnant. Thus society would be punishing the victim of a violent crime by making her a victim again. At the heart

Peter Singer and Infanticide

Australian philosopher Peter Singer, who holds an endowed chair in ethics at Princeton University, has some of the more controversial ideas about abortion and infanticide. He holds a common position in the philosophical community that an important determinant of whether someone is a person is his or her ability to experience a continuing self with an interest in continued life. This presumes a level of consciousness and self-awareness that no fetuses or newborns have and even applies to some severely impaired infants. He and Helga Kuhse put it this way: "When we kill a newborn infant (particularly one that is severely handicapped) there is not a person whose life has begun (or will ever begin). It is the beginning of the life of the person, rather than the physical organism, that is crucial as far as the right to life is concerned." Singer maintains that newborns, up to roughly the first thirty days of life, do not meet the criteria for being a person and that infanticide is justified during that time. He further insists that certain classes of handicapped newborns never will meet the criteria for being a person, and that infanticide is justified in their cases. Singer has had numerous critics, who insist that there is an important difference between being a person and functioning as a person. That is, you can be a person and have those critical functions that Singer describes be latent or temporarily unexpressed.*

*Peter Singer and Helga Kuhse, *Should the Baby Live?* (New York: Oxford University Press, 1985); Peter Singer, *Writings on an Ethical Life* (New York: Ecco, 2000).

of this argument is the premise that a woman should not be held responsible for sex that is forced upon her, and thus should have the right to end a pregnancy that came about through rape or incest.

In response, the number of pregnancies that result from rape or incest is very small—roughly 1 in 100,000 cases. Yet how the pregnancy was conceived is irrelevant to the central question of the personhood of the fetus. This is because the child should not be penalized for the sin of his or her father. This argument can only work if one assumes that the fetus is not a person, since you cannot justify the homicide of another person just to relieve the mental distress of a trauma such as rape.

Many people argue that the pro-life advocate should not victimize the woman a second time by forcing her to continue the pregnancy against her will. Although they hold that the fetus is just as much a person as if conceived through consensual sex, they maintain that the law should allow an exception to permit abortion in cases of rape and incest. The reason for this is not moral but prudential. They believe that unless a proposed law contains this exception, it will have little chance of being enacted into law by any state legislature. Arguing that it is better to save more unborn children than less, one can make a good case that the exception should be adopted. Of course, an inherent problem with this is how to enforce such a law, since it might be difficult to verify the claim of a woman seeking an abortion that she has been raped.

7. Restrictive abortion laws discriminate against poor women.

The argument that restrictive abortion laws discriminate against poor women is based on what happened prior to abortion being legalized in 1973. When women of means wanted abortions, they simply traveled to countries where abortion was legal and paid for them. Obviously, poor women did not have such an option. Thus restrictive abortion laws have the practical effect of discriminating against poor women, who are often the ones who need abortion services the most due to their difficult economic circumstances.

In response, this argument begs the question by assuming that an abortion is somehow a moral good that would be denied to poor women if restrictive abortion laws were enacted. But whether abortion is a moral good is precisely the point being debated. If the fetus is a person, then denying someone an abortion is irrelevant. Society has no obligation to provide equally to all people the freedom to kill innocent others. This argument can therefore be valid only if it assumes that the fetus is not a person.

All of the above arguments for abortion rights commit the fallacy of question begging. This illustrates how important it is to debate the central issue in the abortion question—the issue of the personhood of the fetus. If the fetus is not a person at the point in the pregnancy at which the abortion is being considered, then most of the arguments for abortion rights are valid. But if the fetus is a person, then none of the arguments for abortion rights hold. If the premise that the fetus is a person is applied consistently, it would lead to morally preposterous implications. We now turn to the critical question of the personhood of the fetus.

The Personhood of the Fetus

Most philosophers agree that the fetus either has personhood from the point of conception or it acquires it at some point during the process of gestation. A small minority of thinkers hold that not even the newborn baby possesses personhood, thus making infanticide theoretically justifiable in some cases. But most thinkers agree that once the fetus emerges from the womb as a newborn child, it is a person with full human rights. Thus the question under debate is, At what point in the process of gestation does the fetus possess personhood? A wide variety of different points has been suggested. These are called "decisive moments," referring to a "moment" at which the fetus can be said to be a person. In this section we will discuss these different decisive moments.[14]

Often a distinction is made between the fetus being a human being and the fetus being a person. Such a distinction is highly arbitrary, since the essence of the fetus is unchanged throughout the process of gestation. None of the different decisive moments suggests any relevant change in the essence of the fetus. Thus a constant process of growth and development continues from conception to adulthood.

In the abortion debate one commonly hears voices suggest that no one has a way to determine for sure when personhood begins. Taking an agnostic approach to the issue, these people argue that science has provided no clear answer to the question. They maintain that since it is essentially a religious or philosophical issue and cannot be proven conclusively, it should be left to individual choice.

In response to this, the same can be said of the pro-choice view that allows for abortion. By permitting abortion throughout almost the entire nine months of pregnancy, pro-choice advocates are actually making a strong statement that personhood doesn't begin until birth. We will examine birth as a decisive moment below. In addition, if one is admittedly agnostic about when personhood is acquired, then surely it is preferable to err on the side of life. If we are not sure that the fetus is a person, then society should not permit the taking of the life of the fetus through abortion. For example, if I am hunting with a friend who enters the woods and I then hear what sounds like the rustling of a deer at the same spot where my friend entered, I had better not shoot. After all, I cannot be sure whether the rustling sound was made by my friend or the deer. If in doubt, one should not shoot into the trees. Likewise, if in doubt about the personhood of the fetus, one should not risk the life of the fetus, since it may be a person whose life is being ended by abortion. Uncertainty about the status of the fetus justifies caution, not abortion.

The most commonly proposed decisive moment, and the one currently endorsed by the Supreme Court is *viability*, which is the point at which the fetus is able to live on its own outside the womb. At this point of about twenty-four to twenty-six weeks of gestation, the fetus is able to live on its own, a fact that is deemed significant enough to grant it the status of a person. Although it may still depend on medical technology, it no longer depends on its uterine environment.

One problem with viability as a determinant of personhood is that it cannot be measured precisely. It varies from fetus to fetus, and medical technology is continually pushing viability back to earlier stages of pregnancy. Thus viability keeps changing, which raises questions about its reliability as an indicator of personhood. Viability also varies widely from place to place, as a function of the available medical technology. That is, viability is quite different in a high-technology New York City hospital than it is in rural Nigeria. So what does viability actually measure? Viability has more to do with the ability of medical technology to sustain life outside the womb than it has to do with the essence of the fetus. Viability relates more to the fetus's location and dependency than to its essence or its personhood. Hence no inherent connection exists between the fetus's ability to survive outside the womb and its essence. Rather, viability measures the progress of medical technology in helping the fetus to survive in a different location.

Perhaps the next most commonly proposed decisive moment is brain development, or the point at which the brain of the fetus begins to function, which is about forty-five days into the pregnancy. The appeal of this decisive moment is the parallel with the definition of death, which is the cessation of all brain activity. Since brain activity is what measures death, or the loss of personhood, it is reasonable to take the beginning of brain activity as the indication of personhood. The problem with the analogy to brain death is that the dead brain is in an irreversible condition, unable to be revived. The brain of the developing fetus is only temporarily nonfunctional. Its electroencephalogram (EEG) is only temporarily flat, whereas the EEG of a dead person's brain is permanently flat. Also, the embryo from the point of conception has all the necessary capacities to develop full brain activity. Until about forty-five days gestation, those capacities are not yet realized but are latent in the embryo. Just because a capacity is not exercised is not a necessary comment on the essence of the fetus, since that capacity is only temporarily latent, not irreversibly lost. Thus a fetus without brain activity for the first four to five weeks of pregnancy is significantly different from the dead person who is without brain activity. Therefore, using brain activity as the decisive moment for personhood raises serious questions about its usefulness in determining viability.

A third proposal for a decisive moment is *sentience*, that is, the point at which the fetus is capable of experiencing sensations, particularly pain.[15] The appeal of this point for the determination of personhood is that if the fetus cannot feel pain, then there is less of a problem with abortion, and it disarms many of the pro-life arguments that abortion is cruel to the fetus.

As is the case with the other decisive moments, however, sentience has little inherent connection to the personhood of the fetus. This decisive moment confuses the experience of harm with the reality of harm. It does not follow that the fetus cannot be harmed simply because the fetus cannot feel pain or otherwise experience harm. Even if I am paralyzed from the waist down and cannot feel pain in my legs, I am still harmed if someone amputates my leg. In addition, to take sentience as the determinant of personhood, one would also have to admit that the person in a persistent vegetative state (i.e., irreversibly comatose), the momentarily unconscious person, and even the sleeping person are not persons. One might object that these people once did function with sentience and that the loss of sentience is only temporary. But once that objection is made, the objector is admitting that something besides sentience determines personhood, and thus sentience as a decisive moment cannot be sustained. This counterargument applies to other functional criteria for personhood, such as self-consciousness, awareness of one's environment, and relationality, which are used by abortion rights proponents such as Mary Ann Warren and Peter Singer.

Another idea suggested as a decisive moment is *quickening*, that is, the first time that the mother feels the fetus move inside her womb. Before the advent of sophisticated medical technology such as ultrasound, which can see the fetus from the early stages of pregnancy, quickening was considered the first indication of the presence of life within the mother's womb. Yet quickening as a determinant of personhood cannot be maintained, because the essence of the fetus does not depend on someone's awareness of it. This criteria confuses the nature of the fetus with what one can know about the fetus. Philosophically speaking, this decisive moment confuses epistemology (knowledge or awareness of the fetus) with ontology (the nature or essence of the fetus). A similar confusion is involved in the use of *the appearance of humanness* of the fetus as a decisive moment for personhood. The appeal of this is that as the fetus begins to resemble a baby, it makes it at least emotionally more difficult to consider abortion. But the appearance of the fetus has no inherent relationship to its essence. Also, from the point of conception, the fetus has all the capacities necessary to look like a normal human being. Certainly one would not want to determine personhood on such a subjective criteria as the appearance of humanness.

A few hold that *birth* is the decisive moment at which the fetus acquires personhood. But no essential difference exists between the fetus on the day before its birth and the day after its birth. The only difference is location, that is, the baby now lives outside the womb. But as is the case with viability as the determinant of personhood, the essence of personhood involves more than simply location. It does not follow that my nature as a person changes just because I change locations.

Finally, *implantation* has been proposed as a decisive moment for a number of reasons. First, at this point the embryo establishes its presence in the womb by the "signals," or the hormones, it produces. Second, 20 to 50 percent of the embryos spontaneously miscarry prior to implantation, which suggests that implantation is critical not only for the development of the embryo but to its essence. It would also suggest that we have the obligation to save all of the embryos, something that very few people consider. Third, twinning, or the production of twins, normally occurs prior to implantation, suggesting that individual human personhood does not begin until after implantation.

Although placing personhood at implantation would not justify very many abortions, the implications of this decisive moment are significant. First, it would make any birth control methods that prevent implantation, such as many birth control pills, morally acceptable, since an unimplanted embryo is not considered a person. Further, embryos from in vitro fertilization can be either discarded or used for experimentation without any moral problem, since those embryos lack personhood.

In response to the proposal of implantation as a decisive moment, it does not follow that personhood is established at implantation just because the embryo establishes its presence by the hormonal signals it produces. The essence of the fetus cannot be dependent on another's awareness of its existence, whether it is physical awareness, as in quickening, or chemical awareness in the production of specific hormones. Second, just because up to 50 percent of conceived embryos spontaneously miscarry, it does not follow that personhood comes at implantation, since the essential nature of the fetus is not dependent on the number of embryos that do or do not survive to implant. Even if the embryo is fully a person, we are not morally obligated to save all of them since we have no moral obligation to interfere in the embryo's natural death. Not interfering to prevent a spontaneous miscarriage is not the same as killing an embryo, just as removing life support from a terminally ill patient is not the same as actively killing such a patient. Third, just because twinning occurs prior to implantation, it does not follow that the original embryo was not fully a person before the split. Thus the proposal of implantation as a decisive moment for personhood generates some very significant questions.

In light of the above discussion, it seems most reasonable to conclude that the fetus has full personhood from the moment of conception. The argument could look something like this:[16]

1. An adult human being is the end result of the continuous growth of the organism from conception (this premise has hardly any debate).
2. From conception to adulthood, this development has no break that is relevant to the essential nature of the fetus (this is the debatable premise, but the above discussion shows that all the proposed breaks do not have a bearing on the nature of the fetus).
3. Therefore, one is a human person from the point of conception onward (this conclusion follows from the above two premises).

Also, from conception the fetus has a unique and separate genetic identity, needing only nutrition and shelter to mature into a full newborn baby and later into an adult. From the moment of conception, it possesses all the capacities necessary to mature into a full adult. Thus it is incorrect to say that the fetus is a potential person. Rather, the fetus is a person with the full potential to develop all of its latent capacities. It is a full human being, a person that is in the process of maturing into a fully grown adult, with no breaks in the process of its maturity.

Some abortion rights proponents actually concede that the fetus is a person and argue that a woman should still have the right to abortion. A classic example of this is the widely read argument by philosopher Judith Jarvis Thomson, in which she compares a woman with an unwanted pregnancy to a person who has been kidnapped in order to provide a lifesaving blood transfusion to a world-renowned violinist.[17] The violinist is dying, and the person providing the transfusion is essential to the violinist being able to live. Even though the violinist will die if the person "unplugs" from the transfusion, Thomson argues that there is no moral obligation for the kidnapped person to continue to provide this life-saving service. She then applies this to the case of an intended pregnancy and argues that the woman with an unwanted pregnancy has essentially been kidnapped by the fetus and forced to provide a life-saving service by continuing the pregnancy. She concludes that the pregnant woman has no obligation to save the fetus's life and is morally justified in ending her pregnancy, even though it would result in the death of the fetus.

Thomson's argument would apply at most to pregnancies that result from nonconsensual sex, but surely not to pregnancies in which the woman knew that pregnancy was a possible consequence of sexual activity. Further, Thomson's depiction of pregnancy as analogous to being confined to the transfusion table is actually nothing like a normal pregnancy. During most pregnancies, women live their lives relatively normally, and it's not unusual for women to report that in stretches of their pregnancy, they have never felt better.

The difficulty with Thomson's argument is her starting point. Once she concedes that the fetus is a person, she loses any force to her argument that grants abortion rights. In fact, if the fetus is a person, one can make the argument that the unborn child actually has a *claim* on the mother's body. Take, for example, a mother with her one-year-old child. It is not difficult to argue that the child has a claim on her mother for all that the child needs to survive. In fact, if the mother did not provide those necessities of life for her child, she would be guilty of neglect or even child abuse. If this continued, the child would be taken from her due to her unfitness to be a parent. That is, the child has a claim on the mother for those necessary resources. Even if the mother does not want the child, she is still responsible for ensuring that her child is cared for, either by foster care or adoption. If this is true of a one-year-old child who is a full person, why would the fetus not have a similar claim on the pregnant woman for the resources necessary for the fetus to survive? After all, Thomson has conceded that the fetus is a person and thus no different in moral status than the one-year-old. Thomson may argue that the difference is that the fetus requires the mother's body in order to live, whereas the one-year-old does not. But that difference is surely overstated, since the demands of caring for a one-year-old far outweigh the demands of caring for a fetus in the womb. If one concedes that the fetus is a person, then the only real difference between the fetus in the womb and the one-year-old is location.

Embryo and Stem Cell Research

Since scientists first isolated stem cells in the late 1990s, the possibilities of using stem cells for research and treatment of a variety of diseases has generated some very exciting prospects for patients suffering from illnesses ranging from diabetes to spinal cord injuries. But the use of many types of stem cells has presented a series of ethical challenges. Before I outline the ethical issues, let's look at some background information.

Stem cells are what one scientist called "the biological mother lode." That is, they are *undifferentiated* cells, which can be directed in the lab to develop into any of the roughly two hundred types of cells and tissues in the body. Some stem cells are completely undifferentiated—that is, they have not begun down the developmental pathway that dictates that they become certain types of cells, for example, neurological cells or cardiac cells. These are called *pluripotent* stem cells and in theory can be engineered in the lab to become any of the cells in the body. They cannot become the entire organism; those are called *totipotent* cells, and single-cell embryos are the only cells in the body that are totipotent. Some stem cells have become slightly differentiated however. That is, they have begun down the developmental pathway but still can be directed to become cells of a specific type. For example, there are neurological stem cells, which can become any neurological cell but not blood cells or any other type of cells outside their initial developmental boundaries. These stem cells are called *multipotent* stem cells and are very useful in treating a variety of diseases but do not have the same *plasticity*, or developmental flexibility, that pluripotent stem cells have.

There are two primary sources of stem cells. The first, and uncontroversial, is what has come to be known as *adult stem cells*. These stem cells are harvested from a variety of sources, including a person's bone marrow, the umbilical cord blood of a newborn baby, and various organs in the body. A second source, and very controversial, is *human embryos*, at the three- to five-day stage of development. These embryos are either those left over from infertility treatments (see chapter 6 for further discussion of in vitro fertilization) or they are created by a process known as *therapeutic cloning*. This is the process by which a person is cloned (see chapter 7 for further discussion of this), and the resulting embryos mature to the three- to five-day stage, at which point their stem cells are harvested. The reason human embryos are a controversial source is that to obtain their stem cells

Skin Cells Reprogrammed to Form Embryonic Stem Cells

Two different teams of researchers, one in Japan and one in the United States, have successfully "reprogrammed" adult cells and coaxed them to go backward on their developmental pathway, enabling them to produce embryonic-like stem cells that have all the properties of stem cells harvested from human embryos. They have the potential to become, under the right conditions, any of the roughly two hundred cell or tissue types in the human body. This is a potentially significant breakthrough enabling researchers to use embryonic-like stem cells that can be harvested without either creating or destroying embryos. Many in the pro-life community have objected to using stem cells harvested from human embryos because they believe embryos to be fully human with the right to life. This discovery overcomes the most significant moral obstacle to using embryonic stem cells. "We are now in a position to be able to generate patient- and disease-specific stem cells without using human eggs or embryos," said Shinya Yamanaka from the University of Kyoto, who led the Japanese team. Yamanaka was motivated by his view of embryos to engage in this work. He said, "When I saw the embryo, I suddenly realized there was such a small difference between it and my daughters.... I thought, *We can't keep destroying embryos for our research. There must be another way.*" Although some technological obstacles still remain, this is a substantial breakthrough that, though tempered with caution, is reason for optimism. It may be that technology will resolve an ethical dilemma rather than create one.*

---

*Martin Fackler, "Social Call Led to New Calling," *New York Times*, December 16, 2007; Andy Coghlan, "Human Skin Reprogrammed to Form Stem Cells," *New Scientist*, November 20, 2007.

requires that the embryos be destroyed in the process. To date, an embryo cannot survive the harvest of its stem cells. Embryonic stem cells are pluripotent, whereas many types of adult stem cells are multipotent, though there are some indications that some types of adult stem cells may also be pluripotent. Embryonic stem cells also tend to have greater longevity when multiplied in a culture in the lab.

Stem cells are being used or are anticipated to be used to treat various cancers, blood diseases, immune system disorders, Parkinson's disease, diabetes, and multiple sclerosis (MS). They can also be used for repair of heart tissue and growth of new blood vessels, and there is hope for using stem cells to treat spinal cord injuries. This is only a sample of the potential medical benefits that will come from using stem cells. To date, most of the progress in treating diseases has come from stem cells harvested from adult sources.

The issue of stem cell research raises the question of the moral status of early-stage embryos, particularly those that exist outside the womb (ex utero embryos). Some suggest that such microscopic entities that consist of a handful of cells cannot be a person. They argue that embryos are simply clumps of cells and that destroying them is not immoral, especially when compared to the vast number of potential suffering patients who could be treated. Others insist that size and location are irrelevant to a being's ontological and moral status, and that the continuity of personal identity that applies to fetuses extends to embryos too.

Our common views of a person assume a continuity of personal identity, which, as mentioned above, is consistent with the Bible. For example, we assume that persons continue to be the same person irrespective of time and change. Our social notions of moral responsibility and criminal justice are dependent on this view of personal identity. We assume that when we bring someone to trial for a crime committed years prior, we are trying the same person who committed the crime, regardless of how that person has changed or how much time has elapsed. Philosophically this is called a "substance" view of a person. Another way to say this is that being a person is a matter of one's *essence*, or nature, not the ability to perform certain functions. If being a person is determined by our ability to perform certain functions, such as having self-awareness, relationality, and others, then personhood ends up being a degreed property, something of which one can have more or less. But if personhood is an essential property, then it is an all-or-nothing property, with the result that one either is or is not a person. Only an essential view of a person avoids the problematic idea that being a person is a matter of degree. Once it is admitted that being a person is a matter of essence, then the continuity of personal identity follows. What we saw earlier in this chapter is that once we admit to a continuity of identity, then there is no place along the continuum from conception to birth where there is a valid "decisive moment." The result is that one is a person from conception forward. The single-cell embryo has all the information it needs to mature into a full-grown adult, needing only shelter and nutrients. If implantation does not make a morally relevant difference, as I suggested above that it does not, then whether embryos are implanted in the womb or are stored in the lab is irrelevant to their moral and ontological status.

It is important to see that the moral status of embryos is not fundamentally a scientific question but a philosophical one. Science cannot conclusively determine philosophical matters by scientific observation alone. What science can tell us is what kind of a biological entity an embryo is, whether it is alive, and even whether it is human (embryos that are the sources of stem cells are both alive and human, even when stored in the lab). But whether embryos are *persons* is not a biological question but a philosophical one. It is not fundamentally a religious question, since one could arrive at the same conclusions apart from religious convictions.

The notion that embryos are persons does seem somewhat counterintuitive. Some have suggested that preserving embryos should not be weighted as heavily as the obligation to help patients suffering from various diseases. But we should not forget not only the promise, but also the actual progress being made with adult stem cells. Those are being used today to treat numerous diseases effectively, while progress with embryonic stem cells has been much slower but is still promising.

Some argue that it is immoral not to use leftover embryos to help suffering patients, since they are going to be discarded anyway. In reality the stem cells

Embryo Biopsy

Researchers at Advanced Cell Technology, a Massachusetts biotechnology company, for the first time, harvested stem cells from human embryos without destroying the embryos. This marks a significant technological breakthrough in the ability of science to procure embryonic stem cells without harming the embryo from which they come. This technology is aimed at securing the stem cells from embryos that are going to be discarded, in order to produce cell lines both for research purposes and for potential treatments. Robert Lanza, chief scientific officer at ACT, admits that their procedure cannot tailor stem cells to each individual patient but could provide cell lines that would be helpful to some. Lanza is optimistic that once the procedure is peer-reviewed, having already been replicated in a University of California – San Francisco lab, it could dramatically increase the number of stem cells not only available for research, but also would qualify for federal funding because embryos are not destroyed in the process. Lanza said, "We could triple the number of human embryonic stem cells available within a few months."*

*Andy Coghlan, "Stem Cell Breakthrough Leaves Embryos Unharmed," *New Scientist*, January 10, 2008.

from leftover embryos are not that helpful to patients, though they may be helpful in research. The reason is that they are not likely to be compatible with the recipient. This compatibility is critical for organ recipients and bone marrow recipients since the body is well equipped to keep incompatible tissues and organs out. A further problem is that so far embryonic stem cells have the tendency to form tumors when they are used, mostly benign, but a problem nonetheless. The compatibility problem is the reason why therapeutic cloning is necessary for embryonic stem cells to become widely used in treatments. Therapeutic cloning guarantees a match, since the embryos created by cloning are the identical genetic duplicates of the patient. But this requires a prohibitive number of women's donated eggs in order to grow the cloned embryos (see chapter 7 for more on this), which is why some scientists are now calling for using the eggs of advanced mammals to grow the cloned embryos.

There is hope for technologies that will enable researchers to harvest embryonic stem cells without killing embryos. These involve embryo biopsy, using dead embryos, harvesting stem cells from embryo-like entities, and reengineering adult cells backward to an embryo-like state from which stem cells can be harvested (see "Embryo Biopsy" on page 146).

For Further Reading

Beckwith, Francis J. *Defending Life: The Moral and Legal Case against Abortion Choice*. New York: Cambridge University Press, 2007.

Beckwith, Francis J., and Louis P. Pojman, eds. *The Abortion Controversy: 25 Years after Roe vs. Wade*. Toronto: Wadsworth, 1998.

George, Robert P., and Christopher Tollefson, *Embryo: A Defense of Human Life*. New York: Doubleday, 2008.

Lee, Patrick. *Abortion and Unborn Human Life*. Washington, D.C.: Catholic University of America Press, 1996.

Review Questions

1. What are the major court cases that have set the legal context for abortion law in existence today? What is the significance of each one?

2. What are some of the primary biblical texts that have a bearing on the issue of abortion?

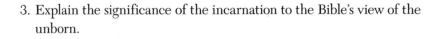

3. Explain the significance of the incarnation to the Bible's view of the unborn.

4. What is the significance of Exodus 21:22–25 to the discussion of abortion?

5. List and evaluate the primary arguments for the pro-choice position on abortion.

6. How do these various arguments beg the question on the moral status of the fetus?

7. Summarize the argument for the fetus being a person. Do you agree with this argument? Why or why not?

8. What are the various "decisive moments" at which it is proposed that the fetus becomes a person? How would you assess each one?

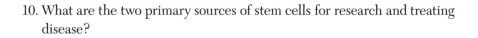

9. Would you make the same argument about embryos being persons? Why or why not?

10. What are the two primary sources of stem cells for research and treating disease?

11. What is the difference between pluripotent and multipotent stem cells?

12. Why is therapeutic cloning necessary for using stem cells to treat diseases?

Cases for Discussion

Case 5.1: The Unwanted Pregnancy

You are the college pastor for your church, and this afternoon you have had a counseling appointment with one of your students and her parents. She is new to your ministry, having recently come to faith in Christ, and her parents do not attend your church. They are distraught with her pregnancy, and you are too, since she is pregnant by one of the young men in your college ministry. They have known each other for roughly six months and are seeing each other exclusively.

They are coming for your counsel on abortion. They are considering facilitating a pregnancy termination and want to know your opinion. Since the parents do not attend your church and are likely not Christians, it is unlikely that they recognize any authority to Scripture.

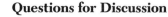

Questions for Discussion

1. What will you tell your student and her parents about the decision to end the pregnancy?

2. How would you defend your advice to the couple from the Bible? How, if at all, would you articulate your view to the girl's parents differently, since they don't appear to have much appreciation for the authority of the Bible?

3. Would you advise the couple to get married? Be sure to explain your reasons for your view on this question.

4. Assuming that they do not terminate the pregnancy and do not get married, would you advise the girl to put the baby up for adoption? Why or why not?

Case 5.2: Aborting the Anencephalic Baby

You and your spouse have found out in the last few weeks that the child with whom you are pregnant has been diagnosed with anencephaly, a fatal genetic disorder in which the cerebral cortex of the brain does not develop at all. The skull is somewhat flat and quite deformed looking. Only the brain stem, which controls all the nonvoluntary actions of the body, such as heartbeat, respiration, and digestion develops. The child will be born in a permanent vegetative state and is not likely to live longer than a few months, though some have lived as long as a year. At present the pregnancy is just into the second trimester.

Your physician has recommended ending the pregnancy as soon as possible. Your doctor wants to avoid labor and delivery for you, and there are some additional risks in a natural delivery of an anencephalic child due to the larger shape of the baby's skull. A cesarean section would not carry those risks, but that is a more invasive way to deliver the baby. You have strong feelings about the morality of abortion when done for nonmedical reasons. You wonder if this child is actually a person, since he or she will be born with only a brain stem and no higher brain.

Questions for Discussion

1. What are the primary moral issues to be resolved in this case?

2. What decision will you make? If you choose to end the pregnancy, what will you tell your neighbor, who knows how you feel about abortion in general? If you choose to carry the pregnancy to term, what will you tell your doctor, who insists that you are carrying a terminally ill child who will die shortly after birth, and you are subjecting yourself to unnecessary risks and emotional heartache?

3. Your physician suggests that ending the pregnancy is parallel to turning off life support from terminally ill patients who are going to die very soon because keeping the person on life support is futile. He argues that your womb is the equivalent of a life support system for the baby and you are simply turning it off because the child will be born with a terminal illness. Do you agree with your doctor's reasoning? Why or why not?

Case 5.3: The Stem Cell Scientist

You have recently received a call from the pastor of your church. One of the members of the church is a prominent scientist who has been doing stem cell research for the past few years. He has been pursuing the research using stem cells from various nonembryonic sources but is being strongly encouraged by the National Institute of Health and his colleagues around the country to begin doing embryonic stem cell research. He sent a lengthy email to the pastor, which he forwarded to you, asking about the morality of stem cell research. The scientist is a Christian, seriously committed to his faith, and wants very much to do his research within biblical guidelines.

Questions for Discussion

1. How would you advise your scientist friend about doing research with stem cells harvested from human embryos?

2. Your scientist friend tells you that he is not the one harvesting the stem cells and thereby destroying the embryos. He is only using the stem cells in his research on a few specific diseases. How, if at all, might that make a difference in the advice you give him?

3. How would this discussion be different if the scientist was not committed to a Christian worldview? Would your advice be any different? Would the reasons you give be different?

Chapter 5 Notes

1. 410 U.S. 113 (1973).
2. 410 U.S. 179 (1973).
3. Ibid., 192–93.
4. 428 U.S. 52 (1977).
5. 109 S. Ct. 3040 (1989).
6. 112 S. Ct. 2791 (1992). For other cases in which limits to abortion were struck down, see *Akron v. Akron Center for Reproductive Health, Inc.* (462 U.S. 416 [1983]), *Thornburgh v. American College of Obstetricians and Gynecologists* (476 U.S. 747 [1986]), and *Ohio v. Akron Center for Reproductive Health* (497 U.S. 502 [1990]).
7. Such dominion involves the freedom to use creation for the benefit of people, but people were also given the responsibility for creation as God's stewards. This responsibility prevents people from exploiting the environment under the guise of dominion over it. See Genesis 1:28–29.
8. For more on this text, see Umberto Cassuto, *Exodus* (Jerusalem: Magnes, 1967), 275; and Gleason Archer, *Encyclopedia of Bible Difficulties* (Grand Rapids: Zondervan, 1982), 246–49.
9. I am indebted to Dr. Francis J. Beckwith for much of the following discussion. For further development of these arguments and the appropriate counterarguments, see his *Defending Life: A Moral and Legal Case against Abortion Choice* (New York: Cambridge University Press, 2007).
10. See, for example, the statements of Dr. Bernard Nathanson, the cofounder of the National Abortion Rights Action League. He has since changed his position and become a pro-life advocate. See his *Aborting America* (New York: Doubleday, 1978), 193.
11. John J. Davis, *Abortion and the Christian* (Phillipsburg, N.J.: Presbyterian and Reformed, 1984), 75.
12. Mary Calderone, "Illegal Abortion as a Public Health Problem," *American Journal of Public Health* 50 (1960): 948–54, cited in Francis J. Beckwith, *Politically Correct Death: Answering the Arguments for Abortion Rights* (Grand Rapids: Baker, 1994), 240. For further discussion of the statistics on illegal abortion, see the discussion in Beckwith, *Politically Correct Death*, 54–59.
13. See Beckwith, *Defending Life*.
14. The pro-life case against abortion focuses on the unborn having personhood from the moment of conception, and is widely considered by pro-life supporters as a conclusive argument against abortion. It is often the only argument offered, as opposed to the various pro-choice arguments. If the argument that the unborn has personhood from conception can be sustained, then abortion is killing an innocent person and is prima facie wrong, or wrong in most cases. One possible exception is the rare case in which the presence of the unborn threatens the physical life of the mother. In order to save the mother's life, abortion would be justifiable, because if the mother dies, the fetus almost always dies too. Another possible exception for abortion is in cases of rape or incest. Some would suggest that the circumstances of an unborn child's conception are irrelevant, and it is wrong to take its life. But others hold that

if a woman does not consent to sexual relations, then she cannot be held responsible for the pregnancy, and thus abortion is justifiable. Still others favor a compromise in the law. Maintaining that abortion is always immoral, they believe that a bill that restricts abortion except in cases of rape and incest has a better chance of becoming law.

15. This is a common view in the philosophical community and is expressed by Bonnie Steinbock in *Life before Birth: The Moral Status of Fetuses and Embryos* (New York: Oxford University Press, 1992).

16. The argument is stated like this in Richard Werner, "Abortion: The Moral Status of the Unborn," *Social Theory and Practice* 4 (Spring 1975): 202.

17. Judith Jarvis Thomson, "A Defense of Abortion," *Philosophy and Public Affairs* 1, no. 1 (Fall 1971).

Chapter 6

Reproductive Technologies

Imagine that you are sitting in your living room with Tom and Joan, two of your closest friends. They have been married for seven years and have been trying to have a baby for the last three years. They have tried all the "home remedies" for infertility that their friends have suggested, such as romantic getaways and ovulation predictor kits, however, none of them have worked. They have difficulty getting excited about their friends having children; in fact, every time another couple they know has a baby, they become more depressed about their own failure to have a child. They have stopped going to church on Mother's Day and Father's Day and other "family" type holidays, such as Thanksgiving and Christmas, because celebrations with families are painful reminders of their desire to have a family themselves. Infertility has shaken their respective senses of manhood and womanhood, because they have realized that a significant part of their identities as man and woman revolve around the ability to have a child.

You and your spouse have only been married for a short time and have not attempted to conceive a child yet, so their frank discussion of their infertility has caught you two a bit off guard. You had assumed that when people wanted to have a child, they were able to accomplish it in fairly short order. You wonder how Tom and Joan can have such trouble conceiving when they would clearly make great parents and so many unwed teenagers are having unwanted babies to whom they cannot be good parents. You feel the pain that Tom and Joan are experiencing and hope that you and your spouse do not have to go through what they have been through. Until they talked to you, you had no idea of the pain that infertility causes a couple.

Tom and Joan have just told you about their first visit to an infertility clinic in the area. The clinic specializes in infertility treatments that you have read about, such as in vitro fertilization. The clinic has presented Tom and Joan with quite an array of technological options, some very expensive that would require borrowing money, since their health insurance does not cover infertility. They are very confused about which option, if any, they should choose. They have been to their pastor, and he doesn't know very much about infertility treatments. He was married at a young age, and he and his wife had the first of their four children within the first year. Two of their children were "surprises." The pastor and his wife clearly had no difficulty conceiving, could not relate, and were not very helpful.

So Tom and Joan have come to you. They know that you are studying ethics at the present time, and they are hoping that you might have something helpful to suggest to them. They want to know which, if any, of the reproductive options available are morally acceptable, or whether adoption is the only alternative. They have Catholic friends who have told them that most of the clinic's options are not right, but they want your opinion. What would you tell them? What moral guidelines would you give them? How would your Christian worldview impact your advice?

Since the late 1970s (with the birth of the first "test-tube baby" in England in 1978), medicine has made some remarkable accomplishments in the field of reproductive technology. The term *reproductive technology* refers to various medical procedures that are designed to alleviate infertility, the inability of a couple to produce a child of their own. These procedures include technologies such as artificial insemination (also known as intrauterine insemination), in vitro fertilization, and surrogate motherhood. Until recently, adoption was the only viable way by which an infertile couple could have a child. Yet in adoption the child is not genetically related to either of the parents. The promise of these reproductive technologies is that they enable infertile couples to have a child to whom at least one of the parents is genetically related.

When successful, these technologies are the miracle of life for couples who have often spent years trying to have a child and have exhausted all other avenues for conceiving a child of their own. But many of these techniques raise major moral questions and can create thorny legal questions that must be resolved in court. Increasingly, judges are looking for direction in deciding these cases, since there is no precedent in the law on which to rely. Legislators are increasingly looking to ethics to help formulate policies to deal with some of these complexities before they arise.

These new technologies now make all sorts of interesting childbearing arrangements possible. Some of the more mainstream uses of reproductive technologies include the following:

- A woman and her husband, who cannot produce sperm, want to have a child. She is artificially inseminated with the sperm from an anonymous donor and conceives and bears a child.
- A couple in their early forties, married in their late thirties and now wanting to have children, are advised by their physician to secure an egg donor

due to the age of the woman's eggs and the increased probability of birth defects.

- A woman is able to produce eggs but is unable to carry a child to term. She and her husband "rent" the womb of another woman to gestate the embryo that will be formed by laboratory fertilization of the husband's sperm and the wife's egg.

Other uses of reproductive technologies that were once considered novel but are mainstream today include these:

- A lesbian couple desire to have a child. One of the women provides the egg. It is fertilized by donor sperm, and the embryo is then implanted in the uterus of her partner.
- Two homosexual males want to raise a child. They can either inseminate a surrogate, who both "donates" the eggs and carries the child to term, or they purchase eggs from a "donor" and have them fertilized in the lab and then implanted in a surrogate who will carry and give birth to the child.
- A single woman who no longer wants to wait for marriage to have a child goes to the local infertility clinic and is inseminated with donor sperm and has a child.

Some of the more novel uses of reproductive technologies include these:

- A couple wants to attempt to have a "designer child." They advertise for an egg donor who has the following characteristics: five feet ten inches tall or above, blond, blue-eyed, athletic, and scored above 1400 on her SAT exam. They are willing to pay up to $50,000 for a harvest of her eggs.
- A couple with three girls wants to "balance their family" with a boy. They can select for gender by sorting the husband's sperm and inseminating the wife with the sperm that will give them a high likelihood of producing a boy.
- A fifty-four-year-old woman who has reached menopause loses her only son in an automobile accident. She wants very much to have another child but cannot on her own. She purchases an egg from a donor, her husband's sperm fertilizes the egg in vitro, and her physician hormonally prepares her uterus for implantation.
- A young man in his midtwenties suffers a fatal head injury in an auto accident. After being pronounced brain-dead and before he is taken of life support, his wife requests to harvest his sperm so that she can "have his child." Surgeons procure his sperm in conjunction with the harvest of other organs obtained for donation.
- A single woman is diagnosed with breast cancer requiring chemotherapy, which normally shuts her fertility down permanently. Prior to beginning

treatment, she undergoes hormone treatments used in other infertility treatments to enable her to release as many eggs in a single cycle as possible. She then freezes the harvest of eggs and keeps them in storage until she is ready to have children.

These new reproductive technologies raise complicated issues, not only for the law, but also for morality. What is society to say about these technologies that in many cases redefine the family and turn traditional notions of reproduction upside down? In addition, what does the Bible teach about these new methods of procreation? Since many of these issues are not directly addressed in Scripture, in what way does the Bible speak to them? What principles touch on these methods? What does the biblical concept of the family and children have to say to these new reproductive technologies?

Overview of Technologies

A wide variety of technologies is available to infertile couples today that range from relatively inexpensive and minimally invasive procedures to very expensive and difficult ones. The following is a brief description of the primary reproductive technologies offered by most infertility clinics. These clinics offer detailed information on these procedures, their success rates, and their current costs on their websites.

1. *Intrauterine insemination* (IUI) is performed when the man's sperm is inferior or there is not enough of it. It is a relatively simple procedure in which sperm from the woman's husband is inserted into the woman's uterus artificially rather than through sexual intercourse. A catheter is used to place a number of washed sperm directly into the uterus. This is usually the first infertility treatment a couple will try because it is simple to accomplish, involves no pain for the woman, and is relatively inexpensive compared with other reproductive technologies. Today it is performed frequently in conjunction with the use of high-powered fertility drugs. This creates a better chance at conception — and also a higher risk of major multiple pregnancies (triplets or more).

2. A related procedure is called *donor insemination* (DI). Here the insemination is performed using the sperm of a donor, someone other than the woman's husband. The donor is usually anonymous, though with their consent, donors can be identified and connected with the children they father.

3. Women can also donate gametes, called *egg donation*. This is analogous to sperm donation but is more technologically difficult and expensive.

The donor woman is given hormonal stimulation so that she can donate multiple eggs. They are retrieved through minor surgery and given to the infertile couple. The normal use of donor eggs is to combine them with sperm in either gamete intrafallopian transfer or in vitro fertilization.

4. *Gamete intrafallopian transfer* (GIFT) is usually the next option for an infertile couple if intrauterine insemination fails. In this process the woman is given hormonal treatments that enable her to release multiple eggs in a single cycle. The eggs are removed by a minor surgical procedure. Once the eggs are extracted, the man's sperm is obtained through masturbation. The sperm are then treated and placed with the eggs in the woman's fallopian tubes. There the sperm and eggs are in close proximity, and the chances of conception taking place are much higher than in the couple's intercourse. Fertilization thus occurs inside the woman's body. The remaining eggs are fertilized by IVF.

5. *In vitro fertilization* (IVF) is similar to GIFT. The woman receives hormonal stimulation and releases as many eggs as possible. The husband's sperm are obtained through masturbation and placed in a petri dish with the eggs in the infertility clinic's lab in the hope that most, if not all, of the eggs will be successfully fertilized. Fertilization occurs in the lab, not within the body as with GIFT. The physician in the clinic will normally take up to four embryos (or fertilized eggs) and implant them in the woman's uterus, in the hope that one or more will successfully implant and the woman will become pregnant. A similar procedure to IVF is called *zygote intrafallopian transfer* (ZIFT), in which the embryos are implanted in the fallopian tubes rather than the uterus.

6. *Surrogate motherhood* arrangements are generally neither new nor sophisticated reproductive technologies. What is different about surrogacy agreements is the presence of brokers, contracts, and lawyers in the process of procreation. *Genetic surrogacy* occurs when the surrogate is inseminated with the sperm of the husband of the couple who contracts her. She conceives, carries, and gives birth to the child and turns over her rights to the child to the contracting couple. The surrogate has a genetic relationship to the child she carries.

   Gestational surrogacy occurs when the surrogate has no such genetic relationship to the child. She provides the womb but not the egg. The infertile couple has eggs removed, sperm obtained, and IVF performed. The embryos are implanted into the surrogate, and she carries and gives birth to the child and relinquishes all rights to the child. Either of these types of surrogacy arrangements can be done for a substantial fee—the normal practice, known as *commercial surrogacy*—or for no fee, which is rare. An arrangement without a fee is known as *altruistic surrogacy* and occurs when a close friend or family member functions as a surrogate solely out of a generous desire to impart "the gift of life."

7. *Intracytoplasmic sperm injection* (ICSI) is a more expensive and more reliable way to achieve pregnancy. The procedure essentially involves injecting a single sperm into an egg, using highly technological and specialized instruments. One concern about this procedure is that it might allow less than a fully healthy sperm to fertilize the egg. The healthier sperm are generally the ones that endure the arduous process of reaching the egg and fertilizing it. ICSI makes it easier for inferior sperm to reach the egg. This may result in a higher incidence of miscarriages, but at this point there are not enough data to determine whether this concern is valid.

Moral Parameters for Reproductive Technologies

People hold a wide spectrum of views regarding the morality of technologically assisted reproduction. Most in the infertility industry reflect the autonomy-based culture and hold that the end of achieving a family makes almost any technological

The Donor Sibling Registry

The Donor Sibling Registry (DSR) is a private, nonprofit vehicle to assist people who were conceived using donor eggs, sperm, or embryos in contacting their genetic "parents" and siblings. For many years gamete donation operated under anonymity, in which it was very difficult for children conceived in this way to make contact with those with whom they shared genetic ties. Both donors and recipients can register on the site and thus be available for mutually desired contact. The site claims to have facilitated the connection of over four thousand half siblings and/or donors. It may be that someone has many more half siblings than they thought, since their sperm donor may have donated multiple times. The registry also recommends sperm banks that are receptive to the needs of recipient families to contact their donors. Some countries have a national registry sponsored by the government, and others require that donors' identity be available for those recipients who want to seek them out. Predictably, in those areas, the number of donors has fallen off sharply. It seems apparent that anonymity is important to many donors, who will not donate without such assurances.*

*Information found at DonorSiblingRegistry.com.

option morally acceptable. By contrast, some are very restrictive in what is morally acceptable, such as the Roman Catholic Church, which prohibits virtually all technological assistance. Others have more moderate restrictions, such as limiting the use of technologies to those that use the genetic materials of husband and wife. Another way to put this is to compare the technological options to stops on a train route. Some insist that one ought not get on the technological train at all. Others argue that one need not get off the technological train anywhere on the line. Still others maintain that though boarding the technological train is acceptable, there are stops where morality requires that they get off the train.

In approaching this subject in general, we should be aware that the use of technology in creating families has changed the language with which the culture describes children and childbearing. For centuries, creating families has been called *procreation*, which refers to the way in which children are brought forth in partnership with God through the loving embrace of a husband and a wife. By contrast, today the culture more commonly refers to starting families as *reproduction*. This is a more product-oriented view of children and families and comes from the use of technology in producing children today. It is not clear that children are necessarily reduced to commodities or products as a result of using technological options to achieve pregnancy, but it is an interesting shift in how this process is described, and some do clearly suggest that children can be analogous to commodities, with traits and gender specifications of the parents met by using various technologies.[1]

Two fundamental questions are raised by all these creative technological methods of conceiving a child. The first is whether any artificial means of procreation should be used at all. If the answer to that question is no, the discussion of these technologies is essentially over. Infertile couples would thus have three options: (1) they could continue to try to achieve conception naturally; (2) they could opt for adoption; or (3) they could accept childlessness as their calling.

If the answer to this first question is yes, that raises the second question, which presents an even more complicated issue: Is it morally legitimate to use third-party contributors (of eggs, sperm, or womb) in the process of procreation? In other words, are the technologies that require sperm, egg, or womb donors morally legitimate? Or are the only legitimate technologies the ones that use the genetic materials of husband and wife?

Let's back up a bit from our fundamental questions and think about the general virtues and principles that we need to take into account in order to properly reflect on the myriad of procreative possibilities these new technologies make available. Of course, no technological ways to procreate children existed when the Bible was written. Although surrogate motherhood was practiced throughout the ancient world, it would have been difficult for Scripture to directly address technologies that did not exist until the present day. However, more general principles and virtues of the Bible can and do apply to these technologies. It is not always easy to determine how these apply, and there may be room for legitimate disagreement among people committed to biblical authority. Perhaps a helpful way to view the contribution of the Bible in this area is to view the various key biblical principles and virtues as "fence posts" that set the parameters for procreation. Any technology that is outside the parameters is problematic, and inside the "fence" of biblical principles and virtues there is freedom for couples to make their own decisions.

In establishing our parameters, we need to begin with the purpose of technology from a theological perspective. For the most part, technological innovations that clearly improve the lot of humankind and help alleviate the effects of the entrance of sin into the world are considered a part of God's common grace, or his general blessings on creation. That is, *medical technology is God's good gift to human beings.* That is our first fence post that helps set parameters for reproductive technologies. As a part of creation and the mandate given to exercise dominion over the earth (Gen. 1:26), God also gave humankind the ability to discover and apply all kinds of technological innovations. This would be particularly true of technologies that enable the human race to fulfill its mandate to multiply and fill the earth. It does not follow, of course, that humankind has the responsibility to use every bit of technology that has been discovered; all of them must be assessed individually. But in general, God's wisdom is embedded in the world, and through general revelation he has given human beings the ability to uncover what he has revealed in his world (Prov. 8:22–36). It would appear that many of the reproductive technologies in question fit under the heading of general revelation and common grace; whether they should be used depends on whether such a use violates a more specific biblical principle or virtue. Or to put it differently, if the use of a specific technology steps outside the parameters at some other point, then that would be morally problematic. Infertility is clearly one of the effects of the *general* entrance of sin into the world, analogous to most other diseases that render a part of the body or system nonfunctional. That is not to say that infertility is the result of a specific sin that the couple could identify. There is no biblical reason why medical technology in general cannot be used to treat infertility or a disease of the reproductive system in the same way that medical technology treats malfunctions of the heart, liver, kidneys, or other organ system. Thus, to answer our first fundamental question, we must look to the purpose of medical technology. What we find in the Bible is a general optimism about medical technology as part of the mandate to establish dominion over the earth. There does not seem to be any good reason to suggest that an infertile couple cannot board the technological train at all. That does not mean that all stops are morally acceptable, only that some technological options are morally appropriate.

One significant challenge to this first fence post is the official Roman Catholic Church teaching on procreation. Catholic teaching accepts the high place for medical technology but not its application to reproductive technologies. The Catholic tradition has emphasized the continuity between normal sexual relations in marriage, procreation, and parenthood. There is a God-designed, natural continuity between sex in marriage, conception, pregnancy, childbirth, and parenthood. Every sexual encounter has the potential for conception, and every conception has the potential for childbirth and parenthood. This is why sex is reserved for marriage and why Catholic tradition makes little room for any reproductive technology that would interfere with a natural process that is the result of creation.

The 1987 official Catholic statement on reproductive technology puts it this way: "The procreation of a new person, whereby the man and the woman collaborate with the power of the Creator, must be the fruit and the sign of the mutual self-giving of *the spouses*, of their love and fidelity ..., in marriage and in its indissoluble unity [is] the only setting worthy of truly responsible procreation."[2] In other words, only in marriage is it morally legitimate to procreate children.

A further statement clarifies the unity of sex and procreation, thereby ruling out most technological interventions for infertile couples: "But from a moral point of view procreation is deprived of its proper perfection when it is not desired as the fruit of the conjugal act, that is to say, of the specific act of the spouses' union ..., the procreation of a human person [is to be] brought about as the fruit of the conjugal act specific to the love between persons."[3]

In other words, in Catholic teaching, there is a unity between sexual relations and procreation. Procreation cannot occur apart from marital sexual intercourse, and every conjugal act in marriage must be open to procreation as the natural result of God's creation design.[4] To put it another way, every time a couple has sex in marriage, the unitive, that is, the "one-flesh" aspect and the procreative aspect, or openness to procreation, must be present. That is why in Catholic teaching, technology cannot replace normal sex in the process of procreation. One cannot have procreation without sex and sex without openness to procreation.

Catholic teaching does not rule out all reproductive technologies but makes an important distinction between a technology that *assists* normal intercourse and one that *replaces* it in the process of trying to conceive a child. Anything that assists sex is considered a part of God's wisdom that can be utilized in reproduction, consistent with its acceptance of medical technology in general. The important aspect is that the unity of sex and procreation is maintained. More specifically, this means that conception must occur according to its intended design. The movement of genetic materials may be assisted, but use of technology may not replace normal intercourse. For example, fertilization must always occur inside the body, and masturbation may not be used as a substitute for sexual relations in order to collect sperm outside the body to be inserted into the womb.

In assessing the Catholic view, it seems ironic and arbitrary that Catholic teaching would view medical technology in general as part of God's blessing, consistent with the notion of general revelation, but significantly restrict its use in the area of procreation. As mentioned above, there does not seem to be any reason not to view infertility in a way analogous to other diseases and organ failures. If infertility is indeed a result of the general entrance of sin into the world, then it is not clear why medical technology cannot be applied to infertility. Just because reproductive technologies enable couples to create a child, in contrast to other medical technologies, is no reason per se to reject some technological assistance in procreation.

Further, it is not clear that the Bible requires that the unitive, or one-flesh, aspect of sex and the procreative aspect always go together. For example, the Song of Songs celebrates the beauty and intimacy of sex in marriage, and appears to treat the unitive element of sex as an all-sufficient end in itself. And in the New Testament, the apostle Paul urges married couples to devote themselves to regular sex so that they will not be tempted to look outside the marriage relationship for the legitimate end of sexual pleasure to be satisfied (1 Cor. 7:1–5). It seems that Paul is treating the unitive element of sex as a sufficient end such that couples should be sure to provide it for each other regularly.

The second and equally foundational fence post in the Bible is that *procreation was designed to occur within the context of a stable, heterosexual, permanent, monogamous marriage.* Children are to be born into families constituted of a husband and wife who love each other, live together, and commit themselves to care properly for their children. Continuity between procreation and parenthood is considered the norm for family life.

In Genesis 1–2, God commanded that Adam and Eve "be fruitful and multiply" (Gen. 1:28 KJV). This command is set in the context of the broad, panoramic account of creation in Genesis 1. However, the complementary account of creation in Genesis 2 contains helpful details that enable us to "read between the lines" in the overarching summary account of Genesis 1.[5]

Genesis 2 speaks not only of the creation of human beings but, more significantly, of their relation to each other and to God. In Genesis 1:26, God declares

Genesis 1:26–27	(Genesis 2:4–25)	Genesis 1:28
Creation of humankind	Details on creation of woman/marriage	"Be fruitful/multiply"

his intention to create human beings, of male and female genders. Genesis 2:4–25 follows chronologically and with additional details. Among those details are the distinction between male and female, the male's aloneness and desire for a mate, and the subsequent creation of the woman. After she is formed and presented to the man, God instructs them about their life together.

In Genesis 2:24, God commands that men and women are to leave their families of origin, be united to each other, and experience unity in all aspects—emotional, spiritual, and physical. It is here that God formally institutes marriage and Adam and Eve become the first officially married couple in creation. The way in which Genesis 2:24 is quoted in the New Testament suggests that whenever it is used, the verse refers to married couples (Matt. 19:5; Eph. 5:31).[6]

In addition, the term "leave" is used to suggest that, against common practice in the ancient world, a man and woman who intend to be married actually separate themselves from their families of origin and form their own family unit. Further, the concept of "one flesh" involves a sexual union that the rest of Scripture makes clear is reserved for married couples. This is underscored by the use of "bone" and "flesh" in Genesis 2:23, the terms used by Adam to describe the woman. The use of these two terms in conjunction normally refers to family relationships (Gen. 29:14; Judg. 9:2; 2 Sam. 5:1; 19:12–13; 1 Chron. 11:1). It would appear that the use of the terms in Genesis 2:23, when Adam declares that Eve is his bone and flesh, suggests that the normative family is in view in the creation account.

If we place the more specific account of the creation of male and female from Genesis 2 back into the broad overview found in Genesis 1, the command to procreate ("be fruitful and multiply," v. 28 KJV) is given to Adam and Eve in the context of their leaving, cleaving, and becoming one flesh (Gen. 2:24). That is, it is within the context of their marriage. Although it is true that Adam and Eve are representative of the male and female of the species, it is clear that this creation model sets the pattern for permanent, monogamous, heterosexual marriage, and procreation within that context as the norm. Not every male and female must be joined in marriage (1 Cor. 7:25–28), but marriage is only to occur between males and females, and procreation is to occur within those confines.

What makes this second parameter quite complicated is the way this creation model is followed in the rest of the Old Testament. God appears to have allowed a number of exceptions to the general model set up at creation. For example, he allowed divorce, which breaks the permanent aspect of marriage suggested by the notion of cleaving to each other. In addition, surrogate motherhood is used by two of the patriarchs, Abraham in Genesis 16—which was disastrous—and by Jacob in Genesis 30—which is treated in a more morally neutral way. Further, polygamy was allowed for reasons that are not entirely clear.[7] God allowed these exceptions to the general rule even though they were deviations from the creation norm. Of course, simply because they occurred historically does not mean that they can occur today. But the point of mentioning them is to indicate that God did allow exceptions to the creation norm. If so, then might other exceptions, such as third-party contributors to procreation, be similarly allowed?

In the New Testament the creation norm carries great weight. This underscores the fact that things like divorce, surrogacy, and polygamy were allowed but never sanctioned and never accepted as the best option. In fact, polygamy comes to be explicitly prohibited in the New Testament. In general, when the New Testament writers appeal to the model set up by God at creation, they consider it to carry considerable weight. For example, when Paul argues against homosexuality in Romans 1, he is appealing primarily to God's creation design for sexuality. In addition, when Paul addresses the roles of women in the church, he considers his appeal to Genesis 1–2 sufficient to end the discussion (1 Tim. 2:12–15). This is also the way in which Jesus treats the creation model when he addresses the subject of divorce (Matt. 19:1–9). This suggests that the creation norm carries great weight. Simply pointing out exceptions to the general rule does not nullify the importance of the creation norm. The weight of biblical teaching suggests that third-party contributors are not

Refusing Infertility Treatments to Single Women

In a case still moving through California courts, two San Diego obstetricians are being sued for refusing to administer intrauterine insemination for a single woman. Dr. Christine Brody and Dr. Douglas Fenton of the North Coast Women's Care clinic refused IUI for their patient Guadalupe Benitez for religious reasons and referred her to another clinic, where she successfully conceived and gave birth to her three children. It has since come out that she is a lesbian, and her cause has been taken up by a variety of gay/lesbian/transgender organizations, namely Lambda Legal, which represents Benitez in her lawsuit. The physicians in the case insist that Benitez's sexual orientation had nothing to do with their refusal of treatment. Rather, it was the fact that she is unmarried. And both Benitez and her partner testified in the initial trial that the physicians were clear up front with them that the issue was that they were unmarried, not that they were lesbian. The sexual orientation of the couple does seem to obscure the central issue in this case — whether the physicians have the right to refuse IUI and, by extension, other infertility services to unmarried individuals, regardless of their sexual orientation. The lower court ruled in favor of the physicians, whose religious freedom was upheld. But Lambda Legal has appealed to the California Supreme Court.*

*William Otis, "Another Type of Conscientious Objector," *Orange County Register*, June 30, 2007.

the norm for procreation. Scripture looks skeptically on any reproductive intervention that goes outside the married couple for genetic material. That would mean that technologies such as donor insemination, egg donation, and surrogate motherhood raise troubling issues and come very close to falling outside the parameters. But if pressed, the Bible does not appear to be sufficiently clear to prohibit all third-party contributors in every case. Technologies that utilize the gametes of a married couple, such as gamete intrafallopian transfer, in vitro fertilization, and intrauterine insemination are generally morally acceptable and clearly fall within the second parameter. Prohibiting third-party contributors would be a prima facie moral rule. Options that would appear to fall more clearly outside of this parameter would be bringing children into "single mother by choice" families or gay/lesbian families.

A third clear fence post is *the moral status of the unborn*, established in chapter 5. If it is clear that from conception forward a full person exists, then fetuses and embryos must be protected in any infertility procedure. This means that any technology that involves discarding embryos or terminating pregnancies falls outside the parameters the Bible has set up. However, it is not clear that freezing embryos per se is outside the fence, particularly if they are successfully thawed, which most often is the case. The dignity of the unborn must be safeguarded.

A fourth parameter is the notion of *adoption as a legitimate rescue operation*, fulfilling the biblical virtue of compassion for the most vulnerable. Adoption is the figure of speech used repeatedly in the Bible to describe the believer's relationship to God (Eph. 1:5); and the virtue that indicates that a person's faith is genuine is a willingness to care for widows and *orphans*, figurative of the most vulnerable in the society (James 1:27). Any view of procreation that downplays adoption as an alternative or even rules it out would appear to fall outside the biblical parameters. This would also include new ways of adopting children, such as adopting embryos that are left over from in vitro fertilization.

Additional parameters that help put boundaries around the use of reproductive technology include the virtue of *trust in God's sovereignty*. As applied to the desire of infertile couples to have a child, this fence post is critical and can be applied to all reproductive technologies, regardless of where the genetic materials come from. That is, dependence on any technological option can undermine a couple's trust in God's sovereignty if it is motivated by desperation or becomes an obsession for the couple. An additional virtue that comes out of this trust in God is that of contentment, as difficult as that is for infertile couples to hear. But the Bible is clear that we are to be content regardless of our station in life (1 Cor. 7:17–28). This does not mean that couples are to accept their infertility passively nor that they are prohibited from using any technological means. Rather, it suggests that use of any reproductive technology could fall outside the parameters if its use is motivated by desperation.

The way the Bible views children is an important fence post that helps establish the parameters for procreation. Throughout the Bible *children are viewed as a gift from God* (Ps. 127:3–5) to be received open handedly and without specifications. The virtue of gratitude naturally accompanies this important truth about children and suggests that specifying gender or choosing traits of children are troublingly close to falling outside the biblical boundaries.

Moral Issues in IUI, GIFT, and IVF

Just because it is clear that technologies that use the genetic material of husband and wife are acceptable, that does not mean that every use of these technologies is morally appropriate. The standard of practice in infertility clinics for some of these procedures raises troubling moral problems, some of which can be managed better than others.

Intrauterine insemination using the husband's sperm (sometimes called *artificial insemination by husband* or *AIH*) would not appear at first glance to present any difficult moral issues. If a simple insemination occurs, that would be true. Even for Catholic teaching, this is not problematic if sperm is obtained through normal sex instead of masturbation. However, IUI is increasingly being done in conjunction with multiple-ovulation drugs that are used with GIFT and IVF. That creates a risk of the woman becoming pregnant with major multiples. In the average case, eight to ten eggs are hyperstimulated to be released in a given cycle, but with IUI done in this way, the eggs are not harvested but left in the womb to be fertilized. With GIFT and IVF one can control the number of embryos in the womb. But that is not the case with IUI when done with potent fertility drugs. In that case the woman runs the risk of having to contemplate selective termination of some of the pregnancies, thereby moving outside the parameters set out above. Since the unborn are persons, reducing the number of pregnancies is the moral and actual equivalent of abortion, which is ending the life of an innocent person. Couples who put themselves in this position risk very difficult decisions, and to avoid such a scenario, IUI should be performed without these strong fertility drugs.

Gamete intrafallopian transfer similarly presents no inherent moral dilemmas at first glance. No third party is necessarily introduced into the procreative picture, though it can be done with donor gametes. As with IUI, if sperm is obtained through normal sex, GIFT can even be done consistently with official Catholic teaching. The moral difficulties with GIFT lie in its connection with IVF. After the initial procedure, in which there are likely leftover unused eggs, those eggs are normally fertilized in vitro and held in storage in case the initial GIFT procedure does not produce a pregnancy. If that is the case, the remaining embryos are thawed and implanted, thus avoiding substantial cost to start the process over again. But if the initial procedure succeeds, the remaining embryos can become "leftover" and unneeded.

In vitro fertilization simply means fertilization "in glass," as in the glass container of a test tube or petri dish used in a laboratory. Because the procedure is so expensive, all of the eggs that are harvested are fertilized in the lab. This is done so that if none of the fertilized embryos are successfully implanted, a second round of implantation of the embryos in storage can occur without much additional cost or lost time, since to harvest eggs again would involve a substantial financial cost. Normally, but not always, three embryos maximum are implanted in the woman's uterus. If more than one embryo does successfully implant, the couple may end up with more children than they originally intended. Twins and even triplets are not uncommon for couples who use IVF. In rarer cases more than three embryos are implanted, which may result in major multiple pregnancies.

In order to keep the procedure as cost effective as possible and to maximize the possibilities of a successful implantation, embryos are frozen in storage to be used later if the first attempt fails. Thus, if the first round of implanted embryos results in a sufficient number of children for the couple, their childbearing days may be over, and they may have a number of embryos left over in storage that they do not intend to use. Embryos are easily kept in storage for at least five years, and the longest storage time on record that produced a successful birth is thirteen years. In some cases, more embryos successfully "take" implant than the woman is able to carry without endangering her health and at times even endangering her life. It may also be that she simply becomes pregnant with more children than she and her husband desire to raise.

What to do with frozen embryos if they are not needed raises significant questions about the moral status of the embryo.[8] Most people recognize that with its potential to become a fully developed baby, the embryo cannot be seen as morally neutral and regarded as a clump of cells. Thus the alternatives would appear to be to keep the embryos in storage indefinitely (at a nominal cost), to destroy them, to allow the couple to donate them to another infertile couple, or to use them for experimental purposes. It is possible to freeze a woman's eggs once harvested, but it has been difficult to thaw them successfully. However, the technology is improving, and more clinics are offering egg freezing for women who wish to delay childbearing, and egg freezing may become more routine for couples who desire to avoid having leftover embryos. Once this becomes widely offered, it could render the problem of leftover embryos a moot point.

For those who view personhood as beginning at conception, the disposition of these embryos presents a complex moral dilemma. Of course, if one views personhood as acquired at some point later during pregnancy, then embryos are indeed just cells and may be disposed of with no moral problem. But if the right to life is acquired at conception, then destroying embryos or using them in experiments is very problematic. Destroying embryos outside the body would appear to be the moral equivalent of abortion, as would donating embryos for research or stem cell harvest, since most experimentation on the embryo and harvest of its stem cells would result in its destruction. Storing the embryos indefinitely only postpones dealing with this issue. Allowing the embryos to die a natural death when they could easily be spared is morally no different from abortion. That leaves donation of the embryos to another infertile couple or implantation of the embryos by the couple themselves as the only viable alternatives. Clearly the couple implanting the embryos themselves is the best of the options, since it maintains the continuity between procreation and parenting. But donation of embryos is acceptable too. Some may see this as problematic since it involves a separation of the biological and social roles of parenthood that many believe to be a significant part of the biblical teaching on the family.

However, it is possible to view embryo donation in a way that is analogous to adoption, as a *preimplantation adoption* in which the couple who contributed the genetic materials to form the embryo consent to give up parental rights to their child after implantation instead of after the child's birth. Though this is emotionally difficult, particularly for multiple embryos, the continuity between gestation and parenting that the "adoptive" couple would have may make it better for the child than traditional adoption, in which the child would be taken from its mother at birth. It would seem that a guiding principle for IVF is that all embryos created in the lab deserve an opportunity to be implanted, either with the couple who "created" them or in adoption by another infertile couple.

A second problem arises not from the failures of implantation, but from its successes. Occasionally a woman is left with more developing embryos than she can carry to term without risk to her health and life, or with more children than she and her husband are willing to raise. In these cases the woman, her husband, and her doctor have very difficult decisions to make. The doctor will normally recommend what is called *selective termination* of one or more of the developing embryos. This is done at times for the sake of convenience, when the couple becomes pregnant with more children than they are willing to raise. At other times physicians will recommend this out of a genuine concern for the well-being of the unborn children. Though there are many anecdotal cases of multiple pregnancies turning out well, in many instances when a woman is pregnant with four or more unborn children, she and the fetuses are at risk for a variety of complications. In these cases the doctor is faced with the decision of which one(s) to terminate and how to make that decision. If the mother's life is clearly at significant risk in carrying all the fetuses to term, then it would appear justified to terminate one or more of the fetuses in order to save the life of the mother. This is analogous to cases in which abortion is justifiable when carrying the pregnancy to term would put the mother's life at grave risk. Of course, those who do not hold to such a high view of the sanctity of unborn life would see no problem with the woman terminating the pregnancy for most reasons, consistent with the law of the land under *Roe v. Wade.* But even for people who do not fit into the pro-life camp, the agony of making such painful decisions must surely be considered prior to utilizing IVF to alleviate infertility.

The general principles that should guide a couple's use of GIFT and IVF are that all embryos created in the lab should have a reasonable chance at maturing. That is, they should all be implanted, either in the woman who initiated the procedure or in an adoptive mother. Embryo adoption agencies are springing up across the United States for the purpose of facilitating donation of embryos rather than seeing them destroyed, as is the case normally when couples are finished with infertility treatments.[9] No embryos should be discarded or be subject to experimentation. Nor should they be allowed to die natural deaths in the storage section of the lab. The couple should inform the clinic that they want to minimize the number of leftover embryos. That will involve limiting the number of eggs fertilized. This will likely mean only one attempt at conception, rather than keeping embryos in storage for future attempts. If every egg could be fertilized successfully in the lab, then the couple could simply tell the clinic that they wanted three eggs fertilized, possibly four, and that's all. They would be fertilized and implanted, and none would be left over. Of course, if the couple did not become pregnant, they would have to start the procedure over again, greatly increasing the cost. But one never knows in advance how many eggs will successfully fertilize, which makes the procedure tricky for the couple. A couple could allow for some eggs that will not fertilize, and if there are leftover embryos, they will need to be committed to making sure that all of the embryos have an opportunity for implantation. Further, the couple should not implant more embryos than can be safely carried. Nor should they implant more embryos than children they wish to raise, should all of the implanted embryos turn into pregnancies. Under no circumstances should a couple authorize implantation of embryos that might make selective termination an option.

Moral Issues with Surrogate Motherhood

Undoubtedly, surrogate motherhood is the most controversial of the new reproductive technologies. In the majority of cases, the surrogate bears the child for the contracting couple, willingly gives up the child she has borne to the couple, and accepts her role with no difficulty. In those cases the contracting couple views the surrogate with extreme gratitude for helping their dream of having a child come true. The surrogate also feels a great deal of satisfaction, since she has in effect given a "gift of life" to a previously infertile couple. But in some cases that have been well publicized in the media, the surrogate wants to keep the child she has borne and fights the couple who contracted her for custody.

The Old Testament records two incidents of surrogacy (Gen. 16:1–6; 30:1–13), and it appears that use of a surrogate to circumvent female infertility was an accepted practice in the ancient Near East.[10]

Today surrogacy does not normally involve any sophisticated medical technology. Normally conception is accomplished either by artificial insemination for a genetic surrogacy or by IVF for gestational surrogacy. What made surrogacy novel at its inception was the legal context in which reproduction occurred. The presence of lawyers, detailed contracts, and even the idea of legal representation for the yet-to-be-born child were the new elements in the previously very private area of procreation.

The Morality of Surrogate Motherhood

Significant debate has taken place not only over the legality of surrogacy, but also over whether it is a morally justifiable way to procreate a child. Viewed from the

The Baby M Surrogacy Case

In a made for TV miniseries scenario, William Stern had a special interest in fathering a child to whom he was genetically related, since he was the only living member of his bloodline, most of his relatives having been killed during the Holocaust. His wife, Elizabeth, had a mild case of multiple sclerosis and believed that pregnancy would be a significant health risk.

The Infertility Center of New York matched the Sterns with Mary Beth Whitehead, who would act as a surrogate mother. She was a woman of moderate means with two children already. Regretting her decision to give up the child to the Sterns, Whitehead sued for custody after the child was born. The Sterns allowed her to take the child for a week, after which time she fled the area with the child. The police later recovered the child by force in Florida and returned the child to the Sterns.

The New Jersey Supreme Court ruled that surrogacy contracts were baby selling, and that genetic parents have a fundamental right to participate in raising their children. Whitehead did not receive custody, however, because the justices held that the child's best interests would be served by custody going to the Sterns.

perspective of the parameters for procreation that come from the Bible, surrogacy can be viewed as analogous to other third-party contributor situations, with some other complicating features. Thus there is a prima facie principle against third-party contributors that surrogacy would appear to violate. In terms of public policy, the case both for and against surrogacy is made on broader, nontheologically oriented grounds. This is the aspect of reproductive technologies in which the law has been most involved.

Much of the discussion of surrogacy is set in the broader context of a long tradition in the Western world of procreative liberty that gives couples the freedom to make their own decisions about childbearing and child rearing. The family has historically been a place in which the right to privacy has reigned, and thus, for the most part, family decisions have been beyond the scrutiny and intervention of the government. Laws have been crafted to ensure as much freedom as possible for parents to make choices concerning their children, and the Supreme Court has upheld procreative liberty in a variety of cases.[11] However, simply because the law may allow for procreative arrangements such as surrogacy, it does not follow that surrogacy is a morally justifiable way to conceive a child.

Is Surrogacy Baby Selling?

Both commercial and altruistic surrogacy raise moral issues, though some of the concerns do not apply to altruistic surrogacy. The most serious objection to commercial surrogacy is that it reduces children to objects of barter by putting a price on them. Opponents of surrogacy insist that any attempt to deny or minimize the charge of baby selling fails, and thus surrogacy involves the sale of children.

Surrogacy violates the Thirteenth Amendment to the Constitution, which outlawed slavery, because it constitutes the sale of human beings. It violates commonly and widely held moral principles that safeguard human rights and the dignity of human persons, namely, that human beings are made in God's image and are his unique creations. Persons are not fundamentally things that can be purchased and sold for a price. The fact that proponents of surrogacy try so hard to get around the charge of baby selling indicates their acceptance of these underlying moral principles as well.

Surrogacy proponents are sensitive to the charge that paying a surrogate a large amount of money for bearing a child for another couple is baby selling. They insist that the fee only pays for *gestational services rendered* and does not constitute the sale of a child. They argue that it is only fair for a woman to be compensated for the time, risk, and sacrifice that pregnancy entails. Just as it is legitimate to pay surrogate *child rearers* in a day-care setting, proponents insist that it should be legitimate to pay surrogate *childbearers*.

However, it would appear that the fee paid to the surrogate, which is beyond her expenses, is for much more than childbirth services rendered. What really counts in a surrogacy arrangement is not only the successful birth of the child, but also the transfer of parental rights from the surrogate to the infertile wife. She must adopt the child for the "deal to be done." In surrogacy cases in which the surrogate supplies both the egg and the womb, she is the legal mother of the child.[12] In cases of gestational surrogacy, in which motherhood is up for debate, the surrogate is not recognized as the legal mother, and the legal charge of baby selling would not apply.

To be consistent, if the fee paid to the surrogate is only for gestational services rendered, the surrogate would be paid the same amount whether or not she turned over the child to the contracting couple. If the fee only pays for childbirth services, it is hard to see how a couple could take the surrogate to court to get the child, since the surrogate would have fulfilled her part of the contract once the child was born. In addition, if she miscarried at some point in the pregnancy, her fee should be prorated over the number of months that she performed a gestational service. But this would make surrogacy very risky for the contracting couple. There would be no guarantee that the couple would get a baby under a "fee for the gestational services" scheme. This would likely be a deterrent to couples wanting to utilize surrogacy.

Proponents of surrogacy will answer the baby-selling charge by contending that the natural father cannot buy back what is already his. But the child is not *all* his. At best, he can only claim the equivalent of joint tenancy in a piece of property, in which he "buys out" his partner, the surrogate, which is still baby selling.[13]

Thus the debate is not whether human beings should be bought and sold; rather, it is over whether commercial surrogacy constitutes such a sale of children. If it does, most would agree that the case against surrogacy is quite strong. As the New Jersey Supreme Court put it in the Baby M case, "There are, in a civilized society, some things that money cannot buy.... There are values ... that society deems more important than granting to wealth whatever it can buy, be it labor, love or life."[14]

Another reply to the charge of baby selling is to admit that children are being sold but that the circumstances are so different from black-market adoptions that it does no harm to exchange parental rights for money. The laws that prevent payment to birth mothers were designed to prevent black-market adoptions, in which birth mothers were exploited based on their financial need and in which the well-being of the children was not considered the highest priority. Surrogacy is a completely different situation. Here the natural father is also the adopting father, and surrogacy results from a planned and wanted pregnancy as opposed to an unwanted pregnancy. Thus the child is not going to a stranger but to a genetic relative, and the surrogate is not coerced into making a decision she will later regret.

Opponents of surrogacy respond that the differences between black-market adoptions and surrogacy are overstated. For example, there is little screening of the contracting couple done in order to ensure that they are fit parents and that the best interests of the child are being maintained. In addition, the element of coercion is not entirely absent from a surrogacy arrangement since it is quite possible that the surrogate could be coerced by the contract into giving up a child that she may end up wanting to keep. Further, given the desperation of the contracting couple to have a child, since they usually do not resort to surrogacy until all other means have been exhausted, it leaves them open to exploitation by the surrogacy brokers. Thus, to say that the environment surrounding surrogacy is free from coercion is not accurate.

Even if the child is treated well and the arrangement comes off without coercion, the problem of baby selling remains. By analogy, during the Civil War era, even if there were cases in which slaves were treated well and considered like family members, the fact remained that they had been bought and sold and had become objects of barter. The circumstance in which such barter takes place is irrelevant according to opponents of surrogacy.

Potential for Exploitation

A second area of concern about surrogacy is the potential for commercial surrogacy to become exploitative. The combination of desperate infertile couples, low-income surrogates, and surrogacy brokers motivated by profit raises the prospect that both surrogates and contracting couples can be exploited. But statistics on hundreds of surrogacy arrangements to date indicate that this potential for exploitation has not yet materialized. Most surrogates are women of average means,[15] not destitute but also clearly motivated by the money. The fee alone should not be considered exploitation, but an inducement to do something that the surrogate would not otherwise do. Money functions as an inducement to do many things that people would not normally do without being exploitative.

However, this does not mean that the potential for exploitation should not be taken seriously. Should surrogacy become more socially acceptable and states pass laws making it legal, it is not difficult to imagine the various ways in which surrogacy brokers would attempt to hold costs down in order to maximize their profit. Some people have suggested that those with financial need actually make the best candidates for surrogates because they are the least inclined to keep the child produced by the arrangement.[16] For example, one surrogacy broker suggested that the surrogates from other countries would only receive the basic necessities and travel expenses for their services. Revealing a strong bias toward exploitation of the surrogates, he said, "Often they [the potential surrogates] are looking for a survival situation — something to do to pay for the rent and food. They come from underdeveloped countries where food is a serious issue." But he also added that they make good candidates for surrogacy. "They know how to take care of children ..., it's obviously a perfect match."[17] He further speculated that perhaps one-tenth of the normal fee could be paid these women, and it would not even matter if they had some other health problems, as long as they had an adequate diet and no problems that would affect the developing child.[18] It is not difficult to see the potential for exploitation of poor women in desperate circumstances, a potential that may come about as surrogacy is *outsourced* to other parts of the world.

Turning a Vice into a Virtue?

One of the most serious objections to surrogacy applies to both commercial and altruistic surrogacy. In screening women to select the most ideal surrogates, one looks for the woman's ability to easily give up the child she is carrying. Normally the less attached the woman is to the child, the easier it is to complete the arrangement. But this is hardly an ideal setting for a pregnancy. Surrogacy sanctions female detachment from the child in the womb, a situation that one would never want in any other pregnancy. Thus surrogacy actually turns a vice, the ability to detach from the child in utero, into a virtue. Should surrogacy be widely practiced, bioethicist Daniel Callahan of the Hastings Center describes what one of the results would be. "We will be forced to cultivate the services of women with the hardly desirable trait of being willing to gestate and then give up their own

Outsourcing Surrogacy

Following the trend of looking overseas in order to attain services at lower costs, couples contemplating surrogacy are more frequently looking to outsource that service to India, employing very poor women for a fraction of the cost of a surrogate in the United States. An Indian surrogate costs around $6,000 to $10,000 compared with the average arrangement in the United States costing roughly $40,000 to $50,000. These desperately poor women make approximately ten to fifteen years' income in one surrogacy contract, often enabling them to buy houses for their families that they would never be able to buy otherwise. This is one of a number of aspects of what is coming to be called "reproductive tourism," in which infertile couples come to other parts of the world in search of donor eggs and rental wombs. Some countries, such as France, have outlawed commercial surrogacy, insisting that the womb is not something for rent or sale to the highest bidder. Other countries allow it virtually unregulated and see it as a valuable market transaction — the couples want the babies and the surrogates need the money.*

*Judith Warner, "Outsourcing Wombs," *New York Times*, January 3, 2008; Anuj Chopra, "Childless Couples Look to India for Surrogate Mothers," *Christian Science Monitor*, April 3, 2006.

children, especially if paid enough to do so.... There would still be the need to find women with the capacity to dissociate and distance themselves from their own child. This is not a psychological trait we should want to foster, even in the name of altruism."[19]

The Role of the Contract

Another serious problem with commercial surrogacy might also apply to altruistic surrogacy. In most surrogacy contracts, whether for a fee or not, the surrogate agrees to relinquish any parental rights to the child she is carrying to the couple who contracted her services. Should she have second thoughts and desire to keep the child, under the contract she would be forced to give up her child. Of course, this assumes the traditional definition of a mother, the woman who gives birth to the child. It is a new phenomenon to have one woman be the genetic contributor and a different woman be the one who carries the child. In some cases of surrogacy, the surrogate provides both the genetic material and the womb. Thus by any definition she is the mother of the child. To force her to give up her child under the terms of a surrogacy contract violates her fundamental right to associate with and raise her child.[20]

This does not mean that the surrogate has exclusive right to the child. That must be shared with the natural father, similar to a custody arrangement in a divorce proceeding. But the right of one parent (the natural father) to associate with his child cannot be enforced at the expense of the right of the other (the surrogate). The problem with allowing the surrogate to keep the child is that it substantially increases the risk to the contracting couple. They might go through the entire process and end up with shared custody of a child that they initially thought was to be all theirs. To many people that doesn't seem fair. But to others it is just as unfair to take a child away from his or her mother simply because of the terms of a contract. Whether this argument applies to gestational surrogacy is open to debate and turns on how one defines the mother in those arrangements.[21]

Defining Motherhood

How one defines the mother in surrogate arrangements is a critical consideration. According to the law established by court precedent, genetic surrogates are recognized legally as the mother of the children they bear since they have both key biological components of motherhood: the genetic connection and the gestational environment. In cases of genetic surrogacy, the charge of baby selling would be applicable and the contract could not force the surrogate to give up her child against her will. By contrast, in cases of gestational surrogacy, the surrogate is considered by the law as a "human incubator" or a "prenatal babysitter" with no rights to the child she is carrying. Under the law, the surrogate cannot be charged

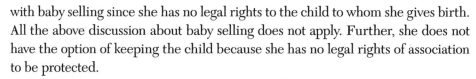

with baby selling since she has no legal rights to the child to whom she gives birth. All the above discussion about baby selling does not apply. Further, she does not have the option of keeping the child because she has no legal rights of association to be protected.

Just because there is a consensus in the law doesn't mean that there is no longer any debate about the definition of motherhood in surrogacy. Some feminists strongly support the rights of gestational surrogates, and others insist that "a deal is a deal" and thus never allow the surrogate to change her mind about keeping the child. This area of the definition of motherhood may be one of those areas in which there is room to agree to disagree, recognizing that a good argument can be made for both key positions.

To be specific, in cases of gestational surrogacy, who should be recognized as the mother—the genetic contributor or the surrogate who is the gestational contributor? The argument in favor of the genetic contributor is the recognition that genetics plays such a key role in determining many of the child's critical traits and features. Genetics has a powerful influence on who the child becomes. Further, until the embryo is implanted in the womb of the surrogate, there is no debate over who the "owners" of the embryo are. They are clearly the genetic contributors—the couple whose gametes created the child. To recognize the rights of the surrogate would involve the very awkward and cumbersome process of transferring maternal rights to the surrogate at the point the embryo is implanted, so that at the child's birth, she can then give up maternal rights back to the genetic contributor. It seems much more straightforward to insist that genetics be weighted more heavily than gestation in terms of its influence on who the child becomes.

Gestational Surrogacy—*Johnson v. Calvert*

Mark and Crispina Calvert hired Anna Johnson to be the gestational surrogate mother for their child. With no genetic connection to the child she was carrying, she "rented her womb" for nine months for $10,000 plus all medical expenses. Toward the beginning of the seventh month, Johnson started having second thoughts about giving up the child she was carrying. A month prior to the child's birth, Johnson sued for custody.

The court ruled that the surrogacy contract was valid and not inherently exploitative. Since Anna Johnson had no genetic stake in the child, she had no parental rights. Thus exclusive custody of the child was given to the Calverts and no visitation allowed. The judge ruled that the genetic connection took precedence over the fact that Johnson actually gave birth to the child and that the best interests of the child would be served by custody of the Calverts in any case.

However, that implies that the womb is a neutral environment that contributes nothing more than nutrients and shelter. That seems to assume that not much occurs in the womb that shapes who the child becomes. But that is not the case. We are learning more about the types of influences that the child experiences while in the womb. It is hardly analogous to prenatal babysitting. What happens in the womb is formative for the child, and not just physically, but emotionally and psychologically too. Further, the surrogate, by virtue of carrying and giving birth to the child, would appear to have made a more significant investment in the child. Her "sweat equity" in the child appears to be greater than the genetic contributor's. Further, the surrogate has the real experience of bonding and relationship with the child, so that if she develops the intention to become the mother over time, it is based on her tangible experience with the child, as opposed to the genetic contributor who can only envision a relationship with the child by the time of birth. It would seem that the case for the surrogate being the mother may be stronger than one would think at first glance. If this is true, then the gestational and genetic surrogates would be situated the same and the charge of baby selling would apply equally to both. But if the genetic contributor is weighted more heavily than the gestational surrogate, then the way the law treats them would be correct—the charge of baby selling would not apply, and the gestational surrogate would have no rights to the child she is carrying. However, some of the other concerns about exploitation and the surrogate distancing herself emotionally from the child still would apply.

Toward the Future of Reproductive Technologies

Some other reproductive technologies are relatively new and not yet mainstream but may become more popular in the future. These include first, artificial wombs. Physicians and neonatologists who manage high-risk pregnancies are already experimenting with synthetic amniotic fluid to assist prematurely delivered newborns. This is the first step toward a full artificial womb. Such a development would likely have a major impact on the abortion debate, since it may be possible for a woman to no longer be pregnant without necessarily ending the life of her child. But to have pregnancy devoid of a relationship with the mother may not be in the best interests of the child, since the prenatal relationship is important to the development of a healthy child in the womb.

A second more novel technology is gender selection, both by prenatal genetic diagnosis, in which embryos are created through in vitro fertilization and screened for gender and the desired gender implanted (see chapter 7 for more discussion of this). Sex selection can also be done by sperm sorting (MicroSort) that will enable

Posthumous Procreation

A thirty-five-year-old former professional football player was left brain-dead from an automobile accident. He had been separated from his wife for some time, though not officially divorced. His father was making decisions about his care and authorized organ donation of all useful organs. In the middle of the night, when the organs were being harvested, his estranged wife, who had just heard of her husband's death, urgently asked for his sperm. The man's father, not knowing quite what to say to such a request, eventually agreed. His sperm was harvested, and she took a vial of it away with her upon leaving the hospital. The man had left no will and no direction about whether he would have wanted his estranged wife to have his sperm after his death.

In a similar case, in order to continue the family lineage, an Israeli man had his sperm harvested after his death at his parents' insistence, even though he had left no will or any indication of his wishes. Soldier Kevin Cohen was killed in active duty in the Gaza Strip in 2002, and his sperm was extracted shortly after his death, then frozen and stored in the hospital where he had been treated. The hospital refused to release the sperm to the parents, insisting that only a deceased person's spouse could make such a request. The family sued to have the sperm released, and roughly four years after his death, an Israeli court ruled that the family could use the sperm to continue their lineage. The family appealed for surrogates (more than two hundred women volunteered) willing to both be impregnated with the sperm and raise the child. The family eventually settled on a twenty-five-year-old woman whom their son had never met to be the mother of his child.*

---

*"Mother Wins Dead Son Sperm Case," *BBC News*, January 19, 2007.

Too Old to Be a Mom?

With egg donation becoming more popular, it is not just infertile couples who are getting pregnant. Women after menopause are now having children by using donor eggs and treatments to prepare the uterus to give birth. Higher risks are involved, such as caesarean section being necessary and higher rates of pregnancy-induced diabetes, but women in their fifties are now giving birth successfully through egg donation. The oldest woman on record to give birth was a sixty-two-year-old woman named Rosanna Della Corte who became pregnant with the help of Italian infertility physician Dr. Severino Antinori. Some are concerned that there are risks to the child from having older parents, especially if the parents die before the child is grown. But others cite the wisdom and experience that comes from being older parents as a good thing for children. The American Society for Reproductive Medicine discourages postmenopausal pregnancies, but others suggest that such a policy constitutes age discrimination.

gender selection prior to conception. Here the sperm is sorted by whether it will produce boys or girls, and only the desired type of sperm is then inserted in the womb by intrauterine insemination.

Technology is also improving the prospects of posthumous procreation, that is, having children after one's death. Given medicine's ability to sustain vital functions after brain death, women can continue to carry pregnancies after brain death is confirmed, and even after an injury or illness leaves them in a permanent vegetative state. In addition, sperm can be harvested after a man's brain death, analogous with other vital organs being harvested for donation. That sperm can then be used in conjunction with IUI to impregnate a woman who desires to have the child of the recently deceased person.

Finally, egg donation is increasingly being used to achieve postmenopausal pregnancies. With egg donation, women in their fifties and sixties are delivering children successfully, though there are questions about the wisdom of having children so late in life. And, of course, human cloning also qualifies as a reproductive technology, which we will discuss in the next chapter.

Conclusion

These new reproductive technologies present some of the most difficult ethical dilemmas facing society today. Given the strong desire of most individuals to have a child to carry on their legacy, it is not surprising to see the lengths to which people will go to have a child that has at least some of their genetic material. People's desires to have genetically related children will likely ensure a brisk business for practitioners of reproductive medicine, and as a result, there will be an ongoing need for ethical discussion and decision making in this area.

For Further Reading

Kilner, John F., W. David Hager, and Paige C. Cunningham, eds. *The Reproduction Revolution: A Christian Appraisal*. Grand Rapids: Eerdmans, 2000.

Mundy, Liza. *Everything Conceivable: How Assisted Reproductive Technology Is Changing Men, Women and the World*. New York: Knopf, 2007.

Rae, Scott B. *Brave New Families: Biblical Ethics and Reproductive Technologies*. Grand Rapids: Baker, 1996.

_____. *The Ethics of Commercial Surrogate Motherhood*. Westport, Conn.: Praeger, 1994.

Ryan, Maura A. *The Ethics and Economics of Assisted Reproduction*. Washington, D.C.: Georgetown University Press, 2001.

Spar, Deborah. *The Baby Business*. Cambridge, Mass.: Harvard Business School Press, 2006.

Review Questions

1. List a few of the reproductive arrangements that are possible with today's reproductive technologies.

2. Briefly describe each of the following reproductive technologies: IUI, IVF, GIFT, ICSI.

3. What are the primary types of surrogate motherhood arrangements?

4. Summarize the official Roman Catholic position on reproductive technologies.

5. Give two examples in the Bible that appear to separate the unitive and procreative aspects of sex.

6. Briefly describe the primary biblical parameters that form the moral boundaries for reproductive technologies.

7. What is the contribution of Genesis 1–2 to your view of reproductive technologies today?

8. What are some of the various exceptions to the Genesis 1–2 model for procreation that were allowed in the Old Testament? How do you deal with these exceptions?

9. How do the New Testament authors tend to weight the Genesis 1–2 model?

10. What technologies involve a third-party contributor to procreation?

11. What does the Bible teach about the role of third-party contributors to procreation?

12. What is the primary moral issue involved with IUI?

13. What are the two primary moral issues involved with IVF?

14. Why is the association of GIFT with IVF potentially problematic?

15. What are the advantages of freezing embryos in IVF?

16. What are the available options for dealing with leftover embryos?

17. What is the argument that surrogacy constitutes baby selling?

18. What is meant by the saying "Surrogacy turns a vice into a virtue"?

19. What are the various determinants of motherhood in a gestational surrogacy case?

20. What technology is used in gender selection procedures?

21. What technology is necessary for achieving a pregnancy after menopause?

22. What is one of the potential problems with artificial wombs?

Cases for Discussion

Case 6.1: Counseling the Infertile Couple

You are sitting across the table having coffee with a couple in their mid-thirties who have been married for six years. For the last three years, they have been trying to conceive a child. Despite no apparent medical indications for their infertility, they have been unable to conceive. In the past few months they decided to see an infertility specialist to whom they were referred by their obstetrician. On their initial visit, they were presented with a confusing array of reproductive options. Some of the proposed infertility treatments involved use of their genetic materials only, while others made use of donor gametes. Since they share your theological convictions, they have come to you for your counsel about what reproductive technologies are within the moral parameters of the Bible. This is difficult for you because you never had to deal with anything like infertility. In fact, just the opposite was the case for you and your wife.

Questions for Discussion

1. How would you counsel this couple? What are the general principles from the Bible on which you would draw?

2. Would you suggest that all reproductive interventions are problematic? On what basis would you say this? Do you believe that the couple should simply adopt?

3. Or would you place more modest restrictions on such technologies? If so, what would some of those restrictions be?

4. Or would you suggest that since the child is coming into a loving Christian home and is the "gift of life" for this couple, that whatever option they feel comfortable with is morally acceptable? Defend your position.

5. Would your advice be any different if you were advising a single woman instead of a married couple? If so, spell out how it would be different and explain why.

Case 6.2: Using a Sperm Donor

You are having lunch with a couple who has been referred to you for your counsel. They are in their early thirties and are infertile because the man is not producing any sperm. The reason for this is that he is sterile because he had the mumps as a child and was not properly treated. His wife is strongly in favor of utilizing an anonymous sperm donor in order to "have their own child." By that she means that the child will have half a genetic connection, which she views as better than none, as would be the case with adoption. She also wants to have the experience of pregnancy and childbirth. They would be able to find out some things about their donor, such as a limited medical history, and see his photo and learn about some of his interests. There is no risk that they would not be the legal parents of the child born to them.

In their community, adoption is not really considered an option, since they place high value on having one's own child. The husband is deeply ambivalent about this, viewing a sperm donor as a "procreative pinch hitter." But he also wants to do what makes his wife happy.

Questions for Discussion

1. Would you encourage this couple to seek out a sperm donor in order to achieve pregnancy? Why or why not?

2. Assuming that the husband was comfortable with conceiving with donor sperm, would you advise them to go ahead with this option?

3. Would you try to encourage them to reconsider adoption? Would you suggest the adoption of an embryo? Why or why not?

Case 6.3: Hiring a Surrogate Mother

You are sitting with a woman and her husband who have a tragic story of infertility. They tried unsuccessfully for three years to conceive a child then finally conceived triplets through the use of in vitro fertilization. Sadly, she miscarried all three babies and had a massive uterine hemorrhage, from which she nearly died. Her physician had no choice but to perform a hysterectomy, in which her uterus was removed.

From the IVF procedure, she and her husband have five embryos in storage. They consider them their children, but once they found out they were pregnant with triplets, they were not sure what to do with them. They would like to implant the embryos themselves, but unfortunately that is no longer an option. They are considering hiring a gestational surrogate to carry and give birth to their embryos.

Questions for Discussion

1. In view of the discussion of surrogacy in this chapter, how do you feel about them hiring a surrogate, or to put it differently, "renting a womb"? Defend your answer.

2. Do you think that this surrogacy arrangement is an example of "baby selling" or just "womb rental"? Be sure to spell out how your answer assumes a definition of motherhood in surrogacy.

3. What other morally acceptable alternatives does the couple have?

Chapter 6 Notes

1. For further discussion of this distinction between procreation and reproduction, see Gilbert Meilander, *Bioethics: A Primer for Christians*, 2nd ed. (Grand Rapids: Eerdmans, 2005).
2. Congregation for the Doctrine of the Faith, "Instruction on Respect for Human Life in Its Origin and on the Dignity of Procreation," *Origins* 16, no. 40 (March 19, 1987): 704–5.
3. Ibid., 706.
4. For further information on Catholic teaching in this area, see Edward Collins Vacek, S.J., "Catholic Natural Law and Reproductive Ethics," *Journal of Medicine and Philosophy* 17 (1992): 329–46.
5. This view of two complementary accounts of creation is the standard evangelical view of Genesis 1–2. This is not to say that the two accounts of creation are in any way contradictory.
6. The exception to this is in 1 Corinthians 6:12–20, where Paul argues against sexual promiscuity on the basis of Genesis 2:24. He is not speaking to married couples exclusively in 1 Corinthians 6, though they constitute a large part of his audience. His point is limited to the one-flesh relationship that occurs whenever two people have sexual relations. This makes promiscuity immoral, particularly since Christ indwells the believer, who is thus joined to another in an illicit way when promiscuity occurs.
7. It may be that polygamy was allowed as part of a social safety net for unmarried women, a mechanism to ensure that they were provided for. Not all polygamy was allowed, however. Solomon's taking on foreign wives to establish political alliances was prohibited because he was to trust God for their national security, not foreign alliances.
8. Leftover embryos can raise some interesting legal problems too. For example, a couple who had utilized IVF had finalized their divorce, and the woman wanted to use the embryos to have a child. Her ex-husband refused, claiming that he did not want his progeny running around without his knowledge even of their existence. The couple went to court to have their dispute arbitrated. The court ruled in favor of the ex-husband, holding that one's procreative liberty also gives him the freedom not to procreate, and thus the embryos could not be used without his consent (see *Davis v. Davis*, 1990 Tenn. App. LEXIS 642 (September 13, 1990). For further commentary on this case, see Alexander Morgan Capron, "Parenthood and Frozen Embryos: More Than Property and Privacy," *Hastings Center Report* 22 (September 1992): 32–33.

   An even more complicated case occurred in Australia. In 1981 a Los Angeles woman and her wealthy husband flew to Australia for IVF. A number of embryos were frozen, and efforts to implant an embryo in the woman were unsuccessful. While the embryos were still in storage in Australia, the couple was killed in a plane crash en route to South America. There were no living heirs to the couple's substantial estate. There are a number of complicated legal questions about inheritance rights, both of the embryos and any woman who "adopted" the embryos to gestate and raise them. They are made more complex by the fact that the sperm that fertilized the embryos was not the husband's but that of an anonymous donor. See George P. Smith, "Australia's Frozen 'Orphan' Embryos: A Medical, Legal and Ethical Dilemma," *Journal of Family Law* 24, no. 1 (1985–86): 26–41. See also Donald DeMarco, *Biotechnology and the Assault on Parenthood* (San Francisco: Ignatius Press, 1992), 104–5.

9. See, for example, the Snowflake program, developed by Nightlight Christian Adoption Agency (www.nightlight.org).

10. Both the Code of Hammurabi (1792–1750 BC) and the Nuzi tablets (1520 BC) authorize surrogacy, and not only for cases of barrenness. Thus surrogacy was not only widely practiced, but was also the subject of detailed legislation to keep the practice within proper limits.

11. This freedom assumes, of course, that parents are acting in the best interest of their children and that no harm comes to children in the exercise of freedom on the part of the parents. See *Meyer v. Nebraska* (262 U.S. 390 [1923]), *Griswold v. Connecticut* (381 U.S. 479 [1965]), *Eisenstadt v. Baird* (405 U.S. 438 [1972]), and *Carey v. Population Services* (431 U.S. 678 [1977]).

12. In cases in which the surrogate does not supply the egg (called gestational surrogacy), there is debate over who is actually the mother, the woman who bears the child (the traditional definition) or the genetic contributor. Good arguments can be made for both genetics and gestation being the determinant of motherhood. For further detail on this, see Scott B. Rae, *The Ethics of Commercial Surrogate Motherhood* (Westport, Conn.: Praeger, 1994).

13. This real estate analogy is taken from Alexander M. Capron, "Surrogate Contracts: A Danger Zone," *Los Angeles Times*, April 7, 1987, B5.

14. *In the Matter of Baby M*, 537 A. 2d, 1249 (1988).

15. The statistics on the annual income of surrogates are a bit misleading because they record the income of women who were selected as surrogates. They do not take into account the women who applied to be surrogates but were not chosen. In a 1983 study by psychiatrist Philip Parker, he found that more than 40 percent of the applicants to provide surrogacy services were receiving some kind of government financial assistance. See "Motivation of Surrogate Mothers: Initial Findings," *American Journal of Psychiatry* 140 (1983): 1.

16. Statement of staff psychologist Howard Adelman of Surrogate Mothering, Ltd., in Philadelphia, cited in Gena Corea, *The Mother Machine* (New York: Harper and Row, 1985), 229.

17. Cited in ibid., 245.

18. Ibid., 214–15.

19. Daniel Callahan, "Surrogate Motherhood: A Bad Idea," *New York Times*, January 20, 1987, B21.

20. In *Stanley v. Illinois*, the Supreme Court stated that "the rights to conceive and to raise one's children have been deemed essential ..., basic civil rights of man ..., far more precious than property rights. It is cardinal with us that the custody, care and nurture of the child reside first in the parents" (405 U.S. 650 [1971], at 651).

21. See Rae, *Ethics of Commercial Surrogate Motherhood*, 77–124, for further discussion of the different positions and merits of each.

Chapter 7

Biotechnology, Genetics, and Human Cloning

In the past decade, various biotechnologies have emerged from the realm of science fiction to everyday reality. What was previously the domain of a handful of molecular biologists restricted to the lab has made it onto the front pages of the newspaper, and in headlines in the evening news and popular newsmagazines. Even a technology like human cloning was the subject of fictional films like *The Boys from Brazil, Blade Runner*, and *Multiplicity*. Then Scottish scientist Ian Wilmutt and his team cloned a sheep (Dolly) from adult cells in 1996. This came only a few years after the first success at cloning human embryos in the lab (1993).

The world of genetic testing has come a long way in the past decade as well. Today ultrasound imaging is considered a routine part of prenatal care for pregnant women, and amniocentesis is regularly offered to pregnant women over age thirty-five. These procedures have become mainstreamed in obstetric care. What is new is the ability of clinics to screen embryos prior to implantation for genetic defects. A couple with a history of genetic disease may consider such a test so that they can implant only normal embryos to avoid becoming pregnant with a genetically anomalous child.

However, the most progress in genetics has come in terms of genetic information. The Human Genome Project has unearthed a gold mine of genetic information. Researchers have traced genetic links of varying degrees to hundreds of diseases. This explosion of knowledge has raised complicated issues relating to privacy and confidentiality and what to do with this potentially life-changing information.

By contrast, the area of gene therapy, popularly known as genetic engineering, has yet to fulfill its promise. Gene therapy protocols are being approved, and some have been a great success, marking the first victories in decades of challenges to make gene therapy a reality. However, there have been some serious setbacks as well, including one that has actually resulted in a patient's death. As genetic engineering moves from the theoretical realm, geneticists are faced with ethical challenges. These include the use of germ line therapy, in which the genetic alteration is passed on to the succeeding generations, and the use of enhancement therapy, which is used to elevate already existing traits rather than correcting obvious defects. Its use for enhancement purposes raises broader questions about biotechnology in general for enhancement of otherwise normal traits. One example of enhancement therapy currently in use is providing the human growth hormone for children who are below average but not abnormal in height.

Genetic Information and the Human Genome Project

The Human Genome Project was one of the most ambitious scientific projects ever attempted and received some of the most substantial funding of any single project of scientific research.[1] The goal of the project was to map the entire human genetic code, thereby finding as many genetic links and predispositions to disease as possible. The project was conducted by molecular biologists all over the world and was essentially completed in 2001. As a result, the amount of genetic information now available to researchers, physicians, and the general public has exploded.

To fully understand the implications of the project would take a degree in molecular biology. Some of the connections between genetics and disease are *direct, causal links*, as is the case with diseases such as Down syndrome, Huntington's disease, sickle-cell anemia, and cystic fibrosis. In these cases, possession of the gene means that the person will develop the disease. The only variable is the time when the symptoms onset. But the project has found that there are more of what are called *predispositions* to many diseases, such as numerous types of cancers, heart disease, and diabetes. This means that a person has a much higher risk of developing the disease, yet in the long run may or may not get it.

To illustrate this, imagine that you are a woman with a history of breast cancer in your family. You have read that the Human Genome Project has discovered two different genetic links to breast cancer, and you are wondering whether you should be tested for the genetic link. If you have the genetic predisposition for breast cancer, it doesn't mean that you will automatically get the disease at some point in your life, but rather that you face a higher risk. You can do a variety of things to help prevent breast cancer, such as watch your diet, have regular mammograms, and be vigilant in self-checking for lumps in the breast area. You might even consider a more radical option, such as preventive surgery to have the breast tissue removed.

Once the genetic connection is found, researchers can develop a diagnostic test for doctors to use. Such tests exist for numerous diseases for which genetic connections have been found. When the information reaches this stage, a variety of issues arise. First, do you want to know whether you have the genetic predisposition? Second, if you undergo such testing and discover that you have the link, what will you do for prevention of breast cancer? Will you have a preventative procedure, in which the breast tissue is surgically removed, as some women have had? Or will you be careful to have regular mammograms and hope for the best? Third, are you concerned about the privacy of your information? Should your genetic information be kept entirely private, or should it be made available to health and life insurance companies or prospective employers? It is not unusual for people to forgo testing out of concerns about the information getting into hands that could do them harm. Although a case can be made for insurers and employers having access to this information, the consensus in the bioethics and legal community is that all genetic information should be kept private. It should only be disclosed with the consent of the individual, and neither employment nor insurance should be

A Walking Genetic Time Bomb

Katharine Moser's grandfather died of Huntington's disease when he was in his early fifties. She watched him lose all of his critical faculties as the cells in his brain began to die off, beginning in his mid-thirties. When she was in her early twenties, she faced the decision of whether to be tested for the gene. She knew that if she had inherited it, she would suffer the same fate as her grandfather. She had done research on the disease as a teenager and had even done a science project for school on it. As her history became clearer (one aunt was diagnosed with HD, and her grandfather's brother also was diagnosed), her desire to be tested herself became more intense. Her mother tried to discourage her from the testing ("Why would you want to know all that?" she asked, assuming that any rational person would not want to know if she or he was going to get an incurable disease). She long suspected that her mother was in the early stages of the symptoms when Moser was a college student. Moser represents something new in the current environment where there is so much genetic information available. When the Human Genome Project was first announced, the question was raised, "What if we gave a genetic revolution and nobody came?" That is, would people really wanted to know all the information? But Moser's desire to be tested and to know her future was clear and determined. In fact, it took some months to convince the hospital that she really did want to know. They finally relented and tested her. The result — she tested positive, and she will get Huntington's disease.*

*Amy Harmon, "Facing Life with a Lethal Gene," *New York Times*, March 18, 2007.

contingent on a willingness to divulge one's genetic information. The reason motivating proponents of privacy is that the makeup of one's genetic code is completely out of a person's control. A person receives the genetic makeup by the natural lottery. For a person to be denied employment or insurance on the basis of his or her genetic code constitutes a classic case of discrimination, on a par with racial and gender discrimination, since those are also factors that are not chosen but received at birth. As a general principle, society should not allow discrimination based on factors that are beyond one's control.

In addition, sometimes the reason for protecting privacy is that a person's genetic makeup constitutes the "sacred ground" of a person's identity. In view of the biblical teaching on the existence of both body and soul, however, a person who wishes to be consistent with Scripture should be very careful about accepting the prevailing scientific assumptions of this kind of genetic reductionism.[2]

Genetic Testing

Prenatal genetic testing has become a part of routine prenatal care for pregnant women. Such tests include simple blood tests such as the AFP test (alpha-fetal protein) to detect severe anomalies such as spina bifida, ultrasound imaging of the unborn child in the womb, and more invasive tests such as amniocentesis, in

Is Happiness Genetic?

A study by researchers at Edinburgh University suggests that our genes may control some of the traits linked to happiness. Researchers studied identical and nonidentical twins and concluded that genetic factors may account for up to half of the traits responsible for maintaining happiness. Dr. Alexander Weiss, who led the research, concluded, "Although happiness is subject to a wide range of external influences, we have found that there is a heritable component of happiness which can be entirely explained by the genetic architecture of personality." However, other researchers on the team suggested that it would be erroneous to conclude that nature had dealt someone an irrevocable hand in terms of happiness. Dr. Alex Linley put it this way: "What it means is that, rather than a single point, people have a range of possible levels of happiness — and it is perfectly possible to influence this with techniques that are empirically proven to work." Although there may be a genetic influence, it is not determinative but still involves what some would describe as self-help techniques and principles. That is, a person can be trained to be content and happy.*

*"Genes Play Key Happiness Role," *BBC News*, March 5, 2008; "Happiness Can Be Inherited, Research Finds," Reuters, March 6, 2008.

which amniotic fluid is drawn out from the woman's abdomen with a needle and the baby's cells in the fluid are analyzed.[3] If the genetic test comes back with bad news, that can be devastating for the expectant couple. At that point they face agonizing decisions about continuing or ending the pregnancy, and genetic counseling is available to help them make these decisions.

Imagine the following scenario. You and your spouse are expecting your first child. You have Down syndrome in your family history, and you have understandable fears that your child will have this genetic abnormality. Your physician strongly recommends that you undergo a variety of prenatal genetic tests to see if your child will suffer from Down syndrome. If you do have the tests, your genetic counselor has strongly suggested that you consider ending the pregnancy if your child has the gene for Down syndrome. You are uncomfortable with that option, but from family experience you are aware of the lifetime of demands of raising a genetically challenged child.

Physicians often suggest amniocentesis when the pregnant woman is over age thirty-five, because of the increased risk of Down syndrome. Although that test does have a small risk of miscarriage (roughly 1 percent), other tests, such as ultrasounds, are relatively risk-free. These risk-free tests can also detect a variety of symptoms of genetic abnormalities, though not with the same degree of accuracy as amniocentesis.

The first issue you and your spouse face is whether you should have the testing done at all. What would you gain by knowing that your child has a genetic anomaly? Or to put it another way, what would you gain by knowing that your child has a clean genetic bill of health? One can make a good case that you have a lot to gain by the testing. That knowledge may not be worth the risk of miscarriage from amniocentesis, but there is no reason why ultrasound per se should not be used for this purpose. A further use for the information might be to prepare for the challenges of raising a genetically defective child. One should not underestimate the daunting task of being a parent to a child born with genetic anomalies. One can make a good case that awareness of the child's condition prior to birth allows the parents critical time to adjust and prepare for the child's arrival.

However, you might want prenatal genetic testing in order to make a decision about continuing the pregnancy. It is not unusual for couples to decide to end a pregnancy when faced with the news that their child has a genetic anomaly. This was one of the difficult decisions that the couple in the second scenario in the introduction faced. With a history of genetic disease such as Down syndrome, one would expect a couple to be very sensitive to the genetic makeup of their child. But if prenatal genetic testing is used for the purpose of deciding whether to continue a pregnancy, that raises different moral questions that a couple must confront.

One should be very careful about using the information gleaned from genetic testing to make decisions about ending a pregnancy. For example, there is widespread agreement that using such testing and ending a pregnancy for the purpose of gender selection is an immoral form of gender discrimination. Although this is not routinely done in most Western nations, there are parts of the world where the abortion of female fetuses is not unusual. This puts some physicians in these countries in a difficult position. They want to provide prenatal care for their patients but are uncomfortable with abortion for gender reasons.

If a couple who is undergoing genetic testing for their child in utero receives bad news from their test, they may understandably wish to end their pregnancy. But using the information from genetic testing for gender reasons raises significant moral concerns. In the first place, ending a pregnancy for reasons of genetic abnormality incorrectly assumes that the genetically anomalous child is less than a full human person.[4] Unless the child in question is not a person, using genetic abnormality to justify ending the pregnancy is no different morally than ending

Selecting *for* Disability

Sharon Duchesneau and Candy McCullough, a British lesbian couple, are both deaf. Believing that there are aspects of life that they appreciate and value as a deaf couple that hearing individuals cannot, they utilized reproductive technologies and genetic testing to do exactly the opposite of what most couples would do — to select for deafness for their child. That is, they used sperm donated by a friend who also inherited deafness. Duchesneau conceived successfully and gave birth to a deaf child. Their story received a good deal of publicity, as one might expect. They also received a substantial amount of criticism for taking a course that many think is not in the best interest of their child. Alto Charo, professor of law and bioethics at the University of Wisconsin, suggested that they had violated their parental duty to secure the best future they could for their child. She said, "I'm loath to say it, but I think it's a shame to set limits on a child's potential." The couple defend their decision as a morally acceptable choice and argue that their child will appreciate rich facets of life that the child could not otherwise appreciate were the child to possess full hearing. Duchesneau put it like this: "It would be nice to have a deaf child who is the same as us.... A hearing baby would be a blessing. A deaf baby would be a special blessing." Sharon Ridgeway, another deaf mother of a deaf child said, "I in no way see deafness as a disability, but rather as a way into a very rich culture — which is one of the reasons I was delighted to learn when I gave birth that my baby was deaf."*

*Jonathan Glover, *Choosing Children: Genes, Disability and Design* (New York: Oxford University Press, 2006), 5.

the life of an adult who is similarly challenged. Yet no one envisions such a scenario, precisely because adults are clearly full-grown persons with the right to life, a right that cannot be compromised by genetic defect. Genetic abnormality should not compromise the full personhood of the unborn child any more than it does the grown adult. If personhood begins at conception and the unborn have the right to life from that point forward, unborn children with genetic challenges are similarly entitled to the right to life.

A second reason why abortion for genetic abnormality is a problem is that it is presumptuous to suggest that the lives of the genetically challenged are less worth living than the lives of those who are genetically normal. Couples attempt to justify abortion in these cases on the basis that the burden of life for the child is too great to put him or her through. However, it is not uncommon to confuse the burden on the child with the burden on the parents to raise the child. Although the burden on the parents should not be minimized, it is a different consideration from the burden on the child, and prospective parents who are considering ending a pregnancy in these cases should be honest with themselves about the underlying reason. As the numerous advocacy groups for the disabled have long contended, for a child with a genetic defect there is no necessary connection between disability and unhappiness. In fact, many disabled persons are happy with their lives and find their purpose for living in overcoming their challenges. If they were asked whether they felt that their lives were less worth living on account of their challenges, or whether they wished they had never been born, they would likely answer that they consider their lives fully worth living and they are glad to be alive. This is one reason that advocacy groups for the disabled are understandably nervous about genetic testing information being used for abortion decisions. They are rightly concerned that abortion due to genetic abnormality might diminish respect for and protection of the adult disabled population.

A third reason that abortion for genetic abnormality is problematic is that the genetic tests, though generally very reliable, are not infallible. More important, the degree of deformity resulting from any genetic disorder is difficult to predict with certainty. For example, it is well known that some children with Down syndrome are seriously impaired, but many others are only mildly affected and live relatively normal lives. In addition, symptoms of some genetic diseases, such as Huntington's disease, do not onset until later in life. Still others, such as cystic fibrosis (CF), though causing death prematurely (generally in the twenties), allow a person to live a satisfying life in spite of the disease. For many of these diseases, treatment of the symptoms has improved, enabling a fuller life.

Couples who have a history of genetic disease or have had one or more genetically anomalous children can choose another way to procreate. Instead of attempting to conceive a child naturally, they can undergo in vitro fertilization and have the embryos screened for genetic disorders prior to implantation. This procedure is known as preimplantation genetic diagnosis (PGD). Only the embryos that do not possess the genetic anomaly would be implanted, and the rest discarded. On the surface, this seems like a very responsible way to procreate, avoiding both the genetic disease and the possibility of abortion. However, for someone who holds to the personhood of the unborn outlined in chapters 5–6, there is no morally relevant difference between aborting a genetically anomalous fetus and disposing of a genetically defective embryo. So although PGD will eliminate the chances of conceiving a child with a genetic defect, it solves one problem only to create another.

For a couple with a history of genetic disease, who are against both abortion and discarding embryos, the prospect of passing along a serious genetic disorder raises questions about the wisdom of procreating naturally. Some would put the issue even stronger and argue that they might have the obligation *not* to procreate naturally. Take, for example, a couple in which the wife has the genetic link for Huntington's disease, a very difficult degenerative neurological disease in which symptoms onset at some point in the mid- to late thirties. She is thirty-one at the time that she and her husband desire to start a family, and she has a 50 percent chance of passing along the gene to her child. Should they attempt to have children naturally? Or should they adopt a child and be sure that their child will not get Huntington's disease? How would you advise them?

The couple in this case went ahead and attempted to procreate naturally and further decided not to have the child tested in utero, since the results would not affect their decision to continue the pregnancy. They also decided to let their child determine whether he or she would be tested. They assumed that as the mother developed symptoms, there would be ample opportunity to tell the child of the disease and the genetic component. Though to say that they had an obligation not to procreate naturally may be too strong, wisdom dictates that couples should think seriously about other options when faced with the likelihood of passing along a serious genetic disorder.

Gene Therapy

Some of the most exciting aspects of the new discoveries in genetics come when these discoveries can be put to use actually treating diseases rather than simply detecting them. The field of gene therapy holds promise for providing treatment for some genetic diseases. One of the earliest and best publicized examples of gene therapy was a program to treat ADA (adenosine deaminase deficiency), the immune system disorder that produced the "Bubble Boy," who could not be exposed to the outside environment because his body could not fight off infections.[5] Gene therapy is being developed for serious diseases such as cystic fibrosis and muscular dystrophy. A disease does not necessarily have to be genetic for gene therapy to be helpful, but genetic diseases are clearly the focus of these experimental efforts.

Gene therapy comes in a variety of forms. The current experimental protocols are all being performed with what is called *gene addition*.[6] For example, in a child with ADA, the immune system does not function properly because of a genetic defect. The gene that triggers the production of a critical enzyme for the immune system is defective because it is not functioning at all. Gene therapy attempts to counter the defect by adding the corrected gene to the body so that the enzyme is produced and the immune system works properly. Millions of copies of the corrected gene are added to the body in the same way that antibiotics would be added to the body to fight infections. It is delivered by a rapidly multiplying virus that enables the corrected gene to spread throughout the body. Repeated gene therapy treatments are necessary. Gene addition therapy either activates inactive genes or counters the effects of harmful genetic defects, as in the case of a disease such as Huntington's disease. This type of therapy affects only the patient; therefore, any genetic material introduced into the body is not passed on to succeeding generations. In other words, gene addition therapy is what is called *somatic cell gene therapy*, affecting only the individual patient.

Somatic cell therapy is different from what is called *germ line therapy*, in which genetic material is added either to very early stage embryos or to sperm or egg cells. In these cases the corrected gene that is added to the cells is transmitted to all succeeding generations. On the one hand, this type of therapy raises ethical concerns about the rights of succeeding generations to inherit a genetic code that is manipulated without their consent. On the other hand, if somatic cell therapy is ethical, then there does not seem to be any reason why correcting a defect for future generations would not also be ethical. One pressing concern for germ line therapy is that given how much molecular biologists still do not understand about the genetic code, the risks to future generations by a genetic alteration are largely unknown. If such alterations turn out to produce unanticipated but harmful effects, there will be no way of stopping such harm to succeeding generations short of ensuring that they do not procreate.

The ideal for gene therapy is what is known as *gene replacement*, in which the defective gene is surgically removed and replaced by the corrected gene. This is done in some cases of germ line therapy, particularly with embryos; however, this type of genetic engineering is still in infancy. When most people think of genetic engineering, this is what they think of, but for the foreseeable future, gene addition somatic cell therapy is what will be available to the public. Gene therapy clinics are springing up in major metropolitan medical centers, and if gene therapy fulfills

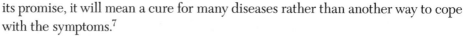

its promise, it will mean a cure for many diseases rather than another way to cope with the symptoms.[7]

One fear of gene therapy is that it might move from correcting clearly defective genes, as in the diseases for which it is now being considered, to being used to enhance already existing traits, such as intelligence or height.[8] It could conceivably also be used for eugenic purposes, the creation of a superior race of human beings, a notion virtually universally condemned as immoral, particularly given the Nazi eugenic experience. But it could also be used for parents to select various traits for their children, such as eye and hair color. Some have even suggested that more novel enhancements should be possible, such as genetic interventions to increase our ability to remain alert with less sleep, enhancing our long-term memory, or even enhancing virtues like generosity.[9]

Enhancement Biotechnology

The prospect of gene therapy to do more than simply cure diseases, to also enhance otherwise "normal" traits in a person, raises the broader question of the use of a wide variety of biotechnologies in this way—not only to treat diseases but to make us "better than well."[10] For example, students sometimes take Ritalin, the drug used to treat attention deficit hyperactivity disorder, even though they have no symptoms of ADHD, in order to improve their concentration and what is called "executive function" around final exam time. Another example that is becoming more widespread is for performance artists and even surgeons to take beta-blockers, which are used to treat social anxiety disorders such as extreme shyness, in order to calm their nerves and steady their hands prior to performances or surgery. Further, drugs such as Prozac that treat depression are being used as "mood brighteners" in people who may or may not be clinically depressed.

As argued in chapter 6, use of medical technology to treat disease can be seen as a part of God's general revelation and common grace to human beings to enable them to further fulfill their mandate to exercise dominion over creation. Thus medical technology in general and even gene therapy that corrects genetic defects in particular are clearly within the creation mandate given in Genesis 1–2. After the entrance of sin into the world, exercising dominion became more difficult for humankind and involved alleviating or reversing the effects of sin. Biotechnology used to treat symptoms or cure diseases plainly falls within the mandate given by God to human beings and for which he has given us the tools to effectively carry that out.

At first glance, enhancement therapies seem quite different than those to treat disease, though in many cases, biotechnologies that treat disease can also be used without adaptation to enhance otherwise normal traits, as is the case in the examples cited above. Enhancing already existing traits does not seem the same as reversing or alleviating the effects of the entrance of sin. Rather, enhancement therapies attempt to improve some already existing condition that falls within the parameters of normal. Using the general criteria—that the goals of medicine are to alleviate the effects of the entrance of sin, which includes disease, decay, and deformity—is a helpful start in attempting to draw some ethical guidelines. But we should admit that this way of stating it, similar to the traditional treatment-enhancement distinction, can be a bit ambiguous when applied to some specific biotechnologies, while accepting those technologies that unambiguously do treat disease.

Think of all the things that parents do for their children that enhance their given traits and tendencies. We send children to school to sharpen their mental capacities, and we even engage a variety of enhancement opportunities for them, such as music lessons and Kaplan courses to prepare for the SAT exam. I doubt there are too many objections to these kinds of *enhancements*, which is what they are, because these involve significant effort and do not become shortcuts for hard work and achievement. Some enhancements are specifically medical or dental. Orthodontics is a cosmetic enhancement, since it is not at all clear that crooked teeth are a result of the entrance of sin into the world. The same could be said for male pattern baldness. It is hard to have a problem with treatments to restore hair growth, though it is not clear that baldness is a result of the entrance of sin into the world. Using this same criteria, it is not difficult to justify many forms of cosmetic surgery that offset the effects of aging, which *is* a result of the general entrance of sin into the world. Yet we are sometimes uneasy with the narcissism that motivates some plastic surgery.

There are, however, some general points of concern when it comes to the widespread use of enhancement biotechnologies.[11] First is the concern about safety of their use. The clearest example of this is the use of anabolic steroids to enhance muscle growth in athletes, which is well known to have some serious side effects. A second concern has to do with fairness, particularly when it comes to the use of biotechnology in competitive situations, such as sports or academics. A related concern has to do with the access to these technologies, a tension that is perhaps clearest when it involves expensive genetic therapies. The use of enhancement biotechnologies runs the risk of widening the gap between the "haves" and "have-nots" and is especially troubling given the inequalities in health-care access that already exist. A fourth concern has to do with the context of personal autonomy and free choice that dominate the cultural landscape today. It may be that use of enhancement therapies begins by free choice but becomes so much a part of the way things are done that participants in certain activities in reality have no choice but to enhance themselves. The prevalence of performance musicians using beta-blockers to calm their performance anxiety may already be an example of this becoming coercive. And it may be naive to expect parents to resist enhancement therapies that will give their children significant advantages. In fact, failure to take advantage of these therapies could be seen as a form of child neglect.[12] Further concerns include how enhancement "short-cuts" can undercut the notions of hard work and achievement, how disorders are increasingly the object of medical treatment (the medicalization of society), and how enhancement undermines acceptance of the "givenness" of life.

Steroids for the Mind

While the efforts to make sports such as baseball and cycling "clean," that is, free from things like steroids and blood doping, are well publicized, what is quietly growing underneath the radar of public scrutiny are performance-enhancing drugs for executives, students, professional musicians, and even poker players. These brain drugs are known as "cognitive enhancers" and include the ADD drugs Adderall and Ritalin, beta blockers such as Inderal, and Aricept, which is used to treat the memory loss in Alzheimer's patients. Though these drugs have clear clinical uses, such as to treat ADHD, heart conditions, and memory loss, their use is increasing by individuals who have none of those problems. Instead, they are being used by people who want to get heightened brain capacity. For example, ADD drugs increase what is called "executive function," which gives people a temporary increase in concentration. Ritalin is sold on the black market on many college campuses as students look to buy it from ADD patients so they can get an edge on final exams or writing major papers. Beta blockers are used frequently by professional performers who want to steady their nerves. And the Alzheimer's drugs are being used more often by fiftysomething adults who want to combat the memory loss that is a natural part of aging. Even professional poker players take Adderall to enable them to focus on the game for long periods of time. Some surveys indicate that roughly 7 percent of college students have tried ADD drugs to help their concentration, and some professional musicians estimate that approximately 75 percent of musicians take beta blockers prior to performances. Even some physicians report taking beta blockers before major medical presentations. Side effects from long-term use are not clear, and some critics suggest that in competitive contexts such as the SAT exam, the use should be prohibited, just as performance-enhancing drugs are prohibited in sports. But those in professions such as air traffic control, airport screening, and surgery might actually be encouraged to take them.*

*Karen Kaplan and Denise Gellene, "Drugs to Build Up That Mental Muscle," *Los Angeles Times*, December 20, 2007; Benedict Carey, "Brain Enhancement Is Wrong, Right?" *New York Times*, March 9, 2008; David E. Rabie, "Generation Adderall," *Los Angeles Times*, March 10, 2008.

Some aspects of enhancement therapies do seem to be more problematic. Traits like eye color, hair color, height, and gender are God-given, and they are the way God designed particular human beings to look and be. God's sovereignty should not be usurped, and gene therapy should not be used to enhance the genetic endowment he has given to a person.[13] The notion of designer children is troubling because it has the potential to undermine the idea of unconditionally accepting one's children as God's good gift.

Human Cloning

For many years, cloning of human beings was the raw material of science fiction. Now it is in the newspapers. Since 1993 scientists have been able to clone human embryos, essentially reproducing in the lab what occurs in the body when identical twins or triplets are produced.[14] Embryos were cloned originally to make infertility treatments less expensive and less demanding on the infertile wife. Thus, if one views embryos as persons, then technically, since 1993 science has been able to clone persons.

However, when most people think of human cloning, they have in mind cloning a mature adult person, not an embryo, known generally as *procreative cloning*. In this type of cloning, scientists take a cell from an adult person (almost any type of cell will do) and remove the nucleus. They then take a woman's egg that has had its nucleus removed and transfer the adult cell nucleus into the egg. It is then chemically "jump-started" so that it begins to divide and multiply and then is implanted into a woman's womb, where it matures like a normal pregnancy. The result is that the child who is born is the identical twin of the adult from whom the cell was originally taken. The technical term for this process is *somatic cell nuclear transfer*. This is the process that made the headlines in 1997 when Scottish researcher Ian Wilmutt announced that he had cloned an adult sheep, which became well-known in the media by her name, Dolly.[15] It is ironic that this process is called *procreative* cloning, since it represents a further technological move away from the traditional idea of procreation and toward the modern notion of reproduction, a distinction mentioned in chapter 6.

The process was far from perfect, since, in Dolly's case, there were 276 failed attempts at cloning before she was produced. After Dolly was successfully cloned, predictions about a timetable for cloning human beings abounded, but the consensus in the scientific community was that replicating this process with human beings would be more difficult and was years away.

Procreative cloning at this point cannot be achieved without significant risk to the cloned embryo/fetus and perhaps even to the woman who carries the cloned person in pregnancy. The reason for so many miscarriages with Dolly was the presence of genetic abnormalities that were incompatible with life. That makes the process problematic, irrespective of the reasons why someone would want to engage in this practice. Assuming that those technological hurdles can be overcome, other questions are raised about cloning per se: whether the process is "playing God," and whether or not cloning violates a person's right to his or her unique genetic identity. It is unclear whether the charge of playing God can be maintained, since it is not an accident but under God's sovereignty and common grace that science has developed this technology. Further, the violation of one's unique genetic endowment does occur naturally when identical twins or triplets are produced, and that would not seem to be an absolute. However, the notion of children as begotten and not made suggests that cloning is problematic and deserves further moral reflection before proceeding.

Not only does the process of cloning itself require moral assessment, but the variety of reasons why someone would want to do it should be subject to moral evaluation. Below are some of the reasons why someone would want to engage in procreative cloning, apart from the more obvious reasons, such as curiosity (seeing whether it could be done) and narcissism (the desire to copy oneself and approach something like immortality):

1. Helping to make infertility treatments more efficient and less costly.
2. Providing embryos for research.
3. Being able to provide a person with an exact tissue match should it be necessary to treat a life-threatening disease (as with a bone marrow transplant).
4. Being able to actually replace a child who died prematurely.
5. Offering organ farming, in which the cloned person is used as a source of biological spare parts.
6. Making a profit from selling one's embryos on the open market, in the case of people like athletes or supermodels.

Helping make infertility treatments less costly (reason 1) could possibly be justified as long as there are no embryos left over at the end of the treatments and no embryos are destroyed in the process of cloning. Providing embryos for research (reason 2) is unethical, since either the research kills the embryo or the embryo is discarded at the end of the experimentation. There does not appear to be any reason why it would not be morally acceptable to be able to clone in order to provide a tissue match (reason 3) so that the cloned person could donate renewable tissue such as bone marrow. The notion of replacing a child who has died prematurely (reason 4) is unlikely to be effective, since it could cement the bereaved couple in grief. The reason for this is that the clone could well be a daily, painful reminder of the child who died. Using clones for organs (reason 5) is virtually universally condemned as a violation of the dignity of the cloned person. Selling cloned embryos on the open market (reason 6) is widely considered problematic, though embryos are sold by some infertility clinics. Further, demand for cloned embryos to produce one's own children is likely to be low, since having one's own child, not someone else's, is highly valued by prospective parents.

Conclusion

The world of biotechnology is here to stay, and the moral dilemmas produced by these sophisticated procedures will only become more complicated. Medical technology can be seen in general as part of God's provision to human beings in enabling them to more effectively exercise dominion over creation, particularly when it comes to confronting the effects of the entrance of sin into the world. The uses of each specific technology must be carefully weighed, and they cannot be exempt from moral scrutiny. The attitude that suggests that a technology must be used simply because it can be used is very problematic. Just because science advances, it does not follow that society is obligated to make every new technology available. Especially in the complex area of biotechnology and human cloning, moral reflection must keep up with scientific progress.

For Further Reading

Kilner, John F., et al., eds. *Genetic Ethics: Do the Ends Justify the Genes?* Grand Rapids: Eerdmans, 1998.

Mitchell, C. Ben, et al. *Biotechnology and the Human Good.* Washington, D.C.: Georgetown University Press, 2006.

President's Council on Bioethics. *Beyond Therapy: Biotechnology and the Pursuit of Happiness.* Washington, D.C.: U.S. Government Printing Office, 2003.

Sandel, Michael. *The Case against Perfection: Ethics in an Age of Genetic Engineering.* Cambridge, Mass.: Belknap, 2007.

Stewart, Gary P., and Timothy J. Demy. *Genetic Engineering: A Christian Response.* Grand Rapids: Kregel, 1999.

Review Questions

1. What was the Human Genome Project? What was its primary goal?

2. What is the difference between a genetic link and a genetic predisposition?

3. What is the argument for maintaining a person's genetic privacy?

4. What are the various types of prenatal genetic testing available today?

5. What does a couple have to gain by having prenatal genetic tests performed?

6. What are some of the moral concerns about using genetic testing to decide whether to end a pregnancy?

7. Why do disability rights advocates become nervous about prenatal genetic testing?

8. What is PGD (preimplantation genetic diagnosis)?

9. What reproductive technology is necessary to use with PGD?

10. What is the difference between gene addition and gene correction?

11. How would you distinguish between somatic cell gene therapy and germ line gene therapy?

12. What are some examples of biotechnology being used for enhancement instead of treatment?

13. Why is the treatment-enhancement distinction not adequate as a criteria for moral evaluation of biotechnology?

14. List some of the concerns with enhancement biotechnologies.

15. How is procreative cloning different from therapeutic cloning (discussed in chapter 5)?

16. Describe the process of somatic cell nuclear transfer.

17. Does procreative cloning constitute "playing God"? Explain your answer.

18. What are some of the reasons why someone would want to engage in procreative cloning? Which ones are morally acceptable?

Cases for Discussion

Case 7.1: Gender Selection for Family Balancing

Your next-door neighbor, who knows you're studying ethics, comes to ask you about a dilemma he and his wife are facing. They have three girls, ages eight, six, and four, and they desperately want to have a boy. They have heard of certain techniques that will increase the chances of having a boy. One involves what is called "sperm spinning" (MicroSort), which has a roughly 80 percent likelihood of producing the desired gender. To use this technology, the couple must achieve conception through intrauterine insemination, with the sperm selected for their desired gender, rather than normal sexual relations. However, the process is not perfect and there is no guarantee that sperm bearing the undesired gender won't get into the womb. A second and more reliable method is to use in vitro fertilization in conjunction with what is known as PGD (preimplantation genetic diagnosis). In this technology, the couple screens the embryos fertilized through IVF and implants only the ones with the desired gender. PGD is commonly used with couples who have a history of genetic disease and want to be sure they do not pass on the disease.

The couple realizes some of the problems with gender selection technologies on a widespread scale, especially in countries and cultures where one gender is strongly preferred over another. But for "family balancing" they don't see any readily apparent problem, and they are asking you for your opinion in the use of these gender selection technologies.

Questions for Discussion

1. How will you advise this couple? Is gender selection for family balancing morally acceptable? Why or why not?

2. If you hold that gender selection is acceptable, does the method used to select make a moral difference? Are both MicroSort and PGD equally acceptable ways to select for the desired gender? Why or why not?

3. Do you think that gender selection is "playing God"? Be sure to spell out precisely what you mean by that phrase.

Case 7.2: An Obligation Not to Procreate?

You are married to a twenty-eight-year-old woman who has the genetic link for Huntington's disease, a degenerative neurological disorder that normally begins to manifest symptoms in the mid-thirties. You have been married to her for three years, and you both are beginning to ask questions about starting a family. There is a 50 percent chance that your child will inherit the genetic link that causes the disease. Of course, you could adopt a child, but even then you have concerns about a child losing his or her mother at a relatively early age. That is in addition to concerns about the child observing her suffer through a progressive decline. You wonder about taking the risk of passing on such a lethal genetic abnormality and think that adoption would be a better option. Yet you both have this desire to "have a child of your own."

Questions for Discussion

1. How would you advise this couple about their desire to procreate naturally?

2. Do you think that the 50 percent risk of passing on the gene for Huntington's gives them an obligation not to reproduce naturally? Why or why not?

3. Given the risk of the mother's decline becoming apparent in the next few years, would you consider adoption a viable option for them? Or should they decide not to have children at all? Explain your answer.

Chapter 7 Notes

1. The literature on the Human Genome Project is voluminous. For example, see Daniel Kevles and Leroy Hood, eds., *The Code of Codes: Social and Scientific Issues in the Human Genome Project* (Cambridge: Harvard University Press, 1992), and George J. Annas and Sherman Elias, *Gene Mapping: Using Law and Ethics as Guides* (New York: Oxford University Press, 1992). Both volumes contain a variety of essays from different perspectives and serve as a good introduction to the issues surrounding the project. For a distinctive Christian perspective on the project and on other aspects of genetic technologies, see Timothy J. Demy and Gary P. Stewart, *Genetic Engineering: Crucial Considerations for Shaping Life* (Grand Rapids: Kregel, 1999), and John F. Kilner et al., eds., *Genetic Ethics: Do the Ends Justify the Genes?* (Grand Rapids: Eerdmans, 1998).

2. For more on the connection between the notion of personhood and genetic technologies, see J. P. Moreland and Scott B. Rae, *Body and Soul: Human Nature and the Crisis in Ethics* (Downers Grove, Ill.: InterVarsity, 2000).

3. For further reading on the details of these tests and some of the moral implications, see Scott B. Rae, "Genetic Testing, Abortion and Beyond," in Kilner et al. *Genetic Ethics.*

4. See the discussion of the personhood of the unborn in chapter 5.

5. LeRoy Walters and Julie Gage Palmer, *The Ethics of Human Gene Therapy* (New York: Oxford University Press, 1997), 17. The "Bubble Boy" was David Philip Vetter, who was born with a genetic disorder called severe combined immune deficiency (SCID). He lived his entire life—twelve years—in a sterile plastic bubble. His battle with SCID gained wide media attention; he died in 1984.

6. Karl Drlica, *Double-Edged Sword: The Promises and Risks of the Genetic Revolution* (New York: Addison Wesley, 1994), 76–77.

7. Todd Ackerman, "Center to Offer Cell-and-Gene Therapy Here," *Houston Chronicle*, August 1, 1999, 1A, 8A.

8. One significant work that discusses the ethical issues in enhancement therapy is Erik Parens, ed., *Enhancing Human Traits: Ethical and Social Implications* (Washington, D.C.: Georgetown University Press, 1998).

9. Ibid., vii.

10. Carl Elliott, *Better Than Well: American Medicine Meets the American Dream* (New York: Norton, 2003).

11. These are summarized from the report of the President's Council on Bioethics, *Beyond Therapy: Biotechnology and the Pursuit of Happiness* (October 2003), 275–300.

12. Ibid., 286.

13. For more discussion on enhancement therapy, see John Feinberg, "Enhancement," in Kilner et al., *Genetic Ethics*, 183–92.

14. Gina Kolata, "Doctor Clones Human Embryos, Creates Twins," *New York Times*, October 24, 1993, 1.

15. J. Madeline Nash, "The Age of Cloning," *Time*, March 10, 1997, 60–71.

Chapter 8

Physician-Assisted Suicide and Euthanasia

Ethics and the end of life were prominently on the evening news and the front pages of the newspaper in the case of Terri Schaivo. Her scenario reminded us that many of the ethical issues surrounding the end of life are still not resolved. Schaivo lapsed into a near vegetative state as a result of a heart attack that deprived her brain of oxygen so that she was severely brain damaged. She eventually required a feeding tube to keep her alive, which was surgically inserted into the lining of her stomach. Her prognosis for recovery was considered very poor. Her husband and her parents shared in her care, and she was cared for in a variety of settings ranging from home to skilled care facilities. Eventually her husband requested that the feeding tube be removed and that Terri be allowed to die. Her parents insisted that she would have wanted to live, and they took her husband to court to prevent him from having the feeding tube removed. Through a long process of appeals that went to the Florida Supreme Court and the federal courts, and eventually included Congressional involvement, a special "Terri's law" (which prevented removal of the feeding tube), and a media circus, eventually her husband was allowed to have her feeding tube removed and she was allowed to die. Part of what made the case so interesting was the deteriorating relationship between Terri's husband and her parents, the charges that her husband was physically abusing her, her husband's fathering two children by another woman while Terri was on feeding tubes, and the intense involvement of activists on both sides of the issue.

There is a long tradition going back to the sixth commandment ("Thou shalt not kill") and the Hippocratic Oath that prohibits doctors from assisting in suicide or killing their patients. And modern medicine has the ability to prolong life in increasingly poor quality of life circumstances, of which Terri Schaivo's case is a compelling example.[1] Her case illustrates the understandable fears among many elderly of being held hostage to medical treatments and technologies that they do not want, and being unable to avoid such a decline in their quality of life.

In recent years well-publicized organizations, such as the Society for the Right to Die, Compassion in Dying, and what was formerly called the Hemlock Society, have worked strenuously for the legalization of assisted suicide. A variety of resources provide detailed instructions on how to be released from the torments of a terminal illness with or without professional medical assistance.[2] Their efforts succeeded in the late 1990s in Oregon, which became the first state to legalize assisted suicide. (Washington became the second in 2008.) However, some states enforced their laws prohibiting such assistance. Michigan pathologist Jack Kevorkian was finally convicted in 1998 after a number of acquittals. He was released from a Michigan prison in 2007. Internationally, prohibitions against assisted suicide and euthanasia exist in some countries in Europe, but in other countries, such as Belgium and the Netherlands, assisted suicide and euthanasia are legal.

There is still vigorous debate on the morality of assisted suicide and euthanasia, and the 1997 decision of the United States Supreme Court in *Washington v. Glucksberg* (see discussion of this case on pages 217–18) has ensured that the debate will continue. In addition, there are fears that the practice of euthanasia would expand beyond acceptable moral limits and include people who are not terminally ill. As a result, most scholars, and even some advocates of assisted suicide, urge caution in determining new parameters for end-of-life medical decisions.

Definition of Key Terms

Termination of Life Support

There are essentially three different ways by which a physician can render assistance to hasten the death of a patient. The first of these is by measures known as *termination of life support* (TLS). This was formerly known as passive euthanasia, but that term is no longer used to describe the process. The reason is that there is nothing passive about withdrawal of life-sustaining technologies; it is a deliberate act. "Termination of life support" generally refers to withdrawing or withholding medical treatment from a dying patient and allowing the patient to die. Such treatments often include withdrawing ventilator support for breathing or withholding CPR (cardiopulmonary resuscitation) from patients for whom it would clearly be futile.

Physician-Assisted Suicide

Physician-assisted suicide is a second form of assistance in dying, and in this situation the physician more actively serves as a causal agent in the patient's death. The physician's role in physician-assisted suicide is normally to provide a medical means by which a patient can take his or her own life. This is generally done through a prescription for a lethal dose of medication. The physician provides the medication and instructs the patient on how much medication to ingest. If the patient follows the instructions and takes the medication, death occurs within a few minutes. In this case death is caused directly by the medication and not by the underlying disease. So far, all of the ballot initiatives that have arisen in various states have attempted to legalize physician-assisted suicide only.

Euthanasia

The general term *euthanasia* derives from classical Greek and literally means "good death." Sometimes patients are too seriously ill and too near death to employ the means of assistance from a physician and thereby commit suicide — they simply are not physically able to do it. In these cases, the physician is more directly involved. This is what the term *euthanasia* technically refers to. It is also sometimes called "mercy killing." It refers to the direct and intentional efforts of a physician or other medical professional to help a dying patient die. It is usually accomplished by a physician administering a lethal injection of drugs into the patient. In euthanasia, the patient is actually killed by the direct action of the physician. The term *euthanasia* is used to refer to this specific kind of aid in dying, though some still use it as an umbrella term for all kinds of aid in dying.

Ordinary and Extraordinary Means

In end-of-life medical decisions, distinctions are often made between *ordinary* and *extraordinary means* of treatment. The term "ordinary means" refers to the course of treatment for a disease that offers a reasonable hope of benefit to the patient without being excessively burdensome. Antibiotics to cure an infection are an example of this type of treatment. "Extraordinary means" are those that do not offer such hope and place undue burdens on the patient. For example, placing a patient on a respirator could be considered extraordinary means. Ordinary means are considered morally obligatory, and extraordinary means are morally optional.

In the past these terms have been used as somewhat rigid guidelines governing treatment decisions, but today there is more flexibility in their application. The terms should be defined relative to the state of medical technology, because many ordinary treatments today were considered extraordinary fifty years ago. In addition, they should be defined relative to the circumstances surrounding a patient. Some treatments may be ordinary in some cases and extraordinary in others, depending on the patient's condition and prognosis. Many bioethicists prefer the terms *obligatory* and *optional* to "ordinary" and "extraordinary" in order to take into account the role that different circumstances play in determining which treatments are morally required and which ones are not.

Living Will/Advance Directive

In some cases patients decide in advance, prior to becoming seriously ill, the kinds of treatments they desire and, more important, the ones they do not. This is called an *advance directive* and is sometimes referred to as a *living will*. In such an advance directive, a person can designate someone else to make medical decisions for him or her should he or she become unable to do so. This part is called a *durable power of attorney for health care* (DPAHC). Some advance directives are quite general, stating that the person does not desire to be maintained on mechanical life-support systems if there is no reasonable hope of recovery or if one's quality of life has dramatically diminished. Others are more detailed, designating the kinds of treatments one desires and refuses. For example, a person can request not to be given food and water by medical means or be placed on a respirator under certain conditions. One common request made by dying patients is a *"do not resuscitate" order*, abbreviated by its initials, *DNR*. This is also called a "no code" order, indicating, for example, that if the terminally ill patient suffers a heart attack, he or she is not to be resuscitated, or that no emergency code is to be announced in the hospital.

The advantage of a living will is that it allows a person to make end-of-life medical decisions before a medical crisis occurs. In a crisis a person may have to make decisions about treatment options without having enough time to thoroughly think them through. The living will allows time to get the necessary counsel from qualified people so that decisions can be considered carefully and made without pressure.

Living wills are becoming more common, and most states make them available at low or no cost. The Patient Self-Determination Act now requires that whenever people are admitted to a hospital, they are to be given information on a living will for their future medical decisions. This is being done so that people can make many of the end-of-life treatment decisions while they are still competent to make them.

Competence

In medical ethics, *competence* ethics refers to the level of the patient's ability to understand the treatment options and give informed consent to the option that is chosen. Patients normally become *incompetent* to make treatment decisions when they lose consciousness, fall into a permanent vegetative state, are in extreme pain, or are under medication to relieve pain. When someone becomes incompetent, it is important for the medical staff to have some idea of the course of treatment desired by the patient. If this is written in a living will, the physicians have some direction to guide them. If the incompetent patient's wishes are not known, a *surrogate*, or *proxy*, decision maker is recognized. This is someone, usually a family member or close friend, who can be trusted to represent accurately the desires of the patient.

Legal Background to End-of-Life Issues

Although many end-of-life cases have gone to court, some have been instrumental in setting the legal context for end-of-life issues. The three discussed below particularly stand out. The Quinlan case dealt with the removal of life support in general. The Cruzan case addressed the more specific removal of feeding tubes. The Glucksberg/Vacco cases marked the first time the U.S. Supreme Court addressed physician-assisted suicide.

In the Matter of Karen Ann Quinlan (1975 – 76)[3]

The Quinlan case marked the first time a U.S. court ruled on the legality of terminating life support. Karen Ann Quinlan had lapsed into a coma as a result of a drug overdose, leaving her brain seriously damaged. She was sustained by a respirator, necessary for her to continue breathing, and a type of feeding tube, necessary for her to receive nutrients. At that time, in the mid-1970s, use of respirators were just becoming more widespread. After five months in the hospital and repeated consultation with the physicians, her parents realized that she would never regain consciousness and requested that the respirator be removed, thereby allowing her to die. They recounted some conversation with her to the effect that if she was ever in a condition like she was in now, she would not want to be kept alive by medical means. But when they asked the physicians to disconnect the respirator, the physicians refused on the grounds that they would be killing Quinlan. They viewed the termination of life support as a departure from standard medical treatment at that time, which was to continue treatment until the patient either died or got better. The hospital viewed it as a form of euthanasia.

The lower court ruled in favor of the hospital, refusing to grant the family's request. That decision was reversed on appeal to the New Jersey Supreme Court, allowing the removal of the respirator on the basis of the right to privacy, which they ruled allowed the family to make end-of-life decisions for loved ones. Interestingly, after the respirator was removed, Quinlan did not die. In fact, she breathed on her own for roughly ten years and lived in a nursing home until her death in 1986. Her case established the legal precedent for the termination of life support that continued to be clarified in subsequent court decisions.

Cruzan v. Director, Missouri Department of Health (1990)[4]

Nancy Cruzan was in a permanent vegetative state as a result of a tragic auto accident. All higher brain activity had stopped, and only the involuntary functions, such as heartbeat, breathing, and digestion—the functions regulated by the brain stem—continued. She had suffered massive head injuries and had to be given life-sustaining food and liquids through a tube surgically inserted into her stomach. Only in her late twenties, she was likely to live in this condition for years, perhaps decades, before the rest of her body aged naturally. The cost of maintaining Cruzan under these circumstances was high, and since her medical condition was irreversible, her family wanted to withdraw the feeding tubes that were keeping her alive. After Cruzan was in this condition for roughly seven years, and seeing that she was not likely to regain consciousness, her parents requested that the feeding tubes be removed and she be allowed to die. This case was slightly different than Quinlan's because it dealt with the removal of feeding tubes, which some people considered basic care and not medical treatment at all.

The lower court ruled in their favor, which was reversed by the Missouri Supreme Court. Though technically the United States Supreme Court denied the request of family to have nutrition and hydration withdrawn, the decision was very significant because it opened the door for patients to request in advance that feeding tubes be withdrawn (or even not begun) should they end up in a *permanent vegetative state* (PVS). The Court's decision contained three important elements:

1. Medically provided nutrition and hydration can be removed with *clear and convincing evidence* of the patient's wishes.
2. Nutrition and hydration so provided qualifies as *legitimate medical treatment*.
3. There is place for *substituted judgment* of a proxy decision maker.

The Court ruled that there was no clear and convincing evidence of Nancy's wishes, thus ruling against the family. However, after the Supreme Court decision, the Cruzans returned to a lower court with additional evidence from Nancy's roommates and coworkers that she did not desire to be kept alive artificially. The lower court then allowed the feeding tubes to be removed, satisfied that the clear and convincing requirement of the Court had been met. She died within two weeks of the removal of the feeding tubes.

Washington v. Glucksberg / Vacco v. Quill (1997)[5]

With the *Washington v. Glucksberg* and *Vacco v. Quill* cases, the United States Supreme Court handed down a landmark decision on assisted suicide and the right to die. The Court was, at the same time, reviewing two different cases in which state laws that prohibit physician-assisted suicide were being challenged. In both cases the lower courts had ruled that there was a constitutionally protected right to die. Thus the laws that prohibited assisted suicide were ruled unconstitutional.

However, the Supreme Court reversed both decisions, ruling that there is no constitutionally protected right to die.[6]

The Court argued that there is a legally and morally relevant distinction between assisting suicide and withdrawing life-sustaining treatments. Patients have the right to say no to life-sustaining treatments because they have the right of bodily integrity—the right to determine what is done to their own bodies. Medical treatment administered against the will of the patient is generally considered battery, to use the legal term, and patients have the right to protect themselves against it. Assistance in suicide is grounded neither in the broader right to die, which the Supreme Court argued was not found anywhere in the Constitution, nor in American legal tradition.

The Court did not say, however, that assisted suicide is illegal. It simply ruled that states are not violating anyone's rights if they prohibit assisted suicide, since there is no constitutionally protected right to die. But if states desire to have laws that allow for assisted suicide, they can do that, too, as the states of Oregon and Washington have done. The Court left the decision about assisted suicide in the hands of the states and as a matter for continued public debate. The Court declined to issue a broad ruling about assisted suicide in general but opened the door for any state either to allow or to prohibit the practice, based on the will of the people of that state.

The End of Life in Biblical Perspective

In the Bible, human life, being made in God's image, is his sacred gift, and thus innocent life is not to be taken. The timing and manner of a person's death belong ultimately to God (Eccl. 3:1–2; Heb. 9:27). With this is the obligation to care for the most vulnerable, which throughout the biblical period, clearly included the dying.

Theologically, death was not a part of God's original design for human beings. It came into the world as a result of the entrance of sin (Rom. 5:12; 1 Cor. 15:21–22). Death can be seen as the ultimate *in*dignity, coming as a result of sin and the fall of man. The late Protestant ethicist Paul Ramsey suggested that death is something wholly alien to humankind, imposed upon humans as a consequence of sin.[7] Since man in Christ is destined for eternal life, Ramsey argued, death is an indignity, inconsistent with man's eternal destiny in Christ.

However, the Bible also affirms that death is a normal and natural part of a person's life "under the sun," or on this side of eternity (Eccl. 2:14–16; 3:19–21; 5:15–16; 9:1–6). Death is seen as both an enemy and a normal part of life, due to the pervasiveness of sin in the world. But from the perspective of the cross and resurrection of Jesus, for the Christian, death is also a *conquered* enemy, having been vanquished by the death and resurrection of Christ. Thus, since death for the Christian is a conquered enemy, it need not always be resisted. Physicians need not always "do everything" to stave off death, especially when it involves no more than simply delaying an inevitable death. In general, when the dying person's prognosis is very poor and further treatment is futile or more burdensome than beneficial, death can be welcomed as the "doorstep to eternity." However, these foundational principles concerning the sanctity of life and the obligation not to take innocent life extend to suicide, making the biblical prohibition of suicide clear. The notion that innocent life cannot be taken because the timing and manner of someone's death belong to God alone suggests that while life support can be removed and death be allowed to run its natural course, physician-assisted suicide and euthanasia are very problematic.

Ethics and the Termination of Life Support

Though the courts have ruled that the decision to remove or withhold life support is legal, that does not mean that no moral issues are involved. Nor does it mean that every decision to terminate life support is morally acceptable. For example, if a person can fully recover from an illness and needs ventilator breathing support

The Value of a Few Months of Life

Harriet and Mort Frank are retired, living on a fixed income of roughly $1,450 per month. Harriet is being treated for lymphoma, which is costing them $2,000 per month for out-of-pocket costs. "So far this medication is working wonders, but I keep thinking, *How are we going to afford it?*" says Mort. Irene Knoll is undergoing treatment for pancreatic cancer but has a monthly income of only $1,200 from Social Security and bills to her various physicians and pharmacies for thousands of dollars. Other targeted cancer drugs, such as Herceptin, used to treat end-stage breast cancer, costs $20,000 for a typical cycle of treatment. Erbitux, approved in 2004 to treat end-stage colorectal cancer, costs roughly $10,000 per month. Other drugs, such as Avastin and Tarceva, can cost as much as $100,000 per year. The costs of many of these specialty drugs are forcing decisions about how much the extra months of life are worth. Patients often refuse these drugs because they know that using them would leave crushing financial burdens on a spouse or other family members after their death. As patients and their families calculate the costs and benefits of these ultra-expensive medications, one wonders about the wisdom of fighting cancer until the end. In fact, some physicians are now raising questions about whether they ought to be prescribing some of these very expensive drugs that will extend life for only a few months to a year.*

*Daniel Costell, "Setting a Price for Putting Off Death," *Los Angeles Times*, March 18, 2007.

temporarily, it would be unethical to terminate that prior to the patient improving. Or if CPR will restart an otherwise healthy person's heart, it would be immoral to withhold it.

In this discussion, a distinction is often made between *withdrawing* and *withholding* treatments. Ethically, if it is acceptable to withdraw a treatment, then it is also acceptable to withhold that same treatment. There is no significant moral difference between the two. But withdrawing a treatment once begun can be more emotionally difficult for family members than simply withholding it. The reason for this emotional difference is that the family sees their loved one being maintained on life support, and the decision to withdraw it often feels more like they are causing the death of their loved one.

When life-sustaining treatments are removed, the physician does not intentionally cause the patient's death. Rather, the disease or condition affecting the patient is simply allowed to take its natural course. Thus the disease, not the doctor (nor the family who makes the decision), is responsible for the patient's death. In some cases death comes quickly when life support is removed; in others it does not. Even though it often feels to the family like they are complicit in their loved one's death, morally that is not the case. Removal of life support does not constitute euthanasia or assistance in suicide, since death is not intentionally caused. In fact, many people who request to have life-sustaining treatments removed do not actually wish to die; they simply desire to live out their remaining time free of unwanted medical technology.

Some suggest that termination of life support is "playing God," that is, usurping a prerogative that belongs to God alone. But that charge is accurate only if TLS is actually killing a patient, which it is not. If it is simply allowing death to take its natural course, then it does not violate the long-standing prohibition against killing innocent persons. This would also be true if the treatment removed is a feeding tube, as opposed to a ventilator. Removal of a feeding tube from a patient who is severely brain damaged can feel like starving someone to death. But removing a feeding tube is no more starving someone to death than removing a ventilator is suffocating someone to death. When a feeding tube is removed, the cause of death is still the underlying disease or condition that is preventing the person from taking food and water by mouth. Thus the condition is being allowed to take its natural course and is like any other form of medical treatment.

Still others insist that termination of life support violates the principle of the sanctity of life—that since life is sacred, medicine ought to be keeping people alive as long as they have breath. Under this view of the sanctity of life, families should not make decisions to remove treatments that would keep their loved ones alive. However, though it is clear that life is sacred, it does not follow that medicine is obligated to keep everyone alive at all times and at all costs. If it is true that death is a conquered enemy, then it need not be resisted at all times. It then is acceptable, in humility, to recognize that death is the doorstep to eternity and not employ life support simply to delay someone's inevitable death and, in doing so, delay his or her homecoming to eternity.

In fact, if the sanctity of life means that medicine is obligated to keep everyone alive at all costs and at all times, then it would seem that the sanctity of life, as understood that way, would involve a problematic theological assumption—that earthly life is the highest good. But that assumption is not supportable from the Bible. It is better to see earthly life as a *penultimate* good—that is, close to ultimate but just below it. The ultimate good for the person in the community of God's people is his or her *eternal* fellowship with God. With earthly life being a penultimate good, it follows then that it is acceptable under the proper conditions for patients and families to say "enough" to life support and allow death to run its natural course.

Some families insist on all treatments to continue in order to give maximum opportunity for a "miracle." Though it is true that miracles do happen in medicine, though rarely, it may be that this desire is simply an unwillingness to "let go" of a dying family member. It is tempting to say to families, "If you want to see a miracle, then let's remove everything!" The miracle that will come is that in eternity their loved one will be healed, not only from this disease, but from all diseases and infirmities. The patient will be healed, but it may not occur on this side of eternity. Further, it is more appropriate theologically to suggest that the paradigm for

Refusing Treatments with Time to Live

When columnist Art Buchwald's kidneys failed, he decided to forgo kidney dialysis. He was older and had seen many of his friends ravaged by end-of-life treatments, their quality of life compromised — and for what? Another few months, or a year or two to live? When he looked at the options, he said, "No thanks." He chose to live out the remainder of his days without treatments, except for those necessary to keep him comfortable. Doctors had little doubt that dialysis could give him more time, but the more he thought about it, the more he was willing to trade off less time for a better quality of life in those final days. He was essentially entering hospice care far earlier than most terminally ill patients take advantage of hospice. His family respected his decision but understandably wanted him to undergo the treatments in order to be around as long as possible. He lived longer than physicians anticipated but not nearly as long as he could have had he decided in favor of dialysis.*

*Susan Brink, "Life on Her Terms," *Los Angeles Times*, February 2, 2007.

end-of-life care is that of eternity and resurrection (1 Cor. 15), rather than hoping for miracles in earthly life.

Finally, some object to termination of life support on the basis that suffering has redemptive value. Though in principle, this is true (James 1:2–5), the suffering that generally has value for a person is suffering that comes on account of one's faith (1 Peter 2:20–24) or suffering that is unavoidable. To say that all suffering is redemptive would be to suggest that someone ought never go to a doctor or dentist! Further, it seems that the value of suffering has to do with the formation of character in this life, since in eternity one's character will be fully formed by virtue of meeting Christ. Thus, just because suffering in general has value, it does not follow that life support can never be removed.

Hence termination of life support is generally acceptable, but not in every case. Determining in which cases it is appropriate requires further criteria, coming under one of three conditions: (1) if a competent adult patient requests it, either in writing in an advance directive or orally; (2) if the treatment is futile or clearly of no benefit

It's Legal for Doctors to Say No to Patients

In July of 2000 California became the first state to provide some degree of legal protection for physicians who want to say no to families who request all-out treatment at the end of life no matter how poor the prognosis. The law was passed in response to a growing number of cases in which families were demanding that physicians "do everything" for their loved ones, when the specific treatments they were insisting upon were either futile or far more burdensome than beneficial. Physicians felt helpless to do what they thought was in the best interests of their patients and were afraid to go against the strong wishes of the family for fear of being sued. The law provides immunity from civil liability for physicians who refuse to provide medically ineffective health care or health care that violates the standard of care for patients in their particular conditions. Of course, physicians must have prior conversations with the family to attempt to persuade them to stop inappropriate treatments, and should those discussions fail, they are obligated to make a reasonable attempt to transfer the care of the patient to a physician who will carry out the family's wishes. Should those attempts fail, the law protects them from liability and from negligence should they refuse to provide futile treatments. The law will not prevent families from suing the physicians, but it will make it very difficult for families to win such lawsuits. Of course, this is not much comfort for physicians, whose desire is to stay out of court to begin with. Some other states have followed California's example and passed similar laws.*

*AB 891, California State Assembly, July 1, 2000.

to the patient; (3) if the burden to the patient outweighs the benefit. In most cases competent adults request termination of life support when their situation is futile or too burdensome. Termination of life support is legal, and competent patients have the right under the law to refuse any form of treatment they do not want.

A treatment is futile if it is of no benefit to the patient. Certain treatments are physiologically futile—they simply don't work—such as prescribing antibiotics for a virus. But more broadly, treatments are futile if they will not reverse an imminent and irreversible downward spiral toward death for the patient. To put it another way, treatments are futile if they will not restore the patient to an acceptable quality of life. Much of the debate about futility has to do with physicians' removing futile treatments even when the family requests that they continue.

More common at the end of life are treatments that have some benefit but are so burdensome to the patient that they actually increase the net level of suffering experienced prior to death—that is, the burden exceeds the benefit, and usually the burden *far* exceeds the benefit. A good case can be made that it is unethical for families to increase the net level of suffering for their loved ones and that treatments in which the burden exceeds the benefit ought to be discontinued. Much of the current debate about the burdens and benefits involves who should be included in that calculation. Should family members and the burdens on them for caring for their loved ones be included in the burdens? Should the calculation of the burdens involve the financial burden on the family for what may be enormous costs of care that must be borne after the patient dies? There is a growing movement that suggests that when weighing the burdens of treatment, the interests of the family and even of society should be considered as well as the interests of the patient.[8]

Withdrawal of Nutrition and Hydration

A closely related and highly controversial issue is the legitimacy of withdrawing medically provided food and water from patients who are in a permanent vegetative state or whose brain function is substantially compromised as result of a stroke or Alzheimer's disease. Patients in a permanent vegetative state are the ones who most commonly require feeding tubes. Those in a permanent vegetative state are those who have lost all higher brain function and for whom the only part of the brain that continues to function is the brain stem, which controls the person's involuntary activities, such as breathing, heartbeat, and digestion. A person in this condition is likely to live to a relatively advanced age as long as food and water are provided. The fact that the patient may not have a terminal illness raises additional questions for the one who permits removal of feeding tubes.

It does seem clear that *medically provided nutrition and hydration are medical treatment*. One of the most helpful aspects of the Cruzan decision was the clear reasoning provided by the Supreme Court on this issue. Once one allows for the general right to refuse life-sustaining medical treatment—a right that is justifiably established in our society—the heart of the issue is whether nutrition and hydration qualify as medical treatment that a patient has the right to refuse.

The phrase "medically provided nutrition and hydration" is used intentionally to underscore the technological nature of the treatment. There is a strong parallel to the ventilator insofar as medical technology is performing an essential function that the body, through injury or disease, can no longer perform itself. Certainly, air to breathe is as basic a human need as food and water. Yet very few question the morality of removing a ventilator under certain conditions since it is considered legitimate medical treatment.

Some suggest that provision of food and water is always required, even if it is through medical means. The primary reason for this is the insistence that nutrition and hydration are necessary to preserve patient comfort and dignity in the dying process. To put it another way, food and water are symbolic of basic human care for the dying, so we don't dare neglect to provide them in light of what that will say about our care for the dying.[9] Some would suggest that it is indeed symbolic, but of something quite different. It is symbolic of someone being held hostage to medical technology, likely against his or her wishes. It may even be symbolic of something further: exile from the human community. Life in a permanent vegetative state can be seen as the modern equivalent of a punishment considered worse than death—exile—in which the person is cut off from loved ones and dies alone.[10] Regarding the need for patient comfort, if the person is in a permanent vegetative state and has no higher brain function, it is difficult to see how he or she can experience pain at all.

Although there is still some debate on this issue, generated by Terri Schaivo's case, the majority of bioethicists hold that it is ethically permissible to withdraw medically provided nutrition and hydration from patients in a permanent vegetative state. The rationale for this is that the right to refuse life-sustaining treatment in general is well established in our society, and this clearly falls under the heading of medical treatment. It is not essential to patient dignity and comfort, nor is it necessarily symbolic of basic human care. The Supreme Court's insistence on clear and convincing evidence of patient desire to refuse this treatment is a necessary safeguard in a matter of life-and-death decision making.

Physician-Assisted Suicide and Active Euthanasia

The discussion of physician-assisted suicide and euthanasia is becoming increasingly public as states have initiatives and bills pending in the legislatures. The debate is no longer confined to physicians, philosophers, and theologians, as many people have to make decisions about end-of-life care for loved ones. When a person has a relative who is dying and perhaps suffering in the process, the arguments for and against physician-assisted suicide/euthanasia are no longer academic; they touch real life. For example, some time ago I was having dinner at a local restaurant with my family and was engaged in conversation with the people sitting next to us. As the conversation unfolded, they confided in my wife and me that their elderly mother had just been diagnosed with end-stage stomach cancer. She had requested an appointment with Jack Kevorkian, the well-known "suicide doctor." They wondered what they should do with such a request and asked our opinion. What would you have told them?

From the context of a Christian worldview, the Bible seems clear that taking innocent life is a prerogative that belongs to God alone. This is the basis for the long-standing prohibition of suicide and laws against murder. Though some would argue that with terminal illness these prohibitions should not apply, and that out of compassion for the dying, physician-assisted suicide/euthanasia should be allowed, there is a consensus among religious believers that physician-assisted suicide/euthanasia violates important moral values that protect the sanctity of life and the dignity of the seriously ill.

However, that is only the beginning of the discussion about physician-assisted suicide/euthanasia. There is also a significant public policy dimension that is still under debate today. In the aftermath of the 1997 Supreme Court decision, many states passed laws prohibiting physician-assisted suicide, and there is still a strong movement to legalize physician-assisted suicide in the United States. Currently there are no efforts to legalize euthanasia, though in some parts of Europe, both physician-assisted suicide and euthanasia are legal. This is a good example of a moral issue that has an ongoing discussion about whether it should be legal. Though physician-assisted suicide and euthanasia are two different things, many of the arguments for legalizing physician-assisted suicide also apply to euthanasia, so the following discussion will consider both together.

Imagine that you are talking with Dr. Kevorkian about legalizing physician-assisted suicide. He wants you to understand why he is so committed to providing suicide assistance for dying patients (or was until he went to prison!) and why he thinks legalizing physician-assisted suicide is so important.

The Argument from Mercy

When confronted by a dying patient who is suffering and wants to die, Kevorkian would conclude that the most merciful thing to do is to stop needless suffering by physician-assisted suicide/euthanasia. After all, one of the principal aims of medicine is the alleviation of suffering, and we have no hesitation about relieving the suffering of animals when they are approaching death. We routinely administer "mercy killing" for animals for whom the end of life constitutes great suffering, though we may also take this action for convenience' sake.

Kevorkian would also appeal to something like the Golden Rule to support this general argument from mercy. Since most people would not like to be subjected to needless suffering at the end of life, supporters of physician-assisted suicide/euthanasia suggest that people should "do unto others" as they would have others do unto them. The argument from mercy is a powerful argument in favor of physician-assisted suicide/euthanasia and usually elicits strong feelings toward the suffering patients when presented in public policy debates.

You might respond to Kevorkian in this way. You would explain to him that the number of cases in which suffering prior to death is so severe that it cannot be adequately controlled is actually very small, though they do occur from time to time. With available pain medication, virtually every patient's pain can be adequately managed. In the vast majority of cases, physician-assisted suicide/euthanasia is simply not necessary to fulfill the goal of medicine to provide relief of suffering. In those cases in which relief of pain is particularly challenging, there are options short of physician-assisted suicide/euthanasia that can be employed. For example, it is acceptable for dying patients to "sleep before they die." That is, if the amount of pain medication necessary to control their pain puts them in an unconscious state before they die, and that is their wish, then there is no reason why that cannot be accomplished. That is not killing the patient, since death still takes its natural course. In addition, if the amount of pain relief necessary to con-

Dr. Kevorkian Goes to Prison

In 1999 a Michigan judge sentenced Jack Kevorkian to ten to twenty-five years in prison for second-degree murder. Already at age seventy, many worried that he would die in prison. He was prosecuted for violating Michigan's law prohibiting assisted suicide, and roughly eight years earlier he had lost his medical license for assisting in a variety of suicides over the years. What seemed to be the last straw for the state was the televised administration of euthanasia for fifty-two-year-old Thomas Youk, who was suffering from Lou Gehrig's disease (ALS). Youk's family was grateful to Kevorkian for his assistance in relieving Youk's suffering, and the defense argued that no useful purpose would be served by sentencing Kevorkian to jail. Prosecutors insisted that Kevorkian had no intention of abiding by Michigan's law, which recently had been affirmed by a 2–1 vote in the state. Kevorkian had been tried four times previously, with three acquittals and one hung jury as the results. Kevorkian was released in 2007 after serving the minimum required prior to his parole.*

*BBC News, June 1, 2007.

trol pain slows down the patient's heartbeat and breathing, it is morally justifiable under what is called "the law of double effect" to prescribe a sufficient dosage of medication to relieve the pain even if one of the possible side effects is hastening the death of the patient.[11]

This law states that an unintended but foreseen negative consequence of a specific action does not necessarily make that action immoral. Here the *intent* is critical. If the intent is simply to end the patient's life quickly and quietly, then that constitutes euthanasia and is the direct killing of the patient. However, if the intent is actually to relieve pain (though not permanently) and the patient's death is hastened, though not caused, as a result of the amount of medication necessary to do that, that is something quite different and may be justifiable as an unintended, though foreseen, consequence of an intended action.

The Argument from Utility

Kevorkian would next bring up the point that when physician-assisted suicide/ euthanasia is performed at a patient's request, it's a "win-win" situation in which everyone involved benefits. Consider the benefits of physician-assisted suicide/ euthanasia in such instances: the patient's suffering is ended, the high cost of expensive terminal medical care is avoided, the family can grieve appropriately and get on with their lives, and the medical staff can avoid the stress and anguish of an unnecessarily drawn-out dying process. He would suggest that he has seen this scenario many times with the people he has assisted, and he fails to see the downside to such a practice.

But you might respond to Kevorkian in this way. Before the calculation of consequences is finished, you must also consider the impact on the public at large, over the long term as well as the short term. There is more to this than simply what happens to the individual patient and his or her family. You would also want to know if the action produces a balance of good consequences in society in general, especially as it relates to future terminally ill patients who might be coerced into consenting to active euthanasia. You could also point out to Dr. Kevorkian that this way of thinking about physician-assisted suicide/euthanasia assumes the adequacy of utilitarian moral reasoning. You could then point out that there are deontological arguments as well that contribute to the discussion, such as the sanctity of life and the prohibition on killing innocent people.

The Argument from Autonomy

When it comes to legalizing physician-assisted suicide/euthanasia, Kevorkian and other advocates appeal to an argument from personal autonomy. What he means by this argument is that the law generally protects the right of individuals to make life's most private and personal decisions on their own, apart from interference by government. For example, decisions about marriage, family, child rearing (except in cases of abuse), procreation, birth control, abortion, and other personal matters are left to people to make by themselves, in ways that reflect their values. Except in cases of abortion, where the life of another person is at stake, it is right that the government leaves people alone to make these decisions as they see fit. This falls under the heading of the "right to privacy," and the law protects the rights of individuals to exercise personal liberty in this way. This is what the Constitution means when it says that people cannot be denied liberty without due process of law.

Kevorkian wants to extend the right to privacy to the end of one's life. He maintains that the timing and manner of one's death are surely as personal and private a decision as those already protected by the right to privacy. That decision reflects one's deepest values about life, death, and the afterlife and should not be subject to interference by a law that makes physician-assisted suicide/euthanasia illegal. This is particularly the case when the patient is terminally ill and death is imminent.

Here is how you could respond to Kevorkian. First, personal autonomy is not absolute; there are things that one cannot morally do to one's body, such as put illegal drugs into it or use it for prostitution. Further, when there has been a conflict between autonomy and the rights of others, the rights of others usually take precedence. This is particularly the case when the exercise of autonomy results in harm coming to others. You can make a good case that by opening the door to euthanasia, others at the end of life are being harmed. The data from the Dutch experience of euthanasia strongly suggest that terminally ill people are being administered euthanasia against their will and without their knowledge. Virtually everyone who advocates euthanasia insists that the practice must be administered only with the consent of the terminally ill patient, that nonvoluntary euthanasia is clearly immoral. But if you can show that by legalizing physician-assisted suicide/ euthanasia, other terminally ill people are put at risk for nonvoluntary euthanasia, that argues strongly that the exercise of autonomy for some is bringing harm to others. In such cases, the reality of harm overrides the right to privacy and personal liberty.

Another way to respond to the argument from autonomy is to insist that if the right to die is grounded in personal autonomy (the common grounding for a right to die), it is a *universal* right. Since everyone has autonomy over these key personal decisions, everyone has the right to determine the timing and manner of one's death. Thus the right to die with physician-assisted suicide cannot be limited to the terminally ill. It must be available to all, regardless of age or illness. Yet most proponents of physician-assisted suicide insist that it be limited, even though it can't be both limited and based on autonomy.

Though Kevorkian is not approaching this from a Christian worldview, we need to be clear that for the Christian the argument from autonomy is a difficult one to maintain. The main element of this argument is that individuals have the right to determine the timing and manner of their death. But theologically this is just not the case. The timing of one's death belongs to God alone. It is his decision, not any individual's. Hebrews 9:27 says, "It is appointed for men to die once and after this comes judgment" (NASB). It is clear from the context that the one who has appointed the time for man to die is God. This echoes the statement in Ecclesiastes 3:2 that there is "a time to be born and a time to die." These times, including death, are appointed by God, who is the sovereign over all of life. This long-standing part of Christian tradition informed, in part, the Supreme Court's decision not to recognize a constitutionally protected right to die. In its deliberations the Court needed to see a long tradition outside the legal arena in which people recognized a right to die. Precisely the opposite is the case in American history, in which there is a strong theological notion of the sovereignty of God over death.

Euthanasia Is Not a Violation of the Hippocratic Oath

Suppose you bring up to Kevorkian the idea of the Hippocratic Oath that all physicians are supposed to respect life. You point out to him that many medical professionals oppose euthanasia because it violates the part of the oath that prohibits physicians from using medical means to kill their patients. Kevorkian might

Euthanasia During Hurricane Katrina

In the aftermath of the most devastating hurricane ever to hit the Gulf Coast, physicians caring for elderly seriously ill patients in New Orleans area hospitals faced an incredibly difficult moral dilemma. With patients either too ill or too elderly to be moved, and with no power, no fresh water, soaring temperatures, flooding in the hospitals, and sanitation breakdowns, physicians were apparently no longer able to take care of their patients. Rather than abandon them, as hospital staffs were alleged to have done, the other option was to mercifully administer euthanasia to them. Some physicians and hospital workers felt it was more compassionate to perform "mercy killing" than to let them die from their deteriorating conditions. The Louisiana attorney general investigated the allegations and looked into six hospitals and thirteen nursing homes in the New Orleans area to see if there was merit to the claim that patients had been administered euthanasia. When the coroner was called in to investigate the deaths, he could not determine the cause of death because many of the bodies were badly decomposed from the heat and the flooding.*

*Jennifer Lahl, "When Is Killing Merciful?: Life Choices in Hurricanes Katrina and Wilma," *Breakpoint Worldview*, January–February 2006, 12–17.

point out to you in response that the oath also prohibits abortion, yet hundreds of thousands of abortions are performed annually. He might also suggest to you that the Hippocratic Oath has become less of a moral requirement than a piece of quaint fiction and is not taken all that seriously in medical training today. He might further suggest that had Hippocrates known of chronic diseases in his time to the extent they exist today, he may have changed his mind and supported euthanasia, since such a significant part of his oath deals with alleviation of suffering for patients in pain. That is, he was not aware of the prospect that many seriously ill people face today, namely, a longer life span in increasingly poor quality-of-life circumstances.

Here is where you can respond to Kevorkian. Had Hippocrates known of the advances in pain management, he surely would not have authorized taking the lives of his patients. This is because he could control pain without physician-assisted suicide/euthanasia being necessary. He could accomplish his overriding goal of alleviating suffering without having to end the life of his patient.

There Is No Morally Relevant Difference between Killing and Allowing to Die

Kevorkian might try to remind you that there is no significant difference between killing through euthanasia and allowing someone to die by termination of life support. Since we have already established the morality of terminating life-sustaining treatment, Kevorkian and other advocates of physician-assisted suicide/euthanasia argue that there is no significant moral difference between allowing a patient to die by stopping life support and killing that patient by administration of euthanasia. Thus both morality and the law should allow for physician-assisted suicide/euthanasia.

Here Kevorkian cites the late moral philosopher James Rachels, who uses a well-known illustration to argue for his point. It is the analogy of the nephew in the bathtub. In this case, a man stands to inherit a fortune if his young nephew, who is the sole heir to his father's fortune, meets an untimely demise. In one scenario, the uncle comes into the bathroom and actively drowns the boy in the bathtub by holding his head under the water. In the other, the uncle walks into the bathroom just after the boy has hit his head on the tub's faucet, and the boy is lying unconscious under the water. The uncle does nothing, allowing the boy to die. In these two scenarios, the uncle is equally responsible for his nephew's death. There is no significant difference between allowing the boy to die and actively killing him. Rachels then applies the analogy to end-of-life decisions and concludes that there is no significant moral difference between killing patients through physician-assisted suicide/euthanasia and allowing them to die through terminating life support.

However, there are ways to respond to this analogy. First, you could suggest that analogies like this are valid only for analogous cases.[12] Since the actions of the uncle in both scenarios are so morally outrageous and cannot be justified, it should not be surprising that other fine distinctions (especially ones about the intent of the moral actor) necessary in the medical setting are lost in this blatant example. This is an example of what is called the "sledgehammer effect,"[13] in which analogies are used with the result that essential distinctions are masked in the process of transferring the analogy to another setting. For example, if I mixed lemon juice into two glasses of wine, one white and one red, no one would be able to taste the difference between the wines because the lemon juice would be overpowering and would effectively mask the subtle differences.

But the most significant criticism leveled at this argument is its inadequate analysis of a moral act. There is more to a moral act than the means used to accomplish the end. *Intent* is a critical component and at times the only determinant of the morality of the case. Consider, for example, the difference between a gift and a bribe. The intent there determines the morality of two otherwise identical acts. It would not be accurate to say that two people who offered money to the same man, but for vastly different reasons, did the same thing. A gift and a bribe are two fundamentally different moral acts, and the only difference between them is the intent of the *moral actor*, the technical term for the person performing the action in question.

We can make the same criticism of Rachels's illustration of Jack and Jill visiting their sick grandmother.[14] He poses a scenario in which Jack goes to visit his grandmother out of good intentions, simply to show kindness to her. By contrast, Jill has ulterior motives relating to her grandmother's considerable estate. Although on the surface they performed the same action, their motives were clearly different. Rachels would argue that different intent only reveals the different character of Jack and Jill. It seems clear, however, that they did two fundamentally different acts. Whereas Jack visited a sick and elderly woman to cheer her up, Jill visited her to secure a place in her grandmother's will. Here intent is not irrelevant but makes all the difference in determining the morality of these acts.

Rachels insists that intent only reveals the character of the moral actor. But certainly character is the tendency to *act* in certain ways and in certain situations. Character is linked inseparably to the actions that demonstrate it. Otherwise, it is not clear how character can be known at all, if intent is separate from the act itself. It seems that either actions and intentions are linked, in which case this part of Rachels' argument fails, or intent cannot reveal character, as Rachels and most ethicists insist it does. Intent clearly does make a significant moral difference in the distinction between killing and allowing to die.

Even though the result is the same, the intent is critical in justifying the termination of life support and raising questions about the legitimacy of physician-assisted suicide/euthanasia. The intent in the termination of life-sustaining treatment is not necessarily that the patient dies. As we discussed earlier in this chapter, most patients who desire to stop such treatments do not want to die; they simply want to live out their remaining days without dependence on medical technology that will not change the downward course of their disease and may be more burdensome than beneficial. Although it is true that in many cases the patient will die soon after termination of life support, it is usually not the intent. By contrast, the intent in physician-assisted suicide/euthanasia is clearly to cause the patient to die.

Not only is the intent different between killing and allowing to die, but the cause of death is also. In cases in which life support is terminated, the underlying disease that is allowed to take its natural course is the immediate cause of death. The treatment was not curing the patient. At best, such treatment was only delaying an inevitable death. Withdrawing treatment does not allow for further delay of the patient's death. The disease is allowed to finish its course, unchecked by any additional treatments. Of course, when the patient chooses this course, the physician is morally obligated to provide for adequate comfort care for the patient, also known as "palliative care." But when a physician assists in suicide or administers euthanasia, his or her action is the immediate cause of death. It is inaccurate to insist that physicians do the same thing in euthanasia as in the termination of life support. They are doing two fundamentally different acts.

Euthanasia Does Not Always Involve Killing a Person

Here Kevorkian might follow Rachels and some others, such as Peter Singer, who distinguish between a person's *biological life*, or physical existence, and one's *biographical life*, or the aspects of one's life that make it meaningful. This is one way of maintaining a distinction between a human being and a person. That is, one can be a human being and not a person by being alive but being so impaired or so seriously ill that it is said of that person that his or her "life" is gone. Some view the unborn in this way; others view certain types of severely handicapped newborns as human beings but not full persons. Some apply this distinction to the end of life as well. They argue that some terminally ill elderly are so debilitated or demented that they cannot reasonably be called persons. They are, for the most part, only bodies from which the persons have already departed. It is common to view patients who are in an irreversible coma or a permanent vegetative state in this way—merely as bodies with physiological function but with no inner life.[15]

Thus Kevorkian and others like him insist that to administer euthanasia or assist patients in suicide does not involve killing a person. It means ending only the physiological functioning of the body—since they maintain that the *person* has already died. So proponents of physician-assisted suicide/euthanasia argue that physician-assisted suicide and euthanasia do not violate the sixth commandment against killing innocent persons.

One's biographical life, according to Rachels, is the sum total of one's goals, dreams, aspirations, accomplishments, and human relationships. These are the things that form the narrative of one's life. According to advocates of this position, modern medicine has enabled one to exist biologically while the person's biographical life has ended. They suggest that a person who is in a permanent vegetative state or is in intense suffering with death imminent can be said to have lost his or her biographical life. Therefore a human being basically exists only as a body and has lost the essence of what makes him or her a person. This is what separates humans from animals. Since it is biographical life that gives human beings their distinctive value, Rachels reasons that when that has been lost, what is essential about personhood has been lost. Therefore, concerns about killing persons by physician-assisted suicide/euthanasia are minimized, thus deflecting much of the sanctity-of-life criticism of his position.

Here is what you might say in response to this distinction. First, biographical life, far from rendering biological life morally irrelevant, rather presupposes it. The capacity to have biographical life is grounded in a person being of a specific kind, namely, a human being. A human being has an essence that is capable of constructing those necessary elements of biographical life.[16] In other words, a thing has certain qualities because it is a thing of a particular kind. The possibility of a coherent full biographical life is grounded in biological life, both of which are part of the essence of being human. Thus personhood is not lost just because the ability to exercise its capacities is lost. Losing the essence is not the same thing as losing the function in the same way that losing the use of my arm is not the same thing as having the arm amputated.

Second, if biographical life is what gives life its value, and if, when it is gone, essentially only a body can be said to exist, then what is to prevent us from stripping the "person" of all his rights? If biographical life alone gives life its value, then that would seem to be the basis for all other rights. But if biographical life is lost, it would seem that the person has lost all other rights too. Could we then bury the "person" and treat him like a corpse? Can we take organs with consent of next of kin? Can we experiment on him, again with appropriate proxy consent? If the essentials of one's life and one's rights are tied up with biographical life, and that is lost, there does not seem to be any consistent way of preventing any of the above scenarios as long as they are done with appropriate respect for the dead.

One could even argue that if rights have been lost with biographical life, not even consent would be necessary for physician-assisted suicide/euthanasia. Opponents of physician-assisted suicide/euthanasia suggest that this move from voluntary to involuntary euthanasia, which is performed without the patient's consent and at times without the patient's knowledge, is already happening in parts of Europe. Thus it is not surprising to them that this biographical-biological life distinction is problematic and could lead to abuses in its administration.

The Case against Assisted Suicide and Active Euthanasia

Opponents of physician-assisted suicide/euthanasia reject the biographical-biological life distinction and uphold the moral difference between killing and allowing to die, and they conclude that euthanasia and assisted suicide involve killing an innocent person. Assisted suicide and euthanasia thus violate both Western social-legal and Judeo-Christian prohibitions on killing innocent people. For most opponents of euthanasia and assisted suicide, the fact that they violate the norm against killing the innocent is sufficient to end the discussion. That is, if the key distinctions made by proponents, such as the distinction between killing and allowing to die and the distinction between biological and biographical life, cannot be maintained, there is no case for euthanasia. The following are other arguments that supplement this principal deontological one.

Physician-Assisted Suicide and Euthanasia Are Ways of Playing God

It is not the place of human beings to take a prerogative that belongs exclusively to God, namely, the taking of innocent life. It is simply not within the purview of human beings to determine the time and manner of their death. Scripture is clear that such matters belong exclusively to God—that is, there are some prerogatives in life that are only God's, the direct taking of life being one of them.[17] Modern medicine does not play God when intervening to prevent death, only when it actively takes an innocent human life. Granted, this argument is limited to people who presuppose God's existence.

Suffering May Be Redemptive

The idea that suffering may be redemptive is a specifically Christian notion rooted in the biblical teaching that suffering produces character. A significant part of the biblical explanation and justification of the existence of suffering (the technical term for which is theodicy, literally the "justification of God" in the face of the reality of suffering) is that it has a redemptive element. People grow and mature out of hardship, and God uses the process as a chisel to chip away the rough edges of a person's character (Rom. 5:3–5; 2 Cor. 4:16–17; James 1:2–4). Suffering further equips the believer to be a source of comfort to others who experience hardship.

However, this argument has limits when applied to medicine, because, as Rachels indicates, if it were applied consistently, it would preclude any medical treatment that alleviates suffering. Just because suffering produces a beneficial result in the believer's life, it does not follow that the medical profession should not work to reduce unnecessary suffering. From a biblical perspective, it is suffering that cannot be avoided, such as suffering for one's faith, that has redemptive value. There is no particular value in enduring suffering that can be avoided; rather, that is foolishness.

In addition, this argument has limits when applied to end-of-life medical decisions, because some suffering occurs when death is so imminent that it is difficult to see how it could be redemptive for the patient. Further, the Bible seems to indicate that the character-refining value of suffering is primarily for this life, since once a believer dies and is united with God, his or her character is made perfect. On that basis, it is difficult to see how it could be redemptive when it occurs so close to death.

Experimental Drugs for the Terminally Ill

Abagail Burroughs was nineteen when she discovered she had cancerous tumors in her head and neck. She was dying, and her last hope, according to her oncologist, was an experimental drug, Erbitux, which they hoped would shrink the tumors. But in 1999, when Abagail was ill, Erbitux was still in the process (a decade-long process on average) of being approved by the Food and Drug Administration (FDA). She died in 2001 at the age of twenty-one, three years before Erbitux gained FDA approval. The FDA's policy is that even the terminally ill cannot legally receive experimental drugs, even though it may be their last and only hope. Some terminally ill patients do get access to these drugs through participation in clinical trials — experiments on human subjects required by the FDA before they will approve a drug for general use. The Abagail Alliance, an advocacy group for the terminally ill, sued to force a change in the FDA's policy. A federal judge dismissed their suit, but the court of appeals reversed the ruling, saying that "a mentally competent, terminally ill adult patient has a right to obtain potentially lifesaving new drugs" that have potential to help his or her illness. However, in early 2008, the U.S. Supreme Court ruled that there is no such right of access to experimental drugs for the terminally ill, arguing that the vast majority of experimental drugs have no benefit and may be harmful to patients.*

*David G. Savage, "Justices Uphold Ban on Test Drugs for the Dying," *Los Angeles Times*, January 15, 2008.

Misdiagnoses Are Possible

Administering euthanasia or assisting in suicide leaves no opportunity to correct a misdiagnosis. Terminal illness cases in which euthanasia could be considered and in which a diagnosis could be mistaken are quite rare. However, some people have made remarkable recoveries from what doctors thought was a terminal illness. In 1984 Sidney Hook, a noted American educator and philosopher, requested that doctors remove all life support from him. He was suffering from a stroke, pleurisy, and violent hiccups that prevented him from taking food orally. The doctors refused, suggesting that it was premature to make that kind of decision. Within one month Hook was out of the hospital, and within six months he had resumed his writing, publishing several articles and another book in the following two years.[18]

As exceptional as a case like this may be, it should be noted that the doctors acted appropriately. The instances in which people come back from imminent death are actually quite rare, though it is undeniable that they do occur.

Euthanasia Will Likely Move from Voluntary to Nonvoluntary Euthanasia

A principal concern of most opponents of euthanasia is that the acceptance of voluntary euthanasia may lead to involuntary euthanasia. It is not hard to see how family pressure and mounting medical bills that eat away at a patient's estate could coerce one into consenting to ending one's life, not because he is tired of living, but because others are tired of his living. The pressure to do one's "duty to die and get out of the way"—as a former governor of Colorado, Richard Lamm, regrettably put it—could be subtle yet significant. This pressure could grow as the baby boomers enter their retirement years in record numbers over the next few decades and pressures to reduce the cost of medical care increase dramatically. Further, if assisted suicide and euthanasia are legalized, the elderly and seriously ill could face the unenviable situation in which they would have to justify their continued existence. That is, in the face of this pressure to end their lives and stop being a drain on society's or the family's resources, they would have to make the case why they should be allowed to *continue* their lives. Such a need to justify one's continued existence is inconsistent with the right to life protected by the Constitution.

Already there is evidence that a movement from voluntary to nonvoluntary euthanasia is occurring. In places such as the Netherlands, it is clear that nonvoluntary euthanasia is occurring at a rate that alarms opponents of the practice.[19] There is a good reason why the movement from voluntary to nonvoluntary physician-assisted suicide/euthanasia is difficult to stop. Any law that would prohibit coercion or pressure on a potential candidate for euthanasia would be impossible to enforce since no one except family members would have access to those coercive conversations. Most of the discussions in which elderly or terminally ill persons could be pressured into making decisions about ending their lives could never be detected without having access to a family's private conversations.[20] Further, a physician who is recommending such a course is in a very influential position over a vulnerable patient and can contribute to coercion.

Additional concerns about heading down the "slippery slope" are voiced by those who fear that euthanasia would not be restricted to the terminally ill but would be extended to people with varying quality-of-life circumstances. Opponents fear that candidates for euthanasia will include the nonterminally ill, such as people with Alzheimer's disease or other degenerative brain diseases, the severely mentally retarded, and handicapped newborns.

The slippery slope arguments frequently brought to bear on this issue often invoke the parallel to the Nazi euthanasia experience in World War II. Although society is rightly fearful of anything that would reproduce the Nazi experiments in medical killing, it is important to realize what the Nazi experience does not teach us about our current situation.[21]

It does not indicate that a practice that began out of mercy will move toward more corrupt ends, since the Nazi experience did not begin out of mercy. It does not indicate that euthanasia for the terminally ill will be extended to other handicapped people, since the Nazi experience did not begin with the terminally ill. It does not indicate that voluntary euthanasia will move toward involuntary euthanasia (though many believe that distinction will be difficult to maintain if voluntary euthanasia is legalized), since the Nazi experience did not begin with voluntary euthanasia. The Nazi program started near the *bottom* of the slippery slope and does not illustrate the movement that many opponents believe it does. However, two important parallels in the *thinking* behind the Nazi experience serve as cautions for us. They are the concepts of the life not worth living and the separation of personhood and its attendant rights from biological life. Both concepts are being heard increasingly in the euthanasia debate.

Conclusion

The issues surrounding end-of-life medical decisions and euthanasia will likely become more complex as medical technology continues to develop, increasing the ability to extend people's life span. Although one should be cautious about any separation of biological life and personhood (or biographical life, to use Rachels's term), one should be equally wary about using scarce and very expensive medical resources on treatment that is futile. There is more to the sanctity of life than simply postponing an imminent death. All life is valuable to God, irrespective of its quality, and the biblical commands against killing innocent people should make society cautious about supporting euthanasia and assisted suicide, as merciful as they seem. Nevertheless, that does not mean that the sanctity-of-life principle demands that every patient receive indefinitely the most aggressive treatment available. In many cases, treatment is clearly no longer helpful to the patient, is no longer desired by the patient, or is more burdensome than beneficial to the patient. Even though death is rightly to be resisted through reasonable medical means, the Christian's eternal destiny is beyond death. In that sense, death for a Christian is by definition a "good death" because it ushers him or her into God's presence in eternal life.

For Further Reading

Callahan, Daniel. *The Troubled Dream of Life: Living with Mortality.* New York: Simon and Schuster, 1993.

Chamberlain, Paul. *Final Wishes: A Cautionary Tale on Death, Dignity and Physician-Assisted Suicide.* Downers Grove, Ill.: InterVarsity, 2000.

Foley, Kathleen, and Herbert Hendin. *The Case against Assisted Suicide.* Baltimore: Johns Hopkins University Press, 2002.

Quill, Timothy E., and Margaret E. Battin. *Physician-Assisted Dying: The Case for Palliative Care and Patient Choice.* Baltimore: Johns Hopkins University Press, 2004.

Uhlmann, Michael. *Last Rights: Physician-Assisted Suicide and Euthanasia.* Grand Rapids: Eerdmans, 1997.

Review Questions

1. Terri Schaivo's case was about which of the following elements: termination of ventilator support, physician-assisted suicide, or removal of feeding tubes?

2. What are the three primary methods physicians can use to hasten a patient's death?

3. What are some common forms of life-support technology?

4. What is the main difference between physician-assisted suicide and euthanasia?

5. What is the literal meaning of the term *euthanasia*?

6. Instead of the traditional terms—*ordinary* and *extraordinary means*—what different terms are more in use today?

7. What is a living will? What is the other term used to describe this document?

8. What is a "durable power of attorney for health care"?

9. What is a DNR order?

10. To what does the term *competence* refer?

11. What was the basic issue at hand in the case of Karen Ann Quinlan?

12. How was the case of Nancy Cruzan different from Quinlan's case?

13. What issue was decided in the Glucksberg/Vacco cases? Which court decided those cases?

14. What are the only U.S. states in which physician-assisted suicide is legal?

15. Name at least one country in Europe in which euthanasia is legal.

16. Briefly summarize the biblical perspective on death.

17. How should death be viewed from the perspective of the death and resurrection of Jesus?

18. What is the difference between *withholding* and *withdrawing* a treatment?.

19. Does the termination of life support (TLS) violate the sanctity-of-life principle?

20. Under what conditions is TLS morally acceptable?

21. What does it mean to say that a treatment is "futile"?

22. Should feeding tubes be considered medical treatment that can be removed under the right conditions? Defend your answer.

23. What are the primary arguments given in support of physician-assisted suicide/euthanasia? How would you respond to each one?

24. Explain why the movement from voluntary to nonvoluntary physician-assisted suicide/euthanasia is likely to happen.

25. Evaluate the use of the Nazi analogy in the discussion of physician-assisted suicide/euthanasia.

Cases for Discussion

Case 8.1: Your Father's Living Will

Your elderly father has recently been diagnosed with terminal lung cancer. His doctors estimate that he has roughly a year left to live before the cancer will overtake him. He is wisely using this as an opportunity to think about what kinds of treatments he wants or wants to refuse as the cancer takes its course. He has seen a number of his friends die on life support in hospitals and wants to make sure that he doesn't die that way. He is asking you to be his medical decision maker should he lose the ability to make those decisions for himself. Specifically, he does not want to be put on ventilator support, especially if it looks like he cannot be weaned off of it. You realize that means that he may die sooner than if he were on such support, and you wonder if you can do that, given your strong view of the sanctity of life. It feels as if you would be killing your dad if you authorized the withholding or withdrawal of ventilator support.

Questions for Discussion

1. Do you think it is acceptable to remove or withhold a ventilator from your father in his condition, even if it means he will die sooner? If not, why not? If so, under what conditions is it acceptable?

2. Do you believe that removing a ventilator would be killing your father? Would it make you complicit in his death? Why or why not?

3. Your father also does not want to be on feeding tubes for his nutrition and hydration should he lose the ability to swallow. Would you consider feeding tubes the same as a ventilator, or are feeding tubes more basic care? Would you say that removing feeding tubes is the same as starving someone to death? Why or why not?

Case 8.2: Performing Physician-Assisted Suicide?

You are a physician specializing in end-of-life care of the elderly, particularly pain management at the end of life. You practice in Oregon, where physician-assisted suicide is legal as long as specific guidelines are followed. You have a patient who is in the beginning stages of a long-term decline in his health due to AIDS. This patient has seen numerous friends die of AIDS, and he has no interest in suffering like many of his close friends have done. He has asked if you would assist him in taking his life should his suffering become unbearable. He doesn't anticipate that anytime soon, but he wants to know that if his pain becomes more than he chooses to bear, you will help him take his life by prescribing and securing an overdose of medication for him. You assure him that you will do everything you can to keep him comfortable, and he asks if that includes physician-assisted suicide.

Questions for Discussion

1. Would you go along with his request for physician-assisted suicide? Why or why not?

2. If you do not go along with his request, you are obligated to treat his pain adequately. Would you be comfortable prescribing enough pain medication that it might put him to sleep for good before he dies? What if the amount of pain medication necessary to control his pain slows his heartbeat and breathing so that he dies a few days sooner?

3. Do you think it is a good idea for physician-assisted suicide to be legal? Why or why not?

Chapter 8 Notes

1. See, for example, the landmark SUPPORT study, which indicated that the experience of dying patients in hospitals in the United States was a great concern. See the SUPPORT Principal Investigators, "A Controlled Trial to Improve Care for Seriously Ill Hospitalized Patients," *Journal of the American Medical Association* 274, no. 20 (November 22–29, 1995): 1591–98.

2. Derek Humphry, *Final Exit: The Practicalities of Self-Deliverance and Assisted Suicide for the Dying*, 3rd ed. (New York: Dell, 2002).

3. 355 A.2d 647 (1976).

4. 497 U.S. 261; 110 S. Ct. 2841 (1990).

5. The cases the Supreme Court reviewed were *Washington v. Glucksberg* (listed in appeals court documents as *Compassion in Dying v. Washington*, 79 F. 3d 790 [1996], and *Vacco v. Quill*, 80 F. 3d 716 [1996]).

6. For further discussion on the right to die, see Leon R. Kass, "Is There a Right to Die?" *Hastings Center Report* 23 (January–February 1993): 34–43, and Yale Kamisar, "Are Laws against Assisted Suicide Unconstitutional?" *Hastings Center Report* 23 (May–June 1993): 32–41.

7. Paul Ramsey, "The Indignity of 'Death with Dignity,'" *Hastings Center Report* 2 (May 1974): 47–62. For more discussion of the theological perspectives on death and dying, see Scott B. Rae and Paul M. Cox, *Bioethics: A Christian Approach in a Pluralistic Age* (Grand Rapids: Eerdmans, 1999), 217–52.

8. For considering the interests of the family, see John Hardwig, *Is There a Duty to Die?* (New York: Routledge, 2000). See also for consideration of society's interests, Daniel Callahan, *Setting Limits: Medical Goals in an Aging Society* (New York: Touchstone, 1987).

9. Gilbert Meilander, "On Removing Food and Water: Against the Stream," *Hastings Center Report* 14 (December 1984): 11–13.

10. Lawrence J. Schneiderman, "Exile and PVS," *Hastings Center Report* 20 (May–June 1990): 5.

11. See, for example, Task Force on Pain Management, "Pain Management: Theological and Ethical Principles Governing the Use of Pain Relief for Dying Patients," *Health Progress* (January–February 1993): 36–38.

12. Tom L. Beauchamp, "A Reply to Rachels on Active and Passive Euthanasia," in *Contemporary Issues in Bioethics*, ed. Tom L. Beauchamp and LeRoy Walters (Belmont, Calif.: Wadsworth, 1989), 336–45.

13. J. P. Moreland, "James Rachels and the Active Euthanasia Debate," *Journal of the Evangelical Theological Society* 31 (March 1988): 89.

14. James Rachels, *The End of Life* (Oxford: Oxford University Press, 1986), 93–94.

15. For example, see Peter Singer, *Rethinking Life and Death* (New York: St. Martin's, 1994), for another example of a view similar to Rachels's. Some in Christian circles hold that patients in a permanent vegetative state have lost their personhood. See Robert Wennberg, *Terminal Choices: Euthanasia, Suicide and the Right to Die* (Grand Rapids: Eerdmans, 1989).

16. For an extended defense of a substance dualist view of a human person, see J. P. Moreland and Scott B. Rae, *Body and Soul: Human Nature and the Crisis in Ethics* (Downers Grove, Ill.: InterVarsity, 2000).

17. There are exceptions to this general principle. Killing in self-defense, killing of legitimate combatants in a just war, and capital punishment are allowed by biblical principles and have been recognized by Christian tradition. Of course, Christian pacifists dispute each of these exceptions.

18. This account is taken from Beth Spring and Ed Larson, *Euthanasia: Spiritual, Medical and Legal Issues in Terminal Health Care* (Portland, Ore.: Multnomah, 1988), 12–13.

19. Numerous studies of this have been undertaken. For further data, see John Keown, "On Regulating Death," *Hastings Center Report* 22 (1992): 39–43; Herbert Hendin et al., "Physician Assisted Suicide and Euthanasia in the Netherlands: Lessons from the Dutch," *Journal of the American Medical Association* 277, no. 21 (June 4, 1997): 1720–22; and Johanna H. Groenewoud et al., "Clinical Problems with the Performance of Euthanasia and Physician Assisted Suicide in the Netherlands," *Netherlands Journal of Medicine* 342, no. 8 (February 24, 2000): 551–56. For a summary of this material, see Scott B. Rae, *Bioethics: A Christian Approach in a Pluralistic Age* (Grand Rapids: Eerdmans, 1999), 248–51.

20. Daniel Callahan, "Self Determination Run Amok," *Hastings Center Report* 22 (March–April 1992).

21. Wennberg, *Terminal Choices*, 214–20.

Chapter 9

Capital Punishment

Whenever there is an execution in the approximately thirty-five U.S. states that have the death penalty, one can usually find both advocates and opponents of capital punishment gathered outside the prison to make statements about the morality of the death penalty. The advocates claim that the condemned murderer is getting what he deserves, that the demands of justice are about to be satisfied. Opponents protest that capital punishment is a barbaric practice, out of place in the modern world and unconstitutional as cruel and inhuman punishment.

Interestingly, religious believers from a variety of religious traditions can be found on both sides of the issue, and usually religious groups hold up signs and placards with biblical references on them. The advocates of the death penalty cite Old Testament passages that speak of the principle of "life for life" and insist that condemned murderers should justly receive death as a consequence of their actions. On the other hand, opponents of capital punishment quote teachings of Jesus with emphasis on mercy, the fact that vengeance belongs to God, and the sacredness of human life. These opposing opinions illustrate that the Christian community mirrors the same debate about the death penalty that exists in society as a whole.

Imagine a situation in which you are a member of a jury that is hearing a murder case. The jury has already convicted the person of first-degree murder. You now proceed to the sentencing phase of the trial. Here you must decide if the crime committed warrants the death penalty. In most states, carefully defined conditions, such as the heinousness of the crime or multiple murders are necessary for a death sentence. You were likely questioned by the attorneys about your view of the death penalty prior to being selected for the jury. Neither the prosecution nor the defense had reservations about your view. But now that it is actually time to make a decision that may result in the death of another person, you are seriously reconsidering your view.

The United States is one of the few industrialized countries that still retains capital punishment. Most countries in Europe have prohibited it, while it remains in force in some Asian countries. Many third world countries and Islamic republics apply the death penalty for a variety of crimes, not just for murder. For example, drug trafficking warrants the death penalty in countries such as Singapore and Malaysia.

The United States Supreme Court has issued two significant decisions concerning capital punishment. The first was the case of *Furman v. Georgia* (1972), in which the Court ruled that capital punishment as currently administered in the state of Georgia violated the Eighth Amendment against cruel and inhuman punishment. In *Gregg v. Georgia* (1976), the Court upheld a death sentence for murder but made sure that juries had careful guidelines to follow in determining the appropriateness of the death sentence. After these two cases, thirty-five states enacted new laws authorizing the death penalty for certain crimes. In 1974, in the wake of growing international terrorism, Congress legislated the death penalty for murder in airline hijacking cases.

Those who oppose the death penalty are known as *abolitionists*, since they favor abolishing death sentences. Although they may disagree about the particulars of some of their arguments, all abolitionists agree that the death penalty is never morally justifiable. Those who favor capital punishment are called *retentionists* because they favor retaining the death penalty. Not all retentionists, however, agree on the particular circumstances that justify capital punishment or on the specific arguments for their position. Inherent in the retentionist view is the sense that capital punishment has been allowed historically and that moral reservations about its use have arisen only within the last century. Thus capital punishment has been traditionally viewed as morally legitimate and necessary in many cultures. Only in recent modern times have objections been raised to what abolitionists call a cruel and outdated form of criminal justice.

A third view has arisen in recent years that occupies somewhat of a middle ground between the two predominant views. I will call this the *procedural abolitionist*. The person who holds this view argues that there is nothing wrong with the death penalty in principle. But since there are a variety of procedural problems with the administration of the death penalty, one should be very careful about having the death penalty at all. The advocate of this view might put a moratorium on capital punishment or even abolish it entirely for these reasons. But one who holds this view might also agree that in rare cases the death penalty could be justified. For all practical purposes, this person fits in the abolitionist camp, but for procedural, not principled reasons.

While most people agree on the general morality of punishment for crime, they disagree on the primary goal of criminal punishment, whether it should be retribution, deterrence, or rehabilitation. Criminal sanctions intend to evoke a respect for the law that is necessary if society is to keep from plunging into chaos. From the biblical perspective, given the reality of humankind's nature, called "total depravity" by theologians, some kind of deterrent is necessary for people to obey the law. Further, respect for those who do abide by the law demands a penalty for those who do not.

The Eighth Amendment of the Constitution protects individuals from cruel and unusual punishment. Specifically, it provides protection from the wanton and unnecessary infliction of pain. That is the reason imprisonment is the principal form of criminal punishment administered in most of the Western world, and it is why the Western justice system rejects much of the Islamic style of punishment. For example, in many Muslim countries that are ruled by Islamic law, theft is punishable by having one's hand cut off, and other crimes are punishable by public floggings. The justice system of the Western world would view such practices in violation of the Eighth Amendment. Second, the Eighth Amendment protects a person from punishment that is out of proportion to the crime committed. Finally, the Constitution protects individuals from punishment without due process of law. Historically, capital punishment has not been considered cruel and inhuman punishment, because when the Bill of Rights was written in 1789, every state allowed the death penalty. Its constitutionality was not substantially challenged until the Furman case in 1972.

Biblical Teaching on Capital Punishment

Many references to the death penalty can be found in the Bible. The Old Testament law in Exodus and Deuteronomy contains most of the biblical references to capital punishment, but references and allusions to the death penalty are also scattered throughout the New Testament. The Old Testament prescribed the death penalty for a variety of crimes. The crimes that merited capital punishment included:[1]

1. Murder (Ex. 21:12–14)[2]
2. Cursing or killing one's parent (Ex. 21:15;[3]Lev. 20:9)[4]
3. Kidnapping (Ex. 21:16; Deut. 24:7)[5]
4. Adultery (Lev. 20:10–21; Deut. 22:22)
5. Incest (Lev. 20:11–12, 14)
6. Bestiality (Ex. 22:19; Lev. 20:15–16)
7. Sodomy or homosexual sexual relations (Lev. 20:13)
8. Premarital sexual promiscuity (Deut. 22:20–21)
9. Rape of an engaged virgin (Deut. 22:23–27)[6]

10. Witchcraft (Ex. 22:18)
11. Offering human sacrifice (Lev. 20:2)
12. Offering sacrifice or worship to a false god (Ex. 22:20; Deut. 13:6–11)
13. Blasphemy (Lev. 24:11–14, 16, 23)
14. Violating the Sabbath (Ex. 35:2)
15. Showing contempt for the court (Deut. 17:8–13)

Compared to other cultures in the ancient Near East, the Old Testament actually limited the number of offenses for which capital punishment was mandated. Except for showing contempt for the court, the capital offenses can be organized around three general classes of violations: (1) violations against the sanctity of life (nos. 1–3 above); (2) violations against the source of life, primarily sexual sins (nos. 4–9); and (3) violations against the purity of the worship of God (nos. 10–14). What these have in common is that they are violations against the sacredness of life, whether directly, as in the case of murder, or indirectly, as in the case of sexual sin (sins regarding the source of life) and the purity of worship (sins against the Creator of life).

The degree to which the death penalty was actually carried out for each of these offenses is not clear from the historical accounts of the Old Testament. The Historical Books and the Prophets contain little information on how the death penalty was administered.[7] Although the Old Testament includes scattered examples of people who received capital punishment in accordance with the guidelines of the Law, it does not provide a thorough sense of how consistently the nation of Israel followed through on the prescribed penalties for many crimes. Of course, this may simply reflect Israel's disobedience in their unwillingness to follow the sanctions laid down by the Law.

Many retentionists use these texts in the Mosaic law to support their position. But there are significant theological questions about the relevance of the Old Testament Law to moral questions today. Simply because the death penalty was widely prescribed in the Law, it does not follow that the death penalty should be prescribed for civil society today. Most advocates of capital punishment recognize some limits on how far to use Mosaic law in support of their view. For example, most retentionists favor the death penalty for murder only under certain circumstances. They do not favor the death penalty for the variety of crimes for which it was prescribed in the Law, such as adultery and idolatry. The abolitionist charges that the retentionist who appeals to the Mosaic law must do so consistently and support capital punishment for the crimes laid out in the Law.

The retentionist will respond that, of course, he does not support capital punishment for all the crimes mentioned in the Law. But the Old Testament texts do give solid support for the principle of the death penalty. The details of the Law may or may not be relevant to the present day, but the Law does support the idea of the death penalty. Even though one might admit that not all the details of the Law are directly, personally applicable, one must admit that at the level of broad, general principles, the Law is certainly relevant for today. For example, believers no longer offer thanksgiving offerings as the Law prescribed. But the principle of being thankful to God for his blessings and publicly expressing thanks is clearly relevant and mandatory today. Or consider the example of the Day of Atonement (Lev. 16). While the church no longer celebrates this festival, one of its underlying principles—the necessity of confessing sin—is surely applicable and mandatory today.

Most agree that the Mosaic law as a rule of life is not applicable in the same way it was in Israel during Old Testament times. The books of Romans, Galatians, and Hebrews all make clear that the Law is not directly applicable today as it was in Old Testament times (Gal. 3:24; see also Rom. 6:14–15; Heb. 10:1). The Law consisted of three parts: the moral law (Ten Commandments), the ceremonial law (laws concerning Israel's religious rituals), and the civil law (laws for maintaining order and justice in civil society). The New Testament clearly teaches that the ceremonial law is neither necessary nor appropriate because of the once-for-all sacrifice of Christ.

When it comes to the civil law, Israel under the Law was a theocracy, or a society in which the law of God was automatically the law of the land. In Old Testament Israel, the people did not vote on the laws to which they were to be subject. No legislative body made the laws, and no executive branch enforced them. People could not change the laws that God had given to Moses on Mount Sinai by "constitutional amendments" or ballot initiatives. The law of God was automatically and unquestionably the law of the land. The reason for this was to make Israel a "kingdom of priests and a holy nation" (Ex. 19:6) by setting up a model society that would corporately bear witness to the reality of God. However, with the coming of Christ, the theocracy ended. The emphasis in the New Testament was on the church as a multinational body that would go out and bring the gospel to different cultures, penetrating them and fulfilling Jesus' mandate to be the salt of the earth and the light of the world (Matt. 5:13–16).

Regardless of the debate on the specifics of Mosaic law for today, most agree that the general principles that undergird the Law are relevant for today and need to be taken seriously. Of course, abolitionists and retentionists will disagree about whether capital punishment is a specific part of the Law or one of its more general principles. At the least, the principle that underlies the idea of capital punishment is the sanctity of life made in the image of God. Whether the death penalty accompanies that principle is at the heart of the debate between those who want to abolish and those who want to retain capital punishment.

One passage in the Bible that was given prior to the Mosaic law and links the sanctity of life and the death penalty is Genesis 9:6, which says, "Whoever sheds the blood of man, by man shall his blood be shed; for in the image of God has God made man." The general principle is "life for life," and the support for it is drawn from the overarching theological truth of man and woman being made in God's image. It is not drawn from any cultural traditions that can be subject to change. The reason that the life-for-life principle is important is that it is based on the unchanging truth that God created human beings in his own image. The life-for-life principle and its link to the image of God in human beings would seem to support the retentionist argument that the sacredness of life necessitates the strongest deterrent—loss of one's own life for taking an innocent life. The *procedural abolitionist* can also appeal to this passage to support capital punishment in principle, though in practice this position is for all practical purposes against capital punishment.

The New Testament makes scant reference to the death penalty, and most references are in the form of allusions as opposed to more direct teaching. Clearly it was in use during the time of Jesus. Romans 13:4 perhaps makes the clearest reference to capital punishment when Paul states that the responsibility of civil government is to maintain civil order as God's servant. Believers and unbelievers alike are to fear the civil authorities in the case of wrongdoing, since "he [the one in authority] does not bear the sword for nothing." Retentionists will argue that Paul assumed the legitimacy of the death penalty as a part of the role of God-ordained government. Abolitionists will counter by suggesting that Paul also assumed the legitimacy of slavery, yet no one considers slavery as a moral option for today. The use of the term *sword* evokes some debate, but it is probably a figure of speech. It may be a metaphor for punishment and law enforcement in general and not necessarily capital punishment. But it may also be a figure of speech for the death penalty, since the sword was normally used as a weapon of death and was likely seen as such by the first-century readers of the book of Romans. Abolitionists sometimes refer to the episode of the woman caught in adultery (John 7:53–8:11) as an example of Jesus setting aside the death penalty. But there are substantial textual issues with this narrative, and there is a lack of clarity concerning its place in the original text. But assuming it belongs in the text, Jesus does not authorize the death penalty, because the situation in which she was brought to him was unjust, since the man who was also guilty was not brought forth. Further, it was clearly a setup to try to trap Jesus, and he refused to participate in the religious leaders' scheme. Finally, Jesus did offer forgiveness to the woman, and no one is suggesting that murderers be forgiven by the state.

Even if one accepts the life-for-life principle, one must admit that the Bible places significant limits on its application. There are some notable exceptions to the life-for-life principle. For example, the first two murderers recorded in biblical history, Cain and Lamech (Gen. 4), were not given the death penalty.[8] In addition, cities of refuge were established in places throughout the land of Israel to provide sanctuary for those who were guilty of manslaughter, or *accidental* killings. The person who committed manslaughter could flee to one of these cities and be free from any retribution. In these cases, a life was not required in exchange for the one that was taken (Num. 35:6–29). Further, taking the life of combatants in war is clearly justified in the Old Testament, as is evident from the numerous wars in which Israel was engaged at God's specific direction. Thus the life-for-life principle was not meant to be applied as an absolute, but within limits laid down by the Law.

One important limit on the administration of capital punishment is described in Numbers 35:30, which says, "Anyone who kills a person is to be put to death as a murderer only on the testimony of witnesses. But no one is to be put to death on the testimony of only one witness." This part of the Law prevented someone from being put to death on the basis of circumstantial evidence alone. The term translated "witness" literally means an eyewitness. Hence it took two eyewitnesses of a murder to justify use of the death penalty. Since this passage comes at the end of the long section concerning the cities of refuge, the term "anyone who kills a person" must be limited to someone who commits murder. The person who commits manslaughter is included in Numbers 35:30. The general principle that is important in this verse is that the judicial system must have a high degree of certainty about the guilt of the murderer. Circumstantial evidence and a single eyewitness were insufficient by themselves. Even the testimony of an eyewitness must be corroborated, and the Law was careful to ensure that no one could be put to death on the basis of one eyewitness who might have ulterior motives for testifying against the accused. In fact, perjury in a capital case was itself a capital crime. Circumstantial evidence leaves room for doubt, and two eyewitnesses were necessary to ensure that eyewitness testimony was corroborated before someone could be put to death for murder. Thus the degree of certainty required for the use of the death penalty seems to be higher than that of the "reasonable doubt" standard that is used throughout the Western legal system today.

If this principle is applied literally to capital murder cases today, both principled and procedural abolitionists insist that the majority of people on death row have been sentenced to death in a way that is inconsistent with biblical guidelines. The procedural abolitionist can argue that the life-for-life principle is valid, but that in terms of procedure, the proponent of capital punishment cannot meet the biblical standard for administrating the death penalty. Since there was virtually no such thing as circumstantial evidence in the ancient world, the way it is handled today is clearly more reliable in assessing guilt than in the ancient world. But most people on death row today were convicted and sentenced without even one eyewitness of the crime, not to mention a second eyewitness to corroborate the account. If advocates of the death penalty desire to administer capital punishment consistently with biblical guidelines, both principled and procedural abolitionists maintain that we must reconsider the cases of many inmates who now sit on death row and move them to a life sentence. Retentionists will respond by insisting that only the general principle of the certainty of guilt is required today, not the ancient specifics that were a part of life under the Mosaic law. They insist that the two eyewitnesses mandate does not adequately take into account the sophistication of other forms of evidence, which are capable of satisfying the general principle of the certainty of guilt. They argue further that opponents of the death penalty are appealing to the details of the law when only the more general principles are required for today.

Arguments for Capital Punishment

The retentionist view accepts capital punishment as appropriate under some circumstances. Advocates of this view do not favor any "across the board" view of the death penalty without careful guidelines to direct the way in which death sentences are handed down. Nor do they generally insist that the death penalty *must* be administered in cases of capital murder. There is a wide variety of opinion concerning the circumstances that would justify use of capital punishment, but all advocates agree that in some cases the death penalty not only can, but should be used in especially egregious cases. The procedural abolitionist can accept all of the following principled arguments while at the same time opposing the death penalty due to procedural concerns—those will be addressed in the arguments against capital punishment. The primary arguments in favor of the retentionist view are:

1. Capital Punishment Expresses an Appropriate Demand for Justice in Society.

According to both the abolitionist and the retentionist, criminal justice in general demands that the punishment fit the crime. When a murder occurs and innocent life is taken, retentionists argue that the only punishment that is proportionate to the crime is the death penalty. Only the death penalty can express society's moral outrage at the taking of innocent life. Justice being satisfied is especially important for a society dependent on due process of law instead of vigilantism to restore the imbalance created by crime. The retentionist has a difficult question for the abolitionist in this regard: he would ask, "What is it that is intrinsically unjust about requiring life for life?" The retentionist insists that there is nothing inherently wrong with such a requirement. The reason for applying the life-for-life principle is that the condemned murderer actually forfeits his or her right to life by virtue of taking the life of another. Failing to require life for life as a general rule would involve a low view of the victim's life that has been needlessly taken. It seems unjust to the retentionist that the condemned murderer could continue with his or her life (albeit in prison) when the victim's life has been tragically and undeservedly ended.

This demand for justice is not inconsistent with the New Testament emphasis on showing mercy and forgiveness and on vengeance belonging to God. However, abolitionists are correct in maintaining that when family members of a murder victim express a demand for justice, they are often masking a desire for revenge that does not reflect the teaching of Jesus. Nevertheless, it is true that the victim's family has personally experienced the loss caused by crime, and thus their demand for justice may be a legitimate demand.

The problem with bringing Jesus' ethic of forgiveness to bear on the issue of the death penalty is the way in which abolitionists confuse personal and social ethics. The New Testament teachings on revenge and forgiveness are part of a personal ethic that forbids individuals from taking revenge and that requires forgiveness when wronged. But that ethic cannot be applied to the state. The responsibility of the state is to punish criminals, not to forgive them. The state may not exercise its role unjustly or indiscriminately, but God has given the state the responsibility of criminal punishment (Rom. 13:1–7; 1 Peter 4:15). The retentionists argue that the biblical emphasis on forgiveness, mercy, and revenge is irrelevant to the morality

The Execution of Timothy McVeigh

Timothy McVeigh was convicted of the worst act of domestic terrorism in U.S. history for the 1995 bombing of the Oklahoma City federal building, which killed 168 people and wounded several hundred more. After only six years on death row, he was executed in 2001 by lethal injection. Surviving members of the victims' families called it "the completion of justice" and felt a long-overdue sense of closure to the bombing and its aftermath. Still others protested McVeigh's execution because they opposed the death penalty in principle. Opponents of capital punishment had their sentiments summarized by one of McVeigh's lawyers, who said, "If there is anything good that can come from the execution of Tim McVeigh, it may be to help us realize that we simply cannot do this anymore. I am firmly convinced that it is not a question of if we will stop, it's simply a matter of when."*

*"McVeigh Execution: A Completion of Justice," CNN.com, June 11, 2001.

of the state-administered death penalty and has nothing to do with the state's legitimate responsibility to uphold criminal sanctions.

2. Capital Punishment Provides a Unique Deterrent against Crime.

The argument that capital punishment provides a unique deterrent against crime has a strong intuitive appeal, particularly since many societies around the world are perceived as becoming more chaotic with less respect for law and morality. Since the fear of death is virtually a universal phenomenon, the death penalty is an unparalleled deterrent for people considering a capital crime. Generally, the harsher the potential penalty, the greater the deterrent value of such a penalty. Deterrence increases with the severity of the penalty involved. Drug trafficking is practically nonexistent in Singapore and Malaysia, where the death penalty is mandated for dealing drugs. The reason why the crime rate is much lower in societies under Islamic law than it is in the West may be because in many cases Islamic law proscribes much harsher punishment than imprisonment. Of course, that is not to say that Islamic law is preferable, only that its severe punishment does act as a deterrent to crime.

A strong view of the sanctity of life is not inconsistent with advocating the death penalty when viewed from the perspective of a deterrent. If society is serious about the sanctity of life, then it will mandate the strongest possible deterrent to keep people from taking innocent life. To deny the legitimacy of the death penalty cheapens life by discounting the life of the murder victim. Retentionists argue that it is not inconsistent to be pro-life and also support the death penalty, since it provides a deterrent encouraging people to think about the consequence of taking the life of an innocent person.

It is undoubtedly true that the death penalty is not a deterrent for certain types of people — for example, terrorists who kill innocents out of a commitment to a cause, whether religiously motivated or not. Although the prospect of the death sentence cannot deter all murderers, that does not mean that it is unable to deter any murderers. Exceptions, therefore, should not undermine the general rule.[9]

Although most people have a strong intuitive belief in the deterrent power of capital punishment, abolitionists will point out that statistically there is no relationship between capital punishment and the murder rate. In fact, the murder rate is lower in Europe in countries that have abolished the death penalty. The murder rate is very complex and is influenced by many factors other than the deterrent force that the death penalty contributes (such as the socioeconomic background of the perpetrator), which makes it nearly impossible to determine the deterrent effect of capital punishment. Thus substantial debate surrounds the subject of the effectiveness of the death penalty as a deterrent.

But that is not the end of the deterrence discussion. Let's consider what is called the *best-bet argument*.[10] First, let's assume that the death penalty works as a deterrent. If society has the death penalty, society ends up in a positive position with regard to capital punishment because murderers are put to death and some innocent people are saved by the deterrent effect. Conversely, if capital punishment is effective and society does not have the death penalty, society ends up in a worse position because murderers live and some innocent people are killed because the deterrent effect of capital punishment is not present.

Now, let's change our assumption. Let's assume that capital punishment does not work as a deterrent. With that assumption and society having capital punishment, society is in a worse off position—some murderers die with no deterrent value. Again, conversely, if we assume capital punishment doesn't work and we don't have the death penalty, society seems in a better position, with murderers living and, the important part, no additional risk to the lives of innocent others. To summarize, if we are unsure about the deterrent effect of capital punishment, we should bet that it does have such a value. The reason is that if we bet on capital punishment and it does work, innocent people are saved. Further, innocent people die needlessly if society does not have capital punishment. By contrast, if capital punishment doesn't work, either way we bet, the lives of innocents are not affected. This argument then asks, "Who should get the benefit of the doubt—the potential victims or the convicted murderers?" The retentionist argues that the obligation would clearly be to the potential innocent victims, not to convicted murderers. Thus, in light of the ambiguity of the ability of the death penalty to deter killers, the retentionist insists that society should retain the death penalty rather than unnecessarily risk the lives of potential murder victims who may die if a potentially effective deterrent is abolished.

3. The Cost of a Life Term Is Not Something Society Should Have to Bear.

The cost of housing, feeding, security, and health care, particularly as the inmate ages and requires more extensive care, could easily run in excess of $1 million, assuming the inmate lives to old age. In some cases, the cost of the various appeals that are filed will not be comparable to the cost of maintaining someone in a life term. To be sure, in some cases the cost of the appeals may exceed the cost of maintaining the inmate over the course of his or her life. Of course, the debate over capital punishment involves much more than the "bottom line," but the argument frequently advanced by abolitionists, that the death penalty is very expensive due to the exhaustive appeals that are normally pursued, needs to be compared with the actual costs associated with a life term in prison. Even if a life term costs less, the retentionist argues that such costs should not be borne by the public.

Implicit in this argument is the assumption that the condemned murderer has forfeited his or her right to life.

4. Capital Punishment Is Not Cruel and Unusual Punishment.

The Eighth Amendment to the Bill of Rights prohibits cruel and unusual punishment, normally taken to mean punishment that inflicts pain in a wanton and unnecessary manner, as well as punishment that is disproportionate to the crime committed. Critics of the death penalty argue that it is inherently cruel and unusual punishment, yet it is administered in a way that does not involve wanton infliction of pain. In fact, retentionists argue that it can be essentially a painless death. There is no reason the death penalty cannot be administered by lethal injection of drugs in the same way euthanasia is performed. Euthanasia is sometimes referred to as "mercy killing," in which a patient is painlessly put out of misery. If that can be done medically for a terminally ill patient as an act of mercy, then proponents suggest that the death penalty can be administered in the same way. Thus, in response to the argument that the death sentence is cruel and

New Jersey Bans the Death Penalty

In December 2007 New Jersey became the first state in forty years to abolish the death penalty, thereby making life in prison the harshest penalty available for convicted murderers. The bill to prohibit capital punishment was introduced following a report from a state commission that concluded that the death penalty does not deter violent crime and could involve innocent people being executed. Some dissenters in the legislature insisted that the death penalty still be available for convicted murderers of police officers and for convicted terrorists. Opponents of the death penalty were pleased with the legislature's action. "New Jersey lawmakers are demonstrating sound judgment in abandoning capital punishment after learning of its costs, the pain it causes victims' families, and the risks the death penalty poses to innocent lives," said Richard Dieter, director of the Death Penalty Information Center. However, proponents of the death penalty noted that one of the convicts on New Jersey's death row is Jesse Timmendequas, who murdered seven-year-old Megan Kanka in 1994. Her brutal murder led to the various Megan's law efforts to better identify and track sex offenders. Proponents argue that someone like Megan's killer does not deserve to live, especially at taxpayers' expense.*

*"New Jersey Lawmakers Vote to Abolish Death Penalty," CNN.com, December 13, 2007.

unusual punishment, retentionists maintain that it can be accomplished in a way that is neither cruel nor unusual.

Retentionists insist that abolitionists cannot argue that the death sentence is out of proportion to the crime committed. It is not unreasonable to demand the life of a person who has taken another's life by first-degree murder. This is not to suggest that the principle of life for life should be followed in all crimes in which an innocent life is taken. However, in cases where someone is convicted of first-degree murder and the criteria for the death penalty are met, such as the crime being particularly heinous, the notion that the life of the murderer be exchanged for the life of the innocent victim does not constitute punishment that is out of proportion to the crime. Sometimes retentionists argue that a life sentence is out of proportion to the crime of murder in some cases, since it would be too light a sentence.

Compared with the alternatives, the death penalty, when quickly and painlessly administered, may actually be less cruel and unusual than serving a life term in a maximum security prison. The indignities and harsh conditions of some prisons can also be considered cruel and unusual punishment. Thus retentionists sometimes argue that if abolitionists are concerned about the death penalty being cruel and unusual, to be consistent, they should object to a life term in prison due to its conditions.

Arguments against Capital Punishment

The abolitionist view is that capital punishment is not justifiable under any circumstances. No crime, however heinous, and no view of criminal punishment can be adequate grounds for sentencing anyone to death. The procedural abolitionist normally does not find the first four arguments (which are more principle based) persuasive, but focuses on the final two concerns. Following are the most common arguments used to support the abolitionist position.

1. The Death Penalty Undermines the Dignity of Persons Made in the Image of God and Cheapens Human Life.

Abolitionists argue that the death penalty undermines the dignity of persons made in the image of God and cheapens human life. This argument suggests that the death penalty is inconsistent with Western civilization's evolving standards of decency and respect for human beings. Thus, by definition, abolitionists insist that capital punishment constitutes cruel and inhuman punishment. While the death penalty has had a long history, that history is for the most part in a barbaric past, with criminal punishment being motivated by the uncivilized desire for revenge. Most other modern nations have seen the inconsistency of capital punishment with civilized thought and have abolished the practice. In a society that so values human life, abolitionists argue that it seems inconsistent for a person to be against abortion and for the death penalty.

For the Christian, God's call is certainly to be consistently pro-life, to be concerned about life after it emerges from the womb too. Abolitionists insist that to put someone to death for any crime is a conflicting message about respect for human life. For the abolitionist, if the state wants to teach a lesson about the sanctity of life, the death penalty is surely an odd way of doing it. It would seem to put the state in the position of saying to its citizens, "Do what I say, not what I do." The state should not compound one wrong (the crime committed) by committing another (putting the criminal to death). Retentionists respond that the murderer has forfeited his or her right to life and is not deserving of any respect. They further insist that the Bible only prohibits the taking of *innocent* life.

2. Reform Becomes Impossible.

The death penalty removes the prospect of rehabilitation that could lead to an individual again becoming a productive member of society. In some cases, with

The Transformation of Karla Faye Tucker Brown

Karla Faye Tucker died by lethal injection in Huntsville, Texas, after spending fourteen years on death row. She was convicted for a brutal double murder and sentenced to death. While on death row, she turned her life around as a result of her conversion to Christianity, and she and those close to her claimed she had become an entirely new person. She never denied her guilt and never asked for a different sentence than what she received. She married the prison chaplain while on death row, and virtually everyone close to her testified to her changed life — that it was genuine and a result of her faith. Although she had no qualms about facing her date with execution, numerous observers suggested that her case illustrated that something was very wrong with the death penalty, that it would preclude someone like her, who has been transformed, from being a contributing member of society. They argued that the death penalty was a waste of her new life. Proponents of the death penalty insisted that her changed life was not relevant to her conviction and subsequent penalty. And she seemed to think that way, too, evidenced by the way she was at peace with accepting her fate.*

*Karla Faye Tucker Brown Research Center, geocities.com.

the process of appealing a death sentence taking as long as it does, a convicted murderer could be a very different person at the execution date than at the date of sentencing. A person could be put to death despite being rehabilitated during the period of time spent on death row. While many criminals do not change while in prison, some clearly do, even some who are awaiting a death sentence.

For example, Paul Crump was convicted of murder in 1955 and given the death penalty. While he was in prison awaiting execution, the prison received a new warden who instituted a series of reforms aimed at the possibility of rehabilitation. It created an environment in which Crump began to change. He learned to read and write and eventually began to write material for publication. He started taking interest in his fellow prisoners and was entrusted with progressively more responsibility over them. Over a period of seven years, his change was so dramatic that the warden testified that he had no qualms about putting Crump back on the streets again, and to execute him would be wasting a changed and productive life. In 1962 the governor of Illinois commuted Crump's death sentence to life imprisonment without parole.[11]

For the Christian, reform includes the prospect of someone coming to faith in Christ while serving a life sentence, of being redeemed and having hope not only of a changed life, but also of eternal life. Implementing the death penalty removes the possibility of someone becoming reconciled to God. Since one of the primary missions of the Christian is to be an agent of reconciliation, working to bring people into a saving relationship with God (2 Cor. 5:17–21), many religious groups suggest that support of the death penalty is inconsistent with that goal. Retentionists reply to this that on death row there are numerous opportunities for someone to be redeemed, and impending mortality can be especially effective in motivating that consideration. Further, the retentionist will insist that reform is not the primary goal of criminal justice; retribution is.

3. Death Sentences Are Usually Accompanied by Long and Expensive Appeals.

Abolitionists use the argument that death sentences are usually accompanied by long and expensive appeals. The reason for the appeals process is to ensure that no mistakes are made. The process normally takes from five to seven years and costs hundreds of thousands of dollars. It creates backlogs in the appeals courts, since approximately half of the appeals heard in the courts in which the death penalty is legal involve death penalty appeals. In many cases, the requests for appeals hearings are requested up until the "eleventh hour," just prior to a person's execution. It would be much simpler and more cost-effective to eliminate the death penalty in favor of life sentences without the possibility of parole. Retentionists insist that the costs of these appeals be compared to the cost of maintaining an inmate for a life term, which may exceed the costs of the exhaustive appeals process.

4. The Demand for "Justice" Is Inconsistent with Jesus' Ethic of Forgiveness and Redemption.

Abolitionists claim that the demand for "justice" is inconsistent with Jesus' ethic of forgiveness and redemption. This is not to say that society does not hold people accountable for their crimes. But the cry for "justice," which in many cases is only a facade for revenge, is inconsistent with Jesus' ethic in the Gospels and Paul's statement that vengeance belongs only to the Lord (Rom. 12:19). Significantly, the cry for "justice" is most often made by surviving family members of the slain victim. In many of these cases, the family members have clearly confused justice with revenge, having little compassion for the person condemned to die. Putting someone to death cannot bring the victim back to life or compensate the family in any significant way. In reality this emphasis on "justice" is an expression of the primitive and uncivilized desire for revenge, which is inconsistent not only with the message of the gospel, but also with the humane standards of civilized societies. Retentionists suggest that though revenge is understandable but not justifiable, the demand for justice can be real and only satisfied by the death penalty.

These final two arguments are more *procedural* concerns with capital punishment rather than principled objection to the death penalty. A person could hold to the death penalty in principle yet have serious reservations about these procedural problems and end up holding to the position mentioned earlier that we called the *procedural abolitionist*. That is, one could agree that there is nothing intrinsically unjust about requiring life for life under certain circumstances, but the procedural concerns, depending on their significance, could make one an abolitionist for all practical purposes. This position is becoming more widespread as the number of people exonerated from death row increases.

5. Mistakes Are Inevitable and Irreversible.

The primary procedural reservation about capital punishment is that given fallible human beings and an imperfect justice system involved at every point in a capital case, mistakes are not just possible, they are inevitable, say abolitionists. Although the Western judicial system most often works well and justice is served, it is undeniable that miscarriages of justice do occasionally occur. Innocent people are sometimes wrongly convicted and sent to prison. In some cases innocent people who maintained their innocence throughout their trial and appeals process have been executed. In other cases convictions have been overturned, leaving the judicial system to acknowledge that injustices were done. When mistakes are made in noncapital cases, the state can compensate wrongly convicted persons and release them from prison. But if the court makes a mistake in a death penalty case, nothing can be done for the person who was wrongly put to death—the state cannot bring people back to life. The death penalty has no room for correcting mistakes that are an inevitable part of an imperfect judicial system. Capital punishment leaves no room for the kind of mistakes that are a well-documented part of the Western system of justice. Religious people who oppose capital punishment sometimes suggest that the reason the Bible required the testimony of two eyewitnesses was to avoid some of the problems that arise when relying on non-eyewitness testimony. And some suggest that that criteria still be used today, thus making one a practical abolitionist, since corroborating eyewitness testimony is very rare today. In some U.S. states, seeing death row inmates exonerated and released has brought about a moratorium on executions. Some people who support measures like this also support capital punishment in principle, but the mistakes that are made periodically make them abolitionists for all practical purposes.[12] The retentionist will respond to this by suggesting that even though the system is not perfect, it does get things right quite often. They insist that non-eyewitness evidence can establish the certainty of guilt in many cases with forensics such as DNA evidence. They argue that because mistakes are sometimes made, that does not mean that capital punishment should be eliminated in all cases.

6. The Way in Which the Death Penalty Is Administered Is Discriminatory.

A further procedural concern is the way in which the death penalty is administered. The majority of convicted murderers who receive death sentences are minority men,

North Carolina Man Exonerated after Fifteen Years on Death Row

Glen Edward Chapman, who was given the death penalty for two 1992 murders, was released from death row after fifteen years of awaiting execution. In 2007 he was given a new trial, and in April 2008 prosecutors dropped all charges against him. He was granted a new trial on the basis of evidence that had been withheld, key documents that had been lost or destroyed, and false testimony by one of the investigators. New evidence came to light after the trial that suggested that one of the victim's deaths may have been due to a drug overdose, not homicide. The trial court judge also cited Chapman's inadequate legal representation — one of his attorneys had been disciplined by the North Carolina Bar Association for drinking during another capital trial. According to the Death Penalty Information Center, Chapman was the 128th death row inmate to be exonerated since 1973.*

*WRAL.com, April 2, 2008.

particularly blacks and Hispanics, who come from the lower socioeconomic classes. Rarely do whites or middle- or upper-class individuals receive the death penalty, and even more rarely are women executed. It is true that minority men commit a higher percentage of violent crimes. But even taking that into account, the incidence of minority men receiving capital punishment is still disproportionate when compared to nonminorities who are executed. Thus abolitionists argue that capital punishment is unjust and discriminatory, and actually oppresses the most disadvantaged groups in society. The reasons that minority men more often receive a death sentence can include inadequate representation, race, gender, jury misperceptions, and geography (some states and even some regions have a higher incidence of death sentences). Procedural abolitionists cite this as a major reservation about capital punishment because they conclude that the current system is incapable of administering it within fundamental norms of fairness. While acknowledging that the problems that contribute to this shortcoming in the system are deep and pervasive, retentionists argue that there is a solution to this—to administer capital punishment more even-handedly. In addition, retentionists, with the life-for-life principle, will suggest that the wrong is not for the ones who receive capital punishment, but for those who receive a life term instead. Unless a mistake was made or the person received poor representation, the retentionists will argue that they have not been wronged by receiving capital punishment.

Conclusion

The debate over capital punishment is ongoing, and society is still divided over both moral and legal aspects of the death penalty. There are now three primary positions that one could hold and have good arguments to support one's case. A person could be a *retentionist*, who holds to capital punishment under some conditions, such as the certainty of guilt for first-degree murder; one could be an *abolitionist*, who opposes capital punishment in all circumstances. Or one could be a *procedural abolitionist*, accepting capital punishment in principle but having serious reservations about how capital punishment is administered.

It would seem that the Bible opens the door to allowing the death penalty in principle as long as the absolute certainty of guilt is established. This is based on Genesis 9:6, coming prior to the law and grounding capital punishment in the notion that human beings are created in the image of God. There is room for legitimate debate over the procedural elements and over whether one should support capital punishment in the current legal and forensic context. Whether or not a person believes in capital punishment in certain cases, what is needed is a sense of compassion for the criminal, the victim, and the victim's family. Often compassion and the hope of redemption for the convicted criminal are overlooked in the retentionist's demand for justice. The demand for justice can too easily become a demand for vengeance and retribution, actions that belong only to God. Also, the victim and the victim's family can too easily be forgotten by the abolitionist. In a desire to protect the rights of the criminal, the abolitionist may too easily forget the life-shattering damage done by the criminal's actions. Thus the Bible commands compassion for both parties but also reminds us that actions have consequences. The debate continues: Should the act of murder have consequences that include the death penalty?

For Further Reading

Bedau, Hugo Adam. *The Death Penalty in America*. New York: Oxford University Press, 1992.

Budziszewski, J., E. J. Dionne, Avery Cardinal Dulles, and Stanley Hauerwas. *Religion and the Death Penalty: A Call for Reckoning*. Grand Rapids: Eerdmans, 2004.

Megivern, James J. *The Death Penalty: An Historical and Theological Survey*. New York: Paulist Press, 1997.

Review Questions

1. What is the significance of *Furman v. Georgia*? *Gregg v. Georgia*? How do each of these cases relate to the death penalty?

2. Briefly identify the three primary positions on the death penalty.

3. What is the point of the Eighth Amendment to the U.S. Constitution?

4. List some of the capital crimes recognized by the Old Testament.

5. How does the teaching of the law of Moses relate to the death penalty today?

6. What is the contribution of Genesis 9:6 to the discussion of capital punishment?

7. What is the primary New Testament reference to capital punishment? What is the point of that passage?

8. What does the account of the woman caught in adultery (John 7:53–8:11) contribute to the Bible's teaching on capital punishment?

9. What does Numbers 35:30 tell us about the procedural requirements to administer capital punishment?

10. What are the primary arguments in favor of capital punishment?

11. What is the "best-bet argument"?

12. What are the main arguments against capital punishment?

13. What is your position on capital punishment? Which of the arguments do you find most persuasive?

Cases for Discussion

Case 9.1: You're on the Jury!

You are on the jury in a first-degree murder case. You and your peers have already unanimously convicted the defendant. The task before you is to decide the penalty, either life in prison without possibility of parole or the death penalty. The special circumstances that made the death penalty an option under state law include more than one murder (he killed two women) and sexual assault prior to the murder of one of the women. You are deliberating on the penalty phase of the trial.

Questions for Discussion

1. How would you vote in this case? Would you vote for the death penalty or for life in prison without parole?

2. If you vote for the death penalty, how do you address the claim that taking the life of another is an odd way of affirming the sacredness of life?

3. If you vote for life in prison, how do you respond to the objection that there is nothing unjust about requiring life for life?

4. How do you understand the teaching of the Bible on the death penalty?

Case 9.2: You're in the Legislature!

You are a sitting legislator in the state assembly, and a bill is up for discussion that would abolish the death penalty in your state. Proponents of the death penalty argue that it is a just punishment for certain types of murder and that the current system is capable of carrying it out in a careful and reliable way. They argue that even though the system is not perfect, the guilt of many murderers is very clear, and the failure to impose the death penalty is an injustice to the surviving members of victims' families. Opponents of the death penalty argue that the system cannot ensure that mistakes won't be made and that the application of the death penalty is discriminatory (more minorities than whites receive the death penalty).

Questions for Discussion

1. How will you vote on this bill before the legislature? Defend your vote.

2. Do you agree that the legal system is too flawed to have the death penalty? Why or why not?

3. As a Christian, how would you respond to the argument that the death penalty precludes the convicted murderer having a chance at redemption later in life?

Chapter 9 Notes

1. This list is taken from R. J. Rushdoony, *The Institutes of Biblical Law* (Nutley, N.J.: Craig, 1973), 235.
2. The death penalty was not prescribed for accidental killing or manslaughter.
3. The term for "attacking" or "striking" one's parent refers to striking with a mortal blow and is the equivalent of killing one's parent.
4. Related to this is the command that the incorrigibly delinquent, criminally rebellious child be stoned to death. See Deuteronomy 21:18–21.
5. It appears from these two texts that the main reason for kidnapping was not to exact a ransom, but to sell the person into slavery or to keep the person as a slave.
6. The reason that this specific crime carries the death penalty is due to the way in which betrothal was viewed as the essential equivalent of marriage in the ancient world. Thus, to have sexual relations with an engaged person was the virtual equivalent of adultery and carried the same penalty.
7. One of the few references to the death penalty outside the Law occurs in Ezekiel 18:12–13, where the crimes of murder, adultery, oppression of the poor, not keeping a pledge, idolatry, and usury are mentioned as deserving the death penalty. However, it is not clear from this passage if the person is to die from a judicial verdict of capital punishment or if a premature death is one of the anticipated consequences of a lifestyle characterized by these things.
8. It may be that the reason why Cain and Lamech were not given the death penalty was because there was no state in existence at that time, and only the state is authorized by God to administer capital punishment. See Rushdoony, *Institutes of Biblical Law.*
9. Also, a life sentence is not an effective deterrent for other types of criminals, including people who commit a murder while serving a life sentence, terrorists, and other forms of revolutionaries, as well as professional killers. This fact supports retention of the death penalty as the only adequate deterrent for some types of people.
10. The classic exposition of this argument is found in Ernest van den Haag, "On Deterrence and the Death Penalty," *Ethics* 78 (July 1968).
11. Ronald Bailey, "Facing Death: A New Life Too Late," *Life*, July 27, 1962, 28–29.
12. "Illinois Suspends Death Penalty," CNN.com, January 31, 2000. The reason for this suspension was the realization that Illinois had released more death row inmates than it had executed since the death penalty had been reinstituted in 1977.

Chapter 10

Sexual Ethics

Sexual ethics refers to the ethical issues raised by the variety of sexual relationships and arrangements both inside and outside of marriage. Cultures throughout the centuries have been concerned about the moral parameters for sexual expression. Since the "sexual revolution" of the 1960s and 1970s, many sexual boundaries have been challenged and longtime prohibitions on certain types of sexual behavior have been rethought.

To appreciate the challenges involved in this area of ethics, think about how you would respond to the following scenarios:

1. You are counseling a high school student who is unsure of his sexual orientation. He feels some attraction for the same sex and has received some very private encouragement from gay teens at his high school. He has doubts about his ability to be attracted to women but is very reluctant to admit that he is struggling with his sexual identity.

2. An engaged couple comes to you for counsel prior to their marriage concerning the subject of birth control. They do not want to become pregnant before they are ready, and they believe that life begins at conception. They believe that children are a gift from God, and they want to know if any birth control is okay. They have heard that some birth control methods actually prevent embryos from implanting in the womb. They don't think that they want to do birth control that way but are not sure if that is any different from a miscarriage that might happen naturally.

3. A gay couple comes to you asking you to perform their civil commitment service. They know you are a minister in the area, and they are committed to each other and plan to stay together and either adopt a child or "procreate" using assisted reproductive technologies.

4. A college student asks you for your opinion on masturbation. He wants to know if that is something that the Bible allows or if it is a practice that should be

discouraged. He acknowledges that it is widespread, and he sees nothing wrong with it.

5. A couple in their forties tells you that they are "done" having children — that their family is just the right size. The man in the couple is considering a vasectomy. He believes that all of their children are gifts from God, but he and his wife feel that they can give them all the attention they need if they hold their family size at what it is today. He wants to know what you think about permanent birth control.

6. An engaged couple on their second marriage participates in your premarital counseling workshop and is taken aback by your view that sex is reserved for marriage. They consider you outdated, especially with people who have been previously married. They insist that marriage is just a "piece of paper," and if they are committed to each other, there is nothing wrong with sex prior to marriage.

Biblical Teaching on Sexual Relationships

Much to the surprise of people who have never read the Bible carefully, there is a wealth of material in Scripture that addresses the sexual relationship. God did not appear to be bashful or embarrassed when he spoke about sex in the Bible, and his teaching is both clear about the need for restraint and explicit about the passion of sex when expressed within the proper parameters. Central biblical passages include Genesis 2:18–25, where the notions of sex and marriage are both introduced; Leviticus 18, a listing of illicit sexual relationships; the Song of Songs, which passionately celebrates sex in marriage; 1 Corinthians 5–7, which addresses the sexual excesses of the church in Corinth; and selected statements in the Epistles that encourage avoiding sexual immorality.[1]

Genesis

In Genesis 1–2 there is a critical link between the man and woman in the context of marriage and the sexual relationship that will eventually result in the procreation of children. Although there are two creation accounts in Genesis 1–2, they are complementary and not contradictory. Genesis 1 provides the broad overview of creation. Genesis 2 views the most important aspects of creation in more detail — the creation of man and woman and their relationship to each other and to God.

In Genesis 2:18–25 both marriage and sexual relations are instituted. Thus this account actually fits into the broader overview of Genesis 1. It occurs after the divine initiative in 1:26 to create humankind and prior to the command to the newly formed couple in 1:28 to begin procreating and populating the earth. The first command given to them is the command to reproduce in 1:28, clearly a result of their becoming "one flesh" in 2:24.

Most scholars believe Genesis 2:24 to be the first reference to the institution of marriage. There are various reasons for this. First, the way that this text is quoted in other places in the New Testament makes it clear that it was originally intended for married couples (Matt. 19:5; Eph. 5:31).[2]

Second, the term "leave" is used to suggest that a man and woman who will be intimately related (as the term "cleave" [KJV] suggests) are to separate from their families of origin and begin a new family unit of their own—contrary to ancient Near Eastern cultural practice in which the bride moved in with the groom and his family.

Third, the concept of one flesh clearly involves a sexual unity (though not limited to that), and throughout Scripture it is evident that sexual relations are restricted to the setting of marriage. Thus it would appear that 2:24 is where marriage as a divine institution begins.

Placing the more specific account of the creation of male and female and the subsequent institution of marriage back into the broader context of the creation in Genesis 1:26, the command to procreate, which presumes sexual relationships, is therefore given to Adam and Eve in the context of their leaving, cleaving, and becoming one flesh—in the context of marriage. This sets the precedent for heterosexual marriage and sexual relationships for the purpose of procreation within that setting. Though it does not suggest that every male and female must be joined in marriage, it does indicate that marriage is to be between male and female, and that only in marriage are sexual relationships and procreation to occur. In other words, God has established sex and procreation to be restricted to heterosexual couples in marriage. There is continuity between God's creation of the family in Genesis 1–2, sexual expression, and the command to procreate within that context.[3] This structure of the family seems to be basic to God's creative design, however extended the family became due to cultural and economic factors.

The term "one flesh" is widely considered to refer to sexual oneness. Since the Hebrew term *basar*, translated "flesh," is used, it appears to emphasize the physical side of the married couple's relationship. Though it certainly also refers to a spiritual and emotional oneness experienced by couples, had the author wanted to stress that and downplay the sexual aspect, he could have used the term *nephesh*, translated "soul." Whatever else it signifies, the use of *basar* clearly involves the sexual relationship. Since it is linked with the terms "leave" and "cleave" in the passage that institutes marriage, it makes sense to say that the Bible intends sex within the bounds of marriage. When Genesis 2:24 is cited in both Matthew 19:5

and Ephesians 5:31, it is clear that the original design for the one-flesh relationship of sex was intended for marriage, since both contexts indicate that married couples are in view.

The seventh commandment, "You shall not commit adultery" (Ex. 20:14; Deut. 5:18), was designed to protect this creation ideal for family life that was instituted in Genesis 1–2. Though adultery (sex between a married person and someone other than his or her spouse) does not encompass all the prohibited sexual relationships in Scripture, it is central since it involves breaking the intimate one-flesh connection with one's spouse. Most cultures around the world have some moral rules to protect the family, and a prohibition against adultery is widely recognized since it breaks the sacred covenant of marriage. The prophets bring out this aspect of adultery by routinely comparing Israel's spiritual breach of covenant with God in their idolatry to the violation of the marriage covenant that occurred when adultery was committed. Just as individuals broke a marriage covenant with their partners when guilty of adultery, so Israel was guilty of spiritual adultery when, through idolatry, they broke their spiritual covenant with God. The irony of the adultery imagery to describe Israel's spiritual condition was that often idolatry did involve adultery. Religious prostitution was a regular part of idolatrous worship in the ancient world and was part of its appeal. So the prophets were correct both literally and figuratively to describe Israel's idolatry as spiritual adultery (see, e.g., Jer. 3:6–10; Hos. 1–3).

Contrary to the original design for monogamous marriage, polygamy (as well as concubinage) was practiced periodically in ancient Israel. The patriarchs, such as Jacob, had multiple wives as did King Solomon, though in Solomon's case, using marriage as a way to solidify foreign alliances was contrary to God's explicit demand that the king trust God, not foreign allies, for Israel's national security. Though polygamy was never sanctioned, nor commanded, it does appear to have been allowed in Old Testament times. The reason polygamy seems to have been allowed is not clear, though it may have something to do with the provision of an economic safety net for women. Remember that in the ancient world there were very few "working women," at least not working in reputable occupations. For the most part, women were provided for either by their family of origin or by marriage. Women who never married or who were widowed were not generally seen as able to financially provide for themselves, though there were some exceptions. This is one reason why the biblical tradition of levirate marriage was commanded in the law—to provide financially for childless widows and to ensure that the lineage of the deceased woman's late husband continue (Deut. 25:5–10; Ruth 4). This may be one of the reasons why polygamy seems to have been allowed in Old Testament Israel. In the New Testament, monogamy is affirmed as the norm. For example, when Jesus teaches on divorce (Matt. 19:1–5), he does so from

Genesis 1–2, presuming monogamy as the standard. Further, when the qualifications for leadership in the church are clarified, elders are to be the "husband of one wife" (1 Tim. 3:1–5). Interestingly, when missionaries bring the gospel message to cultures where polygamy is still practiced, this raises a very sensitive ethical issue. What should be done with multiple wives once someone has come to faith in Christ? It would clearly be callous and uncaring to insist that polygamy be abandoned, virtually putting women into a state of destitution. Rather, many missions organizations suggest that no current marriages be renounced, but that following Christ demands that no additional wives be taken on from that point forward (having multiple wives would disqualify them from serving as elders in the church according to 1 Tim. 3:1–5). This would be a compromise of the standard of monogamy, but in cultures where polygamy is entrenched, it may take a generation or more to move toward monogamy in the culture.

Early on in Genesis (chaps. 19–20), the book describes the destruction of Sodom and Gomorrah as evidence of how far and how quickly the world degen-

Levirate Marriage in Ruth

One of the most interesting sexual ethics questions is raised in the book of Ruth — it's the biblical tradition of levirate marriage. Being a widow and having no surviving children created two significant problems for a woman. First, she had no way to support herself on her own, other than returning to her family of origin. Second, she had no opportunity to carry on the lineage of her deceased husband, a very important concept in the ancient world due to the link between lineage and property. In addition, having a lineage was considered an important form of respect for the person.

In the book of Ruth, Ruth is a foreign, childless widow who returns to Israel with her mother-in-law, Naomi. She attracts the interest and favor of Boaz, a landowner of some means in the town of Bethlehem, where they live. Through elaborate imagery, Ruth and Boaz connect and express their interest in each other. Naomi reveals that Boaz is a close relative, which means that he is a candidate to perform levirate marriage with Ruth. Ruth indicates her willingness to follow what the Law indicates, and Boaz expresses his desire to fulfill his legal responsibility to marry Ruth and provide for her. But there is a relative who is closer than Boaz who, according to the Law, has the first option to marry Ruth. Boaz defers to this relative who is not willing to marry Ruth. Boaz then publicly marries her and they conceive a child who continues Ruth's late husband's lineage. She gives birth to a child whom they name Obed, and everyone appears to live happily after that. Levirate marriage was especially important in this case, since the child born to Ruth and Boaz was the grandfather of King David. We learn later that the lineage of Ruth's deceased husband actually includes Jesus the Messiah, since he is a descendant of David.

erated after the entrance of sin (Gen. 3). It is a common interpretation of this episode to hold that the judgment on the two cities came about as a result of their sexual perversions, which include homosexuality. Critics of the traditional Christian view of homosexuality argue that the sin of the cities was primarily neglect of the poor and materialism (Ezek. 16:49–50), and that even if homosexuality was involved, it was a case of gang rape, not consensual sex. They argue that this kind of gang rape was often associated with dominance and enforced submission in the ancient world, and that this narrative cannot be used to condemn loving, committed, and consensual homosexuality.[4] Those who defend the traditional view correctly point out that the New Testament clarifies the basis for the judgment on these two cities, clearly including a wide variety of sexual perversions, including homosexuality (Jude 7). One should exercise caution in using this account, since the specific instance of homosexuality was clearly nonconsensual. It is not clear that this story can be applied to consensual homosexual relationships, though other parts of the Bible do apply to those.

Old Testament Law

Other parts of the Old Testament Law were designed to safeguard this creation model of the family outlined in Genesis 1–2. For example, the prohibitions against illicit sexual relations assumed that the creation model for sex within marriage was normative and functioned to preserve the family from breakdown. In the sexual code in Leviticus 18 and 20, every sexual relationship except that between a heterosexual couple in marriage is prohibited. All forms of incest (sex with a relative), homosexuality, adultery, cultic prostitution, premarital sex, and even bestiality (sex with an animal) are forbidden. Though there is no specific reason given for these prohibitions in Leviticus 18 and 20, it seems clear that these violate the normative structure of the family that is rooted in creation. Keeping the creation ideal of the family intact and free from influences that would undermine it was considered central to the preservation of Israel as a society set apart as God's holy nation (Ex. 19:6). Though it is true that God's people are no longer under the Law as a rule of life (Rom. 7:1–3), it would seem that the general principle that is relevant is the protection of the creation norm of sexual relationships within heterosexual marriage.

Song of Songs

In contrast to the Law, which stresses sexual prohibitions, the Song of Songs celebrates the beauty of sex in marriage.[5] Throughout the Song there are exquisite descriptions of the lover and his beloved bride, particularly in 4:1–10, where Solomon describes the body of his bride in passionate detail prior to the consummation of their marriage (see also Song 5:10–16; 7:1–9). The imagery for sexual enjoyment is vivid and includes things like the choicest foods, drinks and spices, and water from the freshest springs and fountains (4:11–5:1). It is seen as a sensual delight, entirely blessed by God and to be enjoyed.

However, there is restraint in the premarital period in 1:1–3:5. During courtship, there is a normal and natural longing and deep desire for the other person, but restraint is required even though it is difficult. It is further significant that the book progresses in a rough chronological order. The book can be divided into four major sections: courtship (1:1–3:5), marriage and consummation (3:6–5:1), conflict (5:2–6:3), and reconciliation (6:4–8:14). Restraint is exercised during courtship (2:7; 3:5), and sex is not fully enjoyed until after the wedding procession (3:6–7) and ceremony (3:11). The book appears to assume that sex is to be enjoyed only within the parameters of marriage.

New Testament

The New Testament consistently appeals for the believer to avoid sexual immorality. For example, in 1 Thessalonians 4:3 Paul equates avoiding sexual immorality with the will of God for the believer, one of the few occasions in which it is stated that directly. Similarly, the believer is to avoid even the hint of immorality because it is inconsistent with his or her position as one of God's people (Eph. 5:3). Sexual immorality is seen as a part of the old life of the believer (Col. 3:5), and they are discouraged from associating with those who boast in such immorality (1 Cor. 5:9). Marriage is to be kept pure, particularly in the sexual expression (Heb. 13:4). Sexual immorality is also included in many of the "vice lists"—lists of specific sins that the believer is to avoid (Matt. 15:19; Mark 7:21–23; 1 Cor. 6:9–11; Gal. 5:19–21; Rev. 21:8).

First Corinthians 5–7 is one of the New Testament texts that develops its teaching in more detail, presumably because the church at Corinth was having significant problems with sexual immorality in the church. They seemed to be proud of their accommodation to the sexual morality of the Corinthian culture (5:1–2), and it appears that many in the church came to faith in Christ from a background of immorality (6:9–11). Paul rebuked both their incestuous relationships and the pride that accompanied it (5:1–13). Then in 6:12–20, he laid some theological groundwork for his admonition for sexual purity. He then addressed specific problems related to married and single adults (1 Cor. 7, especially vv. 25–35).

Paul gives three theologically grounded reasons the believer should avoid sexual immorality. First, God the Father will raise the body to immortality at his second coming (1 Cor. 6:14). Because of this, the body is important and should be treated with as much care as the soul. With this point Paul is combating a view that dominated the Greek culture of the day—that the soul was all that mattered about a person. There were for the Greeks, therefore, two options for the body: either the person could severely discipline the body in order to keep it from interfering with the soul's development (also known as asceticism), or he or she could do with one's body whatever one desired (hedonism), since the body was of no consequence to the soul. The Corinthian culture had clearly chosen the latter option, and sexual license was commonplace as a result. Paul is suggesting that there is as much of a future for a person's body as there is for his or her soul. Thus a person's body is to be maintained with the utmost purity and care since God will redeem it at Christ's second coming.

A second reason for sexual purity is that believers are one with Christ the Son (1 Cor. 6:15–17). Since believers are "members of Christ" (v. 15) and one with him, a believer should never become one with someone other than his or her spouse. This is especially true if, in sexual immorality, the believer is actually participating in idolatry through religious prostitution, as was the case in Corinth (v. 16). Not only does immorality result in breaking the one-flesh relationship with one's spouse, but it also violates a person's relationship with Christ by joining him to the person with whom one has sex.

A third reason Paul gives for avoiding sexual immorality is that the believer's body is the temple of the Holy Spirit (1 Cor. 6:19). Thus it is to be revered and cared for, not abused or used in any way that would compromise a person's testimony for Christ. Ultimately, the body does not belong to the believer because it has been purchased by God at the cost of his Son's death. Therefore, the believer does not have the right to do with his or her body whatever he or she desires. The believer's body belongs to God and is to be used to honor him, chiefly by avoiding sexual immorality (6:19–20).

In 1 Corinthians 6:12–20, sexual immorality is prohibited because it violates the believer's relationship with all three members of the Trinity. God the Father will raise the body (v. 14), thus it is to be considered sacred. The believer is one with Christ the Son (v. 15), and thus should not join a part of him sexually to someone other than one's spouse. The believer is also a temple of the Holy Spirit (v. 19), and thus the body is to be used for his honor. The way Paul outlines this passage shows that sexual immorality violates the essence of a person's relationship with God.

Critics of the New Testament teaching insist that Paul's teaching on sexuality must be understood against the backdrop of attitudes on sex in the ancient world. Critics argue that Paul's prohibitions on homosexuality simply reflect his homophobic cultural bias, analogous to his patriarchal views on the role of women. But a close look at these cultural attitudes in the first century reveals a clear plurality of views and sexual practices that were considered acceptable, including homosexuality. For example, first-century Corinth, the city to whom the Corinthian letters of Paul were addressed, illustrated this sexual diversity well (1 Cor. 5–6). It would seem that the New Testament writers, rather than reflecting their culture, are actually being countercultural and are grounding their views in their theology, as opposed to their cultural biases.

Singleness

In the latter part of the decade of the 2000s, for the first time in the United States, the number of households headed by single adults was greater than those headed by married couples. That is, for the first time, single households outnumbered married households. The expectation of marriage may be diminishing as well, as many single adults are no longer viewing marriage as a viable or desirable option. A substantial portion of the culture is single and will remain that way, and the Bible has a bit to say about singleness as well as marriage. Just because sex is reserved for marriage does not mean that the Bible has nothing to say concerning singleness.

First Corinthians 7 is the one New Testament section that directly addresses unmarried adults. The Bible here affirms singleness and suggests that at times it may be a more expedient life choice than marriage. Verses 25–35 argue that singleness is preferable to marriage because of the "present distress" (v. 26) in the culture, which most take as the context of persecution for the faith facing the Christian community there. Given the likelihood of enduring persecution, singleness may be a better option, because being single minimizes a person's vulnerability to persecution. Having a family makes one more at risk for succumbing to persecution, because far more pressure can be brought to bear on a person through persecuting his or her spouse and/or children than by pressuring the person himself or herself.

The passage goes on to affirm singleness by suggesting that marriage is part of this world that is passing away (1 Cor. 7:29–31). That is, marriage is part of the world that will pass away when Christ returns, which the early community anticipated as imminent. Thus marriage and singleness are both on the same level playing field when it comes to their eternal value. It would appear that here the Bible affirms singleness as almost the moral equivalent of marriage, that both have value, though not eternal value in and of themselves.

But perhaps the strongest affirmation of singleness comes when the passage suggests that single adults can serve Christ with undivided loyalty in a way that married couples cannot (1 Cor. 7:32–34). In terms of "undivided devotion to the Lord" (v. 35), it would seem that singleness has advantages over marriage. This passage clearly affirms that both choices, marriage and singleness, are good things and that no one has done wrong with either choice. Of course, there can be a variety of reasons and motives for pursuing marriage or remaining single, some reasons and motives better than others. But the Bible appears to affirm singleness as a morally good choice, while at the same time upholding marriage as the model from Genesis 1–2.

Homosexuality

The discussion on the morality of homosexuality has shifted somewhat from the intrinsic morality of homosexuality/lesbianism/bisexuality to the social arrangements that support homosexuality, such as same-sex marriage. It is assumed in most cultures that homosexuality is a valid alternative lifestyle, and that what is done sexually in private among consenting adults is no one's business except the couple's and is thus exempt from moral scrutiny.

Some of the increasing acceptance of homosexuality comes from religious individuals and groups who are serious about their religious views and are homosexual at the same time. For example, there are hundreds of congregations in the Metropolitan Community Church (MCC) today around the world. The MCC is an association of churches that are attempting to harmonize homosexuality and the Bible. They claim that there is nothing inconsistent with following Christ and being homosexual at the same time. They have written broadly in an attempt to show how homosexuality fits with their interpretation of the Bible.

Society is facing increasing pressure to recognize gay rights and same-sex marriages, both of which presume a moral acceptance of homosexuality as a valid alternative lifestyle. Although one can and should have sympathy for homosexuals who are victims of discrimination in housing and jobs—which is illegal—that does not mean that all parts of the gay rights agenda should be accepted. Similarly, the debate over same-sex marriage assumes that homosexuality is morally acceptable. Some states such as Hawaii recognize such unions, and many states and cities have what are called "domestic partner ordinances," which recognize gay unions and grant whatever benefits they can to these couples.

Defining the Term *Homosexual*

The term *homosexual* can mean many things. Exactly what kind of person is in view with the label *homosexual*? First, it can refer to a true homosexual, one whose sexual preference has been inverted and who prefers only members of the same sex. This is what most people mean by the term, yet it constitutes only about 5 percent of the total persons to whom the term *homosexual* may apply. The latest studies indicate that only 1 or 2 percent of the total adult population are homosexual by sexual inversion. Second, it can refer to someone who is bisexual—someone who can be sexually attracted to either gender.

Third, it can refer to someone called a situational homosexual. This person has had some homosexual experience but does not have a predominant homosexual orientation. He or she has experienced homosexuality in some form, however limited. For example, a relationally needy person will sometimes use a homosexual affair to meet his or her needs for affirmation and love. Here the sexual attraction is not the controlling factor, but the person acts out his or her neediness in a homosexual relationship. The person is attracted to another person because his or her needs are being met, not because of the person's gender. A second example is in the preteenage exploration of one's sexuality. Some of that experimentation may take place with another member of the same sex. This is not particularly uncom-

The Metropolitan Community Church

The Metropolitan Community Church exists as an association of churches that attempt to hold homosexuality and Christianity together. They hold to the historic creeds of the church and attempt to interpret biblical texts in a way consistent with loving, committed homosexual relationships. They argue that none of the often-cited biblical passages actually condemn loving, committed forms of homosexual relationships. For example, they insist that the account of Sodom and Gomorrah is not representative of the kind of homosexual relationships they support, since what occurred in Genesis 19–20 is gang rape, not consensual sex. In addition, they argue that the writings of Paul in the New Testament address perversions of homosexuality, such as homosexuality as an expression of dominance over someone, or homosexual religious prostitution. In their view, what the Bible condemns is the use of sexuality for purposes of dominance and submission. They insist that the Bible does not address the kinds of homosexual relationships in which there is mutual caring and commitment. They insist that Jesus would not discriminate against someone on the basis of sexual orientation, analogous to not discriminating against a person because of race or gender.

Metropolitan Community Church congregations can be found all over the world, and they are spread throughout most regions of the United States and Canada. Their goal is to pose a challenge to the traditional view of homosexuality in Christian tradition. They offer seminary training and online resources concerning their view of the Bible and homosexuality. They view the Bible as one important resource but say that its teaching must be balanced by reason, experience, and tradition. Critics of the MCC insist that they misread the clear intention of the biblical texts and give too much authority to non-biblical sources.*

*Sources: www.christianlgbtrights.org; Mona D. West, "The Bible and Homosexuality," www.mcchurch.org; Nancy Wilson, "Our Story Too: Reading the Bible with New Eyes," www.mcchurch.org.

mon; studies show that up to 30 percent of adolescents have experimented in some way with a person of the same sex.

Myths about Homosexuality

These categories help dispel some of the myths of homosexuality, the first of which proposes that all homosexuals are effeminate. Though some homosexuals are readily identifiable, many are not, and there is nothing in their public lives that would outwardly indicate their homosexuality.

A second myth is that all homosexuals are promiscuous. Though it is true that the average homosexual male has had a relatively high number of sexual partners (the number is less for lesbians), to characterize all homosexuals as sexually promiscuous is certainly unfair. There are also loving, supportive, and committed homosexual relationships.

A third myth asserts that homosexuality is always a chosen way of life. It may actually be learned developmentally and therefore be neither hereditary nor chosen. Adjustment to the homosexual subculture is often difficult, though for many homosexuals that community may be the first place they have felt accepted without having to hide their homosexuality.

A final myth is that homosexuality occurs only in the more artistic professions. Though there may be a disproportionate percentage of homosexuals in those professions as opposed to the rest of society, homosexuality cuts across most cultural and professional boundaries.

Causes of Homosexuality

How does a person acquire a disposition toward homosexuality? No single, specific cause can be pinpointed with any precision, and there is currently great debate about the evidence for a genetic link. The gay community clearly hopes that some genetic predisposition will be found by researchers working on the Human Genome Project (see the discussion of the project in chapter 7).

There do seem to be certain developmental factors that many homosexuals have in common, indicating that a homosexual orientation may be learned rather than chosen. These factors apply primarily to male homosexuality. First, there is the combination of an angry or absent father and a close-bonding and/or domineering mother. This is especially a factor if the boy becomes an emotional substitute "husband" for his mother. Second, the boy does not enter the "boy becoming man" social processes with pleasure. He either does not participate, or if he does, he does not enjoy it, and for that reason is derided by his peers. Finally, the boy's introduction to his sexuality is a crucial factor. Two critical key questions are, With whom was he introduced to sex? and Was it pleasurable? If he was introduced to sex with a male who enjoyed it, that may contribute toward a homosexual orientation.

Though homosexuality is a diverse phenomenon and there is no clear pattern for its development, there may be some common elements that help pinpoint the way in which it developed.

Biblical Response to Homosexuality

Homosexual sex is prohibited in the Old Testament Law (Lev. 18:22; 20:13). However, among all the illicit sexual relations listed in Leviticus 18 and 20, homosexuality is not singled out as being any different or more worthy of condemnation than other sexual sins.

The central New Testament passage that addresses homosexuality is Romans 1:24–27. It is set in the context of the condemnation of those who reject God as revealed in creation or through natural law. It is part of Paul's broader argument for the universality of sin and judgment, setting the need for the believer to be justified by faith in Christ's atoning death on the cross, as outlined in Romans 4–5. Those who reject the available knowledge of God and choose instead to worship the Greek and Roman idols have lifestyle consequences that they cannot avoid. One of these consequences is homosexual behavior. Paul implicitly appeals to the natural order of creation to condemn homosexual behavior (Rom. 1:27). Male and female were created with an innate tendency toward opposite sex attraction, but because of sin, the human race developed the potential for homosexuality. This potential is often realized when certain developmental factors are present. Because of the reality of sin, every person has the potential for homosexuality in the same way that we have the potential for any other kind of sin that the Bible describes.

The reference to homosexuality in this passage has been interpreted in a variety of ways. First, it has been taken to refer to homosexual male religious prostitutes in idolatrous worship ceremonies. Therefore, idolatry, not homosexual relations, is condemned. This is parallel to the description of homosexuality in Deuteronomy 23:17–18, where religious prostitution of all types is condemned. Since idolatry is in the immediate context of the condemnation of homosexual sex, this adds strength to this view.

A second view is that Paul is condemning true heterosexuals who are engaging in homosexual acts. This view comes out of Paul's emphasis on homosexuality as being unnatural. Many homosexuals, however, argue that their orientation is natural for them. An example of homosexuality that is not natural would be true heterosexuals who perform homosexual acts. The debate is over the use of the term "natural," whether that refers to what is natural *subjectively*, based on a person's own individual orientation, or whether it refers to what is natural *objectively*, which is natural regardless of one's orientation.

A third view is that Paul is condemning perverse expressions of homosexuality as opposed to the loving, committed relationships that are possible for homosexuals. Thus Paul's condemnation would be parallel to the way he would condemn heterosexuals for perverse expressions of their sexual identity.

A fourth view is that Paul intended to condemn all homosexual behavior. Paul's appeal to a universal truth about sexual relations linked to the order of creation prevents someone from seeing this passage limited to only certain kinds of homosexual behavior and from seeing Paul as culturally outdated in his teaching. Rather, it provides an appropriate context for a judgment on all homosexual relationships. The phrase "natural relations *with women*" (Rom. 1:27, emphasis added) makes it clear that the natural sexual relationship is heterosexual and objective, and thus is not dependent on a person's individual orientation. This is the only view that does not read into the passage things that are not there.

In applying these passages that forbid homosexuality, some suggest that it is important to make a distinction between homosexual *attraction* and homosexual *sexual relations*. There is a difference between being *homoerotic*, that is, being attracted to a person of the same sex, and *homosexual*, that is, acting sexually on that attraction. It may be helpful to see this distinction paralleled with heterosexual relationships. For a married person to be attracted to a person of the opposite sex other than his or her spouse is not sin. It becomes sin when that attraction is acted upon, either in lust, which is the process of mentally having sex with a person (Matt. 5:27–32), or in sexual overtures. Likewise, it may be that the homosexual attraction in itself is not sin, though at variance with the order of creation. But when that attraction gives way to lust and ultimately to sexual activity, it is sin. Some argue that what the Bible condemns in homosexual relationships it also condemns in heterosexual relationships—lust and sexual involvement outside marriage. Thus the options for the Christian homosexual would be the same as for the Christian heterosexual—either abstinence or heterosexual sex in marriage. Some Christians who struggle with their sexual identity have grasped this distinction and are attempting to be faithful to Christ and sexually pure at the same time. It may be that failure to recognize this distinction between being homoerotic and homosexual has kept the church from being a more accepting place for those struggling with their sexual orientation.

This above distinction may also be helpful in discussing a cure for homosexuality. It is common for gay activists to hold that cures rarely, if ever, happen. But they are using the term *cure* in a way that is not used in treating other kinds of struggles and addictions. There is a critical distinction between being cured of the behavior and cured of the desire. To be cured in the most common psychological and medical usage is to be content apart from the specific behavior in question. For example, the alcoholic who is cured has not necessarily lost the craving for alcohol. Rather, he has learned to be content apart from drinking. The same is true for the homosexual. He or she may not be cured of the attraction for persons of the same sex but is content apart from acting out sexually on that attraction.

Whether or not a person accepts this distinction, it is important that the church not view homosexuals as somehow outside the boundaries of God's grace. The church needs to be a place where those struggling with their sexual identity can come and receive grace, truth, and compassion.

Responses to Homosexuality in Addition to Scripture

Crafting an argument against homosexuality that is addressed to a secular audience is more difficult than interpreting the biblical teaching. Three primary arguments have been attempted. The first is a public health argument. It is based on the statistics that clearly link the transmission of AIDS to homosexual sexual activity. Proponents of this argument insist that homosexuality constitutes a threat to public health, and thus it should not be embraced. While one should be honest with the statistics and admit that there is a significant link between certain types of behavior (unprotected sex, particularly homosexual sex, and intravenous drug use) and the spread of AIDS, one should also admit that AIDS has spread to the heterosexual community, although with far less incidence than in the homosexual community. Further, at best this argument would seem to support being careful about all unprotected sex—not just homosexual sex, though some suggest that homosexual sex is more likely to spread AIDS than heterosexual sex.

A second argument is a historical argument. It is based on the precedent that no civilization has ever survived the destruction of the traditional family. Homosexuality as a valid lifestyle clearly undermines the model of the family that has characterized most societies throughout the history of civilization—husband, wife, and children. Thus, to ensure the best prospects for the flourishing of society, one of its major institutions, the family, should be encouraged, and any competing institutions that tend to undercut the family should be resisted. However, historical arguments, though they can be very persuasive, always have the possibility of exceptions to which the gay rights activist may appeal.

A third argument comes from the moral philosophy of Immanuel Kant, whose system was based on the categorical imperative, or the principles deduced by reason alone.[6] One way Kant formulated his moral duties was in terms of what he called the "principle of universalizability"—if a certain moral rule can be comfortably made universal, then and only then is it a valid moral rule. For example, Kant held that truth telling should be a universal moral duty because it is necessary to a functioning society. If people stopped telling the truth, the prospect for meaningful communication in society would be slim, because one could never know if he or she was being told the truth. In other words, what might happen if no one held to the moral rule in question? As in the case of truth telling, social relations would be severely damaged. The same kind of argument might be applied to homosexuality. What would happen if no one obeyed the moral rule that prohibited homosexuality? It is likely that procreation would decline significantly unless reproductive technologies were employed on a massive scale, and the existence of the next generation might be at stake. Of course, one must adhere to Kant's ethical system, and though there are many moral philosophers who do not, his way of fashioning moral duties has survived in the popular culture.

Same-Sex Marriage

Related to the above discussion is the issue of same-sex marriage, particularly in the arena of public policy. Though many states have formally defined marriage as between a man and a woman, there is a significant movement to legalize same-sex marriage at the state level. Some countries in Europe have laws that recognize same-sex couples as legally married, analogous to heterosexual couples.

The primary argument in favor of legalizing same-sex marriage is the principle of fairness. Advocates of same-sex marriage insist that it is unfair to deny same-sex couples the designation of marriage and benefits accorded to heterosexual couples. They argue that this is simply another way of discriminating against gays and lesbians. In the past, discrimination in the workplace and in housing has been eliminated by the force of law. Proponents of same-sex marriage argue that this is the last bastion of discrimination that must also be dealt with by the law.

Opponents of same-sex marriage reply that there is nothing wrong with defining marriage as exclusively between a man and a woman. Nor is there anything

California and Same-Sex Marriage

The California Supreme Court heard oral arguments in March 2008 on the legality of same-sex marriage and in May 2008 ruled that the state's prohibition on same-sex marriage was unconstitutional. The case came about when city officials in San Francisco allied with civil rights activists challenged the state's prohibition of gay marriage on the grounds of equal protection under the law. The plaintiffs argued that denial of same-sex marriage treats same-sex couples differently under the law than heterosexual couples, thereby violating the equal protection clause of the Constitution. The state appeals court upheld the state's ban on same-sex marriage in 2006, overturning a San Francisco ruling that held that the ban was unconstitutional. The State Supreme Court upheld that ruling.* In 2008, California voters approved Proposition 8, a constitutional amendment defining marriage as between a man and a woman.

*Howard Mintz, "California High Court Plans to Hear Gay Marriage Arguments," *San Jose Mercury News*, February 7, 2008.

unfair about such a definition, because virtually all of the benefits available to married couples under the law are available to same-sex couples under domestic partner ordinances, which are the law in states that do not recognize same-sex marriage. Critics of same-sex marriage wonder what exactly the proponents are seeking in the designation of marriage if so many of the benefits they claim they are being denied are actually available through domestic partnerships. Critics argue that proponents of same-sex marriage are seeking the social and moral validation of marriage more than any of the specific benefits. That is, they are seeking the symbolic affirmation of same-sex relationships by putting them under the designation of marriage. But this is precisely what the critics are attempting to prevent—the symbolic approval of types of relationships that they believe are morally problematic.

A second reply of the critics of same-sex marriage relates to the way in which the argument for same-sex marriage is grounded. Underlying the argument from fairness is the notion of personal autonomy—that a person has the right to make life's most significant decisions, especially the ones that are value laden, apart from judgment or the intrusion of the law. Because of personal autonomy, whether a person chooses same-sex or opposite-sex relationships is irrelevant—the law should recognize them both because they are the informed choices of consenting adults. Critics insist that this grounding in personal autonomy opens the door to any type of relationship between consenting adults, including various forms of incest and polygamy. Some have even argued that there can be consenting relationships between adults and children, and others suggest that even relationships with animals (known as bestiality) be acceptable if they are based on a person's informed desires. Critics of same-sex marriage are understandably concerned about what else beside same-sex marriage may emerge on the basis of the same personal autonomy that supports same-sex marriage. They point out that there are already some countries in Europe that have recognized same-sex marriage that are also legally recognizing multiple marriages as the equivalent of monogamy. When defending fundamentalist Mormons who are being prosecuted under state law in Arizona and Utah, the ACLU points out the similarity to the defense of same-sex marriage. One ACLU attorney in Utah put it this way: "Talking to Utah's polygamists is like talking to gays and lesbians who really want the right to live their lives and not live in fear because of someone they love. Further, other law scholars recognize the connection between support for same-sex marriage and increased receptivity to multiple marriage."[7]

Birth Control

Two primary issues arise in dealing with birth control—whether birth control is acceptable at all, and if so, what types of birth control are within biblical parameters. Except for official Roman Catholic teaching, which prohibits all forms of artificial birth control, the consensus among most religious believers and the culture at large is that birth control is not only acceptable but desirable. Further, there is no moral distinction between temporary birth control and sterilization—vasectomies and tubal ligations (in which the woman's fallopian tubes are tied). The debate over birth control is primarily a religious one—most nonreligious people in the culture take birth control for granted.

Nowhere does the Bible prohibit the use of birth control. The only instance in which birth control was practiced was in Genesis 38:9–10 with the "sin of Onan." Onan engaged in what is called *coitus interruptus* and, by doing so, refused to fulfill his responsibility as the "kinsman redeemer" by fathering a child to carry

Polyamory and Multiple Marriage

In September 2005 Victor de Bruijn and his wife, Bianca, took on another woman, Mirjam Gevan, in a ceremony recognized by the notary in the Dutch town of Roosendaal as a "cohabitation contract." They exchanged wedding rings and held a reception and celebrated a honeymoon immediately afterward. This is the first instance of a publicly recognized multiple marriage in the West, though it was not technically a marriage or a state-sanctioned domestic partner agreement (the way same-sex marriages are recognized in the Netherlands). Interestingly, both the women in the arrangement are bisexual and the man is straight. The bisexual nature of the relationships suggests that multiple marriages are different from same-sex marriages, but they do share the same basis in personal autonomy. Social commentator Stanley Kurtz makes this observation: "Increasingly bisexuality is emerging as a reason why legalized gay marriage is likely to result in legalized group marriage. If every sexual orientation has a right to construct its own form of marriage, then more changes are surely due. For what gay marriage is to homosexuality, group marriage is to bisexuality. The De Bruijn trio is the tip-off to the fact that a connection between bisexuality and the drive for multipartner marriage has been developing for some time."

Although polygamy exists in parts of the non-Western world, the new movement, known as "polyamory," is seen in some fundamentalist Mormon communities in Utah, Arizona, and Texas. It is endorsed by the Unitarian Universalist Church, which desires to become the first denomination to welcome multiple marriages into their church. It has also made its way into the media, in the HBO series *Big Love*. Legal justifications are being published in major law journals in the United States such as the *Stanford Law Review* and the New York University *Review of Law and Social Change*.*

*Stanley Kurtz, "Here Come the Brides," *The Weekly Standard*, December 26, 2005, 19–27; Megan Busham, "Pushing for Polygamy," *National Review Online* (April 18, 2005).

on the lineage of his deceased brother. He was unwilling to do this because he didn't want the burden and responsibility of raising and supporting the child. So he practiced a crude form of birth control by having sex and withdrawing just prior to inseminating the woman.

Some argue that the original mandate given to human beings in Genesis 1–2 ("be fruitful and multiply") makes it mandatory for married couples to procreate children. In chapter 6 I noted that the view of procreation that must always link the unitive and procreative aspects of sex is a more rigid view than Scripture makes necessary. I pointed out that the Bible seems to separate those aspects of sex and holds that the unitive (the one flesh) aspect of sex is a sufficient end in itself. If those two components of sex do not always have to be connected, then married couples can have sex without procreation without violating any moral norm. In addition, notice in Genesis 1:27 that the purpose for human beings procreating was to "fill the earth," thereby enabling human beings to more effectively exercise dominion over all of creation. If part of the original purpose for procreation was to fill the earth, one can easily make the case that the earth is full (perhaps even overfull) and that the mandate to procreate, and thus fill the earth, has been fulfilled. So assuming that it is done for the right reasons, a couple who chooses not to have children would not be violating the mandate to "be fruitful and multiply."

Even conceding that the mandate to procreate is still in effect, the Bible nowhere indicates when or how many children a couple is to have. Advocates of birth control insist that couples have stewardship responsibilities both to their family and to the broader world and therefore should avoid having more children than they can properly parent and provide for, and further avoid contributing to overpopulation and taxing the world's resources. It may be that birth control is used only for the purpose of spacing out one's children, affecting not necessarily the numbers but the timing of children. This seems consistent with the notion of stewardship by avoiding overwhelming parents with children spaced very closely together.

Opponents of birth control insist that children are a gift from God, and that God's good gifts should not be refused. However, proponents of birth control respond that, of course, if God gives a couple a child, they should see the child as God's gift and the child should not be refused or abandoned. But they insist that it does not follow from that that a couple is obligated to have as many children as they biologically can bear. Nor does it follow that reasonable means to control the number of children can't be used, knowing that the ultimate decision on the number of children a couple has belongs to God. Even though birth control is used, God can still give a couple a child should he so desire. It appears that God has ordained limits on procreation that are biological in nature when a woman starts menopause and stops releasing eggs monthly. Thus the mandate to procreate has a time limit on it that is God-ordained.

If temporary birth control is acceptable, there does not seem to be any reason why more permanent sterilization measures could not be utilized. Of course, this must be done wisely and not prematurely. But for couples who have reached their limit in terms of the number of children they have, nothing seems to prohibit sterilization. In fact, such measures may be consistent with obligations of stewardship toward one's family and toward the broader community.

A second area of discussion about birth control concerns the specific methods of birth control. Most agree that *contraceptive* methods are morally acceptable — that is, methods that prevent conception are not problematic. The methods that are *abortifacient* are the ones that generate discussion. Given a view of the moral status of embryos defended in earlier chapters, abortifacient methods are intrinsically problematic because they cause the death of human persons, either by preventing implantation or by expelling the embryo form the uterus. IUDs prevent implantation, and RU-486 causes an implanted embryo to evacuate the uterus. Both are morally problematic from the view that embryos have full moral status. Of course, if one views embryonic status differently, these methods that cause the embryo's destruction are not immoral.

The controversial method in this area is the birth control pill — a very common birth control method used by vast numbers of women around the world. The pill acts by suppressing ovulation and thickening the cervical mucous in order to prevent sperm from reaching the egg. There is nothing problematic about the contraceptive part of the pill. But what is under debate is the abortifacient aspect of the pill — whether it has one and how significant it is. Some argue that there is a secondary effect of the pill that affects the lining of the uterus, making it inhospitable for an embryo to successfully implant. Others insist that no such mechanism is involved, or if it is, it is impossible to quantify how often it occurs. There is still considerable debate over this, and no consensus exists among specialists who are sensitive to the moral status of the embryo. For couples considering the pill, it is best to consult with your physician and be very open with him or her about your values and concerns about birth control. Until more of a consensus is reached, it is a matter of one's individual conscience.[8]

Masturbation

This is an area on which the Bible is almost entirely silent. It is common to suggest that the "sin of Onan" refers to masturbation, but as mentioned above, that narrative is about Onan's unwillingness to fulfill his obligation as a kinsman redeemer (Gen. 38:8–10). In fact, it is coitus interruptus, not masturbation, that is occurring in that narrative. So that narrative is entirely unrelated to the issue under discussion.

As noted in chapter 6, masturbation is necessary to obtain sperm samples for in vitro fertilization, gamete intrafallopian transfer, and intrauterine insemination. In addition, it may be that couples may experience some periods where sex is either not possible or more difficult, such as during pregnancy or while nursing small children, or even post-menopause. Nowhere does the Bible suggest that there is anything inherently wrong with masturbation. However, the Bible is clear that the sexual fantasy that normally accompanies masturbation is lust, and that is very problematic. Lust is equated with adultery (Matt. 5:27–29), and what is done in the mind is just as troubling as what is done in the body. Thus, for example, if it is done with one's spouse and done apart from lust or sinful sexual fantasy, it can be acceptable. In the cases in which sexual fantasy is involved, that is the problem with masturbation, not the action itself.

Sex Change and Transgender

The Bible is silent about sex change and transgender because the technology to effect sex changes did not exist in biblical times and the biblical writers could not have been expected to anticipate issues like these. But there are some principles that seem to apply to this, particularly trust in God's providence in the assignment of gender to individuals. Accepting one's gender as one of life's "givens" seems most consistent with a Christian ethic, analogous to accepting one's race and traits that are genetically given. Of course, not everyone who would call themselves transgender would opt for sex-change surgery. Transgender simply refers to a person whose gender identity is at variance with his or her sex at birth. It has a variety of manifestations, ranging from cross-dressing (transvestites) to being a transsexual, one who desires to live full-time as a member of the opposite sex. Transsexuals generally seek medical interventions to change their sex.

In some cases a child is born with ambiguous gender, in which it is not clear whether the child is male or female. One form of this is known as *hermaphroditism*. Ambiguous gender results from a genetic abnormality, and normally the parents select a gender at birth, which then requires corrective surgery and hormone replacement therapy. There are some medical indicators that help parents make a good decision when gender is selected. However, it seems reasonable to assume that mistakes are sometimes made in that selection, which then generates a later desire for sex change. In cases where sex change is done to correct a mistake made at birth, it would seem appropriate to allow medicine to make such a correction. That seems different from someone who is unable or unwilling to accept his or her gender as one of the givens of life.

Premarital Sex and Abstinence

The general term in the New Testament that is translated "sexual immorality" is the Greek term *porneía*, from which the English word *pornography* is derived. Though at times it does refer to a more specific type of sexual immorality,[9] in general it refers to all illicit sexual relations. These are listed in Leviticus 18, as we discussed earlier, and the New Testament repeatedly urges the believer to avoid sexual immorality and thus restrict sexual expression to marriage (Eph. 5:3; Col. 3:5; 1 Thess. 4:3; Heb. 13:4). In the Song of Songs, the various figures of speech used to describe sex also suggest that sex is reserved for marriage. Solomon compares sex to a garden, spring, and fountain, and compares his bride's virginity to a locked garden, sealed spring, and enclosed fountain (Song 4:12–5:1). Prior to his wedding night, he realizes that he cannot enjoy the fruit of her sexual garden or the water of her sexual spring and fountain. After they have consummated their marriage, he speaks of having entered the garden and tasted its choice fruits and spices. Thus the way that the sexual imagery is used in the Song of Songs strongly suggests that full sexual enjoyment is not an option prior to the marriage ceremony.

Sexual Purity versus Safe Sex

It is one thing to outline the biblical case for premarital sexual restraint, but it is quite another to apply it consistently in a society that is inundated with sexual stimuli. Even with the growing fear of AIDS and other sexually transmitted diseases, as well as the long-standing fear of pregnancy (though less today due to the availability of abortion), practicing sexual purity is still a significant challenge. People are being encouraged to practice "safe sex," and there is a great deal of debate about how *safe* sex can actually be. Public awareness of the failure rate of many types of condoms is growing. Condoms fail to prevent sperm penetration in roughly 15 percent of all cases, and it is becoming clearer that many brands of condoms are incapable of preventing HIV transmission and fail to do so in as many as one-third of the cases. The following illustration suggests that condoms may not provide entirely safe sex. A few years ago a professional association of approximately eight hundred sex therapists was asked if they would have sex with a partner whom they knew was infected with HIV, using only a condom for protection. None of them responded that they would. As advertised in society, safe sex may not be nearly as safe as its advocates would like the public to believe. There is even a sense that the term *safe sex* is an oxymoron. One writer put it this way: "Consider the notion of 'safe sex.' Surely, the two words are ludicrously contradictory. Sex can be many things: dark, mysterious, passionate, wild, gentle, even reassuring, but it is not safe. If it is, it is not very likely to be sexy. How to abandon oneself to another, how to give your body into someone else's care and control, and remain safe? Sex is dangerous. It's supposed to be."[10]

In moving toward sexual self-control, it is important to realize that individuals are capable of controlling their sexual urges in the same way that they are capable of controlling any other desire. Abstinence is routinely dismissed as unrealistic today because adolescents are simply going to "do it." But such language is actually insulting to teenagers because it suggests that they are incapable of self-control in this area. It likens them to animals for whom sex is qualitatively different than for human beings. Individuals do have choices about sex beyond whether to use adequate protection. They also have choices about whether to become sexually involved.

Given the way that sex outside of marriage is viewed in the popular culture, making the right choice to keep its full expression within the boundaries of marriage is difficult. Many people who desire to keep themselves for marriage are thus viewed as hopelessly out of date, belonging to the Victorian era of a few centuries ago. And many who desire sexual self-control are frustrated by their inability to maintain it consistently. There is a great deal of encouragement for sexual self-control in Christian circles but not much advice on how to make it a reality. The culture at large treats abstinence as though it is not a possibility, and its main concern is with preventing pregnancy and sexually transmitted diseases.

Winning the Battle for Sexual Purity

There are a variety of things that a person can do in the battle for sexual purity. First, it is important to avoid sexually tempting situations in the same way that one should avoid other potentially morally compromising situations. Paul puts it in a simple and straightforward way when he says to "flee . . . immorality" (1 Cor. 6:18). The comparison of this advice with Peter's later advice to believers to resist Satan (1 Peter 5:8) shows the power of the sexual temptation. Believers are encouraged to *resist* Satan, but to *flee* sexual temptation. This involves conscious decisions to limit one's intake of sexually stimulating media and avoid situations in which a person could end up sexually involved. This may also require some sort of accountability from a trustworthy friend to whom permission is given to ask hard questions about what is happening in one's sexual life.

A second element of sexual self-control is to realize that sex is not the glue that holds a relationship together. If anything, sex is the dessert, and the main course of the meal of marriage is the emotional and spiritual relationship of the couple. Sex is simply not like the media portrays it. On television or in the movies, every time a couple goes behind closed doors, it is assumed that fireworks and magic result.

Rarely does one get the impression that anything disappointing ever happens in the bedroom. Yet many married couples will testify that sex, particularly without emotional intimacy and commitment, is overrated. A healthy sexual relationship does not happen like spontaneous combustion. It takes work, adjustments, and communication—none of which are ever portrayed in the media. It is not unusual for the average married couple to take up to a year to initially adjust to each other sexually, and it is not uncommon for couples who have been happily married for five to ten years to say that they are just now beginning to enjoy the sexual aspect of their marriage. There are actually more conflicts about sex than about anything else in marriage except money. It is hardly the glue that keeps a relationship together, even though it is treated as such by the popular culture.

A third element in the move toward sexual self-control is to accurately assess the damage that premature sexual relations can do to a relationship. For example, when a couple gets sexually involved, the physical aspect of the relationship normally begins to dominate and can short-circuit the development of the emotional and spiritual sides of the relationship—the ones that are important for long-term sexual enjoyment. Most sexual problems in relationships are not physical, but relational in origin, and the solution has nothing to do with sexual technique. It lies with relational harmony and contentment. Couples who get sexually involved prior to marriage risk mortgaging long-term sexual development for short-term pleasure if a dominant sexual aspect of the relationship stunts emotional and spiritual growth. In addition, for many Christian couples there is a good deal of guilt involved in premarital sex, and for many couples there is often pain and frustration if the relationship does not last. There can also be a loss of objectivity about the direction of the relationship when the physical aspect is dominant, since sexual involvement often communicates a greater sense of commitment than may actually exist. Finally, sex before marriage can sow seeds of mistrust. If a person cannot control his or her sexual desires before marriage, then what assurances are there that he or she can control sexual desire after marriage when the complicating

Advertising Adultery

The Ashley Madison Agency (www.ashleymadison.com) promotes itself as the largest *married* dating site in the world. It uses the catch line "When monogamy becomes monotony." The site boasts almost two million members, and it enables married individuals to meet someone in order to start dating outside marriage. Of course, the site promises 100 percent confidentiality, making it "safe and secure for people just like you." It claims to have been seen on major media outlets such as *Dr. Phil* and *20/20*.

factors of pregnancy and children enter in? Control of sexual desire thus tends to build trust in one's partner that is essential to good sexual enjoyment in the long term.

Restoring Sexual Purity

Frequently in discussions of sexual morality, one's moral obligation is clear but the person is disturbed by failure to live up to that obligation. Of more interest than how to maintain sexual self-control is the question of what to do when someone sins sexually. An extension of the garden imagery for sex in the Song of Songs is particularly helpful here in addressing a lack of sexual self-control (Song 4:12–5:1). It may be that a person has unwisely allowed someone to enter his or her garden, and as a result the garden is in a state of disarray. Or worse, it may be that someone has forced himself or herself into a person's garden through rape or sexual abuse. Solomon's bride kept her garden locked until the appropriate time, but she is the ideal, and many people's actual experience falls discouragingly short of that. If someone came to you and asked what to do about sexual failure, perhaps you could tell him or her something like this:

> If I were a gardener and someone had broken into my garden and overturned the flowers and fairly well spoiled it, I suppose I would be the best person to go in and fix it and place things back like I wanted them. I could accept the problem and restore the garden to its original beauty. You are the garden of your Creator. He is the One who made you, and He knows how you are best prepared for marriage. He can accept the problem and remake the garden. He can accept the broken flowers of your life and forgive them. And He can give you instructions for your part in the restoration of the garden.[11]

Even though physical virginity cannot be restored, it appears that emotional and spiritual virginity can be. In his forgiveness and grace, God can heal the emotional scars of past sexual promiscuity and restore a person's hope for a fulfilling sexual relationship in marriage. The individual's responsibility is not to let anyone in the garden while the divine gardener is at work restoring it. One woman who wrote to Dear Abby put it this way:

> Dear Abby:
> I was raped by a relative when I was a teenager. I spent the next five years searching desperately for love through numerous brief sexual encounters. I felt cheap and dirty and was convinced that no one could love or want me. Then I met a very special young man who convinced me that God loved me just the way I was, and that I was precious in His sight. I then let go of my burdensome past, and by accepting God's forgiveness, I started on the long road to forgiving myself. It works. Believe me.
>
> Free and Happy

For Further Reading

Grenz, Stanley. *Welcoming but Not Affirming: An Evangelical Response to Homosexuality.* Louisville: Westminster John Knox, 1998.

Wold, Donald J. *Out of Order: Homosexuality in the Bible and the Ancient Near East.* Grand Rapids: Baker, 1998.

Wolfe, Christopher, ed. *Homosexuality and American Public Life.* New York: Spence, 1999.

Review Questions

1. What types of sexual relationships are prohibited in the Mosaic law?

2. What is the general norm for sexual relationships in Genesis 1–2?

3. Israel's idolatry was compared to what sexual sin? Why was that specific comparison made?

4. Why was polygamy allowed in Old Testament times?

5. Which book in the Bible celebrates the sexual relationship in marriage?

6. In 1 Corinthians 6:12–20, what is violated when sexual immorality occurs?

7. Why does 1 Corinthians 7:25–35 affirm singleness?

8. What are the different meanings of the term *homosexual*?

9. What are some of the primary myths about homosexuality?

10. What are some of the developmental factors that sometimes account for a homosexual orientation?

11. What does Romans 1:24–27 teach about homosexuality?

12. What are some of the other suggested interpretations of Romans 1:24–27?

13. What is the difference between being homoerotic and homosexual?

14. What are the arguments outside the Bible that are sometimes used to address homosexuality?

15. What is the primary argument for legalizing same-sex marriage? Against it?

16. What is the difference between contraceptive and abortifacient types of birth control?

17. What does the "sin of Onan" refer to?

18. What is the primary argument against the use of birth control?

19. What arguments support birth control being acceptable?

20. What is the clear moral difficulty in the discussion of masturbation?

21. What are the main concerns with the notion of "safe sex"?

22. What things can be done to maintain sexual purity?

23. How can the garden imagery from the Song of Songs help someone to recover from sexual failure?

Cases for Discussion

Case 10.1: Wrestling with Sexual Orientation

You are counseling a college student in your church who has come to you very privately with ambiguity about his sexual orientation. He doesn't understand why it is difficult for him to sustain interest in opposite-sex relationships, and he thinks he might be gay but is not sure. He wants to know what you think about homosexuality—he knows you have religious views on this, and he wants to know what you think.

Questions for Discussion

1. What would you tell this young man about your views on homosexuality? What does the Bible contribute to your view on this issue?

2. Suppose he ends up deciding that he's gay and holds similar religious views to yours. Is it possible for him to be a Christian and a homosexual at the same time? Why or why not?

3. Assume that this person has no interest in any of your religious grounding for your view. How would you articulate your view in a way that is not exclusively dependent on the Bible?

Case 10.2: Legalizing Same-Sex Marriage

You are a state senator in your state, and there is a bill in your committee that would provide for the legalization of same-sex marriage. It would go beyond simply recognizing the rights of same-sex couples, as civil unions do in your state and many others. This bill would actually confer the designation of "marriage" on same-sex couples who go through a ceremony similar to the justice of the peace performing heterosexual marriages. Opponents of the bill insist that this will undermine the traditional family—the most important structure that transmits values in the culture. Proponents of the bill insist that this is basic fairness for same-sex couples.

Questions for Discussion

1. How will you vote on this bill giving same-sex couples the designation of marriage? Would you extend that designation to other forms of constructing a family, such as multiple marriage?

2. What do your religious views have to say on this issue? How do you feel about your religious views informing your public policy position?

Case 10.3: Sex Change and Christian Ethics

I recently received the following inquiry from a church leader. Think about how you would respond to this request for counsel.

> Dear Dr. Rae,
>
> I work at _____ Church with Pastor _____ . Recently, a person called our church and said that they had a sex change from a man to a woman. (His male organs were changed to female organs.) He does not view this as a problem and wants to know if our church would accept him into our congregation. My current view is that this type of behavior is sin, but the pastor and I want to know how you might handle this situation. What Scripture would you cite relating to this issue? Do you have any advice on how we should handle this situation? Is this an acceptable thing to do for someone who says he is a Christian?
>
> I appreciate your help.

Questions for Discussion

1. How would you answer this inquiry from this church leader? Do you think that a sex change is compatible with Christian ethics?

2. What biblical resources would you bring to bear on this discussion?

3. How does your decision on the sex-change operation affect your decision to receive this person into the church?

Chapter 10 Notes

1. Paul's teaching on homosexuality in Romans 1:18–32 will be discussed in this chapter in the section on homosexuality.

2. The exception to this is in 1 Corinthians 6:12–20, where Paul argues against sexual promiscuity on the basis of Genesis 2:24. He is not speaking to married couples here. Rather, his point is limited to the one-flesh relationship that is associated with sexual intercourse, thus making promiscuity wholly inappropriate for the believer. This is magnified by the indwelling Christ in the believer, so that Christ is actually joined to the person with whom one has had an affair.

3. This is not to say that single-parent families are any less genuine families in the sight of God, only that procreation cannot occur in that setting. Single-parent families usually began as two-parent families, and procreation occurred in the proper context. Divorce, however tragic, does not prevent the resulting single parent and children from being a legitimate family.

4. Though not a supporter of these critics of the traditional view, Donald Wold makes this same cultural observation about the connection between homosexual gang rape and forced submission in his book *Out of Order: Homsexualitiy in the Bible and the Ancient Near East* (Grand Rapids: Baker, 1998).

5. I am assuming a more literal interpretation of the Song of Songs and reject the allegorical interpretation that views the relationship between Solomon and his bride as symbolic of the relationship between Christ and the church. Although that comparison is certainly appropriate in the light of Ephesians 5:22–33, the consensus among recent commentators is that Solomon's primary intent was to address literal sex in a literal heterosexual marriage. For more on this, see S. Craig Glickman, *A Song for Lovers* (Downers Grove, Ill.: InterVarsity, 1978). See also Richard Hess, *The Song of Songs* (Grand Rapids: Baker, 2005).

6. See chapter 3 for more detail on Kant's deontological ethical system.

7. Cited in Megan Basham, "Pushing for Polygamy," *National Review Online*, April 18, 2005.

8. For further reading on this, see Linda K. Bevington and Russell DiSilvestro, *The Pill: Addressing the Scientific and Ethical Questions of the Abortifacient Issue* (Deerfield, Ill.: Center for Bioethics and Human Dignity, 2002).

9. For example, see Matthew 5:19 and 19:1–10, where Jesus discusses divorce. There is a great deal of debate on what exactly *porneía* means in this context. Some hold that it means premarital sex, while others hold that it means adultery. Whatever one's interpretation of these difficult passages, it is clear that *porneía* is used to specify a particular type of sexual immorality.

10. Kari Jenson Gold, "Getting Real," *First Things* 39 (January 1994): 6.

11. Glickman, *Song for Lovers*, 115–16.

Chapter 11

The Morality of War

In 2003 the United States launched an invasion of Iraq, with the initial intention of ousting Saddam Hussein and generating a stable democracy in the Arab Middle East. Many people saw it as a part of the response to the 9/11 terrorist attacks on the World Trade Center, a response that also included the war in Afghanistan, which was aimed at destroying terrorist bases of operations there. In the days leading up to the commencement of the invasion, there was a good deal of debate, both in Congress and in the media, over whether this was a war that should be undertaken. To be sure, there was a strategic component to the debate—that is, whether it was feasible to take on an invasion such as this. But a substantial degree of the discussion was about the *morality* of such a war—whether the Iraq war was a morally justified operation.

Interestingly, much of the debate centered on an idea that was at least a thousand years old—the idea of *just war*. Although this concept was clarified and codified in the Middle Ages, its criteria for determining the justice of a war were still being appealed to in the debate over the Iraq war. Even people who disagreed with the final decision to go to war frequently appealed to the just war criteria to articulate their opposition to the war. Of course, some participants in the debate rejected the just war idea altogether and argued that going to war is never justifiable. These groups, known as *pacifists*, insist that the idea of a just war is an oxymoron—they argue that all wars are unjust and that all participation in war is immoral. The Iraq war contributed to somewhat of a resurgence of pacifism. Pacifists today sometimes prefer the term *peacemakers* to describe their position and consider the term *pacifism* to be a bit out of date.[1]

The wars in recent history, especially since World War II, are grim reminders that humankind possesses greater skill and machinery to bring death and destruction in war than at any other time in human history. Even though the Cold War is over and there is not the same fear of nuclear weapons that there was at its peak, there is a sufficient nuclear arsenal to destroy the earth many times over. In addition, the remarkable rise of international terrorism in recent decades means that the traditional ways of conducting warfare have changed dramatically. Some suggest that concepts like the just war are actually obsolete because of these developments.

Imagine that you are sitting in on a panel discussion of the morality of the Iraq war. Others on this panel include an officer currently serving in the military, a Catholic priest, and a Protestant minister. All three have different views of the morality of war in general and the morality of the Iraq war in particular. Here is what the panelists might say to summarize their positions.

Officer on Active Duty

My position is that the world is a very dangerous place today, and many of the heads of state in certain parts of the world are aggressive, ruthless tyrants that support and facilitate international terrorism. War is necessary to defend ourselves from them. I further hold that in certain cases preventive strikes against enemies that are poised for imminent attack are also justifiable. I hold that both the wars in Iraq and Afghanistan are morally justifiable in the ongoing defense of our country against terrorism.

Catholic Priest

I believe that my military colleague has gone too far in defending which wars can be justified. My view is that the only wars that are justifiable are wars of self-defense. I hold to what is called the *just war theory*, which states that once aggression is visited upon a nation, the properly constituted authorities in that nation are morally justified in meeting force with force and defending their people from a hostile aggressor. I cannot support any aggressive use of military force. It cannot be used unless and until another country has initiated a conflict. The only wars that are morally allowable are those fought in self-defense, such as the West's efforts in defeating the Nazis in World War II. Since Iraq did not initiate aggressive military action against the United States directly, and it is debatable whether Iraq was involved with the 9/11 attacks, I have major reservations about calling the Iraq war a just war.

Protestant Minister

I think you both are wrong and out of step with clear biblical teaching on this subject. Both Jesus and the early church were pacifists. Jesus taught his followers to "turn the other cheek," to leave vengeance to God and not to use violence in any way to accomplish any purpose. The Beatitudes tell us, "Blessed are the peacemakers," and I take that to mean that any involvement in war, either as a combatant or noncombatant, is inconsistent with that. In addition, the people who were closest to Jesus chronologically were also pacifists. The early church for about the first three centuries had nothing to do with the military. Only when Christianity became the official religion of the Roman Empire and had "national interests" that needed defending did the use of violence get church sanction. Thus, not only do I believe that the Iraq war was totally unjustified, but I hold that all use of violence is wrong.

What do you think of the panelists' statements? Which position do you find most persuasive to you and most consistent with your moral views? As you read this chapter and these views are more fully explained, come back to this panel discussion and think about what you would say if you were one of the panel members.

You could probably have the same kind of panel discussion for a variety of conflicts that have occurred in the past few years. For example, the conflicts over portions of the former Yugoslavia, such as the fierce fighting that took place in Bosnia and later in Kosovo, both involved the intervention of international military forces from the United States and Europe in order to keep peace (under the commission of the United Nations). Similarly, in the Darfur region of the Sudan, genocide is occurring, prompting requests for international intervention. The same questions the panelists raise about the Iraq war could also be raised about these other conflicts. That is, is the use of military force justified in these situations? Under what understanding of war are they either justified or condemned?

Although this discussion impacts those who serve in the military most directly, it affects more people than just those who serve in the military. Some pacifists hold that *any* participation in war in any form violates Jesus' command to be peacemakers. So the morality of war creates moral tension not just for the soldier or officer, but might also for the person who is employed by a company that manufactures weapons or equipment for the military. Perhaps even someone involved in financing these defense industries might face moral tension. For example, a banker whose loan portfolio includes some of these defense-based companies might experience some moral conflict with Jesus' command to be a peacemaker. Or it could be that owning stock in companies that supply the military could raise moral questions too.

War in the Bible

The debate over the morality of war is set against the backdrop of war in the Old Testament. Throughout the Old Testament, Israel was commanded by God to go to war. Some of these wars were designed to secure Israel's boundaries and could be called preventive strikes (2 Sam. 5:17–25; 11:1–2). Others were clearly wars of national defense, fending off the attacks of a belligerent foreign nation (1 Kings 20). But others were aggressive in nature, designed to push Israel's enemies out of the Promised Land (Josh. 6–12). Military force was one of the methods God used to help accomplish his purposes for his chosen nation Israel. What is particularly difficult about some wars in the Old Testament is that God commanded total annihilation of certain enemies because of their idolatry (Deut. 25:17–19; 1 Sam. 15:1–3). This is commonly seen as God exercising his judgment in a more temporal way rather than the norm, which was to delay judgment until one's death.

Simply because God commanded and sanctioned Israel's wars in the Old Testament does not mean that war is justified today. Nothing necessarily follows from this observation except the notion that there is nothing *intrinsically* immoral about war. Important differences distinguish Israel in Old Testament times from the nations living in the present age. First, Old Testament Israel was a theocracy, literally one nation under God, in which the law of God was the law of the land. God had a unique relationship with Israel under the Law that has never been duplicated. No nation today can say that God is commanding them to go to war in the same way that he commanded Old Testament Israel.

Second, Israel was promised the land of Canaan as a national homeland, a place in which God would fulfill the covenant he made with Abraham. One way that was accomplished was through the Messiah coming from the lineage of Abraham. But another way was the manner in which Israel lived together as a community of God's people in the land that God had selected for them. It was a strategic plot of land, in the center of commerce and travel between the empires of Egypt and Mesopotamia, maximizing the visibility of Israel's ideal society for their unbelieving neighbors.

Third, Israel was placed in the land of Canaan because of their vulnerability to military attack. Generally, when Israel was obedient to God, they experienced peace in the land; when they were disobedient, they experienced war. The period of the Judges gives a variety of examples of this trend. To develop Israel's trust in God to protect them from their enemies, he placed them in a particularly vulnerable piece of land that necessitated their possession of it. No nation can say that of its relationship with God today. Thus one should be very careful about drawing any conclusions validating military force from the Old Testament, since God is not dealing with the church or the nations today as he did with Old Testament Israel. The case for war cannot be made from the precedent in the Old Testament alone.

It is true that the New Testament reflects a spirit of pacifism. For example, the Sermon on the Mount forbids resistance or retaliation with respect to evil (Matt. 5:38–42), enjoins love for enemies (5:43–48), and blesses peacemakers, calling them sons of God (5:9). Similarly, the apostles encouraged submission to persecutors (1 Peter 4:12–19) and to civil government, even to the tyrannical Roman Empire (Rom. 13:1–7). During the first few centuries of church history, this same spirit is carried forward. No mention is made of Christians serving in the military, and the early Christian martyrs offered little resistance to their persecutors.

Critics of pacifism will suggest that there were good reasons why there were few early Christians in the military.[2] Many of the first Christians were Jews, and to join the Roman army would have been unthinkable, as it would have been for Gentile Christians once the Roman persecutions began, because the Roman military was the primary persecutor of the early Christian community. But more important, joining the Roman legions normally involved swearing an idolatrous oath of loyalty to Caesar, which believers clearly were unwilling to do. Thus, just because there were few if any Christians serving in the military in the early days of the church, it does not necessarily follow that pacifism is the biblical teaching on war. Nor does that conclusion follow from the admonitions to avoid personal resistance and retaliation. Many advocates of the moral use of military force argue that Jesus is addressing personal relationships, not the government's role in society. They remind us that Paul clearly sanctions the state's valid use of force to maintain justice and public order (Rom. 13:1–7). If that role of the state is valid, then the critics of pacifism can argue that a believer is not prohibited from involvement with the state in its divinely ordained function. Neither the Gospels nor Acts have

Pleas for God's Justice

Many of the psalms contain what are called *imprecations*, or pleas for God to take vengeance on a person's enemies. They come in one of three forms — a request for vengeance against a society enemy, against a nation, or most commonly, against a personal enemy. Here is an example of an imprecation from Psalm 9:

> Arise, O LORD, let not man triumph;
> > let the nations be judged in your presence.
> Strike them with terror, O LORD;
> > let the nations know they are but men. (vv. 19–20)

John Day, in his book *Crying for Justice*, argues that the imprecations are still appropriate for today. He concludes, "It is legitimate for God's present people to utter prayers of imprecation, or pleas for divine vengeance — like those in the Psalms — against the recalcitrant enemies of God and His people. Such expression is consistent with the ethics of the Old Testament and finds corresponding echo in the New Testament." He finds such a view consistent with the idea of justice in the Old Testament, as governed by the notion of "an eye for an eye."* Even though the New Testament ethic is characterized by love of enemies, Day holds that there is still a place allowed for pleas for divine vengeance, though human beings are never allowed to personally carry out vengeance. Critics of this view argue that the notion of love of enemies is so strong in the New Testament that it renders the imprecations an Old Testament phenomena at best. Others insist that the imprecations are figures of speech that communicate a person's loyalty to God to disassociating himself totally from God's enemies.

---

*John N. Day, *Crying for Justice: What the Psalms Teach Us about Mercy and Vengeance in an Age of Terrorism* (Grand Rapids: Kregel, 2005), 109.

any record of soldiers being converted and then being asked to give up their profession (Luke 7:1–10). When John the Baptist was preaching, some soldiers were strongly influenced by his teaching. When asked what they should do in response to John's message, he did not require that they give up their occupation in the military. He only required that they not misuse their authority for oppressive purposes (Luke 3:7–14). New Testament scholar Richard Hays suggests that despite the overall peacemaking message of the New Testament, "these narratives about soldiers provide one possible legitimate basis for arguing that Christian discipleship does not necessarily preclude the exercise of violence in defense of social order or justice."[3] Pacifists rejoin that the state may be permitted to use violence to fulfill its God-ordained mandate, but the Christian cannot participate with the state in those instances.

Major Views on the Morality of War

Although many fine distinctions can be made among the different positions on the morality of war, most major views essentially correspond to one of two positions. For lack of a better term, we will call the first position *pacifism*. Although there are numerous varieties of pacifism, both in secular and religious arenas, which make generalizations difficult, pacifists basically hold that participation in war is never justifiable. The primary difference between the varieties of pacifism is the definition of "participation." Some pacifists hold to what is called *nonviolent pacifism*, which precludes the use of violence in any form. As a result, the nonviolent pacifist cannot be involved in war as a combatant, because that necessarily involves the use of lethal violence against another person. Neither can the nonviolent pacifist use violence against any personal attack. But other pacifists hold to what is sometimes called *nonparticipation pacifism*, the view that participation in war of any kind is not justifiable, including "behind the scenes" work that supports a war effort or national defense in peacetime. This would include, for example, being employed by companies that make military weapons and/or provide essential support for the military. Some pacifists argue that governments should not ever undertake war efforts, but most of the discussion of pacifism in recent years has focused on an individual's use of violence and participation in the military.

The second major position is commonly referred to as the *just war* position. Advocates of a just war concept hold that participation in war can be morally acceptable under certain conditions, outlined in the just war criteria that we will discuss later in this chapter. Again, the primary difference is one of definition, namely, the definition of a "just war." Some people within this camp favor the more traditional idea of the just war, that is, war is justifiable only when it is undertaken in self-defense, when one has been the victim of aggression by an outside intruder. A common example of this appeal to the just war notion occurred during World War II, when the United States attacked Japan in response to the attack on Pearl Harbor. Others define the just war more broadly to include preventive strikes that ward off imminent attack. Advocates of this position hold that this is a similar form of self-defense that only operates prior to an attack instead of solely in response to it. A commonly used example of this is the preemptive strike that Israel undertook against the Arab nations in the Six-Day War of 1967. A third version of the just war concept is that it is justifiable to participate in wars that reverse clear cases of injustice visited upon a vulnerable group or nation by a stronger aggressor. Proponents of American intervention in the first Gulf War in the early 1990s appealed to this version of the just war concept to justify expelling Iraq from Kuwait. Let's look more carefully at each of these positions.

Pacifism

Pacifists insist that all uses of violence, particularly the use of lethal force cannot be justified. Most pacifists agree that participation in war is always immoral and that even the use of violence in self-defense cannot be justified. This view we referred to earlier as *nonviolent pacifism*, and it is the prevalent form of pacifism being articulated today. Though many pacifists who hold their views out of religious convictions (both Eastern and Western religions), other pacifists have no such religious inclinations. Similarly, some nonparticipation pacifists have adopted

The Six-Day War as a Preemptive Strike

In June 1967 the state of Israel launched a preemptive strike against the three Arab nations amassed on its borders — Egypt to the south, Syria to the north, and Jordan to the east. Due to intelligence reports, the Israelis had good reasons to think that their neighbors were preparing to invade, with their goal to destroy the Jewish state entirely. Egyptian President Nasser had mobilized the military forces of Egypt, Syria, and Jordan together to launch the invasion, which Israel preempted by destroying the Egyptian air force and moving into the Golan Heights, held by Syria, and the West Bank, then held by Jordan. Advocates of the just war notion argue that this kind of preemptive strike makes sense — there is no reason to wait until your enemy has crossed your border to engage in self-defense. Critics of the preemptive strike argue that launching such strikes puts the nation that does so in the position of the aggressor.

their views out of a religiously grounded worldview, but others hold pacifist convictions out of nonreligious worldviews.

Some pacifists would insist that one's personal ethic cannot be imposed on society and made into a social ethic. Thus, since the society at large does not claim to follow Christ, it cannot be expected to follow his mandate for nonviolence. Certainly they desire that such a view of war would permeate the general society, but the expectation of nonviolence is only addressed to believers in Christ. As a result, some Christian pacifists do not suggest that the state cannot be involved in war, only that Christians cannot participate with the state when it does wage war. Some versions of secular and other religiously grounded pacifism suggest that the state should not ever go to war, but the support for these versions of nonviolence usually is based on the harm caused by the ravages of war, both to people and the environment. Those who would uphold pacifism as social policy would oppose efforts to create a strong national defense. They would also argue that the money used to support the defense effort could be and should be better spent on social programs aimed at helping the poor and other vulnerable groups in society.

Most religious versions of pacifism are premised upon a strict separation of the church from the world. Violence, pacifists claim, characterizes the world's way of doing business and accomplishing its ends. Therefore Christians can have no part with the world in using force. Christ's kingdom is not of this world (John 18:36), and the Christian does not wage war with the weapons of the world (2 Cor. 10:3–4). Since the Christian's citizenship is in heaven (Phil. 3:20), and since Christians are called to hold values separate from the values of the world (Rom. 12:1–2), use of violence cannot be consistent with following Christ. Some pacifists suggest that a major indicator of the advance of Christ's kingdom is the degree to which nonviolence is practiced in society.

Christian versions of pacifism are grounded in several central passages of Scripture. These include selections primarily from the Sermon on the Mount (Matt. 5:38–48; Luke 6:27–36), Paul's teaching on vengeance in Romans 12:19–21, and Peter's doctrine of nonresistance to persecution in 1 Peter 2:18–24. Undoubtedly, the primary text used to support most forms of pacifism is Jesus' teaching in the Sermon on the Mount. The heart of this passage as it applies to war is as follows:

> You have heard that it was said, "Eye for eye, and tooth for tooth." But I tell you, Do not resist an evil person. If someone strikes you on the right cheek, turn to him the other also....
>
> You have heard that it was said, "Love your neighbor and hate your enemy." But I tell you: Love your enemies and pray for those who persecute you, that you may be sons of your Father in heaven. (Matt. 5:38–40, 43–45)

According to the pacifist, Jesus here is teaching nonresistance to an evil person. The circumstances are not narrowly circumscribed to exempt combatants in war. Rather, that would seem to be the case in which the passage would most directly apply, because in times of war, your enemies are the most intense and most clearly defined. According to pacifists, Jesus' teaching that commands believers to love their enemies is inconsistent with being a participant in war. The context also appears to be broader than simply referring to persecution. It refers to the way in which a believer is to treat enemies in war, in persecution, in business, and in the church. According to most pacifists, one cannot ever justify using violence, not even in self-defense. That is not to say that the one is to stand by idly while being overrun by evil and evil people. They are to resist by any means that do not involve violence. These may include nonviolent ways of making their task more difficult, similar to the way in which Operation Rescue advocates make procuring an abortion more difficult, as well as prayer, love, and other spiritual means to resist evil.

A second central passage is a teaching of Paul on nonretaliation:

> If it is possible, as far as it depends on you, live at peace with everyone. Do not take revenge, my friends, but leave room for God's wrath, for it is written: "It is mine to avenge; I will repay," says the Lord. On the contrary: "If your enemy is hungry, feed him; if he is thirsty, give him something to drink. In doing this, you will heap burning coals on his head." Do not be overcome by evil, but overcome evil with good. (Rom. 12:18–21)

The beginning admonition sets the context for the rest of the passage. The goal for the believer is to be at peace with everyone, while realizing that a person cannot control the two-way street that being fully at peace involves. Just because someone cannot control all aspects of being at peace with another, according to the pacifist, that does not justify the use of violence. Rather, the rest of the passage lays out the believer's response when someone is intent on being at war. The pacifist argues that both violence and retaliation are ruled out by this passage, and that the classic case of being overcome with evil would be to take revenge or act violently in response to it. This is Paul's way of stating what Jesus made clear in the Sermon on the Mount, that you are to love your enemies. Whatever that does involve, certainly it does not leave room for using violent force in the view of the pacifist.

A third central text occurs specifically in the context of Christian persecution. Pacifists argue that 1 Peter 2:18–24 reinforces the nonviolent thrust of the New Testament and grounds it in the example of Christ, strongly suggesting that it is normative for the believer today. The heart of the passage is the section that refers to the nonresistant model of Jesus on the cross:

To this [suffering] you were called, because Christ suffered for you, leaving you an example, that you should follow in his steps.... When they hurled their insults at him, he did not retaliate; when he suffered, he made no threats. Instead, he entrusted himself to him who judges justly. (1 Peter 2:21, 23)

Because nonresistance is such a significant part of the identity of Christ on the cross and following Christ in his sacrifice is such a significant part of the Christian's lifestyle, the pacifist concludes that trusting God and using nonviolent means of resisting evil are the only appropriate responses to evil for the Christian. Thus genuinely following Christ and participation in war are mutually exclusive. Some critics of pacifism would point out that Jesus' and Peter's teaching, if taken in the kind of absolute sense that pacifists take them, would also rule out nonviolent resistance to evil. Jesus seems to be very clear that the believer is not to resist evil, and on the cross he did not simply avoid the use of violence with his enemies, but he did not resist at all. In the Sermon on the Mount, Jesus instructs his disciples to go the extra mile, and if someone takes your coat, let him have other parts of your clothing. To the critic of pacifism this does not sound much like nonviolent resistance to evil. Rather, it sounds like complete nonresistance.

Nonviolence and Nonparticipation

As a result, some Christian pacifists oppose more than simply participation in war as combatants. They are nonparticipation pacifists who would oppose any involvement in a specific war effort because of the Christian's calling to be a peacemaker (Matt. 5:9) and our role as ambassadors of reconciliation, bringing men and women back to God (2 Cor. 5:18–21). Supporters of this more extreme version of pacifism (although they would not call it more extreme, but more consistent with Jesus' teaching) suggest that it is inconsistent to be involved in any way with a system that, by waging war, kills people for whom Christ died. Not only can the believer not be personally involved in the use of violence (which for some pacifists would rule out involvement in law enforcement as well), but anything that contributes to the overall war effort is seen as on the same moral level as being a combatant. Thus the believer in Christ cannot be involved in support of the defense industry, such as working for companies that make weapons and other materials used in war. They would suggest to the nonviolent pacifist that they are making an artificial and somewhat ad hoc distinction between combatant and noncombatant aspects of war. That is, it seems arbitrary to allow the believer to support every other aspect of the war effort, but not to be a combatant. They hold that if they were consistent, they would realize that there is little moral difference between the direct combatant role and other indirect supporting roles.

The supporter of nonviolent pacifism, that is, the more moderate pacifist, would respond by insisting that the teaching of Jesus prohibits only the personal use of violence in resisting evil. In addition, they might respond that nonparticipation pacifism leads to a position in which it is impossible to draw any meaningful lines that distinguish participation from nonparticipation in war. To prohibit someone from supporting the defense industry would make many jobs off-limits. For example, consider the companies that do some business with the defense establishment, while the majority of their business is not related to the military. Rubber companies that make tires for commercial airplanes, for instance, also make them for military airplanes. Separating military from nonmilitary use of the company's product would seem to be virtually impossible or, at the least, would make someone go to absurd lengths to be consistent with their view of the Bible's teaching. Or consider companies that bottle water for sale. Most of their business is clearly nonmilitary use. Yet they played a very important role in supporting the troops engaged in the Iraq war in the desert. Should the Christian who owns a company

What about Hitler?

Philosopher Robert Brimlow in his book *What about Hitler?* attempts to wrestle with his commitment to pacifism as it confronts the reality of evil in the world. He honestly faces the difficult questions that pacifism must face in order to be credible in the world today. He offers a penetrating critique of the just war theory and rejects it as being inconsistent with following Christ. In his conclusion he summarizes his response to the question that the title of the book raises. That is, how should someone who desires to follow Christ and takes nonviolence seriously respond to someone like Hitler who embodies evil in the world? He puts the response like this:

> At this juncture it is time for me to respond to the Hitler question: How should Christians respond to the kind of evil Hitler represents if just war theory is precluded? We must live faithfully; we must be humble in our faith and truthful in what we say and do; we must repay evil with good; and we must be peacemakers. This may also mean as a result that the evildoers will kill us. Then, we also shall die. That's it. There is nothing else — or rather, anything else is only a footnote to this. We are called to live the kingdom as he proclaimed it and be his disciples, come what may. We are, in his words, flowers flourishing and growing wild today, and tomorrow destined for the furnace. We are God's people, living by faith. The gospel is clear and simple, and I know what the response to the Hitler question must be. And I desperately want to avoid this conclusion.*

*Robert W. Brimlow, *What about Hitler? Wrestling with Jesus' Call to Nonviolence in an Evil World* (Grand Rapids: Brazos, 2006), 151.

that bottles water refuse to sell it to the military? Or should the Christian who works for one of these companies quit when they start selling water to the army, even though this is a small part of the company's overall business? To be consistent with this more extreme pacifism, the Christian would need to separate military from nonmilitary use. However, more moderate pacifists would argue that this simply cannot be done in most cases and is not necessary because the Bible only prohibits personal use of violence.

Criticism of Pacifism

The primary criticism of pacifism is not necessarily related to involvement in war, but to the use of violence in general. The classic scenario that is often invoked goes as follows: Imagine that your wife and children were being brutally attacked by someone who had broken into your home and intended to kill them. He is a crazed killer who has chosen your home at random, and unless you intervene personally, your family will all be killed. There is not enough time to call the police. What should you do? What would be most in keeping with your calling as a Christian? One response would be to attempt to disarm him and detain him until the police arrive. If that can be done, that would be the best option, although it could be argued that you still used violence in disarming him. In this case, it may be that the only way to disarm him would be to inflict some kind of bodily harm on him in order to get him to stop his murderous rampage. But what if the only way to stop him is to kill him? If you don't, your family, and likely you, will be killed.

Most people have a strong intuitive opposition to pacifism because of cases like this. Somehow they think it cannot be right to stand by and let their family be harmed, or even killed because they are not willing to use violence when necessary. One can argue that using force is justified here because a person has a higher moral obligation to protect his family than to obey the mandate for nonviolence; that is, there is a conflict between two moral absolutes, the command not to use violence and the command to protect and provide for one's family (1 Tim. 5:8). Augustine expressed it a bit differently, and in the course of church history, opened the door to legitimizing the use of force. He held that at times, the only way that someone can obey the law of love (the biblical mandate to "love your neighbor as yourself," Lev. 19:18) is to use violence when another person is threatened with deadly force. The only way I could truly fulfill the law of love for my wife and children is to do whatever is necessary to repel their attackers, even using lethal force in response if necessary. Refusing to take such action would not be loving toward my family. Seen in this way, it is argued that the use of violence can be justified as a fulfillment of the higher law of love (Rom. 13:8; Gal. 5:14).

A further criticism of pacifism comes from the view of the state in Romans 13:1–7. There Paul suggests that the state legitimately employs force ("wields the sword") to keep order and secure justice. The state exercises these responsibilities under the authority of God himself. Since it is legitimate under God for the state to use violence in the God-given exercise of its responsibility to protect its citizens and maintain order, and since Christians are called to support and be involved with government in its legitimate role, then it is difficult to see why someone cannot be involved with the state in a role that involves the use of force. This would open the door for involvement in internal law enforcement as well as external military affairs that protect its citizens from harm, both from inside the state as well as outside it.[4]

The Just War Theory

The just war tradition goes back ultimately to the time of Augustine but was not systematically well developed until Catholic theologians did so in the Middle Ages. For some time it has been the dominant justification for the use of force. More recently its adequacy has been called into question with the development of nuclear weapons capable of destroying the planet and the advent of terrorism as a means of waging war. Advocates of the classical view hold that war is justifiable under certain carefully worked out conditions, namely, when it is a response of self-defense to unprovoked aggression. Some just war advocates have taken the view a bit further and justified preventive wars, or those that anticipate certain aggression, and wars to reverse clear injustices visited on vulnerable nations by stronger aggressors. Both are justified as just wars, but the definition of what constitutes a just war is different.

Traditional Criteria for the Just War

Proponents of the classical just war tradition maintain that only wars of self-defense are justified. They admit that war is an atrocity but is sometimes regrettably necessary to maintain security and justice within one's borders. Any just war must meet a series of conditions that specify when a war is just in order for a war to be engaged. They are generally structured in two distinct categories—*jus ad bello*, a Latin phrase that refers to justice in going to war, and *jus in bello*, or justice in the conduct of war. Criteria 1–4 are classified as *jus ad bello* criteria and 5–7 are in the category of *jus in bello*. The criteria are as follows:

Jus Ad Bello Criteria

1. *The war in question must be prompted by a just cause*, defined as a defensive war; that is, no war of unprovoked aggression can ever be justified. Only wars that are a response to aggression already initiated are morally legitimate.

Thus, after the Japanese attack on Pearl Harbor during World War II, the United States had just cause to respond to Japanese aggression by declaring war. Whether the war was entirely just depends on how well it measures up to the rest of the just war criteria, but the just cause rule is a critical one. But simply because a nation has a just cause for war does not mean that the war can be morally justified. It must meet the rest of the criteria.

2. *The war in question must have a just intention*, that is, its intent must be to secure a fair peace for all parties involved. It cannot be undertaken with the aim of securing a peace that is to one's clear advantage, not only a peace that insures one's security. This criterion rules out wars of national revenge, economic exploitation, and ethnic cleansing. Many would argue that the Allies in World War II had a just intention to secure a just peace, as evidenced by the Marshall Plan to help rebuild Europe.

3. *The war in question must be engaged in as a last resort.* All diplomatic efforts to resolve the conflict must be exhausted prior to engaging in defensive war. This criterion also implies that diplomatic efforts should continue once the war is begun in an effort to settle the hostilities at the negotiating table rather than on the battlefield.

4. *The war in question must be initiated with a formal declaration by properly constituted authorities.* Warfare is the prerogative of governments, not individuals, vigilante groups, or paramilitary units operating outside legitimate government authority. A just war is declared and engaged in by the highest authority in government and must be recognized by appropriate legislative bodies, assuming they operate in the nation in question. This criterion does not mean that individuals do not have the right of self-defense, but on the surface, it would seem to preclude wars of national liberation by paramilitary groups operating against the government.

Jus In Bello Criteria

5. *The war in question must be characterized by limited objectives.* Wars of total annihilation, unconditional surrender, or wholesale destruction of a nation's infrastructure and ability to rebuild following war are not moral. The overriding purpose for a just war is peace, not the humiliation and economic crippling of another nation. It may be that insuring the victor's future security may involve disarming the enemy nation and crippling its offensive military capabilities, but it must not involve destruction of its potential to survive as a nation.

6. *The war in question must be conducted with proportionate means*, that is, the amount of force used must be proportionate to the threat. Only sufficient force to repel and deter the aggressor can be justifiably used. Total destruction,

perhaps by nuclear attack, is ruled out. The defending nation, in responding to the attack, must not be guilty of "burning down the barn to roast the pig." Many critics of just war theory aim their criticism right here, that any use of nuclear weapons violates this criterion, and thus any war in which nuclear weapons are engaged cannot be just. They would therefore conclude that American attacks on Hiroshima and Nagasaki violated just war doctrine. But advocates of the bombing of these two cities could respond by saying that if conventional war had continued and an invasion of Japan had taken place, far more lives would have been lost than were lost as a result of the nuclear bombing. However, the final criterion poses even greater problems for nuclear weapons.

7. *The war in question must respect noncombatant immunity.* Only those individuals who are representing their respective governments in the military can be targeted in the course of the war. Civilians, wounded soldiers, and prisoners of war cannot be objects of attack. Since most nuclear weapons are indiscriminate in their destructive capacity, they would not be considered implements in a just war. It may be that strategic nuclear weapons will be perfected, but until then, noncombatant immunity poses significant problems for any nation's nuclear arsenal within the just war tradition. This would also rule out other weapons of mass destruction, such as chemical and biological weapons and terrorist attacks on innocent civilians. It also raises questions about one of the strategies employed in World War II, the firebombing of cities both in Britain by the Nazis and in Germany by the Allies.

Use of Waterboarding Justified?

Waterboarding, an interrogation technique that simulates drowning, was accepted by the Bush administration in early 2008 for use in "extraordinary circumstances," such as when a prisoner has information about an imminent attack. This renewed the debate about the use of harsh techniques that could be construed to constitute torture. Many consider the law to prohibit these kinds of methods, arguing that their use is a "black mark" on the United States. The CIA has testified that waterboarding was used on a handful of al-Qaida suspects, including Khalid Sheikh Mohammed, the alleged mastermind behind the 9/11 attacks. Critics insist that use of such techniques only aids the enemy and puts U.S. soldiers at risk for the same treatment. Advocates argue that if it is the only way to get information that will stop an imminent attack and save lives, then it is justified.*

*Greg Miller, "Waterboarding Is Legal, White House Says," *Los Angeles Times*, February 7, 2008.

Responding to the Pacifist's Biblical Support

Only if a military campaign meets the above seven conditions can it be termed a just war in the traditional sense. In their attempts to justify the use of force to resist evil, Christian just war theorists must respond to the pacifist's appeal to New Testament teaching in the central passages mentioned above.

The primary central text to which pacifists appeal is from the Sermon on the Mount (Matt. 5:38–48). Here Jesus makes a general statement expressing a contrast with the traditional understanding of the religious leaders of his time, "You have heard it said, 'Eye for eye, and tooth for tooth.' But I tell you, Do not resist an evil person" (vv. 38–39). He then follows this with four specific examples that spell out in more detail precisely what he means by the general statement "Do not resist an evil person." These examples include turning the other cheek when struck (an insult, not a life-threatening assault), giving up one's cloak in response to being sued for one's tunic, going the extra mile, and not turning away someone who wants to borrow from you (vv. 39–42). These refer to the oppressions that a persecuted minority suffered at the hands of a dominant and powerful majority. The important aspect to notice is that they do not refer to any kind of life-threatening situation for the individual or those close to that person. Jesus is insisting that his followers do not respond with retaliation when insulted or taken advantage of by a persecuting power. The just war advocate argues that the text here does not address the types of life-threatening scenarios that are commonly cited by opponents of pacifism. Thus one cannot use these examples to support nonviolence in all circumstances. Jesus is prohibiting revenge, not self-defense or defense of others when threatened by lethal force.

Paul's teaching in Romans 12:19–21 reinforces this teaching of Jesus. The just war advocate argues that Paul is here prohibiting revenge and retaliation and encourages his readers to leave that to God (v. 19). He maintains that the offended individual's responsibility is to stop the cycle of revenge and to do good to one's enemies as a way of promoting peace. However, he acknowledges that peace may not be possible with everyone (v. 18). The emphasis here is on nonretaliation, not self-defense. Nothing in the text precludes the individual from taking measures to ensure the safety of himself and others close to him. But once the offended person is victimized, revenge is to be left to God. One way it is left to God comes out in the very next passage in the book—Romans 13:1–7, which as we have already seen, outlines the responsibility of the state, under God's authority, to keep order and secure justice, by force if necessary. The reason that the individual can trust God with this is because he has entrusted the state as his instrument to uphold justice, particularly for those who are oppressed. According to the just war theorist, Paul is thus not prohibiting self-defense or defense of others, but retaliation for wrongs suffered.

Peter's teaching in 1 Peter 2:19–24 comes in the context of persecution for a person's faith—that is assumed to be the source of the unjust treatment received. In the face of persecution for following Jesus, the person is to follow the example of Jesus, which is summarized in verse 23 when Peter says, "When they hurled their insults at him, he did not retaliate; when he suffered, he made no threats. Instead, he entrusted himself to him who judges justly." Though it is the case that the believer is to endure persecution willingly by following Jesus' example, even if it is life-threatening, that is different than being the victim of a life-threatening assault in general. The just war advocate holds that Peter is not prohibiting self-defense in general. He is addressing it only in the context of enduring persecution for one's faith.

The just war advocate, then, insists that the use of violence under specified conditions is not inconsistent with the New Testament texts often cited by the pacifist. The central focus of those texts is the prohibition of revenge and retaliation, not self-defense or defense of others.

Another way that just war theorists attempt to justify the use of force is by taking a hierarchical view of God's commands;[5] that is, one has a higher obligation to defend oneself and one's family against the imminent threat of harm over and above the obligation not to use violence. This way of approaching the problem concedes that the pacifist has a valid point about the Bible prohibiting the use of violence. But nonviolence is not an absolute under this view and can be outweighed

Just War and the Supreme Emergency

Philosopher Michael Walzer, in his landmark book *Just and Unjust Wars*, argues that the rules of war may be overridden in cases of what he calls "supreme emergency." He addresses two commonly held violations of the just war theory—the decision to bomb German and British civilian populations during World War II and the American decision to drop the atomic bomb on Hiroshima and Nagasaki at the end of the war. The purpose of both decisions was "the destruction of civilian morale," and to thereby hasten the end of the war. In the case of dropping the atomic bomb on Japan, the United States thought about the decision to shorten the war in terms of lives saved by the decision. Walzer puts the question like this: "Should I wage this determinate crime (killing of innocent civilians) against the immeasurable evil (a Nazi triumph)?" Walzer suggests that a supreme emergency occurs when a defeat is not only likely but would "bring disaster upon a political community." In those rare cases, he argues, the normal rules of war may be suspended.*

*Michael Walzer, *Just and Unjust Wars*, 3rd ed. (New York: Basic Books, 2000).

by the higher mandate to love one's neighbor as oneself. Most pacifists find all of these explanations unconvincing, and they insist that one of the weaknesses of the just war tradition is its inability to explain what appears to many to be the clear teaching of Jesus and the apostles advocating nonviolence.

The well-known German theologian and pastor Dietrich Bonhoeffer seems to use reasoning like this to explain his personal involvement in the attempt to assassinate Hitler toward the end of World War II. In his writing Bonhoeffer defended nonviolence as part of the "cost of discipleship." He made it clear that he considered it one of the nonnegotiable components of faithfully following Christ. Yet he was one of the conspirators in the plot to kill Hitler in order to stop the evil of Nazism and the genocide of Jews. He saw himself as caught between two evils—using violence and allowing Nazism and genocide to continue. He reasoned that either choice was evil, for which he would obtain grace and forgiveness, but he felt obligated to choose the lesser evil and participate in the use of violence against Hitler. He saw the danger in pacifism allowing evil to go unchecked but also saw his use of violence against Hitler as the lesser evil and thus his moral duty. Critics of pacifism cite Bonhoeffer as an example of why pacifism cannot be consistently held in the face of a world of evil. When faced with the reality of evil and the opportunity to stop it, critics of pacifism hold that pacifism is indefensible, dangerous, and a refusal to face the facts of evil in the world.[6]

Just war advocates defend the use of force with a set of other, more theologically grounded arguments. First, they insist that the sinfulness of people and the biblical demand for justice make the use of force necessary in society. The inhumanities against the human race in the twentieth century alone, which have surpassed any in the history of civilization, make it apparent that force is sometimes necessary to maintain social control and to keep societies from moving toward chaos. The biblical demand both for love and justice, coupled with the depravity of people, make the use of force necessary to deter and repel aggression. Some just war advocates argue that pacifism might actually contribute to the spread of evil by not resisting it when it comes and by not deterring it before it comes. Just war proponents find pacifism very unsatisfying when directly confronted with the reality of evil. What pacifists call faithfulness, just war proponents might call capitulation to evil.

A second just war argument is based on the role of the state in Romans 13:1–7. In this passage Paul outlines the God-given role of the state to maintain order and justice by enforcing the law and punishing those who break it. God entrusted the state with maintaining social order and restraining sinful, self-interested people. The state is to be not an instrument of personal vengeance, since that prerogative belongs exclusively to God (Rom. 12:19), but rather an agent that enforces restraint on a person's pursuit of his or her self-interest. When Paul says that the state "wields the sword" (13:4) in accomplishing this, at the very least this is a figure of speech for the use of force. At a minimum the state is authorized by God to use force to maintain order and secure justice. Based on this, the just war argument is as follows:

1. The state is entrusted by God with a divinely given responsibility to wield force only as necessary to maintain social order and secure justice.
2. In the Bible individuals participated with the state in the exercise of its God-given responsibilities.
3. Citizens are called to support the state in the exercise of its God-given responsibilities as long as the state does not command something that the Bible forbids.
4. If the state is exercising its legitimate, God-given authority by using force to maintain order, there is no reason Christians cannot be involved with the state today in the exercise of the same legitimate God-given role. This does not mean that individuals are commanded to use force in participation with the state, only that they are permitted to do so if necessary.

Pacifists might respond to this argument by insisting that their view of the Christian's relationship to the state and society is different from the just war theorists. And they would be correct. To this the just war theorists would respond that their view of the Christian's involvement in society more closely reflects Jesus' teaching that the church is to be the salt of the earth and the light of the world (Matt. 5:13–16).

Extending the Just War Theory

Once you accept the basic position of the just war theory, that the Bible allows the use of force under certain conditions, then it may be difficult to stop with traditional just war doctrine. Proponents of a broader definition of what constitutes a just war argue that two extensions of just war theory follow logically. First, a preventive strike would seem to be morally acceptable. If your enemy is poised for an imminent attack and capable of dealing you a damaging blow, it makes little sense to wait until formally attacked to defend yourself. In other words, a preventive strike can still be essentially a war of self-defense if the signs that you are in imminent danger from military attack are clear.

The classic example of a justifiable preventive strike was undertaken by Israel in the 1967 Six-Day War. It would have been foolish, and perhaps suicidal, for Israel to wait until their enemies crossed their borders to respond with their own military action. It was a strike that had self-defense as its goal. One can argue that once you accept the idea of a just war of self-defense, there is no moral difference between self-defense taken *in response* to attack and self-defense taken *in anticipation* of imminent attack. The only difference is the timing, that is, when the strike for self-defense occurs. Of course, one has to be careful that preventive strikes do not become a disguise for hiding aggressive intentions toward a nation's enemies. The threat of attack must be clear and imminent in order to justify a preventive strike.

Again, if you accept the basic moral acceptability of the just war, it can be argued that another type of war follows logically. If war is justifiable to prevent or restrain the spread of evil by a hostile aggressor nation, would it not also be justifiable to use force to reverse injustices perpetrated on vulnerable nations? If it is legitimate to prevent evil from spreading to another's territory, then certainly it is legitimate to use force to reverse injustices that have already been visited on a vulnerable people. This is the way the Gulf War was justified and the way many people argued for international intervention in the former nation of Yugoslavia, particularly to the atrocities in Bosnia, and in the eruptions of catastrophe in various parts of sub-Sahara Africa, most notably the Darfur region of the Sudan.

Some argue that the just war notion is in need of updating because it cannot account adequately for the presence of nuclear weapons. Further, it is argued that the just war "founders" did not anticipate anything like international terrorism as it exists today. Since the notion of nuclear deterrence played such a significant role in keeping the peace during the Cold War, it is argued that such a successful concept would have been ruled out by the just war criteria. Just war advocates suggest that even though nuclear weapons were not in existence when the just war doctrine was first put forth, its authors did clearly anticipate both the targeting of noncombatants and the disproportionate use of force. Perhaps this is why nuclear weapons have only been used twice in recent history, both at the end of World War II. Our intuitions appear to be quite consistent with the just war notions that the force used be proportionate to the threat. Further, the principle of noncombatant immunity is consistent with our caution taken to safeguard civilians from harm whenever possible. This principle also explains our innate revulsion at terrorist attacks that target innocent noncombatants. Just war advocates argue that the criteria, far from being out of date, rather, reflect our basic intuitions about what constitutes just conduct in war.

The most recent challenge, not solely to the just war notion, but to the morality of war in general, has to do with the morality of the use of torture. The just war idea as well as basic human rights, operating on a deontological foundation of the principle of human dignity, insists that torture is immoral and should not be used. Critics of this view construct a scenario in which a prisoner has critical information that must be obtained in order to save many lives. Operating within a utilitarian framework, one could argue that the benefits could be so substantial in terms of lives saved that torture of a prisoner of war could be justified. The greater the benefit, the more likely torture could be justified from a utilitarian perspective. For example, if torture were to gain information that would save an entire city from being destroyed, it is not difficult to imagine the justification for use of torture in that setting. The opponent of torture would insist that no utilitarian calculus can justify something as intrinsically, from a deontological view, as repulsive as torture.

Conclusion

Jesus predicted that wars and rumors of wars will be with us until his second coming. With the end of the Cold War, it may be that the threat of a global nuclear catastrophe waned about two decades ago. But tribal and ethnic conflicts are continuing with increasing ferocity and are likely to remain for some time. As society becomes more violent and people become more fearful of being victims of violent crime, even the use of force in matters of personal self-defense is becoming an issue for more people. Thus the questions that are at the heart of the debate over the morality of war affect people personally, beyond the decision that concerns actually going to war. Whether the Christian can use force and violence, even lethal force if necessary, goes beyond questions of war and participation in it to issues of personal safety and protection. Therefore the age-old debate between pacifists and advocates of the just war will likely remain until Christ, the Prince of Peace, returns and brings a real and lasting peace. The prophet Isaiah predicted this final, universal peace in vivid terms: "They will beat their swords into plowshares and their spears into pruning hooks. Nation will not take up sword against nation, nor will they train for war anymore" (Isa. 2:4).

For Further Reading

Brimlow, Robert W. *What about Hitler? Wrestling with Jesus' Call to Nonviolence in an Evil World.* Grand Rapids: Brazos, 2006.

Charles, J. Daryl. *Between Pacifism and Jihad: Just War and Christian Tradition.* Downers Grove, Ill.: InterVarsity, 2005.

Clouse, Robert G., ed. *War: Four Christian Views.* 2d ed. Downers Grove, Ill.: InterVarsity, 1991.

Johnson, James Turner. *The War to Oust Saddam Hussein: Just War and the New Face of Conflict.* Lanham, Md.: Rowman and Littlefield, 2005.

Review Questions

1. What are the two primary forms of pacifism described in this chapter? How are they different?

2. Why were so few of the first-century Christians members of the military?

3. What are the various extensions of the just war theory?

4. How does Matthew 5:38–45 support pacifism? How does the just war advocate understand this passage?

5. How do proponents of pacifism understand Romans 12:18–21? First Peter 2:18–24? How do just war advocates interpret these texts?

6. What are the primary criticisms of pacifism?

7. How does the just war proponent justify the use of violence under some circumstances?

8. Summarize the view of the state presented in Romans 13:1–7. What is the argument for the just war from the role of the state?

9. What is the difference between the *jus ad bello* criteria and the *jus in bello* criteria for just wars?

10. What are the criteria for a just war?

11. How would you evaluate nuclear weapons under just war criteria?

12. Which part of the just war criteria does terrorism violate?

13. How did Dietrich Bonhoeffer attempt to harmonize his pacifism with his support for killing Hitler?

14. How does the just war theory relate to terrorism? Torture?

Cases for Discussion

Case 11.1: Iraq as Just War

You are sitting around the table with a group of college students in the first few weeks after the outbreak of the war in Iraq. You and your friends are debating whether the invasion of Iraq was justified—in other words, did it constitute a just war? Some of your friends argue that Iraq was not a threat to the security of the United States. Others insist that the war was about securing access to oil in the region. Some of your friends took the other side and insisted that the war was critical to the war on terrorism in general, especially given the widely held belief at that time that Iraq had weapons of mass destruction (though there is considerable debate about that today). As you reflect on the just war criteria, you wonder yourself—was this a just war?

Questions for Discussion

1. How do you assess the war in Iraq according to the just war criteria outlined in this chapter? Does it constitute a just war?

2. Does your view of the war change knowing that the suspected weapons of mass destruction have not been found?

3. What do you think about other recent wars—do they fit the just war criteria? What about the first Gulf War in the early 1990s, in which coalition forces expelled Iraq from Kuwait? What about the interventions in Bosnia in the mid-1990s? Vietnam? World War II? Which, if any, of these constitute an example of a just war? Explain your answers.

Case 11.2: Pacifism and Self-Defense

You and your family are asleep in the middle of the night when an intruder who has broken into your house startles you awake. As he bursts into your bedroom, it is apparent that he is high on some drug and does not seem to be in control of his faculties. He is threatening you and your wife, and it becomes clear to you that he intends to kill you both. You fear for your safety, but more importantly, for the safety of your wife and of your children who are sleeping in other bedrooms down the hallway.

This intruder has created a major moral dilemma for you because you are a Christian pacifist. You don't believe that the use of violence is ever justified. In fact, you hold to Jesus' teaching in the Sermon on the Mount where he says, "Do not resist an evil person" (Matt. 5:39). Later in that same chapter, Jesus advises his followers to "turn the other cheek," "love your enemies," and "go the extra mile." You believe that Paul repeats this teaching later when he exhorts the Romans to "overcome evil with good" (Rom. 12:21). You further are reminded of the example of Christ on the cross, trusting God and not resisting the people who wanted to do him evil (1 Peter 2:23).

Questions for Discussion

1. As a pacifist, how should you respond to the intruder who is threatening your own life and that of your family?

2. Do you believe that the Bible teaches pacifism? If so, what would you do in the situation above? If not, how do you explain what appears to be a clear teaching of the Bible?

3. If you would kill the intruder, on what basis would you justify taking his life?

Case 11.3: Torture and Interrogation

You are in the military's special forces, stationed in a part of the world where terrorists organize and train. You are responsible for interrogating and maintaining suspects who are captured in raids into those camps. This is part of an ongoing effort to strike back at the terrorists who organized the 9/11 attacks and who are part of the insurgency in Iraq. Many of these suspects are extremely difficult to question and are very resistant to conventional methods of interrogation. One technique you have found to be effective is known as *waterboarding*, a method that gives them the experience of near drowning and thereby produces extreme fear in the suspects. Human rights advocates have condemned this method as torture. They accuse you of using other types of methods that are even worse.

Questions for Discussion

1. Do you believe that waterboarding constitutes torture? Why or why not?

2. Do you think that torture is an acceptable method of interrogating suspects? Defend your answer.

3. When assessed by the just war criteria, do you think torture is justified? If not, what part of the just war criteria does it violate?

4. If you generally oppose the use of torture, are there any circumstances under which you think it could be acceptable?

Chapter 11 Notes

1. See, for example, the work of Stassen in Glen Stassen and David P. Gushee, *Kingdom Ethics* (Downers Grove, Ill.: InterVarsity, 2003), 149–74.

2. For further reading on this important subject, see Darrell Cole, *When God Says War Is Just* (Colorado Springs: Waterbrook, 2002), and J. Daryl Charles, *Between Pacifism and Jihad: Just War and Christian Tradition* (Downers Grove, Ill.: InterVarsity, 2005).

3. Richard B. Hays, *The Moral Vision of the New Testament* (New York: HarperCollins, 1996), 334–36.

4. For an insightful criticism of pacifism, see C. S. Lewis, "Why I Am Not a Pacifist," in *The Weight of Glory* (New York: Macmillan, 1949).

5. For a brief discussion of the three main ways of viewing ethical conflicts, see chapter 2, "Christian Ethics." Bonhoeffer appears to have taken option 2 of the ways of resolving moral dilemmas.

6. For further discussion of Bonhoeffer and his involvement in the plot to kill Hitler, see Robert W. Brimlow, *What about Hitler? Wrestling with Jesus' Call to Nonviolence in an Evil World* (Grand Rapids: Brazos, 2006), 117–24. Brimlow rejects the way Bonhoeffer handles his moral dilemma for much the same reason we cited in chapter 2 in the criticism of option 2 for dealing with moral conflicts—that having a duty to sin is inconsistent with the character of God. Brimlow puts it like this, "I cannot bring myself to believe that there are situations in which being faithful means that I *must* sin" (p. 124). I agree with his view of handling moral conflicts, that God does not put us in a position where we are obligated to sin—this is why option 3 is preferred from our discussion in chapter 2. I would hold that Bonhoeffer did the morally justifiable thing in participating in the plot to kill Hitler and did nothing for which he needed to ask forgiveness.

Chapter 12

Ethics and Economics

Think about all the companies that have been associated with ethical scandals in the past few years—companies like Enron, Countrywide, and AIG. The collapse of many banks and mortgage companies that led to the financial crisis in 2008–9 contributed to a general sense that these industries lost their way and failed to serve the community. There is a widespread perception in the general public that the business community has lost its moral compass and that greed is the overriding principle governing how business is done. "Business ethics" is widely considered an oxymoron.

But the excesses and scandals of the past few years have also made people realize that ethics does matter and that doing business in the right way morally makes a difference. A special issue of *Business Week* was devoted to "25 Ideas for a Changing World." At the top of the list of these ideas was the idea of integrity. As they put it, "Trust, fairness and integrity matter, and they matter to the bottom line."[1]

The intersection of ethics and economics, particularly in an increasingly *global economy*, raises substantial issues that are current in public discussion and are commonly considered a matter for politicians and public policy as well as managers and executives. These issues include the following:

Outsourcing of domestic jobs to foreign countries

Sweatshops with subsistence wages and questionable working conditions

The use of child labor

Widely variable environmental standards around the world

Global climate change

Economic justice in the distribution of the world's resources, such as food, energy, and health care

Resurgence of slavery and human trafficking worldwide

Then there are issues related to *business ethics*, such as information disclosure/bluffing; issues in sales, marketing, and advertising relating to truth in marketing, product safety, environmental ethics, and corporate social responsibility; issues in accounting and finance related to accurate disclosure of information and fairness in the access to the market (i.e., insider trading); and issues in human resources management, such as sexual harassment, the right to privacy in the workplace, and conflicts of conscience among employees.

Finally, there are issues of *personal financial management* that have to do with a person's attitude toward money and possessions, the issues of "how much is enough," the balance between generosity and responsibility for oneself and one's family, and the exercise of proper stewardship of one's finances.

Of course, each of these areas could be the subject of entire books, and many volumes have been written on each of these general areas. A full treatment of all of these areas of current discussion is well beyond what we can do in a single chapter such as this one. But I can introduce you to the main issues in this area and help you integrate your worldview into this critical area. In this chapter you will receive an introduction to the primary fundamental questions in economic ethics. Some have to do with the moral assessment of the market system of global capitalism. Others have to do with ethical behavior in the workplace. You will also receive a brief introduction to some of the more specific debated issues, such as sexual harassment and insider trading.

Economic Life in the Bible

The Bible has a great deal to say about money and wealth. In fact, there are more references to money in the Bible than there are to eternity. Integrating the Bible's teaching with many of these debated issues is often very challenging, because the Bible was written to a very different socioeconomic culture than the one you work in or will soon work in. In fact, it would be hard to imagine two worlds more different when it comes to economic life.

That does not mean that the Bible has nothing of relevance for today's economic world, only that we must use the Bible carefully when applying its general principles of economic life to current times. A direct application of many biblical commands relating to economic life would be impossible today, because the system to which those commands were addressed has dramatically changed. Rather, we are seeking from Scripture general principles or norms that govern economic life and can be applied to different economic arrangements. Of course, some commands apply directly, for which the differences between the ancient world and today's society do not affect the application of the text. For example, the repeated admonitions of Scripture to take care of the poor remain directly applicable, even though the means by which that is done may have changed. By contrast, the Old Testament commands the people of Israel to keep a sabbatical year, allowing the land to lie fallow for one year in seven (Lev. 25:1–7), and the Year of Jubilee, in which all land was returned to its original owners every fiftieth year (vv. 10–17). These principles cannot be directly applied today, because they were written to a society that revolved around agriculture, not a modern information age economy in which very few people are tied to the land to make their living. Rather, we must glean a general principle from each of these commands that can be applied to the different setting of today.

The pursuit of wealth in the ancient world was fraught with potential problems, which made it easy to view those who possessed wealth with moral and spiritual skepticism. Although the temptations facing the pursuit of wealth today should not be minimized, some important differences exist between the modern and ancient economic systems that may partially account for the strong cautions in the Bible about wealth. For example, in the ancient world, as a general rule, people became wealthy differently than in today's market system. The ancient economic system was largely centered on subsistence agriculture with limited commerce and trade. Real estate was the predominant productive asset. The ancient economy is best described as what is called a "zero-sum game." The pool of economic resources was relatively fixed, so that when one person became wealthy, it was usually at the expense of someone else. Stated differently, the economy was like a pie. When someone took a larger piece, someone else received a smaller piece. This set up numerous opportunities to attain wealth abusively by theft, taxation, or extortion.

One of the most common instances of this abuse involved those who loaned money to the poor at terms they could not repay, requiring what little land the poor

Godly Materialism

Theologian John Schneider argues in his controversial book *Godly Materialism: Rethinking Money and Possessions* (follow-up edition entitled *The Good of Affluence*), that there is nothing wrong with having wealth and that God intends his people to enjoy material abundance. Schneider cites the guilt that wealthy religious people often feel about their wealth and argues that "there is a godly way of living the life of material delight." He points out that God promised Israel in the Old Testament a "land *flowing* with milk and honey," which he insists is a figure of speech for abundance. Yet he also recognizes that wealth does bring numerous temptations about which to be careful.*

*John Schneider, *Godly Materialism: Rethinking Money and Possessions* (Downers Grove, Ill.: InterVarsity, 1994), and *The Good of Affluence: Seeking God in a Culture of Wealth* (Grand Rapids: Eerdmans, 2002).

owned as collateral. Then when the debtors inevitably defaulted, the lender appropriated their land. The debtors became tenant farmers or slaves or were reduced to dependence on charity. This form of taking advantage of the poor occurred regularly in the ancient world and is one of the reasons why the Bible so frequently condemns exploitation of the poor. In these cases, literally, the rich became richer at the expense of the poor, and when someone was wealthy, more often than not, they had acquired it through some immoral means. In addition, the misuse of political power to extort money unjustly was common. Thus the wealthy were viewed with suspicion, and great emphasis was placed on the potential temptations of becoming wealthy, because the ancient world had so few morally legitimate avenues to acquire great wealth.

This may also be the reason why there is so little in the Bible about ambition. Social mobility in the ancient world was very limited—there were no "rags to riches" stories in the ancient world. As a result, the Bible does not have much to teach about ambition, since moving ahead economically was so difficult to do. This may also explain why the Bible has a lot to say about contentment, and why the opposite of contentment is not ambition, but envy.

Today the zero-sum game view of economic life is no longer the dominant paradigm for viewing the economy. The market system is in various stages of development in different parts of the world, but in more mature market systems, the economy is anything but a zero-sum game. In modern industrial and information economies, the size of the economic pie itself is constantly increasing. Wealth is being created instead of simply being transferred. In fact, every time a company makes a profit, wealth is created and the size of the pie grows larger. For this reason, the rich can become wealthy while at the same time the poor can also be better off. That is why the incomes of the poor can and have increased at the same time the wealth of the rich accumulates, though admittedly at very different rates. Someone like Bill Gates or Warren Buffett simply having extraordinary wealth does not mean that the poor are necessarily worse off. Nor does it necessarily follow that Gates's or Buffett's wealth was gained at the expense of someone else. In a modern market economy, wealth is constantly being created, so it is possible for someone to become wealthy without necessarily succumbing to the temptations about which Scripture warned. Today's market economy makes it far easier to be wealthy and virtuous than did the agricultural subsistence economy of the ancient world.

Biblical Teaching on Wealth and Possessions

At first glance, the Bible appears to condemn the accumulation of wealth. Classic passages of Scripture, such as "It is easier for a camel to go through the eye of a needle than for a rich man to enter the kingdom of God" (Luke 18:25) and "Blessed are you who are poor" (Luke 6:20), suggest that possession of wealth is suspect while poverty is virtuous. These texts should be balanced by others that present wealth in a different perspective. These include the sayings of the Old Testament Wisdom Literature that regard wealth as God's blessing to be enjoyed (Eccl. 5:18–20) and a result of one's diligence (Prov. 10:4–5). Similarly, in the New Testament, while Paul counsels Timothy to keep wealth in proper perspective (1 Tim. 6:6–19), Paul acknowledges that God gives liberally to his people for their enjoyment (v. 17). Yet this acknowledgment is balanced by admonitions not to trust in one's wealth because of the temptation to arrogance and of the uncertainty involved in retaining wealth (see also Eccl. 5:8–6:12), and thus, conversely, to be content with one's economic station in life.

The Bible distinguishes between possession of wealth and love of wealth. Only the latter is condemned (1 Tim. 6:10). The love of wealth and desire to become wealthy bring a variety of temptations and have the potential to shipwreck one's spiritual life (v. 9). The reason that this is stated in such stark terms may be a result of the way people attained wealth in the ancient world—normally through morally questionable means. If this is true, then there were numerous temptations that confront someone attempting to become wealthy that have to do with the very way they attain wealth. This is in addition to the common temptation for wealth to become a source of trust instead of God.

The members of the early church and the crowds who followed Jesus covered the socioeconomic spectrum from the poor to the wealthy. From what we know of Jesus' background and his trade as a carpenter, it would appear that he lived a modest middle-class lifestyle in contrast to many portrayals of him in poverty. It does not appear that the possession of wealth per se is problematic in Scripture, but hoarding one's wealth when surrounded by poverty is a sign of selfishness and greed. Throughout Scripture, the wealthy are condemned for their callousness to the needs of the poor (Amos 4:1–4; James 2:1–7). The early days of the church were characterized by an extraordinary generosity toward the poor, many of whom constituted the majority of the membership in the early church (Acts 2:43–47). Although the pattern of the early church did not involve a socialistic style of holding property in common, it did involve heightened sensitivity to the needs of the poor. Though the Bible affirms the right to private property, this right is not absolute. It is tempered by the reality that all property belongs to God and that we are trustees, or stewards, of God's property. God has entrusted his property to us both for our personal needs and enjoyment, and for use to achieve God's purposes (such as meeting the needs of the poor). To summarize the Bible's teaching on wealth, *God owns it all* and has entrusted what he owns to us for responsible use and enjoyment. Human beings are but *trustees* using God's resources wisely. God commands *generosity*, especially toward the poor and vulnerable. Clearly since he owns it all, *there is more to life than our material possessions.*

Work and Calling in the Bible

The Bible not only has much to say about money and possessions, but it also addresses the subject of work in substantial detail. Work has *intrinsic* value because God ordained it *prior* to the entrance of sin into the world. If you look at the Genesis account of creation closely, you will see that God commanded Adam and Eve to work the garden *before* sin entered the picture (2:15). God did not condemn human beings to work as a consequence of the entrance of sin. Work is not a punishment on human beings for their sin. To be sure, work was affected by the fall, making it more arduous and stressful and less productive, but that was not the original design (3:17–19). God's original idea for work was that human beings would spend their lives in productive activity, with regular breaks for leisure, rest, and celebration of God's blessing (Ex. 20:8–11). Even in the pre-fall paradise, God put Adam and Eve to work. Work was a part of God's original design for human beings from the beginning, and because of that it has intrinsic value to God. Work will also be a part of the world after the Lord's return. The prophet Isaiah envisions the world after Christ's return as one in which nations "will beat their swords into plowshares and their spears into pruning hooks" (Isa. 2:4). The obvious point of the passage is to show that universal peace will characterize the kingdom when it is fulfilled. But what often goes unnoticed is that weapons of war will be transformed *into implements of productive work* (plowshares and pruning hooks). That is, there will still be productive work when Christ returns to bring his kingdom in its fullness. So work has intrinsic value because it was ordained before the fall and will be a part of life when the kingdom comes in its fullness. In the paradise settings at the beginning and end of human history, work is ordained by God.

What makes work so valuable to God is its connection to another mandate from creation, the command to exercise dominion over the creation. That is, work is one of the primary ways that God had in mind for human beings to do what he commanded them to do in the world. Work is intricately bound up with the dominion mandate over creation. God ordained work so that human beings could fulfill one of their primary roles for which they were created. Work is not something that we do just to get by or to finance our lifestyles. It is not a necessary evil that will be done away with at some point. Work is not what we do just so that we can enjoy our leisure. Work has inherent dignity because it is the way God arranged for human beings to fulfill a part of their destiny on earth, that of exercising responsible dominion over creation. That mandate is still in effect today, and God is still empowering human beings to be effective trustees of his world. Thus work has intrinsic value because of its connection to the dominion mandate. Adam and Eve were doing God's work in the world by tending the garden and doing their part to be responsible trustees over creation. We do God's work in the world in our jobs because they are connected with the task assigned to all human beings to exercise dominion over the world. We are junior partners with God in the advance of his dominion over the creation, which after the fall also involves alleviating the effects of the entrance of sin.

So work has intrinsic value because it was created before the entrance of sin and is the means by which we partner with God in the exercise of dominion over the world. But there is a more foundational reason why work has value to God: God is a worker, and human beings are workers by virtue of being made in God's image. In other words, we work because that is who God is and who we are in his image. Of course, God is much more than a worker, and so are we. But God mandates work because that is a part of who he is and part of who he made us to be in his image.

Look carefully at the way God is portrayed when it comes to work. One of the first portraits of God in Genesis is as a worker, fashioning the world in his wisdom. God is portrayed as a creative God in Genesis 1–2, with initiative, ingenuity, passion for creation, and innovation all a part of his work in creation. God is portrayed with what we might call "entrepreneurial" traits in Genesis 1–2. From the beginning of the biblical account, God is presented as engaged in productive activity in fashioning and sustaining the world. At the end of the creation account, Genesis 2:2–3 gives the Sabbath model as a day for God to rest from all his work. God blessed the Sabbath because "he rested from *all the work of creating* that he had done" (emphasis added). The pattern for the Sabbath was to rest because God rested (Ex. 20:11) and, conversely, to work because God worked in creation (v. 9). The pattern for creation became the pattern for human beings. They worked six days as God did and rested one day as God did. We work because it is part of what it means to be made in God's image and to be like him. This is why Ecclesiastes can proclaim the goodness of work in this way: "A man can do nothing better than to eat and drink and *find satisfaction in all his work*. This too, I see, is from the hand of God, for without him, who can eat or find enjoyment?" (Eccl. 2:24–25, emphasis added).

Moral/Theological Principles for Economic Life

Though the Bible is not a textbook on economics, a variety of theological principles can be drawn from Scripture that relate to macroeconomics.[2] These are general principles—remember that using the Bible in economics is complicated by how different economic life was in the ancient world. There is considerable agreement on these general principles—the debate is over how they should be applied and what that application should look like. That is, there is much more controversy over the *means* for accomplishing economic justice than over the *ends* themselves. Most agree that the ends are proper and consistent with biblical teaching. Following are some of the primary principles governing economic life:[3]

1. *Though tarnished by sin, the created world is intrinsically good because it is God's creation.* The Bible is clear that the material world is good because it came from God and that the reality of sin has not eradicated the essential good of creation. When God saw his creation at the end of the process, he declared it "good" (Gen. 1:31). It is also clear that the Creator, not the creation is to be worshiped, in contrast to much of the ancient world's worship of the material world and their assignment of gods to aspects of the creation.

2. *God is the ultimate owner of all the world's productive resources.* Though private property is affirmed, human beings are not the final owners of the world's resources. God clearly affirms his ownership of the earth's means of production. For example, in the Mosaic law, the reason for such institutions as the Year of Jubilee and the right of redemption is that God owns the land. As a result, in Old Testament Israel, land could not be permanently bought or sold, only leased. Leviticus 25: 23 puts it this way, "The land must not be sold permanently, because the land is mine and you are but aliens and my tenants. Throughout the country that you hold as a possession, you must provide for the redemption of the land." Private property is affirmed in laws prohibiting theft, but the use of one's property was to reflect that human beings are the *penultimate* owners, not the ultimate ones.

3. *Human beings are stewards of these resources, charged with their responsible and productive use.* Human beings are seen by God as trustees of his resources. This is a critical part of the dominion mandate (Gen. 1:28) that gives human beings both use of and responsibility for God's resources. The dominion mandate does not give human beings the right to do with the world whatever they please only for their own benefit. Rather, they are to put them to productive use for their owner, analogous to managers working for their owners. Adam and Eve managed the garden for God (Gen. 2:15), thereby setting a pattern for their descendants to manage God's productive resources.

4. *Responsible wealth creation is part of the dominion mandate and a way of honoring God.* Exercising dominion over God's good creation involves unlocking what he has embedded in creation by means of his general revelation. Technology and entrepreneurial activity are consistent with creatively extending God's dominion over the world. After the entrance of sin into the world, the task became more complicated. Productively using God's resources necessarily involves generating wealth, as resources are utilized in ways that meet human needs and wants. Wealth creation is simply an indication that God's resources are being put to productive use.

5. *Human beings are created with freedom and a need for community, making them more than autonomous economic agents.* Human beings are created in God's image, both free to act and by nature relational. Just as the Trinity necessarily involves relationships between its three persons, so also human beings are fundamentally relational beings. They are much more than simply economic agents acting to satisfy their desires. Created as free moral agents, human beings can take initiative and act creatively in the world—but they are not simply out to satisfy their desires. This principle affirms the place of initiative-driven entrepreneurial activity and the freedom to pursue economic goals. It also affirms the need for community and relationships, not just material gains, as part of a full and good life.

6. *Work is inherently good, though marred by sin.* As outlined earlier in this chapter, work is intrinsically good because it was ordained by God *prior* to the entrance of sin into the world. The presence of sin and its effect on work (Gen. 3:17–20) are the causes of alienation, dissatisfaction with work, exploitation of workers, and ethical lapses and quandaries in the workplace.

7. *Human beings who are capable of working are responsible for supporting themselves and their families.* The Bible is clear that if a person is able and does not work, he or she has no share in the community's goods (2 Thess. 3:9–12). Rather, people are to "settle down and earn the bread they eat." The Bible further makes clear that the person who does not provide for his or her family has committed a very serious omission analogous to denying the faith (1 Tim. 5:7–8). The norm in God's economy is that individuals work to support themselves and their families and to have some to give to the poor (Eph. 4:28).

8. *The community is responsible for taking care of the poor—those who cannot support themselves.* The poor in the Bible are those who are unable to work and take care of themselves, and they are deserving of access to the community's goods. The Bible makes provision for the poor and repeatedly reminds the community of its obligation to be generous toward the poor (Deut. 15:7; Gal. 2:10). The Bible also recognizes that some people become poor through misfortune that is out of their control and provides for regular opportunities to make a fresh start. This seems to be the purpose of many of the real estate laws that kept someone from permanently losing his land (Lev. 25:8–53).

9. *Human beings are not to exploit the economically vulnerable, but to take care of them.* The Bible again and again prohibits what it calls "oppression" of the poor—taking advantage of someone's economic vulnerability for one's own benefit (Prov. 14:31; Ezek. 22:29; Amos 2:7). Jesus compares taking care of the poor to showing regard for him (Matt. 25:31–46). Micah suggests that "doing justice" is one of the things required by God, in addition to loving mercy and walking humbly with God (6:6–8). Communities are to have "safety nets" that can take care of the

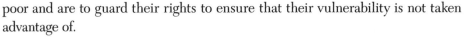

poor and are to guard their rights to ensure that their vulnerability is not taken advantage of.

10. *Economic justice is the provision of access to the productive resources necessary for self-support.* Part of the mandate for any economic system is to make available the resources (jobs, capital, labor, etc.) that are required for a person to support himself or herself. These resources are not to be hoarded but made available to those seeking to support themselves. This principle does not mandate community ownership of these resources, only that individuals who are capable of working not be without opportunity for self-support.

11. *Distributive justice in the Bible is based on a combination of merit and need.* The goods that society produces must be distributed in an orderly and fair way. The Bible makes clear that there is nothing intrinsically problematic with the accumulation of wealth as long as one is generous toward those in need. Though initiative and diligence are rewarded, thus the place of *merit* (Prov. 10:4–5), there is also a place for *need* as a criteria for a minimum level of provision. It is expected that hard work, initiative, and investment would be rewarded—an indication that merit does have a place in a system of distributive justice.

Moral and Theological Critique of Global Capitalism

The debate over the morality of market capitalism has been ongoing since the writings of Adam Smith. A variety of critics, ranging from Karl Marx to the liberation theologians, have offered critiques of the market system. With the fall of communism in the late 1980s, many thought that the debate was essentially over. Rather, the discussion has intensified, since market capitalism in some form appears to be the only surviving economic system. In more recent years, some of the past criticism has reemerged due to the rapid global expansion of capitalism. Many of the former critics of Western-style capitalism now offer the same critique of globalization.

Perhaps the most common criticism of market capitalism is that *it is based on greed.* It is often attributed to Adam Smith that "greed is good," when in reality he said nothing of the sort. Critics argue that since greed is clearly a vice condemned in most religious traditions, there must be something problematic about an economic system that is premised on greed. Certainly there is ample evidence to suggest that greed is a significant motivator for many companies and individuals who go to seemingly absurd excesses to increase their company's profits or their own net worth. The common public perception of Wall Street is that it is dominated by greedy companies willing to do whatever it takes to maximize their profits. This perception is often applied to large companies, especially multinational corporations, that ship domestic jobs overseas in search of higher profits.

Defenders of global capitalism respond to this charge by distinguishing between greed and self-interest. They agree that greed is a vice, but that is a different thing from companies and individuals pursuing their self-interest. The Bible nowhere condemns self-interest—rather, it calls individuals to balance their self-interest with the interests of others (Phil. 2:4). Further, as mentioned above, the Bible commends the pursuit of self-interest necessary to take care of one's own needs and that of one's family. Though it is true that greed sometimes permeates the conduct of business, that is different from the insistence that greed is the "engine of capitalism." As suggested above, trust, not greed, is what makes the system run smoothly. A properly functioning market economy presumes a modicum of virtue among the participants—otherwise it is more difficult to do business efficiently. It may be that there are some cultural contexts that are better suited to the market than others. Smith envisioned that capitalism would flourish in settings in which the participants had the internal moral resources to restrain their self-interest. He realized that greed run rampant would actually have a negative impact on a company's profitability.

A second common criticism of global capitalism is that *it causes poverty by leading to an unequal concentration of wealth and resources.* It is often said that first world prosperity is causing third world poverty, and that there exists a clear cause-and-effect relationship between the two. Critics cite the world's energy use, for example, that the United States has roughly 3 percent of the world's population and uses 25 percent of the world's energy resources. Critics see the vast inequalities in wealth between the industrialized West and the rest of the world and attribute it to the abuse of the system of global capitalism. They accuse the West of becoming wealthy at the expense of the rest of the world. The statement that "the rich are getting richer and the poor are getting poorer," suggests that the rich are causing the poverty of the poor.

Defenders of globalization insist that there is a different cause-and-effect relationship between market capitalism and poverty—that the introduction of capitalism actually raises people out of poverty rather than causing it. They point out that since the introduction of the market system in many parts of the world, virtually three billion people have been lifted above the poverty line. To be sure, there are still three billion below it, which is a cause for ongoing concern. And there are certainly examples of companies who have left the local communities in which they operate worse off. But there are numerous examples of nations with few natural resources that are experiencing significant economic growth because of the introduction of a free market system. Countries such as Singapore, Hong Kong, and South Korea (especially in contrast to North Korea) have been growing for some time as a result of the introduction of market-style economics. In countries such as India and China, which are still mixed systems at best, their growth is commonly accounted for on the basis of the introduction of market mechanisms.

Defenders further point out that the way resource use should be measured is in comparison not to their population but to their productivity. If that is the standard, then one can make the argument that the distribution of wealth and resources reflects productivity as opposed to an immoral inequality. Those who defend the market system also argue that this criticism that the market causes third world poverty assumes a zero-sum game view of economics that does exist in some parts of the world, but is not the case for a properly functioning market system or the system that exists in much of the industrialized and information societies of the world. As mentioned earlier, the zero-sum game notion clearly fits the ancient world and does accurately describe some underdeveloped parts of the world today.

Defenders of capitalism recognize that though the market system is efficient at creating wealth, distribution of wealth is another matter altogether. They realize that distribution cannot be entirely merit based—that there is a place for consideration of need as a criteria for distributing society's goods. As mentioned above, the combination of merit and need seems to reflect the Bible's emphasis on initiative yet balances that with recognition that some are not able to support themselves. They constitute the poor, and based on their need, they deserve the compassion and support of the community.

A third common criticism of global capitalism is that *it brings human suffering through outsourcing and unemployment.* One of the most common features of the global market system is that jobs are sent overseas where wages are much lower and working conditions are more hazardous to workers. The criticism is that this is endemic to the system and it causes predictable human suffering due to loss of jobs, income, and self-esteem. Many factory jobs, for example, have been sent overseas, leaving factory workers unemployed and in some cases unable to get comparable work. Even jobs that require education and a high level of skills are being outsourced today—for example, software engineering and computer programming are increasingly being done in other parts of the world, putting those jobs at risk too.

Defenders of global capitalism respond that there is an upside to the outsourcing of jobs—holding down wages, which enables prices of goods and services to remain competitive. Further, companies should be free to locate where they can obtain the most competitive wage rates in order to keep their costs down. Critics reply that these companies are making high profits and do not need to outsource to stay profitable. It is true that the process of "creative destruction" coined by the economist Joseph Schumpeter, can cause difficulty as resources are transferred from unproductive sectors to productive ones. For example, when the telephone was invented, telegraph operators all eventually lost their jobs. When automobiles came on the scene, the horse and carriage industry became obsolete. The same pattern followed with other innovations, particularly with the advent of the digital age. Defenders of the market system argue that the benefits of innovation and change are overall more positive than the costs of people losing their jobs.

A fourth common criticism is that *the system of global capitalism encourages consumerism*, which in turn produces moral and spiritual poverty. Critics cite the egregious examples of overconsumption and point out that economic growth is premised on consumers purchasing all sorts of things that they do not need. They further point out that many of the goods available on the market have little socially redeeming value yet are continually produced and made available. This seems all the more egregious when compared with the scarcities that exist in many other parts of the world. Critics argue that such overconsumption reflects a callousness to the poor around the world.

Defenders of the market readily concede that overconsumption and materialism exist and are the result of the prosperity produced by the market system. But they point out that materialism is fundamentally a matter of the heart and has existed regardless of the specific economic system. Because human beings are self-centered and sinful, consumerism can emerge in any economic system. Overconsumption is a matter of character, not economic system. However, we should recognize that given the affluence of the information economy nations, the temptations to overconsume are multiplied.

"Two Cheers for Sweatshops"

New York Times columnist Nicholas Kristof, after making repeated trips to Asia and seeing sweatshops firsthand, offers an alternative view, different from the conventional wisdom on outsourcing and globalization. He admits that the working conditions in many of these Asian factories are oppressive and that workers are abused — conditions that all call for change. Interestingly, more Western companies who contract with these factories are auditing their working conditions more regularly and refusing to do business with those who do not make the necessary changes. Ironically, a cottage industry of consultants has arisen, helping the factories "pass" their audits — in reality, enabling them to continue their oppressive practices. But Kristof also admits that "the simplest way to help the poorest Asians would be to buy more from sweatshops, not less." This is because work in these factories helps the poorest to better their situation and escape from poverty. He urges accepting sweatshops as part of the price of development, while at the same time recognizing that there is a place for workplace monitors and improving conditions.*

*Nicholas Kristof and Sheryl WuDunn, "Two Cheers for Sweatshops," *New York Times Magazine*, September 24, 2000.

It may be that there are some goods and services that should not be distributed according to market mechanisms. That is the reason why many countries have laws prohibiting the sale of organs and body parts, and why adoption law does not allow birth mothers to be paid for their adoptable children. Part of the reason why some goods and services ought to be off the market is that if everything was a market transaction, there would be no place for uncompensated altruism. There is debate over some goods being on the market, such as a woman's eggs (used in infertility treatments) and renewable body components, such as blood and sperm. Further debate exists over having reproductive services such as surrogacy be market services.

Ethics in the Workplace

In contrast to the macro issues of the global economic system, the intersection of ethics and economics also includes issues commonly understood as relating to *business ethics*. These have to do with how a person conducts himself or herself in the workplace when confronted with ethical challenges. Remember, we have already discussed a model for making ethical decisions (chapter 4) that can be used when you are in a situation in which you have a conflict of values.

There are some more fundamental questions that we need to address first. They relate to how a person approaches ethical behavior in the workplace and the connection between ethical behavior and successful business. It is common to presume that you cannot adhere to ethical standards at work and still compete successfully. This presumption begs the two issues we will address next—the issue of a dual morality and the relationship between good ethics and good business.

Although Adam Smith viewed business as a morally serious calling and a form of honorable service to the community (analogous to the other professions, such as medicine and law), the culture views business with a degree of cynicism today. The corporate executive is the most common villain in current films and television. Think back through some of the movies you have seen lately and see if you see evidence of this cynical view of business.

Dual Morality

One common strategy for dealing with ethical challenges in the workplace is to create two separate worlds that you operate in—your life in the workplace and your private life. Each sphere then has its own set of rules and guidelines that you follow. That is, you have one set of moral rules for the workplace and a different and presumably higher set of rules for your private life. You realize that the workplace is a very competitive place that requires you to set aside some of your Christian virtues, such as love, compassion, and sometimes even fairness. You insist that those values are fine for private life, but the environment of business is such that you must play by a different set of rules in order to succeed.

You see colleagues of yours who claim to be Christians but who are involved in some very questionable business practices, and you admit that this way of compartmentalizing your life is maybe not that unusual. Perhaps a lot of people accept what Albert Carr wrote years ago, that "a sudden submission to Christian ethics by businessmen would bring about the greatest economic upheaval in history."[4] What he meant is that if a person practiced Christian ethics consistently in the workplace, he or she would not be competitive. Or take the statement by Ray Kroc, founder of McDonald's, who claimed to be a Christian: "My priorities are God first, family second, and McDonald's hamburgers third. And when I go to work on Monday morning, that order reverses."[5] He meant that he had two sets of priorities, one for the workplace and the other for private life, and a corresponding set of rules for each.

From a Christian worldview, compartmentalizing your life is full of difficulties. The Bible is very clear that we are to live all our lives under the lordship of Christ, that he is the boss over every aspect of our lives. No part of our lives is to be exempt from his scrutiny and direction. Following Christ is not something that we reserve for the weekend—it is a full-time vocation (Matt. 6:33; 1 Cor. 10:31; Col. 3:17).

The Smartest Guys in the Room

In their book *The Smartest Guys in the Room*, *Fortune* magazine senior writers Bethany McLean and Peter Elkind chronicle the rise and fall of Enron, the company that became synonymous with corporate scandal. The book became a movie by the same title. Enron was an oil and gas trading company that grew to be the seventh-largest company in the United States, reaching its peak in 2000–2001. It fell precipitously in late 2001 and filed for bankruptcy, resulting in millions of dollars of losses for investors, many of whom were long-term Enron employees. Through very complex financial instruments and special purpose entities (SPEs), the company hid massive losses, and when the stock price began to fall, the carefully constructed financial edifice crumbled within a few months. Never before had such a seemingly successful company experienced such a rapid decline in its fortunes. The title of the book reflects the culture of the company that also contributed to its decline.*

*Bethany McLean and Peter Elkind, *The Smartest Guys in the Room* (New York: Portfolio, 2003).

$

Good Ethics and Good Business

Hidden in the statements of Ray Kroc and Albert Carr is the assumption that having integrity in the workplace is not good business, that is, it is costly to one's bottom line. But most people have the intuitive sense that that's not true, that doing the right thing in the workplace will pay off somehow.

From a Christian worldview, good ethics is always good business. This is because from God's perspective, what constitutes good business is much broader than a company's bottom line. Good business from a biblical perspective includes how you do business. The company that makes a lot of money using immoral means or providing an immoral product or service is viewed by God as a failure regardless of the company's profitability. We should also realize that just because a company or an individual has strong ethics does not necessarily mean that they will be profitable. They could have integrity but be incompetent in running a business or have an inferior product or service.

Ethics at Arthur Andersen

Barbara Ley Toffler was hired by Arthur Andersen — at the time one of the major public accounting firms — to be the partner in charge of Andersen's Ethics and Responsible Business Practices consulting service, their ethics consulting practice. Andersen was the accounting firm that provided both auditing and consulting services for Enron, and shortly after Enron filed for bankruptcy, Andersen was indicted by the Justice Department and later convicted of obstruction of justice for their involvement with Enron. The once proud accounting firm was seriously crippled by the conviction. Toffler recounts Andersen's role with other companies who were guilty of accounting scandals, such as Waste Management and Sunbeam, both of whom had to restate their earnings. She tells how she attempted to institute the same ethics standards and procedures at Andersen that she was implementing with her clients.

> My job as head of the Ethics and Responsible Business Practices group was to sell other companies services that would help them act more responsibly. Yet I was constantly being undermined by one simple fact: While we at Arthur Andersen thought it was important that *you* the ethically challenged corporate client get its house in order, we didn't feel the same compulsion to do any navel-gazing of our own. How do you sell as "essential programs and services" those that your own firm refuses to embrace? How do you respond to the question, "If this stuff is so necessary — how come your firm's not doing any of it?"*

*Barbara Ley Toffler, *Final Accounting: Ambition, Greed and the Fall of Arthur Andersen* (New York: Broadway, 2003), 186.

In the short term, good ethics is usually costly. If it were not, everyone would do the right thing! And this discussion would be unnecessary. But the Bible is full of references to the prosperity of the wicked. The psalmists regularly lament the prosperity of the wicked (Ps. 73:1–9). Some of the most profitable industries today are those that we would classify as "wicked," such as pornography and the illegal drug trade. It is also true that the righteous man prospers (Prov. 13:21), but in the Bible there is no necessary connection between righteousness and prosperity.

In the long run, however, integrity usually pays off. Here's why: Integrity builds trust, and trustworthiness is a critical component in building a successful business over time. People will generally go out of their way and sometimes even pay higher prices to do business with people they trust. And more important, they will take pains to avoid doing business with people they don't trust.

One of the great myths of the business world is that greed is the engine of our economic system. Adam Smith, the ideological founder of capitalism, never said that phrase that is often attributed to him, "Greed is good." He held that enlightened self-interest is the engine of capitalism and that the free market would never work unless the individual participants had the moral values necessary to restrain their self-interest.[6] For Smith those came from Judeo-Christian morality. Greed run amok will alienate most of the parties that are necessary to build a lasting business, such as suppliers, employees, customers, and partners.

The reality is that *trust* is the engine of the market economic system. Without trust, business relationships are more difficult to maintain, and the costs of doing business increase. Think about all the transactions that take place every day that are premised on trust. Literally millions of them occur every day. Every time someone buys something on credit, trust is assumed. Every time you go to work, you are trusting that you will get paid on payday. The reason that e-commerce has taken off in the past few years is that more people trust that their personal and financial information will not be misused.

Consider how the costs of doing business go up when organizational trust is low. When that happens, the need for costly oversight and monitoring mechanisms rises. Further, when trust is low within an organization, employees are usually less committed to their work, less receptive to change and new ideas, and less willing to "go the extra mile" for their employer. To extend this notion internationally, think about how expensive it is to do business in cultures where interpersonal trust is low. It is not an accident that countries and cultures where this is the case have great difficulty attracting foreign investment.

I got a vivid lesson in the importance of trust when I met Tedla. He was one of my graduate students in philosophy who came to Talbot School of Theology from Ethiopia. A few days after he arrived on campus, I had the opportunity to take him out to lunch. We went to a local popular restaurant down the street from the school and had a delightful time getting to know each other better. When it came time to pay for the meal, I handed our server my credit card. Tedla had never seen a credit card before and was unfamiliar with paying for goods or services on credit. When the server brought the bill back, I signed it and we got up to leave. I'm not sure Tedla quite understood that I had just paid for the meal. He explained to me that in his country, this was very rare. In fact, he told me that sometimes buyers and sellers of commodity have a routine in which the buyer holds on to the money and the seller holds on to the product and they both release their grip at the same time, thereby making the exchange. I used the occasion as a "teachable moment" and said that the restaurant trusts that my credit card company will pay the bill. Further, my credit card company trusts that I will pay my bill when it comes in the mail. Of course, if I don't pay the bill, they won't extend me credit any longer. But that transaction in the restaurant was premised on trust, and without it, a good deal of the business that is transacted every day either would not happen or would be more costly and cumbersome to transact.

Good business actually requires not just trust, but some other important virtues. Hard work, diligence, thrift, initiative, creativity, promise keeping, and truthfulness are just a few other virtues that are at the root of successful individuals and companies. Business actually encourages these virtues, and for long run success, they are generally considered very helpful character traits for which employers are always on the lookout. Of course, the converse is also true. Business can encourage

The Place of Trust

Social critic Francis Fukuyama has written about trust in an international context. In his book *Trust: The Social Virtues and the Creation of Prosperity*, he maintains that cultures in which interpersonal trust outside blood relatives is high are the most fertile ground for market capitalism to take root in. By contrast, in cultures in which trust is limited to that among family members, the market system is established more slowly if at all. He argues that in Protestant Europe, particularly England, and the United States, relationships of trust outside family members formed the basis for the trust that came to be between community members involved in business together. He attributes the development of interpersonal trust in these cultures to the growth of church and other voluntary organizations. These groups fostered relationships of trust and expanded the network of people with whom one could engage in business. Fukuyama suggests that this was a critical component in the rise of market capitalism and prosperity in England and the United States.*

*Francis Fukuyama, *Trust: The Social Virtues and the Creation of Prosperity* (New York: Free Press, 2003).

greed too. In fact, the prospect of enormous payoffs in the past few years has made the temptation to cut corners ethically very difficult to resist. But people who act unethically usually have difficulty staying in business and prospering in the long run. The temptation is to get in, make your money however you can, and then get out. In the past decade in the dot.com boom, this pattern was something to which people aspired. It is perhaps not an accident that the vast majority of those companies are no longer in business today. Such a short-term outlook, looking for a quick gain without much consideration for the long run creation of value, turned out to be a very costly way of seeing the world.

Specific Issues in Business Ethics

Though it is true that new issues continue to arise, primarily as a result of new technologies and new ways of doing business, there are a variety of issues in business ethics that have remained constant for some time. This section will introduce you to the principal debated issues in business ethics that will likely be under discussion for some time to come.

Much of this discussion falls under the heading of *corporate social responsibility*. That is, what is a company's responsibility to its various *stakeholders*, or the parties that are affected by the company's way of doing business? Actually, a significant part of the discussion is *to whom* do companies have responsibilities? Is it only the shareholders, or the owners of the company, or do companies have responsibilities to other stakeholders besides their shareholders?

In a classic article published in 1970, the late economist Milton Friedman argued that a company's only social responsibility was to increase its profits.[7] That is, the shareholders were the only party to whom companies had any responsibilities—to maximize their wealth. To show how widespread this view is, ask someone studying in a business school or any businessperson this question: What is the goal of a corporation? They will likely answer you with the standard view that they probably learned in business school—that the sole goal of a corporation is to increase the wealth of its shareholders.

Friedman suggested that companies serve the community substantially in three specific ways: (1) by providing goods and services that are in demand, (2) by employing people from the community, and (3) by paying their taxes to support community services. Friedman insists that any activity a company undertakes that is not designed to maximize the shareholders' wealth is actually stealing from them, or at the least, he maintains, it constitutes taxation without representation. For example, if a company makes charitable contributions, unless they are for public relations purposes (in which case they constitute a business expense, not a charitable contribution), they are taking the shareholders' money and using it for a nonbusiness purpose. Friedman argues that the executives are using someone else's money (the shareholders') without their consent. Further, he suggests that it's not a particularly virtuous act to do something charitable with someone else's money. If I give to help the poor but steal from you to do it, that seriously undermines the charitable nature of the act.

By contrast with Friedman, an alternative view has arisen in recent years known as the *stakeholder view*.[8] Proponents of this view argue that there are a variety of stakeholders, or affected parties, to whom companies have social obligations. These include employees, suppliers, the community, the environment, and, of course, the shareholders. They argue that companies incur obligations by virtue of the effect they have on various parties—if a company's production harms the environment and the surrounding community, then since they caused that harm, they have the responsibility to prevent it. The majority of large publicly traded corporations, at least in the West, have an office or officer responsible for corporate responsibility, and it is now widely accepted that companies do have obligations to the communities they serve, at the least, to avoid doing harm to them in the process of conducting their business. Most companies have mission statements that affirm excellence in the service or product of the company, service to the community, and a *reasonable* return to their shareholders. How consistently they act according to such a mission is another question, but

Supercapitalism

Robert B. Reich, secretary of labor under former President Bill Clinton, published a scathing criticism of the corporate social responsibility (CSR) movement in 2007, arguing that it usurps the proper place of government to make the rules for the common good—to protect communities and the environment from harm. That is government's job, not business's, claims Reich. He further argues that CSR is often a "sideshow," that the vast majority of the ways that a company does good is by doing well in terms of its profitability—by putting out good products and hiring its employees. But Reich offers a third criticism, a common one, that CSR involves doing good with other people's money, namely the shareholders'. A January 2008 special report in *The Economist* suggests that CSR amounts to nothing more than "enlightened self-interest." Their point is that when CSR is also good business, it is a powerful combination. It produces good for the community and profit for the business.*

*Robert B. Reich, *Supercapitalism: The Transformation of Business, Democracy and Everyday Life* (New York: Vintage, 2007); "The Next Question: Does CSR Work?" *The Economist*, January 17, 2008.

it does appear that many companies accept something like a stakeholder model even in the way they state their mission.

International Business Ethics

When business is conducted in other parts of the world, ethical issues emerge when cultures collide. When different moral standards in different cultures come into conflict, ethical issues emerge. For example, in many non-Western cultures, *child labor* is very common and necessary for families to make it economically. Yet in the United States, child labor is illegal, and even as children approach the age of eighteen, there are state-imposed limits on how much they can work. Much of the criticism of sweatshops around the world is that they employ children, and it is widely assumed that this constitutes exploitation. Yet the issue of child labor is quite complicated. Many argue that there is no good reason to prohibit children from working if it is critical to their family's economic survival.

A second example of this collision of cultures producing ethical issues concerns *bribery*. Bribery is very common in many parts of the world, and it is widely viewed as essential to doing business successfully in some parts of the world. Yet bribery is illegal in much of the West, and the Foreign Corrupt Practices Act prohibits U.S. companies from bribing foreign entities in order to secure a competitive advantage. Many other forms of bribery are practiced around the world, ranging from payments made to civil servants to secure prompter service (arguably analogous to paying a premium for overnight mail or other expedited service) to paying off customs officials in order to get people or equipment into a country (which is more like extortion than bribery).

Other examples of international ethical issues include different standards of worker safety, which some argue puts employees at risk, and different environmental standards, which many suggest puts the environment at risk. Safety standards vary widely around the world, and it may be that in some cases employees are being harmed, which is clearly unethical and should also be enforced by the law. But in other cases, it may be that more stringent safety standards do not serve a useful purpose or do not reduce harm to employees. The same holds true for different environmental standards. Some countries argue that more stringent standards do not contribute significantly to protecting the environment (this is the argument made routinely by skeptics of global warming), and that even if they did, countries should have the right to set their priorities according to their needs. Some countries maintain that it is more important to provide jobs and income to lift people out of poverty than it is to protect the environment. Of course, this argument is more difficult to sustain the more a country's environmental damage spills over into other countries and communities.

In dealing with international ethical issues, you should beware of relativism, which insists that whatever is the moral consensus of a culture is to be accepted and no judgments be made. But as we pointed out in chapter 3 in the critique of relativism, that view is flawed and cannot be of much help when heinous practices enjoy a cultural consensus. To resolve some of these ethical conflicts that arise when cultures collide, one must appeal to some sort of universal principle that transcends culture. It may be that the cultures actually share the principles in common but differ on the application. It is required that fundamental human rights be protected, fair competition be encouraged, and employees be protected from harm.

Ethics in Human Resources Management

Ethics issues in the area of human resources often revolve around employee rights in the workplace and include the rights of free speech, conscience, protection from harm, and privacy. At a minimum, a Christian worldview requires that employees be treated with dignity and respect, consistent with being made in God's image. This can be in contrast to the way employees are often treated—as impersonal, replaceable parts of a corporate machine. Many states have what is called *employment at will* as part of state law, which gives employers the right to hire and fire employees at will. Of course, employees can leave their company at will too. There are exceptions to employment at will. For example, companies cannot discriminate against someone and terminate their employment simply because of their race, gender, or sexual orientation. Neither does employment at will give employers the right to break mutually agreed upon employment contracts. Supporters of this concept argue that employers ought to have this right because employees can leave their jobs without reason and that this gives employers the same rights to let employees go for any legal reason. They also suggest that since the employees are assets of the company, the company has the right to use or not use those assets in whatever legal way it desires. Critics maintain that employment at will treats employees like property that the company can dispose of whenever it so chooses. They further argue that it creates an atmosphere of fear and insecurity in the workplace that makes employees less productive.

Consistent with respect for fundamental human dignity, at the least, employees have the moral right to have their contracts upheld, be paid in a fair and timely way, work in a safe workplace (free from discrimination and sexual harassment), have some due process prior to termination, and have a modicum of privacy. Other legal rights are set forth in the law, such as the right to family leave and the right to exercise one's conscience in the workplace (protection for whistleblowers).

Some of the most debatable issues in this area have to do with privacy rights for employees. It is widely assumed that employees have privacy at work like they do at home, and that they can exercise free speech at work like they do outside the workplace. But the protected right of free speech in the First Amendment to the Constitution only protects a person from the reach of *government* censoring their speech—that is, one cannot be arrested by the state for one's speech. But that does not give employees the unqualified right to say whatever they want at work without consequences. For example, if employees are consistently being critical of their employer, they may be terminated for their impact on morale. The exception to this is if they are exercising their legal rights as whistle-blowers, pointing out that the company is engaged in illegal or unethical behavior.

It is further assumed that the right to privacy means that one's employer cannot read an employee's email or have access to his or her desk. It is certainly true that a presumption of privacy is good management practice, but the email and desk are owned by the company and are to be used for company business. Periodic monitoring of email and Internet use is now standard procedure for most companies and has been upheld in the courts as a justifiable invasion of privacy.

Employees do have *rights of conscience* that deserve protection in the case of pointing out illegal or unethical behavior. However, this should be balanced by the company's right to protect itself from harm should the allegations be false or improperly motivated by an employee's desire to damage the company's reputation. This is also the reason why a company may put some limits on how employees conduct themselves off the job. Employees may be terminated for engaging in illegal behavior off the job and for engaging in activities that bring harm to the employer. The right of conscience also extends to employees who do not want to serve clients or do work they find morally objectionable. Companies usually show some flexibility if the individual has been a good employee. But companies also reserve the right to suggest that employees find work elsewhere at a place where their conscience is not so troubled.

A final area of discussion that is emotionally charged is the issue of *sexual harassment*. This can take two forms. One is the "quid pro quo" form, in which sexual favors are exchanged for hiring, promotion, or job security. This is both illegal and unethical and assaults the victim's dignity. A second type—behavior that creates a hostile work environment, is more difficult to define and tends to be a bit more subjective. This could include inappropriate touching, making sexually suggestive comments, or repeated requests for dates (especially difficult when the relationship is between a superior and subordinate). One should be careful to protect the right of due process for the accused, since in sexual harassment this is one of the few areas in which it is culturally common for the accused to be presumed guilty until proven innocent (though not legal to do so).

Environmental Ethics

With the recent discussion of global climate change, environmental ethics is again at the forefront of business ethics and public policy. The conflict between economic growth and development and the environment has been ongoing, with the conflict between the logging industry and the protection of the spotted owl being one of the most public. Today, dealing with climate change and the impact on economic growth is the newest expression of conflict in this area.

There are conflicting views of the environment itself too. Many proponents of environmentalism hold to what is called a *biocentric* view of the environment, suggesting that it should be protected because it has intrinsic value. A contrasting view argues that the environment has value not in and of itself, but because of its value to human beings. This is known as an *anthropocentric* view of the environment. The problem with biocentrism is that it makes it difficult to rank priorities because it is clear that human priorities are sometimes primary. A problem with anthropocentrism is that if unchecked by stewardship, it can lead to environmental irresponsibility. From a Christian worldview, what is called a *theocentric* view gives the environment intrinsic value because it is God's good creation but places it under human dominion and trusteeship for human beings to use responsibly for their benefit.

Product Safety

Companies have the obligation to produce safe products—there is no ethical issue about that. The issues revolve around how the responsibility for ensuring that products are safe is to be shared. Some argue that the consumer has primary responsibility for this: "Let the buyer beware" is an often cited admonition. This view puts much of the responsibility on the market as the vehicle through which consumer choices can influence companies. It is argued that if a product is unsafe, consumers will stop buying it and companies will be forced to make changes if they want to stay in business. The problem with this view is that even if consumers have the expertise to make that judgment themselves, which they often do not, there is still a time lag for the market to make that information available to the company. During that time period, people invariably are harmed.

A second option is for government to take primary responsibility through regulatory mechanisms. The benefit of this is that the necessary expertise is brought in, but the danger is excessive regulation limiting consumer choices. For example, government often protects individuals from engaging in risky behavior, such as driving without seat belts or riding a motorcycle without a helmet. Those may be acceptable limitations on individuals, but there is justifiable concern about what behaviors will be restricted next.

A third option is to put the primary responsibility on the company to make their products safe, and the mechanism for enforcing this is primarily the courts.

The benefit of this view is that the producer takes the majority of the responsibility for safety. The disadvantage is that it leads to frivolous lawsuits that drive up a company's costs and inhibit innovation. In reality all three parties are involved in ensuring that products and services are safe—consumers should beware, government has a role in providing outside expertise, and companies are held accountable for their moral and legal obligation to put out safe products.

Ethics in Accounting and Finance

Issues in these areas have been significantly in the news in the past few years as Wall Street has come under increasing scrutiny for alleged abuses in stock options manipulations and hedge fund abuses. This, combined with accounting scandals in which public companies and their accountants have been implicated, has created a backlash in the law to try to stop such abuses. The law has helped in some areas. For example, it mandated that investment banking firms separate the role of stock analysis and the role of investment banking (the term for helping companies raise large amounts of capital). The result was that stock analysts regained some of their objectivity that had been lost when they were pressured to issue positive analysis on companies who had hired the firm for its investment banking services.

Perhaps the most visible issue in this area is that of *insider trading*. This refers to people who have access to inside information about a company (that has not yet been made public) using that information to make stock trades for themselves. For example, if a company is on the verge of a significant technological breakthrough or is announcing a new product, the stock price will usually rise once that becomes public. Insider trading enables a person with advance knowledge of that information to buy the stock prior to its price increase, thereby making a considerable profit.

Some argue that there is nothing wrong with insider trading—that the market will efficiently adjust to this and that there are really no victims when it occurs. It is what some call a "victimless crime." But opponents insist that it creates an unfair advantage for insiders and could erode trust in the capital markets if investors were not sure that they were not being taken advantage of. Insider trading is currently illegal in the United States, primarily because of its unfairness to those who are not insiders. However, it is legal in other parts of the world.

Conclusion

This chapter has been an introduction to the very complex field of business ethics. We have seen the importance of ethics and character for business to function well. The law is a very blunt instrument that is often not well suited to regulate the fine points of morality. Ethics is critical because the law only provides the moral minimum. Regulation and compliance provide the moral floor, not the ceiling—it is not the full moral requirement, but the minimum. Many of the key ethical issues are unresolved by the law and call for an emphasis on character to be effective in the workplace.

For Further Reading

Blank, Rebecca M., and William McGurn. *Is the Market Moral? A Dialogue on Religion, Economics and Justice*. Washington, D.C.: Brookings Institution, 2004.

Claar, Victor V., and Robin J. Klay. *Economics in Christian Perspective: Theory, Policy and Life Choices*. Downers Grove, Ill.: InterVarsity, 2007.

Hill, Alexander. *Just Business: Christian Ethics for the Marketplace*. 2nd ed. Downers Grove, Ill.: InterVarsity, 2008.

McDaniel, Charles. *God and Money: The Moral Challenge of Capitalism*. Lanham, Md.: Rowman and Littlefield, 2007.

Neuhaus, Richard John. *Doing Well and Doing Good: The Challenge to the Christian Capitalist*. New York: Doubleday, 1992.

Rae, Scott B., and Kenman L. Wong. *Beyond Integrity: A Judeo-Christian Approach to Business Ethics*. 2nd ed. Grand Rapids: Zondervan, 2004.

Stevens, R. Paul. *Doing God's Business: Meaning and Motivation for the Marketplace*. Grand Rapids: Eerdmans, 2006.

Review Questions

1. What is the biblical tradition of the sabbatical year? Year of Jubilee?

2. What are some of the main differences between economic life in biblical times and today?

3. What is meant by the term "zero-sum game"?

4. Why does the Bible have so little to say about ambition?

5. What are some of the primary biblical texts that speak to wealth and possessions?

6. Why is it so hard for a "rich man to enter the kingdom of heaven"?

7. What is the difference between the intrinsic and instrumental value ascribed to work?

8. When was work ordained by God — before or after the entrance of sin into the world?

9. What makes work so valuable to God?

10. How is work connected to the dominion mandate?

11. How does work relate to the image of God in human beings?

12. What are some of the primary biblical principles for economic life?

13. Summarize the biblical obligation toward the poor.

14. How would you distinguish between greed and self-interest?

15. How would you respond to the criticism that in capitalism "the rich get richer and the poor get poorer"?

16. How would you reply to the charge that global capitalism causes great human suffering through outsourcing of jobs?

17. Respond to Ray Kroc's statement, "My priorities are God first, family second, and McDonald's hamburgers third. And when I go to work on Monday morning, that order reverses."

18. What is the connection between good ethics and good business (profitability)? Is there a difference between the short term and the long term with regard to this question?

19. What virtue is the engine of the market economic system?

20. What other virtues are required of "good business"?

21. What is the difference between the view of Milton Friedman and the stakeholder view of corporate social responsibility?

22. What are some of the main ethical issues raised by the collision of cultures in international business?

23. What is employment at will?

24. Distinguish between quid pro quo and the hostile environment types of sexual harassment.

25. What is the difference between a biocentric and anthropocentric view of the environment? How does a theocentric view compare with these?

26. What is insider trading? What are the reasons that it is illegal?

Cases for Discussion

Case 12.1: Downloading Music

You and your friends have a substantial collection of music that you have downloaded from the Internet using one of the free software tools, such as LimeWire. The music is for personal use only. You have it stored on your laptop computer, and you put various songs on your iPod. Most of the music you have downloaded is copyrighted, and therefore it is technically illegal to download it without paying for it—it constitutes a copyright violation. Yet virtually everyone you know has done the same thing and nobody considers it wrong. In fact, more music groups are allowing their music to go out uncopyrighted, and therefore for free, since they realize that the way music is marketed is changing significantly. When you discuss this with your friends, they see no ethical issue at all. In fact, some of them have a small collection of movies on their computers too.

Questions for Discussion

1. Do you consider downloading of copyrighted material morally wrong? Why or why not?

2. How do you evaluate the observation that "everyone is doing it" as a rationale for thinking that downloading copyrighted music is morally acceptable?

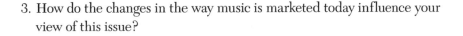

3. How do the changes in the way music is marketed today influence your view of this issue?

Case 12.2: International Business and Product Safety

Your company makes the glue that is used in the manufacture and repair of shoes. The company exports the glue all over the world, and it is used in large factories where shoes are made and in small family-owned shoe repair shops. In addition to its legal use with shoes, it can also be sniffed to get a very inexpensive "high." This can create an addiction as well as bringing harm to the person who sniffs it. For people who engage in this practice regularly, they are at risk for brain damage. For this reason, in some countries, including the United States, the law requires an additive in the glue that acts as a very powerful deterrent to glue sniffing but does not otherwise affect the product in its intended use. This additive adds to the cost of producing the glue such that it would differentiate you from your competitors in terms of price. In many countries where you sell the glue, such as in Latin America, there is no law requiring the additive. You have been selling the glue in these countries for some time and now learn that street kids are using it to get high.

Questions for Discussion

1. Do you continue to market the glue in these countries where the law does not require an additive? Why or why not?

2. If you continue to sell the glue, do you put in the additive, even though it will put you at a price disadvantage? Why or why not?

3. How do you assess the argument that "it's not our problem that street kids are using it—that's the government's problem"?

4. How do you respond to the argument that many products can be misused—so why be alarmed about misuse of the glue?

Case 12.3: Conflicts of Conscience

You are a graphic artist working for a video game manufacturer that produces a variety of very popular video games. They produce games for all audiences, and you have been involved in the work for many of them. Most of the games are well received and contain little objectionable material aside from some periodic violence and foul language. However, your company also produces games with far more violence and sexually explicit material. The company has found this to be a very profitable niche market, and they are careful not to advertise these games in places that would attract underage children. You have been asked to work on the next release of a game that would serve this market. The game will include gratuitous violence, prostitution, sexual assault, and murder of law enforcement officials. You have some reservations about the game—you would not play it, and you certainly would not allow your kids to play it—but you need your job and cannot afford to risk alienating your superiors.

Questions for Discussion

1. What would you do when you are asked to work on this new game the company is producing? Defend your answer.

2. How do you respond to the criticism that these games are harmful to people and desensitize them to sex and violence?

3. Do you think there is a benefit in continuing to work on a project to which you have moral objections? What might those benefits be?

20

Chapter 12 Notes

1. "After Enron: The Ideal Corporation," *Business Week*, August 26, 2002, 68.

2. For a fuller discussion of these principles, see Stephen Mott and Ronald J. Sider, "Economic Justice: A Biblical Paradigm," in David P. Gushee, ed., *Toward a Just and Caring Society: Christian Responses to Poverty in America* (Grand Rapids: Baker, 1999), 15–45.

3. These are taken from Scott B. Rae and Kenman L. Wong, *Beyond Integrity*: A *Judeo-Christian Approach to Business Ethics*, 2nd ed. (Grand Rapids: Zondervan, 2004), 215.

4. Albert Z. Carr, "Is Business Bluffing Ethical?" *Harvard Business Review*, January–February 1968, cited in Rae and Wong, *Beyond Integrity, 28.*

5. This widely quoted statement from Kroc in 1955 was one of the company's first mottos. It appears in many sources. See, for example, Margaret J. King, "Empires of Popular Culture: McDonald's and Disney," *Journal of American Culture* 1, no. 2 (7 June 2004), 424–37; John Mortimer, "The Biggest Bunfight in History": Review of *McLibel* by John Vidal, *Sunday Times* (U.K.) 13 (April 1997).

6. It is worth noting that Adam Smith was first a moral philosopher, who attempted to apply his views to broader economic life. See his work of moral philosophy, *The Theory of Moral Sentiments*, which was published prior to his more well-known work, *The Wealth of Nations*.

7. Milton Friedman, "The Social Responsibility of Business Is to Increase Its Profits," *New York Times Magazine* 33 (September 13, 1970): 122–26, reprinted in Rae and Wong, *Beyond Integrity*, 131–35.

8. One of numerous expressions of stakeholder theory is Kenneth Goodpaster, "Business Ethics and Stakeholder Analysis," *Business Ethics Quarterly* 1, no. 1 (January 1991): 53–73, reprinted in Rae and Wong, *Beyond Integrity*, 136–45.

General Index

Scripture Index